THE CITY AFTER
ABANDONMENT

THE CITY IN THE TWENTY-FIRST CENTURY

Eugenie L. Birch and Susan M. Wachter, *Series Editors*

A complete list of books in the series
is available from the publisher.

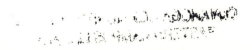

THE CITY AFTER ABANDONMENT

Edited by

MARGARET DEWAR

and

JUNE MANNING THOMAS

PENN

UNIVERSITY OF PENNSYLVANIA PRESS

PHILADELPHIA

Published by
University of Pennsylvania Press
Philadelphia, Pennsylvania 19104-4112
www.upenn.edu/pennpress

Printed in the United States of America on acid-free paper

10 9 8 7 6 5 4 3 2 1

Library of Congress Cataloging-in-Publication Data

The city after abandonment / edited by Margaret Dewar and June Manning Thomas. — 1st ed.
   p. cm. — (The city in the twenty-first century)
  Includes bibliographical references and index.
  ISBN 978-0-8122-4446-5 (hardcover : alk. paper)
  1. Urban renewal —United States. 2. City planning—United States. 3. Urban policy—
United States. I. Dewar, Margaret E. (Margaret Elizabeth), 1948– II. Thomas, June
Manning. III. Series: City in the twenty-first century book series.
HT175.C49 2012
307.3'4160973—dc23   2012007885

CONTENTS

III. WHAT *SHOULD* THE CITY BECOME
AFTER ABANDONMENT?

Introduction: The City After Abandonment

Since the early 1970s, observers of American cities have noted residential abandonment, concentrated in low-income, often minority-race or minority-ethnic neighborhoods.[1] Loss of neighborhoods reached shocking levels in places such as the South Bronx, where by the mid-1970s entire blocks of apartment buildings became uninhabitable and were demolished. By the early part of the twenty-first century, abandonment had become much more than an issue facing certain neighborhoods. Rather, vacant structures and vacant lots dominated the landscape of a large number of previously industrial cities of the Northeast and Midwest as well as other cities such as New Orleans. Neighborhoods reflected this disinvestment, but, in addition, large industrial sites sat vacant; former commercial corridors featured a few stores among boarded up buildings and vacant lots; downtown occupancy fell, and the number of downtown parking lots increased. By 2010, numerous cities had lost so much of their peak population and employment—the households and businesses for which the physical city had been built—that the extent of decline called for new perspectives. The challenge was no longer simply one of revitalizing neighborhoods but rather of restructuring the built city to adapt to new realities.

Population, households, and housing units declined substantially in many cities after World War II. A few examples illustrate this. Of the nation's 200 largest cities in population in 2000, 21 lost more than one fourth of their residents between 1950 and 2008.[2] Cities with more than 100,000 in population that had lost more than 10 percent of their peak population concentrated in the Midwest and Northeast but scattered across the South as well with a few in the West.[3] Beauregard showed that nine of the nation's fifty largest cities lost population in every decade between 1950 and 2000: Baltimore, Buffalo, Cincinnati, Cleveland, Detroit, Philadelphia, Pittsburgh, St. Louis, and Washington, D.C. One other—New Orleans—lost population every decade after 1960. Four-fifths of the large cities that experienced loss between

1950 and 2000 had population decline in multiple decades. Beauregard wrote, "A population drop confined to a single decade is a temporary setback; losing residents from one decade to the next is a cause for alarm. The latter hints at a structural, rather than a circumstantial, impediment to the city's ability to grow . . . this is a more daunting problem for residents, investors, and public officials."[4]

Table I.1 looks more closely at Beauregard's large cities that lost population in every decade from 1950 or 1960 through 2000. The table also includes two smaller cities—Flint and Youngstown, the subjects of chapters in this book. Although all lost at least one-quarter of their peak population, their situations differed. Six cities lost more than half their population between their peak years and 2010—Detroit, St. Louis, Youngstown, Cleveland, Buffalo, and Pittsburgh. The change in number of households from peak year to 2010, a strong indicator of change in demand for housing units, differed from the rate of loss of population. Seven cities lost more than 30 percent of their peak number of households, but Philadelphia lost only 7 percent. Washington, D.C., had more households in 2010 than in any previous census year, despite a 25 percent drop from peak population, a reflection of smaller household size. Loss in housing units lagged behind the loss of households, indicating that high housing vacancy rates, property disinvestment, demolition, and increases in vacant land will continue. The nine cities with housing vacancy rates over 15 percent face more disinvestment and property abandonment than do Philadelphia and Washington.

No consistent data exist to describe the extent and location of vacant land and vacant structures that have resulted from loss of population, households, and businesses in these and other cities.[5] No data allow for a consistent description of property abandonment across numerous cities. The exodus from many areas has been so profound as to make demolitions attractive compared to the alternative (unsafe standing structures), with vast tracts of cleared land then requiring continued maintenance to prevent illegal dumping or reversion to a condition that mimics prairie. Some chapters in this volume provide estimates of vacant land and structures for the cities they examine and, therefore, offer a sense of the extent of physical change.

Throughout this book, we define "abandonment" of a property as occurring when the owner stops taking responsibility for it. "Neighborhood abandonment" or "city abandonment" refers to places where large levels of population and household loss have led to large amounts of property abandonment, manifested in a high percentage of vacant houses, buildings, lots,

Table I.1. Household and Population Decline for Beauregard's "Persistent Nine" Large U.S. Central Cities plus New Orleans, Youngstown, and Flint, Peak Decennial Year to 2010

Central cities, in order of percent decline in households	Change in households (peak year[a] to 2010)	Percent change in households (peak year[a] to 2010)	Percent change in population (peak year[b] to 2010)	Percent change in housing units (peak year[c] to 2010)	Housing vacancy rate (2010)
Detroit	−245,392	−47.7	−61.4	−36.9	22.8
St. Louis	−116,079	−45.0	−62.7	−33.1	19.3
Youngstown	−17,852	−44.8	−60.6	−35.0	19.0
Cleveland	−102,401	−37.9	−56.6	−26.6	19.3
Flint	−20,459	−33.6	−48.0	−20.1	21.1
Buffalo	−56,550	−33.4	−55.0	−24.7	15.7
New Orleans	−64,277	−31.1	−45.2	−16.1	25.1
Pittsburgh	−54,675	−28.6	−54.8	−20.4	12.8
Cincinnati	−28,407	−17.6	−41.1	−6.7	17.2
Baltimore	−39,446	−13.6	−34.6	−2.9	15.8
Philadelphia	−42,409	−6.6	−26.3	−2.3	10.5
Washington[d]	0	0.0	−25.0	0.0	10.1

Sources: U.S. Census Bureau, "Households," "Total Population," "Housing Units," and "Occupancy Status," Census 1930–2010; Robert A. Beauregard, "Urban Population Loss in Historical Perspective: USA, 1820–2000," *Environment and Planning A* 41 (2009): 514–28.

Note: "Persistent Nine" are U.S. central cities among the top 50 in size that lost population every decade, 1950–2000. Another city, New Orleans, lost population 1960–2000. For discussion see Beauregard, "Urban Population Loss in Historical Perspective."

[a]Peak decennial year for households, counted as highest number of households during year of a regular U.S. Census survey, was 1950 for Pittsburgh and St. Louis; 1960 for Buffalo, Cincinnati, Cleveland, Youngstown, and Detroit; 1970 for Baltimore, Philadelphia, and Flint; and 1980 for New Orleans. Washington had a larger number of households in 2010 than in any other census year.

[b]Peak decennial year for population was 1950, except for Flint and New Orleans (1960) and Youngstown (1930).

[c]Peak decennial year for housing units was 1950 for St. Louis; 1960 for Buffalo, Cleveland, Detroit, Pittsburgh, and Youngstown; 1970 for Baltimore and Flint; 1980 for Cincinnati, New Orleans, and Philadelphia. Washington had more housing units in 2010 than in any previous census year.

[d]Washington had more households and housing units in 2010 than ever before; therefore, the city had no changes in these numbers compared to the peak year.

and/or blocks, which jeopardize the quality of life for remaining residents and businesses.[6]

Several forces have caused the losses in population, households, and employment and the large amount of property abandonment since World War II. The first was suburbanization of employment and population. Manufacturers sought larger, therefore suburban, sites when technological change made greater efficiency possible with single-story production and access to highways for transportation by truck. Large numbers of white households moved to the suburbs. This exodus originated in part in the search for new housing outside crowded cities, in part in the choice of residential location in relation to jobs in the suburbs, and in part in racially driven white flight from the cities. In addition, federal and state policies encouraged municipal balkanization as they supported suburban development through transportation, tax, fiscal, home rule, and housing policies. Public policies, the refusal of banks to make mortgage loans to African American and other minority-race households, and the hostility of white neighbors in the city and the suburbs kept particularly African American households in segregated neighborhoods in the cities. The cities' residents became increasingly isolated as the metropolitan areas remained segregated by race and by certain ethnicities.[7] In comparison to support for suburbanization, federal support for central-city revitalization was paltry by any measure that took into account both direct expenditures and indirect expenditures, such as forgone tax revenue for home mortgages. Retail and consumer services also moved to outlying areas, either leading or following customers and workers.[8]

After World War II, the suburbs grew at the expense of the central cities. But beginning around the mid-1970s, industrial restructuring in response to international competition and changing technology led to large-scale plant closings that dramatically reduced the number of manufacturing jobs, particularly in the heavily industrial regions of the Northeast and Midwest. Growth in manufacturing jobs occurred in the South and the West and in lower-wage countries.[9] The loss of jobs and income meant that population growth slowed in many metropolitan areas that had depended on manufacturing.

As the fortunes of many historically industrial central cities continued to decline through the early 2000s, middle- or working-class families of all races and ethnicities left for the suburbs in search of better housing and schools, better public services, safer neighborhoods, and easier access to decentralized employment and shopping. An increasing share of remaining residents lived in poverty. Continuing loss of businesses and residents meant loss of property tax and other revenues for city governments that then lacked the resources to provide adequate police protection and public services, and therefore more residents desired to leave.

Neighborhood change reflected the loss in demand for housing. In lower-income, minority-race neighborhoods initially, homeowners sold to households with lower incomes or to landlords. Disinvestment progressed as landlords made few improvements in property and more owner-occupied houses became renter-occupied. Often the housing in older neighborhoods no longer provided what households sought—more than one bathroom or a larger kitchen, for example. Landlords walked away from properties they could no longer rent. Homeowners, some of whom had inherited property when an elderly owner died, found they could not sell or rent a house, and they, too, walked away.[10]

Corruption marked this process, sometimes in nationwide scandals and sometimes in locally concentrated problems, affecting African American households disproportionately. In the late 1960s, the Federal Housing Administration (FHA) began to insure mortgages in neighborhoods where African Americans lived. Widespread fraud in the appraisal, underwriting, and sale of homes with FHA-insured mortgages, however, meant that households purchased homes requiring repairs they could not afford. The foreclosures and abandonment that followed "devastated entire neighborhoods in such cities as Detroit, Cleveland, and Chicago," according to Alex Schwartz.[11] In the late 1990s, the largest securities fraud case in Michigan's history involved the bankruptcy of RIMCO, a company that owned thousands of homes in Detroit. Most of these homes became blighted. The growth in the use of high-risk mortgages in central-city, minority-race neighborhoods, even when the borrowers had high credit scores, led to thousands of mortgage foreclosures in these older industrial cities beginning in the late 1990s. This situation exacerbated exodus and property abandonment on a massive scale.[12]

Why Study Cities After Abandonment?

Why does the widespread abandonment of many central cities matter? Why should anyone interested in cities want to know more about such places left behind as population fell? A first reason is that many people continue to live in abandoned sectors of cities even after most people have left and that those who remain deserve a functional place to live. The implications of population decline and property abandonment for remaining residents can be profound. For lower-income residents, access to jobs, adequate schools, and supportive services becomes proscribed, leading to other problems such as underemployment, lack of educational readiness for job markets, vulnerability to crime, and poor health; all reflect lack of connection to broader society and possibly a concentration of poverty. For higher-income residents who choose to live in a city experiencing high levels of abandonment, the benefits of such residence—access to traditional central business districts and employment, sports and entertainment venues, affordable housing in established neighborhoods or downtowns, and major educational and health institutions, for example—may not outweigh numerous problems in quality of living—such as high insurance costs, poor public services, high tax rates, crime, and a context of poverty.

In addition to the need to consider the quality of life for remaining residents, anyone interested in urban studies needs to understand these cities and how to address their special circumstances for other reasons. Increasingly, the metropolitan area is the scale at which "local" economies function because of the many interconnections of employment, commerce, and industry at that level. A central city with high levels of property abandonment and a high-poverty population requires high levels of social services and public assistance, as well as intergovernmental transfers. In addition, the image of a central city—that is, the way people in global contexts and markets view that city—often affects both the image and the reality of the entire metropolitan area. Central cities that have declined drastically in social and economic circumstances are at a disadvantage within their metropolitan economies, and their status may affect the economic viability of the entire region. Hence, a negative image of a central city such as Cleveland or Pittsburgh or Detroit may dampen tourism or business investment in surrounding cities or suburbs, no matter how attractive or economically viable nearby areas may be.

Another key concern suggesting the importance of studying the city after abandonment is the need for better environmental sustainability. Compact cities are more environmentally responsible than sprawling metropolitan areas characterized by expanding boundaries and large areas of abandonment in built-up inner cities. Continued flight from central cities associated with further construction of roads, water systems, schools, shopping areas, and subdivisions in sprawling land use patterns leads to the opposite of compactness. Leaving behind thousands of miles of roads, sidewalks, street-light networks, and water and sewer pipes, unrepaired and ultimately untended, while building new ones beyond city borders, creates high costs for society.[13]

This book therefore focuses on the cities that have experienced extensive property abandonment. In particular, the book looks at the local planning and policy implications of population loss and property abandonment for U.S. cities and their neighborhoods, particularly those neighborhoods that community-based organizations serve. Some strategies or strategic frameworks may assist such cities to create a better future.

The problems of population, household, and employment loss and ensuing property disinvestment affect cities elsewhere in the world as well.[14] This book focuses on U.S. cities rather than taking an international perspective because countries differ so much in culture, context, and political systems that comparisons become difficult. In particular, American metropolitan areas are characterized by municipal control of land use within the limits of powers that state governments delegate, decentralized settlement patterns, and residential segregation by race and ethnicity, important conditions that differ in other countries.

The chapters in this book tackle three principal questions regarding cities that have experienced large-scale property abandonment. The sections below explain these questions and the reasons for examining them.

What Does the City Become After Abandonment?

Most visitors to very abandoned areas of cities primarily notice expanses of vacant lots and derelict structures.[15] This focus on destruction and emptiness led a writer for the *New Republic* to exclaim, "Stop slobbering over abandoned cityscapes!"[16] "Read the paper," wrote another journalist, "and you see a wasted landscape; go there, and you see the sprouts emerging from the soil."[17] Indeed, much more remains to be discovered about areas in central cities where few people now live. Individuals and groups respond to conditions of abandonment in a range of ways that no one has fully described.

A look at one quite vacant 54-block section of northwest Detroit near the city boundary, a census tract in an area called Brightmoor, provides glimpses of the people who live there, their circumstances, and some of their responses to abandonment.[18] This tract sits in the southern half of Brightmoor and stretches from several blocks east of Eliza Howell Park to the western edge of a public housing project. About 1,676 people lived in this area in 2010, fewer than five people per acre. The population had fallen more than 60 percent in just the previous twenty years. About 79 percent of the residents were African American, and almost 16 percent were white, a smaller share of African Americans and a larger share of whites than in the city as a whole. About 70 percent of residents lived in poverty in the period 2005–9, nearly double the rate for the city, which had the highest big-city poverty rate in the nation in 2009. Of those who held jobs, more than 70 percent worked outside the city. About 14 percent of the labor force was unemployed, a considerably smaller percent than the city's 22 percent unemployment rate.[19]

About 31 percent of the area's residents were children in 2010, slightly higher than for the city. Only 7 percent were over sixty-five compared to about 11 percent for the city. Of residents over twenty-five, one-fifth had not completed high school or received a GED, a slightly smaller percentage than for the city. About one-third had completed high school but no further education.[20]

In 2010, the residents lived in 582 housing units, all single-family structures in this section of Brightmoor, a housing density of between one and two houses per acre; 31 percent of houses were vacant, a considerably higher vacancy rate than for the city (see Table I.1). In 2009, a survey classified 68 percent of residences as in good condition, but 22 percent as "vacant, open, and dangerous," a city blight classification, and/or fire damaged. Close to 56 percent of residential properties were vacant lots. Around 43 percent of households owned their homes in 2010, less than the city's 51 percent. Households were more transient than in the city as a whole, with 14 percent of homeowners and nearly 60 percent of renters having lived in their current residence less than five years.[21]

The street on the north border of the area, Fenkell, had once served as the commercial corridor for the neighborhood, but by 2010, few retail stores and services remained. A post office, hardware store, locally owned restaurant, and several other enterprises still operated. Homes in the area averaged more than a mile's distance to the nearest grocer; 91 percent of residents lived in a "food desert," as defined by the U.S. Department of Agriculture. Almost forty residents operated home-based businesses that provided services that might once have occupied commercial buildings: hairdressers, barbers, day care providers, and cosmetologists, for instance.[22]

In the first four-and-one-half months of 2011, the area experienced close to 70 crimes that residents and others reported to police. Compared to the same period for the entire city, the area in Brightmoor had lower rates of burglary, larceny, arson, and murder; a slightly higher assault rate; and about the same robbery rate.[23] In community meetings, residents talked about other crimes, such as dog fighting and prostitution, that did not show up in the reported statistics.

Children lived in the attendance areas of an elementary-middle school and an elementary school that were not making "adequate yearly progress"; scores on standardized tests did not show enough children reaching proficiency in a range of subjects. They lived in the attendance area of a high school with a 47 percent graduation rate.[24]

Numerous residents, especially homeowners, purchased or took over vacant lots adjacent to their homes. Forty-six households had consolidated at least three properties as of 2010. Nearly one hundred vacant lots had become part of these consolidations. Homeowners fenced these areas, built additions to their homes, added driveways and garages, installed swimming pools and storage sheds, created gardens. They took control of and remade their environment. Other property owners had also purchased or taken over more than 150 individual next-door lots to add to the area around homes.[25]

Some of the remaining vacant lots had positive uses although no nearby owner had fenced them; twenty had gardens in 2010. On the other hand, the lack of control over property showed in the prevalence of illegal dumping; 166 vacant lots (more than 17 percent of the lots that no nearby resident controlled and that did not serve as gardens) had become dumpsites as of fall 2010.[26]

When property owners stopped paying property taxes, usually the last stage in abandoning property, the county government foreclosed on the properties and offered them at auction. Eighteen percent of all Brightmoor properties (covering a wider area than the 54 blocks) went through this process from 2002 through 2010, and only 18 percent of those offered at auction sold, even for the low price of $500 per property. Purchasers included landlords, a nonprofit developer seeking to build affordable housing, and speculators aiming to obtain property someone else wanted. The unsold properties remained in the ownership of the County Treasurer's Office until the City of Detroit accepted them. Therefore, the city and county owned many properties in the area.[27]

"You can do anything you want with your property; the city won't stop you," said (paraphrased) a resident of another area of Detroit in fall 2010 meetings to develop a plan for the city. "But you also can't expect anyone to respond when you ask for services." Indeed, this characterization seemed to describe the experience of the residents of the very vacant area of Bright-moor. No city official apparently interfered with their stewardship and take-over of property without ownership or with their modification of property in ways that did not conform to codes, but, in addition, no official appar-ently enforced blight codes or antidumping laws.

The residents of the 54-block area faced changing city policies. Tackling a budget shortfall of hundreds of millions of dollars, Mayor Dave Bing an-nounced in 2010 that the administration would encourage residents to move out of emptier areas of the city into denser neighborhoods. He aimed to save city funds by cutting services and halting investments in infrastructure in nearly empty areas. In addition, shoring up demand for housing in destina-tion neighborhoods might slow disinvestment there, some argued, although no one had demonstrated relocated residents' ability to pay for housing in those areas.[28]

The chapters in the first section of the book look at actions that individu-als, small groups of people, and nonprofit organizations take that remake the built city. They operate within an environment that municipal action (or inaction) and legal institutions create. These chapters and the sketch of the residents and their experiences in a very vacant area of Detroit inevitably overlook much about residents' range of adaptations to living in an area of a city with concentrated poverty but with few nearby neighbors. They do not explain the interaction of residents with the numerous nonprofit and faith-based organizations that work in their area. They do not show what makes people commit to stay in such a place if they can choose to leave. Additional research could likely uncover a host of informal actions that shape the city after extensive property abandonment—sites of insurgent citizenship, in Holston's terms, that create an insurgent urbanism.[29] "Shrinking" opens op-portunities for individuals' actions whether scavenging, squatting, farming, or doing something else with urban space.

What Makes a Difference in What Cities Become After Abandonment?

Several questions undergird the second section of the book. What conditions, institutions, policies, and actors affect responses to abandonment, and why do some efforts have more impact than others? The strength of the regional economy has a major influence on whether a central city holds on to residents or attracts new ones and whether demand for property remains strong enough to encourage owners to invest. However, economic conditions do not provide enough explanation for what cities become after extensive loss of population, households, and employment. If two cities experience many of the same challenges in population decline or property abandonment, why does one city develop a more effective response to this situation than another? And why might one set of institutions, whether public or private, launch a more effective strategy than another? The answer to these kinds of questions lies in understanding a broader political and organizational framework—mayoral and city council leadership, the corporate role, the work of city agencies and nonprofit organizations, laws and ordinances, and state and local policies, for instance.

Understanding the forces that distinguish choice of strategy and the strategy's effectiveness helps identify the levers for bringing about change under similar, weak market conditions. Policy makers and planners seek such levers. Differences in outcomes raise numerous questions that chapters in this book begin to address. Why do the leaders and citizens of one city adopt an approach that breaks with the tradition of growth coalitions while those in another city do not? Growth after five or six decades of decline seems improbable, but local elected officials and development boosters such as downtown landowners and investors, corporate leaders, and the press continue to focus primarily on encouraging growth.[30] What enables members of a city council, elected from districts, and a mayor with electoral strength in certain places to agree to devote many resources to a targeted approach to reinforcing some neighborhoods but not others? Evaluation of the Richmond, Virginia, Neighborhoods in Bloom program showed that focused public investment, even in very disinvested areas, through a participatory process in partnership with strong community development organizations, led to more private investment than would have occurred otherwise and increased demand for property in the area.[31] Nevertheless, efficiency-driven policy recommendations such as this do not necessarily get far in urban politics.

What makes a city or state agency unable to deal with abandoned property in a way that brings about change? Although agencies usually lack resources to address the scale of abandonment, the inability to have an impact also originates in other factors. For example, laws governing property tax foreclosure and the inheritance of property could create barriers to the reuse of abandoned property. What enables or prevents grassroots organizations from addressing abandoned property issues effectively? Such place-committed organizations remain in disinvested areas long after many property owners, all unsubsidized for-profit developers, and most businesses have left. Their determination to serve people who remain makes them an asset in reimagining and reconfiguring abandoned areas, if they have the capacity. At the same time, they, like elected officials, have difficulty accepting that their area of the city might not revitalize. Why can nonprofit developers in one city reuse large amounts of abandoned property while they cannot do so in another with the same demand for housing and land? What leads nonprofit developers to target their resources—or not—for greater neighborhood impact?

This book leaves numerous questions unaddressed about what makes a difference in adjusting to a much smaller population and built environment. For example, when do city officials succeed in reducing investments in infrastructure and provision of public services in a much emptier city? How can a city government become smaller and still work effectively with little tax base? How can central cities' leadership ally with suburban leadership to address the challenges of an abandoned city as blight spreads into the suburbs? What difference does metropolitan-wide action make under the same weak market conditions? Minneapolis-St. Paul, Minnesota, and Portland, Oregon, instituted metropolitan planning and growth controls that helped maintain the demand for property in the central cities as suburbs grew. However, their regional economies have been much stronger than those of the formerly industrial metropolises where central cities have lost large shares of their peak populations. The Twin Cities and Portland suburbs could grow at the same time that their central cities remained desirable places to live. What leads to just policies in addressing shrinking cities for people who remain in disinvested cities? These residents may have few choices about where to live; most live in poverty, and most continue to face racial discrimination in labor and housing markets. They may also have remained committed to the place as their neighbors left and made the best of the situation of disinvestment surrounding them through property stewardship and neighborhood activism. They can become important contributors to remaking the city after abandonment into a place with a better quality of life. What participatory processes can lead to just outcomes for remaining residents? These and numerous other questions remain only partially answered because of a focus in urban planning and policy making on encouraging growth and a lack of attention to providing a better quality of life in places that experience decline.

What *Should* the City Become After Abandonment?

The third section offers possibilities for the future, but purposefully imagining a different kind of city is difficult. This different city would not become revitalized and redeveloped to anything like its past condition. Rather, it would have less density but also less blight and would again become a place where people would choose to live, with safe neighborhoods and schools that educate children well. What frameworks help in thinking about how to plan for cities that have experienced major population decline and property abandonment?

The forces that have caused extensive abandonment of cities are greater than any person, group of neighbors, organization, or city government can change. Structure indeed matters in determining outcomes, but, the chapters in this third section assume, so does agency. Individuals can address intractable problems with sufficient effort. Leaders and citizens can make a difference in what cities become after abandonment. Making a difference does not mean a full solution so much as a mitigation of circumstances, using resources in wise, effective ways with a framework for planning the future city.

One framework is to assume that growth is not always the goal and that smaller can be better. City officials and others need to shift perspectives to find ways to make a better city without much growth and with development only in some places to achieve "smart decline." According to Hollander and coauthors, "Planners are in a unique position to reframe decline as an opportunity: a chance to re-envision cities and to explore non-traditional approaches to their growth."[32] Such a framework, however, does not necessarily offer specifics about what to do next. If city officials and residents accept that a city is becoming smaller, with less intense land use because of abandonment, what conceptual frameworks can aid in identifying strategies to move toward better cities?

No one has yet produced an approach in any city that officials elsewhere find compelling enough to adopt as well. Youngstown's 2010 land use plan innovated in accepting that Youngstown was a smaller city and in involving a wide range of residents and other stakeholders, resulting in strong support for the plan. The Kent State University Urban Design Collaborative has offered ways to reimagine Cleveland as a place with plentiful land that can make the city more livable and more environmentally sustainable.[33] An American Institute of Architects Sustainable Design Assessment Team working in Detroit exhorted the city to create more jobs and more compact neighborhoods, among other recommendations. Perhaps the most important was to engage in a planning process "by which the entire community comes to understand the new reality [of a city with a much smaller population], and participates in the process of framing the strategies that reflect that reality."[34]

While such documents help frame the possibilities, they cannot specify exactly what will happen or how to get there. Local politics and the capacities of local governments and community-based organizations will have considerable impact on outcomes. Environmental sustainability principles offer ideas for ways to guide changes. A physical framework for land use changes needs to match the circumstances, perhaps as a "polycentered" city, as one chapter suggests. Earlier chapters suggest other elements as well, such as attending to issues of land stewardship, effective low-income housing programs, or spatial targeting strategies.

This book aims to help readers, especially urban planners and policy makers, develop greater clarity about how their roles might change in a city that needs to adjust to a much less extensive built environment. Many possibilities exist for understanding much more about the cities that have lost large shares of their population, households, and employment and for making a difference in what they become.

PART I

What Does the City Become
After Abandonment?

CHAPTER 1

Community Gardens and Urban Agriculture as Antithesis to Abandonment: Exploring a Citizenship-Land Model

Laura Lawson and Abbilyn Miller

In abandoned cities, vacant land not only signals ongoing depopulation and deindustrialization; it also concerns residents because of its vulnerability to illegal dumping and crime and the associated perceptions of blight. Though many residents may dream of restoring their neighborhood to its past vitality, realistically all the vacant land cannot be redeveloped to its former uses—residences, industry, or retail and services. With city agencies often overwhelmed and underresourced, the responsibility falls on residents and neighborhood organizations to shift vacant land from being perceived as abandoned to having purpose. The inspiring stories of neighbors transforming trashed lots into community gardens lead some observers to suggest a more intensive application of urban agriculture to revitalize abandoned neighborhoods.[1] The emerging patchwork of backyard gardens, community gardens, school gardens, and for-profit urban farming suggests a conversion from brownfields to green fields and the promise of food, natural systems, and citizen engagement. Planners and designers, buoyed by the growing body of research, implicate gardening as a way to address not only vacancy but also concerns about food security, immigrant community cultural knowledge, neighborhood revitalization, and economic development.[2]

While "green cities" and "agricultural urbanism" have emerged as evocative ideas driving planning and design proposals, important groundwork remains to address the reality of effort—the labor and dedication of the gardeners and farmers—and the resources and returns to sustain such efforts.[3] These realities are particular to community gardening and locally based, small-scale, urban agricultural ventures, distinguishing these from larger, more centralized, market-driven farming efforts with considerable capital investment that offer substantively different obstacles and opportunities. Ultimately, the decision to commit to community gardening rests on a desire to act on some personal or community need and some assurance of a return on investment—the idea that this personal commitment of time and energy is worth it. In the absence of rigorous strategies to protect gardeners' investments, these reworked lands remain vulnerable to owners' selling the land when opportunities for other development arise.

Given the need to consider who will steward the land and why and what assurances of permanence such efforts will receive, this chapter draws out the essential elements of garden sustainability: participation, land, and institutional support. Rather than take citizen participation for granted, we develop a citizenship-land model that accounts for the necessary resources to sustain citizen participation, including government commitment to citizen-controlled land and organizational support. Particularly in the context of the city with extensive abandonment, attending to land reclamation efforts matters, as does the long-term function of the repurposed land itself. If community gardening is to serve as an effective urban revitalization strategy, it must be conceptualized as a process involving long-term participation, sustained material resources, and institutional supports. Urban gardens and farms that are appropriated for traditionally defined "higher uses," such as economic development, only temporarily address the socio-spatial abandonment of urban neighborhoods. To develop this model, we first look at the historical evolution of community gardens and community-based urban agriculture in order to underscore the motivations inspiring such efforts even as short-term land access and temporary leadership structures discouraged a view of such investment as a long-term resource. These land and leadership strategies changed with more recent community gardening efforts, though ambivalent attitudes about land tenure remained a concern, particularly when land development pressures increased. This overview sets the stage for us to explore recent urban gardening efforts advocated in abandoned cities for a range of reasons—from addressing local food scarcity to catalytic engagement intended to grow into a larger social agenda—that still remain somewhat ambiguous in addressing land tenure and citizen control. We concentrate on two abandoned cities in the Midwest: Detroit and St. Louis, both of which have experienced overall depopulation and have neighborhoods with concentrated vacancy and abandoned properties. We chose these cities because, while both have experienced some of the most severe population losses in the nation, each manifests a different approach to urban gardening that is shaped by its abandonment-redevelopment dynamics, institutional and organizational support, and approaches to land tenure. This framing of each city provides a contextualized lens to understand the relationship between citizen practices and land control and suggests policies that enable self-determinism and address escalating resident concerns in the processes of abandonment and revitalization. The result is a return to the idea of the "commons" as frame for community gardeners, as citizens of the city, to invoke their rights to collective spaces. We conclude with some suggestions for how to secure the commons in scenarios of revitalization and ongoing abandonment through practices of land trusts and land banking.

From Community Gardens to a Citizen-Land Model

Community gardens illustrate citizen action to reclaim and reuse vacant land. According to the American Community Gardening Association website, a community garden is a piece of land gardened by a group of people and associated with myriad benefits, from producing nutritious food to creating a community commons.[4] As defined by landscape architect Mark Francis, community gardens are "neighborhood spaces designed, developed or managed by local residents on vacant land."[5] This term emphasizes both the people and the place they create: the garden. Neither definition accounts for the political and economic systems that provide context for community gardens, both legally and spatially. We politicize these concepts as "citizen" and "land," acknowledging the relationship between gardeners and the land they work, as well as the economic reality of the site as land that has both use and exchange value, if not now then potentially in the future.

Too often, municipal policies to encourage urban gardening on otherwise abandoned land either frame the project as temporary or ignore the possible increased value (and development potential) of that property.[6] As a result, while governments benefit from citizen initiative, such governments fail to ground the return on investment—the land as a claimed property—due to the citizens enacting the benefit. The model we propose (see Figure 1.1) acknowledges that cities' abandonment-redevelopment dynamics and different organizational approaches to facilitating gardening both affect site

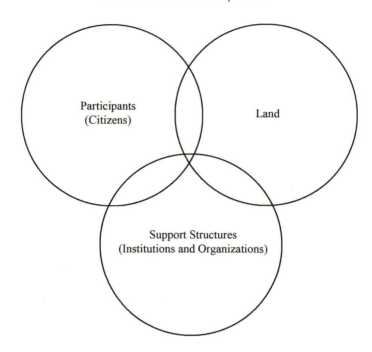

Figure 1.1. The citizenship-land model, balancing citizen action, support structures, and land tenure.

security and citizen participation. Each of the individual parts relates to the others. For instance, while gardeners may have increased capacity due to institutional support, inattention to land tenure could mean the loss of their garden to redevelopment. Conversely, guaranteed land without community buy-in (both individual and institutional) perpetuates the problem of unclaimed and untended city spaces.

Persistence of the Urban Garden Idea, But Is It a Solution?

While the contemporary "guerrilla gardening" discussion often frames urban cultivation as revolutionary and new, urban gardening has been a persistent impulse in American cities since the late nineteenth century.[7] Specific campaigns include the vacant lot cultivation associations during the 1893–97 depression that assisted unemployed laborers through food production and sales; the school garden movement from the 1890s to 1920s that established gardens for educational purposes; a civic gardening campaign from the 1890s to 1910s to promote beautification; the war garden campaign of World War I; the subsistence and work relief gardens during the 1930s depression; victory gardens of World War II; and the grassroots activism of 1970s community gardens. The social, economic, and political context shaped each of these campaigns, yet they shared many of the same beliefs about gardening as a way to promote health and nutrition, psychological restoration, social engagement, environmental restoration, and development of productive citizens. Episodic interest intensified during periods of societal crisis—war, economic depression, civil unrest—when governments and people turned to gardening as a direct, tangible means to address the local manifestation of larger crises without instituting structural changes. Table 1.1 shows how each period related to the citizenship-land model's organizational support, participants, and land.

Although many of the same benefits have been associated with gardening advocacy since the 1890s, varying organizational structures and intentions for participation in each phase created different degrees of participant control, organizational support, and land tenure strategies. In the late nineteenth and early twentieth centuries, well-intentioned reformers started many garden programs to help vulnerable populations achieve self-sufficiency through gardening. For instance, in 1893 Detroit's Mayor Hazen Pingree first proposed using private unused land for allotment gardens and farms for the poor and unemployed citizens of the city; many cities then emulated this model program. In most cases, the supporting organizations asked land owners to let gardeners use the land during the economic crisis.[8] At the same time, civic improvement groups and education advocates encouraged school gardens, vacant lot gardens, and other beautification projects, with the hope that changes in the physical environment would produce changes in people's behavior. During this period, such advocates organized support for gardens along philanthropic lines, viewing them as educational in intent and interim in structure. The tone of promotional literature was paternalistic, particularly when directed at recent immigrants or children.[9] Figure 1.2 depicts the top-down control of state-organized gardening programs, in which the participants themselves had little voice or control, except in the choice to participate or not. In the most telling cases, charity organizations sought to separate the "worthy" from the "unworthy" poor seeking financial relief.

Table 1.1. Historic Phases of Urban Garden Promotion

Phase	Primary goals and benefits	Organizational support	Participants	Land
Vacant lot cultivation/ allotments (1890s)	Food and income Moral reform Decongestion	Private committees and charity organizations	Urban laboring class, often recent immigrants, many unemployed	Donated land, often on outskirts of city; land held in speculation and meant to be temporary
Civic and school gardens (1890s–1910s)	Beautification Civic mindedness Back-to-nature Education reform	Philanthropic organizations, women's clubs, and civic improvement groups	Urban residents in crowded districts; children of all ages and circumstances	Vacant lots, backyards, school grounds
World War I (1917–1919)	Food and conservation Patriotism Personal gain	Federal, state, and local agencies; philanthropic and civic groups	Everyone, "good" citizens	Vacant lots, backyards, parks, company grounds, railroad rights of way
Subsistence and relief gardens (1930s)	Food Subsidized public relief Morale Back-to-nature	Local charity organizations and city relief agencies; shifting to state and federal agencies	People who had applied for public assistance; sometimes gardening required for aid	Donated land, both public and private
World War II (1942–1946)	Patriotism Morale and recreation Food Beautification	Federal agencies, national nongovernmental organizations, civic and philanthropic organizations	Everyone	Vacant lots, backyards, parks, company grounds, railroad rights of way

Source: Laura Lawson, *City Bountiful* (Berkeley: University of California Press, 2005).

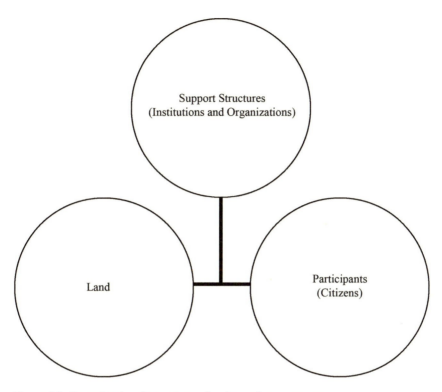

Figure 1.2. Organizational structure of early garden programs.

During these times, notions of a good, productive, self-reliant citizen circulated widely.

During the world wars and the Great Depression of the 1930s, urban gardening again surfaced as a resource, this time primarily orchestrated and funded through state and federal programs and facilitated by volunteer organizations at the national, state, and local levels to reach more participants. Through war gardens, relief gardens, and victory gardens, individuals could garden to express engagement or commitment to the nation, and in this collective effort, these hundreds, thousands, or millions of individual gardeners produced impressive results in the acreage of gardens and the amount of food produced. Gardening efforts generated praise for participants' citizenship, patriotism, and self-reliance. Supporters also viewed gardening as a democratizing activity, and media accounts often highlighted families, neighbors, and co-workers (even boss and staff) gardening side by side. Overall, though, the gardens were located on borrowed or donated land for short-term use during the crisis and not intended to be permanent.[10]

Urban gardening took on a new meaning as grassroots activism in the 1970s, as individuals, buoyed by new ideas about civil rights, the environment, and community, began to work together to build gardens on vacant land, often in neighborhoods experiencing social conflict. From New York, Boston, Philadelphia, Detroit, and other cities came stories of neighbors who cleared abandoned cars and debris out of vacant lots to plant gardens. As in past eras, though, gardening efforts did not come purely from individuals—municipal, state, and federal programs and policies emerged to encourage gardening as a solution to abandoned urban land. Some financially strapped municipalities—struggling to maintain abandoned buildings and acres of cleared land in the inner city—realized the opportunity to hand over care through rent-a-lot programs and other short-term incentives. Many gardens of this era were opportunistic efforts that did not dwell on who owned the land or whether owners would want it back. Advantages existed for individuals and municipalities under these programs, but ultimately citizens bore the responsibility as they worked to transform lots with no guarantee of permanence.

Urban gardening received a big institutional boost in 1977 when the U.S. Department of Agriculture (USDA) Urban Gardening Program established extension offices in selected cities to teach and demonstrate urban gardening. With this federal funding came new opportunities for educational programs and assistance in organizing garden groups.[11] Extension agents joined staff and volunteers from nonprofit gardening organizations such as New York City's Green Guerillas, Boston Urban Gardeners, and Philadelphia Green to form the American Community Gardening Association (ACGA) in 1978. By the late 1980s, most large cities had nonprofit organizations and/or municipal agencies that supported community gardening.

While interest has continued to develop since the 1970s, the conditions in neighborhoods have changed why and how garden organizations work. Based on two surveys conducted by the ACGA in 1990 and 1996 on efforts in twenty-three cities, the number and types of gardens have increased, including neighborhood, public housing, mental health, senior center, and job training or entrepreneurial gardens.[12] In cities that reported loss of gardens, the primary reasons were gardeners' lack of interest in maintaining the garden (49 percent), loss of land to a public agency (20 percent), and loss of land to a private developer (15 percent). Garden organization efforts to secure land ownership or longer lease agreements seemed on the rise; however, only 5.3 percent of all reported gardens in 1996 were protected through land trusts or other ownership, and just 14 cities reported significant municipal policies to secure gardens in land use planning. The ACGA responded to these findings with increased focus on training gardeners in leadership development, organizational capacity, and alternative strategies for land security, including ownership, land trusts, and advocacy for municipal policies to secure garden sites through land use planning and zoning.[13]

This overview of the changing balance in support structure, participants, and land leads to questions about strategies for the contemporary abandoned city. Historically, in the context of urban gardening, promoters have evoked citizenship, individual self-help, and patriotism, suggesting that the benefits associated with this effort would last beyond the supported programs. Self-help and self-reliance remain core values associated with community gardening in the abandoned city today. However, ideas about the relationship among the gardener, the support system, and the land have radically changed from top-down and temporary toward more participatory and long term. These shifts began in the 1970s and 1980s, when gardening acted as a grassroots response to disinvestment and a resource for community engagement. Like earlier periods of gardening, though, the fragility of the gardens became clear in the 1980s and 1990s, as stories emerged from New York, Los Angeles, and other cities about gardens lost to development.[14] In these conflicts, both citizens and governments claimed their rights to land; citizens made claims collectively from a standpoint of use and sweat equity, governments from a standpoint of aiding residents through transfer of property ownership to developers.

Today, in abandoned cities with land that has little market value or purpose, the return to the idea of productive urban gardens and farms is seductive. If framed as stop-gap measures, such efforts run the risk of burdening community volunteerism without attention to organizational and government supports. Gardening in areas with large-scale land vacancy is not a hobby; it is hard work involving substantial sweat equity. Addressing how the investment of labor in land yields returns (that is, who profits) remains critical.

With background on the persistence of the idea to provide land to people to garden, the many benefits, and the land tenure considerations and with healthy skepticism about the capacity of individuals to sustain gardens, we now look at two cases of abandoned city urban gardening/farming to describe manifestations of the citizen-land model.

Case Study Cities

We chose the cities of Detroit and St. Louis for this study because both have experienced large-scale abandonment with differing legacies and current developments of urban gardening projects, offering an opportunity to identify and illustrate the conditions that facilitate or interfere with gardening in cities where vacant land is plentiful. The cities differ in size, governance, and current abandonment-redevelopment dynamics, offering different sets of conditions within which to examine gardening/farming efforts. The differences across the cities make them desirable for understanding how abandonment/revitalization dynamics, organizational support, and land issues shape strategies to sustain community-based gardening and farming efforts (see Table 1.2).

Developing the case studies required multiple methods of data collection and analysis. Historical research provided a context for understanding how each city followed or deviated from national trends in community gardening. We learned recent history from newspaper archives and organizational publications. Interviews with community garden organizers and informal discussions with staff of related organizations provided understanding of the local political structure and how gardening organizations worked in each city. We mapped vacancy and demographic information and, when available, the locations of urban gardens and farms. Site visits helped reaffirm conditions and also give a sense of place to each city's efforts.

Along national trends, each of the two cities experienced phases of urban gardening activity from the 1890s to present, though at varying degrees of intensity. Each city, experiencing disinvestment and depopulation that began in the 1950s, had residents who participated in gardening programs in the 1970s. In Detroit and St. Louis, the city government proposed low- to no-cost short-term leasing programs to encourage residents to take over care of vacant land.[15] Both cities also benefited from the USDA Urban Gardening Program, with Michigan State University Extension and University of Missouri Extension providing technical assistance and education from the mid-1970s until the early 1990s. According to a 1979 report, Detroit's program

Table 1.2. Comparison of Detroit and St. Louis

	Detroit	St. Louis
Area	139 sq. miles	62 sq. miles
1950 population	1,849,568	856,796
2000 population	951,270	348,189
2010 population	713,777	319,294
Percent population decline 1950–2000	49	59
Percent population decline 2000–2010	25	8
Vacancy estimates	90,000 lots	9,397 parcels
Percent of land vacant	18	Not available
Population-land density, people/sq. mile, 2000	6,843	5,616
Urban garden estimates	875	210

Sources: U.S. Census Bureau, "Total Population," Census 1950, 2000, and 2010; Margaret Dewar, "Selling Tax-Reverted Land," *Journal of the American Planning Association* 72, 2 (2006): 167–80; Audrey Spalding and Thomas Duda, "Standstill," policy brief 27, Show-Me Institute, April 2011, http://www.showmeinstitute.org/publications/policy-study/red-tape /507-standstill.html; Garden Resource Program Collaborative, http://detroitagriculture.net /urban-garden-programs/garden-resource-program/.

involved 6,995 participants in the extension programs, and St. Louis reported 1,107 participants. Various long-term and short-term nonprofit garden advocacy groups formed in Detroit and St. Louis to encourage and train potential gardeners.[16] In a 1990 ACGA survey, Detroit organizations reported sixty-two gardens, five on permanently owned sites; and St. Louis's Gateway Green reported forty-four gardens, none on permanently owned land.[17] Since about 2005, both cities have experienced an upswing in organizational interest in starting gardens for nutrition and food security.

Detroit

Spanning 139 square miles with 90,000 vacant lots in 2001 (18 percent of the area),[18] Detroit has more vacant land than anyone knows what to do with it. In 2010, a Detroit City Council member publicly stated that "Detroit is not like Boston or San Francisco or New York, where land is at a premium. Land is in abundance in this city."[19] A 2009 grant of $47 million in federal Neighborhood Stabilization Program funds from the U.S. Department of Housing and Urban Development (HUD) allowed the city to raze thousands of buildings, rehabilitate other buildings, and build infill housing.[20] In addition to the federal funding, in 2009 the City of Detroit created the Detroit Land Bank Authority, an organization that takes advantage of the State of Michigan's land banking legislation and offers new opportunities to the City of Detroit in processing and transferring vacant land.[21] The city continued to depopulate, with a 25 percent decrease between 2000 and 2010, indicating that the city's abandonment issues persist.[22]

ORGANIZATIONAL SUPPORT

Detroit citizens have engaged in three essential efforts regarding urban gardening: developing networks and collaboration, emphasizing food security, and promoting locally oriented economic development around food production. Detroit organizations demonstrate motivation for self-determination in their gardening efforts, reminiscent of the bootstrap self-reliance espoused during the Pingree Potato Patches of the 1890s.[23] Networking and collaboration have taken place on a large scale with significant efforts from institutions such as Michigan State University Extension and Wayne State University, as well as many independent grassroots efforts. [24]

Various organizations formed the Garden Resource Program Collaborative (GRP) in 2003 to coordinate efforts to help residents access resources, education, and other support they need to grow food in the city. The GRP consists of Greening of Detroit, Detroit Agriculture Network, Earthworks Urban Farm/Capuchin Soup Kitchen, and Michigan State University, as well as other grassroots groups. The GRP provided support to more than 875 urban gardens and farms in 2009. Many of the urban gardens are small and maintained by a few dedicated individuals. The GRP responded to this self-determined style of gardening by providing materials and training but not interfering with the operation of these gardens. It has also developed a cluster model that groups areas of urban gardening into smaller, more manageable networks. These clusters are meant to encourage collaboration among urban gardeners, as well as provide more resources in an efficient manner. Earthworks Urban Farm and Greening of Detroit also offer training programs to educate residents about how to garden, to encourage more grassroots start-ups in urban farming. Coordination and collaboration in training opportunities have led to successes, such as training in biointensive techniques, hoop houses, and crop rotation that have extended the growing season to ten months to provide fresh produce as long as possible.

Gardening and the creation of small markets provide residents with one part of the solution to enhance local food security. Various groups, such as Sustainable Food Systems Education and Engagement in Detroit and Wayne State University (SEED Wayne) and the Detroit Black Community Food Security Network (DBCFSN), have been instrumental in developing programs. SEED Wayne, a community-university partnership, has taken a systemic approach to food security through creation of several initiatives, including a farmers' market on a main street in midtown Detroit and the Detroit FRESH program, which provides ways for small corner stores to carry fresh produce.[25] Detroit Agriculture Network's (DAN) "Grown in Detroit" cooperative strives to provide multiple venues for gardeners to sell their produce and promote local buying. DAN's website states, "'Grown in Detroit' fruits and vegetables are grown by families & youth in community gardens and urban farms throughout Detroit, Hamtramck, and Highland Park."[26]

DBCFSN has addressed issues of food in more political ways, engaging City of Detroit policies to connect individual needs and broader concerns of justice and equity. The group aims to change community residents' thinking about food, including where it comes from and who controls it. The organization engages in activities to "build food security in Detroit's Black community by: 1) influencing public policy; 2) promoting urban agriculture; 3) encouraging co-operative buying; 4) promoting healthy eating habits; 5) facilitating mutual support and collective action among members; and 6) encouraging young people to pursue careers in agriculture, aquaculture, animal husbandry, bee-keeping and other food related fields."[27] Recognizing the need for more locally grown produce, DBCFSN created an urban garden called D-Town Farm, which uses a plot of park land in northwest Detroit. The coalition also recognized the need for the City of Detroit to engage with citizens to realize DBCFSN's efforts in improving the local food system. They have pursued policy-oriented goals, including the 2009 formation of the Detroit Food Policy Council, as well as City Council adoption of a City of Detroit Policy on Food Security and the formation of a City Council Green Task Force, which has called for more vacant lot gardens in the city.[28]

DETROIT LAND ISSUES

The extreme and sustained levels of vacancy over such a large area, coupled with institutional support and resident participation, have led to a proliferation of urban gardens, including family plots and various sizes of community gardens. State, county, and city programs assist gardeners with obtaining legal use of vacant lots, but they do so through different methods. The Michigan Land Bank Fast Track Authority sells lots adjacent to an owner's other property for $100 plus a $35 processing fee[29] and leases lots for community gardens on a one-year contract for $25 or a three-year contract for $75 with an option to renew.[30] Wayne County does not have a formal leasing option but auctions tax-reverted property in the second of two annual auctions for an opening bid of $500 per lot, and the county treasurer transfers all property not sold at auction to the City of Detroit. The city has maintained an adopt-a-lot program intermittently since the 1970s and in 2010 folded this program into the new Detroit Land Bank Authority. Adopt-a-lot programs do not guarantee tenure for any period of time, but those who adopt a lot receive special consideration for purchase of the specific adopted vacant lot(s).[31]

In the context of Detroit's persistent abandonment, concerns about food access and community resilience tend to dominate, and discussions neglect issues of land tenure.[32] Plentiful land seems to imply for gardening organizations that gardening sites will not need to be taken as land for redevelopment, providing land security through high supply and low demand. To paraphrase Ashley Atkinson, director of project development and urban agriculture for Greening of Detroit, there is just so much land, so who's worried about not having enough?[33] In light of this perspective, the organization primarily focuses on training and tends to downplay organizing around protection of land tenure. Attending to the potential loss of land tenure to development, the Detroit Policy on Food Security, developed from collaboration between the DBCFSN and Detroit City Council, calls for community, school, and home gardens and mini-farms to be "protected and supported through local, state and federal legislation."[34] The Policy on Food Security also calls on the city government to "protect [gardens and farms] as resources that will not be taken over for other types of development."[35]

As illustrated in Figure 1.3, locations of gardens do not necessarily align with areas with the highest vacancy. Each property has a distinct situation that may make it vulnerable to redevelopment. Given a city strapped for resources and eager for development, land is one incentive that the city officials can use as leverage to draw in developers who might be more attracted to particular areas than others. For instance, the proposal for a 70-acre for-profit farm using abandoned property in Detroit, known as Hantz Farms, polarized opinions on whether urban gardening and agriculture should remain a community effort or become a subsidized private venture. In his 2009 proposal to start a farm that would provide food, energy, and other

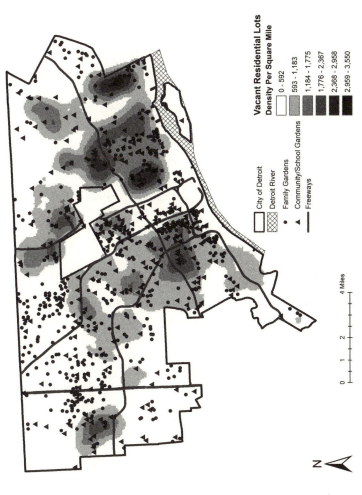

Figure 1.3. Detroit gardens in relation to vacant residential lots, approximately 169 community gardens, 40 school gardens (not shown), and 359 family gardens. Detroit Residential Parcel Survey, 2009, http://www.detroitparcelsurvey.org/; ESRI, Census 2000 TIGER/Line Files; Garden Resource Program Collaborative website, http://www.detroitagriculture.org/GRP _Website/Home.html; Jon A. Miller, "Small Farm Movement Takes Root in Motor City," *Small Farmer's Journal* 33, 2 (2009): 74–78. Map by Robert Linn, 2011.

benefits, CEO John Hantz stated, "Hantz Farms will transform this area into a viable, beautiful and sustainable area that will serve the community, increase the tax base, create jobs and greatly improve the quality of life in an area that has experienced a severe decline in population."[36] As an economic development strategy, the Hantz Farms proposal has the potential to meet these goals. The type of agriculture he describes, however, differs from the existing community-based efforts that focus on food security. Hantz Farms includes among its marketable items pumpkins, Christmas trees, and more pricey foods, and what Hantz refers to as "high-margin edibles: peaches, berries, plums, nectarines, and exotic greens."[37] Malik Yakini of DBCFSN has expressed concern with the plans for Hantz Farms, calling attention to the business's lack of racial diversity and lack of empowerment opportunities for residents beyond providing some jobs.[38] Hantz Farms would use a substantial chunk of land, and if proposals for large-scale, for-profit urban farming get off the ground, grassroots gardeners may face redevelopment pressure. With qualitatively different products and aims, the addition of for-profit farming and loss of citizen-driven community gardening could negatively affect local food security initiatives.

St. Louis

St. Louis, a smaller city in population and physical size, faces different issues from Detroit. St. Louis suffered one of the largest population declines in the country, losing 59 percent of its population from 1950 to 2008. Despite this decline, the percentage of vacant land is substantially less than that of Detroit. Swaths of vacant land remain, particularly on the north side, but revitalization efforts tend to focus on downtown and its surrounding neighborhoods.[39] St. Louis has taken the approach of many cities, turning the downtown area into an entertainment district with a new stadium, casino, bars, restaurants and nightclubs, and new loft developments. While downtown and surrounding neighborhoods revitalize, the city as a whole is experiencing population decline, losing 8 percent of its population between 2000 and 2010. One critic of St. Louis redevelopment, highlighting the discriminatory nature of the city's plans, noted strategies that discouraged development in areas of "spotty City services" for fear that such scattered investment would "sap the city's too limited fiscal resources."[40] In this atmosphere, gardening generally occupies a marginal role in the redevelopment plans of the city.

ORGANIZATIONAL SUPPORT

Gateway Greening supports almost all St. Louis urban gardens. Gateway Greening, a nonprofit organization, promotes gardening as a form of community development through technical assistance, plant materials, soil and mulch, planning and coordination assistance, and Master Gardener expertise. Begun in 1983 as Gateway to Gardens, the program evolved into Gateway Greening, with programs mirroring the ACGA's agenda to focus not only on gardens but also on the leadership and organizational capacity needed to sustain the effort. When groups come with a plan to start a garden immediately, Gateway Greening encourages them to slow down and attend to organizational structure and community outreach first.[41] While it emphasizes self-determination and self-sufficiency, Gateway Greening has recognized the need for gardeners to network and is developing a cluster approach modeled after Detroit's.

Gateway Greening also developed collaborative programs, including Urban Roots (downtown beautification), school and children's garden programs, and City Seeds, a program that engages homeless men in gardening. City Seeds provides a horticultural therapy program for those with mental illness and/or substance abuse and a horticultural training program where the men grow food and sell it at farmers' markets.

As of summer 2010, Gateway Greening was swamped with requests for gardens, many from institutions such as schools, juvenile detention centers, and daycare centers. Executive director Gwenne Hayes-Stewart felt that demand came out of need—teachers responded to children's coming to school hungry and to obesity among their students. She found that new applications for assistance were more ambitious and better organized than previous ones. However, she insisted on grassroots community involvement as a necessary step—engaging residents around the garden whether it was part of an institution or in a neighborhood. "If it is not grassroots, and if money is top down, it is not going to work. Residents are tired of being told what is good for them," she said. While some people chafe at the requirements Gateway Greening imposes, Hayes-Stewart argues that the training and orientations help assure success. Furthermore, she sees a positive response from city officials: "The stricter we are, the more cooperative they [city officials] are in supporting community gardens." Public policy researchers Mark Tranel and Larry Handlin observed that "Gateway Greening typically does not choose neighborhoods that are so depopulated that they have no life or hope, nor those stable neighborhoods that have well-developed human and capital resources. Rather they opt for the neighborhoods experiencing declining conditions but with a group seeking to pursue a nontraditional community improvement project."[42] This can mean that neighborhoods with abundant land may not meet the requirements to receive organizational support. In this context, community gardens are considered tools to bolster destabilizing neighborhoods rather than address abandonment directly.

ST. LOUIS LAND ISSUES

In the 1970s and 1980s, city government owned many lots, and officials established an adopt-a-lot program whereby community groups could lease properties for one dollar per year. As part of the contract, gardeners agreed to a thirty-day eviction notice if the city sold the land for development.[43] To purchase a lot, gardening groups must submit an application to the Land Reutilization Authority (LRA), which controls all city-owned vacant land, 9,397 parcels as of 2009.[44] This process has political aspects, as LRA application instructions require groups to submit a letter from their alderperson with the application. Policy researchers and advocacy groups have critiqued LRA for its unwillingness to sell vacant land, finding that in 2003–10 LRA rejected 43 percent, countered 33 percent, and accepted only 24 percent of applications for vacant land.[45] Community gardens, therefore, still largely operate under tenuous lease terms, leaving them in jeopardy in revitalizing neighborhoods. The inefficiency and political nature of St. Louis's land transfer system make land acquisition for gardening difficult for many.

Land security issues hit home in the early 2000s, as some neighborhoods in St. Louis experienced population increase and stabilization.[46] Gardeners with sites in "up and coming" neighborhoods found that developers were interested in their leased sites. Newspaper articles cited cases in which gardeners, priding themselves in "taking back the neighborhood," now found that their gardens were vulnerable to development.[47] A 2004 news article summed up the paradox: "Gardens' success sows seed of their demise."[48] In response, city staff stated that their goal was to "put these lots back into a productive, permanent use . . . [and to] generate tax revenues."[49] As Hayes-Stewart of Gateway Greening remarked, "These [gardens] are the heart and soul of many neighborhoods. They represent hope. If you take away a community garden, you have taken a magnet out of the neighborhood that is attracting development"[50] (see Figure 1.4).

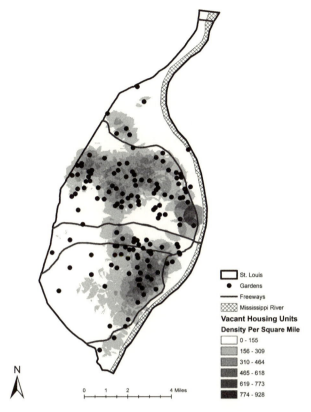

Figure 1.4. St. Louis other vacant housing with approximately 70 percent of Gateway Greening garden sites, all those for which addresses were determined. U.S. Census Bureau, "Vacancy Status," Census 2010 Summary File 1, Table H5; ESRI, Census 2000 TIGER/Line Files; Gateway Green, data file, 2011. Map by Robert Linn, 2011. "Other" vacancy offers an estimate of permanently vacant housing.

In response to these concerns, Gateway Greening sponsored the Whitmire Study that analyzed census tract demographic information from 1990 to 2000 to study the impact around community gardens versus the larger census tract area and the city as a whole. The study found that community gardening had positive effects on neighborhoods and quality of life, including retaining a higher percentage of population, increasing rates of home ownership, and generating higher rates of investment in housing.[51] At the same time, more affluent residents coming into the area did not displace low-income households. Home values and costs increased in areas surrounding gardens more than in areas without gardens in the same census tract, and neighborhoods attracted households with incomes above the average for city and surrounding census tracts.[52] Hayes-Stewart summarized its findings, from both the Whitmire Study and ongoing observation, that the presence of urban gardens in revitalizing neighborhoods was often a stabilizing force; so far, community gardens are a gentle contributor that have not led to displacement.[53]

As the primary advocate for urban gardens, Gateway Greening seeks to "be at the table" in discussions of development, primarily through ongoing dialogue with aldermen and providing strict rules for gardens to assure leadership development and participation. In light of land security issues, Gateway Greening has also developed a land trust to hold garden sites permanently. Criteria for the land trust's purchase of land are as stringent as LRA criteria and include location, cost associated with purchase, political support, long-term viability, history of investment, organizational ability, and long-term community support. In 2000, in discussions around formation of the land trust, Gateway Greening identified fifteen gardens at risk of removal for development. By 2010, three gardens from this list, all in revitalizing areas, had entered the land trust.

The Citizenship-Land Model as New Commons?

As the two city descriptions suggest, demand for access to gardening and the existence of support organizations drive urban gardening efforts. The cases highlight different organizational strategies that grow out of the local context, as well as different approaches to land tenure. Both cities' support organizations frame urban gardening as a community resource with the capacity to improve quality of life. The cases also reveal challenges to implementation and sustainability. With these cases in mind, we turn to the citizenship-land model, which accounts for community gardens as products of people, with interdependent elements of participation (linked to neighborhood population density), support structures (materials/knowledge/training), and land. The three elements in this model exist in a delicate balance. Too much land without enough people, as in parts of Detroit and

St. Louis, results in too great a burden on the few residents. In St. Louis, enough people and resources exist, but some land is contested as some neighborhoods revitalize. Detroit has an abundance of vacant land, but with greater average population density than St. Louis and efforts underway to address land transfer practices, increased capacity exists to tackle the vacant spaces, made even more possible by the strong network of resources available to gardeners.

A balanced citizen-land model might benefit from equating urban gardens with the "commons" concept.[54] Between private or public land might exist a type of property whose use value has been divorced from its income/exchange value: the commons.[55] The commons operates under different assumptions than the ownership model: collective claims to property based on use, occupation, and need trump individual claims to property based on legal ownership.[56] Municipal policy makers have paid little attention to this model, but residents may consider their gardens as symbols of community even when an outside entity owns the site. Geographer Nicholas Blomley, in discussing conflict between neighborhood residents and developers, states, "The unitary claim of the developer is challenged by the argument that the poor also have a legitimate property interest in, and claim to, the site. This interest is a collective one—note the frequent invocation of 'us'—and also a clearly localized one ('the community'). This property interest . . . is predicated on use, occupation, domicile and inherent need."[57]

Thinking about urban gardens as commons should shift discussion from land use to property claims.[58] When considered an issue of land use, urban gardens are susceptible to being treated as temporary and mobile, capable of existing in any abandoned site. As a particular type of property, whose value stems from the many hours of work and resources and the continued commitment of its users, urban gardens can no longer serve as moveable green squares on a land use map—they indelibly link to the people who created and maintained them.

Relying on a model of citizenship-land, or the commons, creates policy implications for urban gardening. In consideration of the long-term prospects for urban gardening/farming in abandoned cities, the demand for land in the city matters: is the trajectory toward ongoing abandonment or toward eventual and possibly spotty revitalization? The following two policy scenarios address land tenure in conditions of revitalization or ongoing abandonment.

Scenario 1: Policies in Light of Revitalization

Revitalization may occur citywide or in scattered pockets. Gardens in those revitalizing areas would be vulnerable for displacement, given that city officials often do not consider gardening a "highest and best use."[59] In this case, if ongoing support/engagement in gardening exists, groups working the land might transition the land into recreation, leisure, and/or open space. Land trusts, such as Chicago's NeighborSpace and OpenLands, support community gardens as collective property. Incorporated in 1996, NeighborSpace aims to provide open space and to coordinate public agencies' support for neighborhood groups' gardening through a board that consists of representatives from key public agencies connected with community gardening and/ or holding properties in the city, such as the Parks Department and Public Works. NeighborSpace focuses on protecting small neighborhood gardens and parks by purchasing, holding, and providing insurance for the spaces.[60] They require only that the land continue as an open space without structures.[61] As described by Ben Helphand, executive director of NeighborSpace, the ongoing partnerships among government, nonprofits, and community groups have established a condition for urban gardens to thrive.[62] OpenLands Project has similar goals, stating that "planners, developers, and city officials believe that there is always another higher and better use for a piece of open land . . . we work to show that open space is a higher and better use . . . open space has to be part of the urban infrastructure, and not just a social service."[63]

Land trusts play a critical role in reforming values associated with land by challenging the notion that municipalities are necessarily the "best" entity to control community/public space. While municipalities are charged with a responsibility to their entire public, whether they achieve this or not, land trusts engage in the practice of citizens controlling land as a communal resource. Land trusts also offer a more intimate scale of action, as neighborhoods or smaller communities of interest engage in decision making around open spaces.[64] In their capacity to hold land for "the public," land trusts ensure that urban gardens' value continues to be based on use, much as low-income cooperatives do for affordable housing. Such trusts operate in specific ways for urban gardens, in that gardens must remain publicly accessible and not become spaces for an individual's private gain. Their regulations also remove the possibility that the gardeners may wish to convert their hard work into exchange value by selling an improved lot. As law professor James

Kelly states, "A [land trust] does not merely focus its efforts on long-term collective needs but also elevates its goals to provide for those whose needs are most likely to be neglected by market activities in the neighborhood. Although democratically controlled, the [land trust] structure as a tax-exempt 501(c)(3) organization challenges, and to some extent requires, its resident constituents to act as trustees for the resources that have been trusted to it."[65] Land trusts cannot, however, inspire community dedication to a space, which is the reason they can facilitate urban garden permanence, but not create urban gardens.[66]

Scenario 2: Policies in Light of Continuing Abandonment

In cities with persistent abandonment, residents face a challenging set of issues, including upkeep of land and access to municipal services. In situations such as Detroit's, where land is abundant and tenure seems less challenged than in revitalizing cities, gardeners may not need land trusts. As an alternative, urban gardeners could secure long-term leases from land banks that respond to the capacity of the community organization. These leases would resemble the leases cities provide through adopt-a-lot programs; however, the implications for land tenure could differ. City officials often sell land to speculators and developers, while land banks can instead protect property from speculation. Legislation could also restrict land banks from repossessing land without the gardeners' consent, resulting in greater gardeners' control of the property's future. Residents could garden while avoiding the burden of owning land in perpetuity, with the taxes and long-term responsibilities associated with ownership. Another advantage is that, if continuing disinvestment and abandonment result in the demise of the garden, the land bank can repossess the property. This transfer of property, while more bureaucratically cumbersome, frames land in terms of "use" value.

Conclusion

Community gardens are symbolic as much as they are material. How city officials approach community gardens says a lot about how they value citizen-led initiatives. Quick to invoke the virtues of gardening in times of crisis, when the crisis lessens, the state (in most cases, city government) often changes the story of the garden—it becomes land to be used as a resource for the "public good," defined narrowly as a site for private development. The garden also helps anchor the term "citizenship" to land rights (collectively) within the city. As with gardens, the state historically has invoked the term "citizenship" to encourage desired citizen practices in times of crisis. But the citizen-land model acknowledges that citizens cannot carry out these practices effectively in the long term without some level of resources and security of land tenure, as the case studies suggest.

Respect for the efforts of individuals to steward gardens requires taking such sites off the "vacant" property books and acknowledging them as valued community resources. City officials also cannot rely on individual gardening efforts without offering some guarantee of continued land tenure and resources. Acknowledging and sustaining such efforts involve shifting out of the language of abandonment to that of community commons, a new "highest and best use." These sites may serve as catalysts for community revitalization, or they may bring resources to a disenfranchised community. In either case, the resulting urban gardens link indelibly to the citizens who make the transformation and the land they have claimed.

CHAPTER 2

Building Affordable Housing in Cities After Abandonment: The Case of Low Income Housing Tax Credit Developments in Detroit

Lan Deng

A consensus exists that housing policy should reflect local market conditions. In cities that are growing rapidly, promoting affordable housing production is necessary to accommodate the rising demand. Yet in cities like Detroit where continuous population loss has created an oversupply of housing units, the rationale for subsidizing affordable housing production may not be self-evident. In discussing guiding principles for housing policy, Schill and Wachter argue that production subsidies are appropriate only where special circumstances, such as barriers to supply or the desire to promote neighborhood redevelopment, justify their use.[1] Given this view, we can justify affordable housing production in cities like Detroit on the grounds that it promotes neighborhood redevelopment. Mallach echoes this point, arguing that housing strategy in weak market cities should focus on building neighborhoods, not just houses.[2] Particularly in cities with extensive abandonment, where many neighborhoods have suffered from disinvestment, building subsidized affordable housing often represents a rare opportunity to channel resources into these neighborhoods.

The Low Income Housing Tax Credit (LIHTC) program has offered such opportunities. Enacted as part of the Tax Reform Act of 1986, the LIHTC program provides tax credits for low-income rental housing owners and investors. It now gives states the equivalent of nearly $8 billion in annual budget authority to issue tax credits for the acquisition, rehabilitation, or new construction of rental housing targeted to lower-income households. Since the LIHTC funding is largely distributed to states as a block grant, each state can exercise its discretion in allocating the credits to individual housing projects. States may aim to expand affordable housing supply in low-poverty suburban neighborhoods so as to improve the social and economic opportunities for assisted households. Meanwhile, many states also emphasize the need to spur neighborhood revitalization by investing in distressed areas.[3] In major central cities LIHTC was much more often used to provide better housing in poor neighborhoods than to provide affordable housing in higher-income neighborhoods.[4] As a result, LIHTC is not only the largest affordable housing production program but also a critical tool for neighborhood redevelopment, especially for cities that suffer from disinvestment. In the city of Detroit, for example, the LIHTC has supported the rehabilitation of over 6,000 housing units and produced over 5,000 new units from 1987 to 2007, a major component of the city's housing development efforts during this period. Given its significance, surprisingly little has been written on the use of LIHTC in those places, a gap this chapter attempts to fill. In particular, by examining how the LIHTC developments are sited and whether they have contributed to neighborhood redevelopment in Detroit, this chapter also adds to our understanding of how government investment has shaped the physical landscape of a city facing disinvestment and abandonment.

The Low Income Housing Tax Credit Program

The Internal Revenue Service (IRS) and state housing finance agencies jointly administer the LIHTC program. Developers who wish to build low-income rental housing apply for a tax credit allocation from their state housing finance agencies. As long as the aggregate tax credits allocated do not exceed the cap amount, each state may set specific allocation criteria under very general IRS guidelines. The IRS initially set the cap at $1.25 per state resident but in 2002 raised it to $1.75, indexed for inflation. Once awarded, developers sell the tax credits to private investors who, in turn, contribute equity to the development in exchange for an ownership position that allows them to use the tax credits and other possible financial benefits from the project. When LIHTC first took effect, investors were concerned about the risks associated with affordable housing development. As a result, the price for tax credits was quite low, only about 30 or 40 cents per tax credit dollar. In weak housing markets, developers often had difficulty finding investors to purchase their tax credits. However, after the LIHTC program became "permanent" in 1993, investors grew more confident. The price for tax credits has steadily increased, reaching 80 to 90 cents per dollar in the late 1990s and early 2000s.[5] Even in distressed places like Detroit, developers could easily find investors for their affordable housing projects until the recession began in 2007. The LIHTC has thus become a very effective means of raising development funds for such places.

This ability to raise development funds has faced serious challenges in recent years. Due to the housing crisis that began in 2007, many financial institutions that were formerly major buyers of tax credits withdrew from this market. Therefore, many developers who received tax credit allocations could not find buyers or could not get the price they needed to raise enough equity. As part of the economic recovery effort, the federal government provided temporary assistance to this industry by allowing investors to trade in unsold tax credits for direct development subsidies.[6] But the long-term impacts of the housing crisis remain to be seen. Economic recovery might not bring back much of the LIHTC demand as investors remain more cautious about real estate deals. If so, distressed places like Detroit or Cleveland will continue to have difficulty selling their tax credits.

An example illustrates the importance of this program to Detroit before the housing crisis. The Michigan State Housing Development Authority (MSHDA) allocates tax credits in Michigan. In 2006, the tax credit cap was $1.90 per state resident. With a population of about 10 million, MSHDA could allocate about $19 million in tax credits. The LIHTC program authorizes two types of tax credits, the "9 percent" credits and the "4 percent" credits. The 9 percent credits apply to both rehabilitation and new construction. The rate declines to 4 percent if the project receives other federal subsidies or uses tax-exempt bond financing. The 4 percent tax credits awarded for bond-financing projects, however, are not subject to the tax credit cap. Thus, in addition to the $19 million allocation limit, MSHDA also awarded about $5 million in tax credits to bond-financing projects. The total tax credit allocation in Michigan reached about $24 million in 2006.[7]

MSHDA allocates tax credits through a statewide competition. How much goes to Detroit varies from year to year. In 2006, MSHDA allocated about $8 million in tax credits to projects in Detroit, of which about $1.5 million went to tax-exempt bond financing projects.[8] Since investors can claim the tax credits in equal installments over ten years and only the first-year tax credits are counted in the allocation, the total amount of tax credits committed from the Treasury is effectively ten times the allocation. This means that, in 2006, Detroit received about $80 million in tax credits. Assuming a tax credit price of 85 cents per dollar, this allocation would generate $68 million in development funds, larger than the amount of Community Development Block Grant (CDBG) money Detroit received in a year. The LIHTC, thus, offers important resources for neighborhood redevelopment in Detroit.

LIHTC Development Activities in Detroit

Developers carried out 255 LIHTC projects (12,297 units) in Detroit from 1987 to 2007. Table 2.1 presents the characteristics of the LIHTC development portfolio in Detroit. Developers did far more rehabilitation projects than new developments, a phenomenon common in many older central cities with deteriorating housing.[9] Only 76 projects were new construction. These new construction projects produced 5,156 units. Since the first new construction project finished in 1990, we can compare the number of LIHTC new units with the total housing units built in the city from 1990 to 2007. The city added 11,051 new housing units during this period, with a margin of error of about 2,612 units.[10] The LIHTC developments thus accounted for 38 percent to 61 percent of all new housing units. This is striking if one compares Detroit with other large cities. Table 2.2 shows the contribution of LIHTC developments to citywide new housing construction in the country's ten largest cities. LIHTC developments were most dominant in Detroit. In the other cities, they represented only a small share of new housing development. The significance of LIHTC developments in Detroit reflects the severe population decline the city has experienced in the last several decades. Without public subsidies, private developers did not have much interest in carrying out new development in Detroit.[11]

Focusing on new construction projects alone understates the importance of LIHTC developments to Detroit, given that most of the funding has supported rehabilitation. Table 2.1 lists the total number of units and the number of low-income units produced by both new construction and rehabilitation projects. Low-income units are affordable to families that make less than 50

Table 2.1. LIHTC Development Portfolio, Detroit, 1987–2007

		No. of projects	Percent of total projects	No. of units	Percent of total units	No. of low-income units	Percent of low-income units
Development type	Acquisition and rehabilitation	175	69	6,788	55	6,507	62
	New construction	76	30	5,156	42	3,634	35
	Both	4	2	353	3	353	3
Developer type	For profit	190	75	8,523	69	7,589	72
	Nonprofit	41	16	2,507	20	2,505	24
	Missing	24	9	1,267	10	400	4
Project size	Under 50	169	66	2,044	17	1,994	19
	50–99	49	19	3,228	26	3,163	30
	100+	37	15	7,025	57	5,337	51
Total[a]		255	100	12,297	100	10,494	100

Source: U.S. Department of Housing and Urban Development, "National Low Income Housing Tax Credit (LIHTC) Database: Projects Placed in Service Through 2007" (last updated Feb. 15, 2010), http://www.huduser.org/Datasets/lihtc/tables9507.pdf.

[a]Number of projects in each section; percent may not add to 100 due to rounding.

Table 2.2. Contribution of LIHTC Projects to Citywide New Housing Construction in 10 Largest Cities, 1990–2007

City	LIHTC developments			ACS estimate		Percent share of LIHTC NC units in total new housing units built citywide
	No. of projects	No. of units	No. of NC^a units	Total housing units built citywide	Margin of error^b	
New York	1,386	72,422	28,794	235,189	13,406	12 ~ 13
Los Angeles	352	21,932	10,758	128,652	9,048	8 ~ 9
Chicago	308	27,575	7,450	110,723	8,484	6 ~ 7
Houston	136	26,685	15,980	184,049	11,545	8 ~ 9
Philadelphia	465	10,022	3,807	34,193	5,369	10 ~ 13
Phoenix	44	6,250	3,286	167,795	10,368	2
San Antonio	68	9,613	6,952	144,665	10,481	4 ~ 5
San Diego	81	8,153	3,628	100,302	8,323	3 ~ 4
Dallas	120	20,238	7,968	98,343	8,396	7 ~ 9
Detroit	255	12,297	5,156	11,051	2,612	38 ~ 61

Sources: U.S. Department of Housing and Urban Development, LIHTC Database, 2010; U.S. Census Bureau, "Year Structure Built," American Community Survey 2007 1-Year Estimates, Table B25034.

Note: ten largest cities based on population in 2000.

^aNew construction. All new construction units were completed after 1990.

^bACS estimates have a wide margin of error. I added and subtracted the margin of error from the ACS estimate to get the range of the total housing units built citywide. I then used this range to calculate the share of LIHTC NC units in total housing units built citywide.

or 60 percent of the Area Median Income (AMI) and thus qualify for the tax credits. The two numbers differ due to the existence of mixed-income developments that contain "unqualified" units for higher-income families. As Table 2.1 shows, almost all the rehabilitation units are low-income units, while only 70 percent of the new construction units are low income. However, most of these mixed-income projects were built in the early 1990s. Since 1995, such developments have become rare. Two possible reasons may explain this. First, given the continuing population loss, mixed-income development may have become more difficult. Second, since developers can claim tax credits only for low-income units, they may have chosen to designate all their units low-income to maximize the subsidies. Such action was financially attractive given the rising sales price of the tax credits after 1995. As a result, developers commonly built projects that were 100 percent affordable, a phenomenon that is also observed nationwide.[12]

Table 2.1 also presents the distribution of the LIHTC projects and units by developer type. Despite Detroit's weak housing market, for-profit developers have dominated LIHTC developments. For-profit developers built over 70 percent of the LIHTC projects and units in Detroit; nonprofits built only about 20 percent (developer information was missing for the remainder). The nonprofits' share of LIHTC housing production in Detroit was even lower than the national average of 29 percent.[13] Several reasons may explain this. First, the ease of selling the tax credits before the housing crisis made the program popular among for-profit developers. With the tax credit subsidies, developers could quickly put together the financing and get the projects built. In return, they earned the developer fees as well as property management fees if they also managed these properties by themselves. While nonprofits also found such opportunities attractive, many nonprofit organizations in Detroit were small and could not compete with for-profits in the LIHTC allocation process. In places where large-scale regional nonprofits operate, the nonprofit sector has produced a large share of LIHTC housing,[14] but such regional nonprofits do not exist in Detroit. According to a survey conducted by Community Legal Resources in Detroit, the median number of employees for Detroit CDCs was about three.[15] In addition to capacity constraints, many Detroit nonprofits also faced practical barriers that may have thwarted their housing development efforts. Land assembly was one example. Despite the amount of city-owned land, getting such land for affordable housing development could be challenging.[16] The limited participation in LIHTC developments was a lost opportunity for Detroit's nonprofits. The funds and experience acquired from developing LIHTC projects often contributed to the growth of the nonprofit sector in other places.[17]

Table 2.1 also categorizes the LIHTC projects by their project size. About two-thirds of the LIHTC projects were small projects, with fewer than fifty units. Ninety-six of these projects were single-unit rehabilitations carried out by a few local landlords, who often used the LIHTC to renovate single-family housing units and rent them out to Section 8 tenants. All the single-unit rehabilitation projects were funded before 1996. After 1996, the LIHTC database listed no such projects. According to the developer of most of these single-unit rehabilitation projects, this was partly due to a change in IRS inspection rules.[18] On the other hand, while no longer supporting single-unit rehabilitation, MSHDA favored scattered-site, new construction projects. Developers build such projects with single-family housing units close to each other to facilitate construction and operating efficiencies and, one hopes, to create the synergy for neighborhood improvement. LIHTC projects' size distribution may also reflect MSHDA's allocation preferences. Throughout the program history, MSHDA has discouraged large-scale developments by setting maximum project sizes or limiting developer fees. Still, as Table 2.1 shows, while developers built only 37 large-scale projects with over 100 units per project, together these accounted for over half the LIHTC units in Detroit.

The program's broad income targeting made LIHTC developments particularly popular in Detroit. Units targeting households with income below 50 or 60 percent AMI, defined for the metropolitan area, qualify for the tax credits. The presence of affluent suburbs north and west of the city means that the AMI for the metropolitan area is high. As a result, the maximum rents allowed for LIHTC units, calculated at 30 percent of targeted household income, exceed the prevailing market rents in many neighborhoods. In 1999, for example, the U.S. Department of Housing and Urban Development (HUD) specified the AMI for the Detroit MSA as $60,500. With a 50 percent AMI target, the maximum rent allowed for LIHTC units was about $756 per month. Yet, according to the 2000 census data, the median gross rent citywide was only about $486 per month in the same year.[19] This had three implications. First, LIHTC's rent limits were fairly high. Since developers could easily meet this requirement, LIHTC was useful for many developments in Detroit. Second, as the rent comparison shows, not much difference existed between market-rate housing and LIHTC housing in Detroit. Thus the relationships between LIHTC projects and their surrounding neighborhoods in Detroit may have been quite different from those in other places. The

NIMBY (Not-In-My-Backyard) attitude, for example, may not have been a big concern for such developments. In many of Detroit's neighborhoods experiencing property disinvestment and abandonment, newly built or renovated LIHTC projects may have provided an opportunity to move up for residents who lived in deteriorated housing units.

Not only could the new housing units be attractive to neighbors, but the broad income targeting also meant that the program might have helped the city retain working-class families. For example, in the 1990s, the median family income in the city of Detroit was only about half the metro area's AMI. Thus, targeting households making 50 or 60 percent of AMI was essentially targeting the city's median-income population. However, the syndicator who has underwritten most of the LIHTC projects in Detroit argues that, except for projects located at prime locations such as downtown or riverfront areas, LIHTC projects would have taken risks in only targeting the city's median-income population, since these households had plenty of other options. Thus, LIHTC projects targeting households with lower income would have been more solid in achieving occupancy. But these projects would have had very restricted rent flows. As a result, the syndicator preferred projects that combined other types of government subsidies such as project-based housing vouchers to ensure financial stability.[20]

Examining the Neighborhood Impacts of LIHTC Projects in Detroit

Existing literature suggests that affordable housing developments can generate significant impacts on the surrounding neighborhoods. According to Schill and Wachter, housing has the potential to replace disamenities with amenities and help create neighborhood stability.[21] In New York City, for example, studies have found that the city's ten-year housing development efforts, which began in the mid-1980s, have contributed to neighborhood revitalization by transforming once abandoned areas into thriving low- and moderate-income neighborhoods.[22] Researchers who have studied Housing Opportunities for People Everywhere (HOPE VI) developments report similar findings. Created to redevelop the nation's most distressed public housing properties, HOPE VI projects have sought not only to improve the properties' physical quality but also to promote social and economic transformation in public housing complexes and their surrounding neighborhoods.

Many of those projects have strengthened their surrounding neighborhoods through a reduction in crime rates and a boost in property values.[23] However, as these studies often point out, affordable housing developments are only one necessary component of revitalization efforts, not enough by themselves. Other factors such as changing market forces and strong, visionary local institutions are equally important.[24] When these factors are not present, evidence suggests that affordable housing development can concentrate poverty and accelerate neighborhood decline.[25] Next, I will examine which scenario best characterizes the effects of Detroit's LIHTC developments.

To examine the neighborhood impacts of the LIHTC projects in Detroit, this analysis will consider LIHTC projects built between 1990 and 1999.[26] In this study, I use census block groups to represent neighborhoods. By comparing the 1990 and 2000 census data, I demonstrate how neighborhoods hosting the LIHTC projects have changed after these developments. I conduct analysis in two steps. First, using the 1990 census data, I apply a hierarchical cluster analysis to sort all census block groups into different neighborhood clusters. Table 2.3 lists the 16 variables used for the cluster analysis. The hierarchical cluster analysis maximizes the similarity of block groups within each cluster on these variables. Since neighborhoods in the same cluster have a stronger similarity than neighborhoods between clusters, this analysis helps identify comparison groups for LIHTC neighborhoods. Second, for

Table 2.3. Variables Used for Cluster Analysis

Demographic variables	*Social variables*
Total population	Persons with no high school degree
Percent of non-Hispanic white	Persons with college degree
Percent of Black	Persons who are foreign born
Percent of Hispanic population	
Economic variables	*Housing variables*
Unemployment rate	Home ownership rate
Poverty rate	Rental vacancy rate
Median household income	Percent of single-family housing units
	Median gross rent
	Median housing value
	Median age of housing structure built

Source: U.S. Census Bureau, Census 1990 Summary File 1 and 3.

each LIHTC neighborhood, I identify a comparison group that includes all the non-LIHTC neighborhoods in the same cluster and also within the same zip code area. I then compare changes in this LIHTC neighborhood with the mean changes experienced by the comparison group, which allows me to see how LIHTC neighborhoods have evolved compared to similar nearby neighborhoods.

Identifying Neighborhood Types Using Cluster Analysis

The cluster analysis shows that, according to 1990 census data, six clusters of neighborhoods exist in Detroit. Figure 2.1 presents the spatial distribution of the six clusters of neighborhoods. In defining these clusters, I have used the metropolitan median household income as a benchmark to evaluate the neighborhood economic status. Consequently, all neighborhoods in Detroit

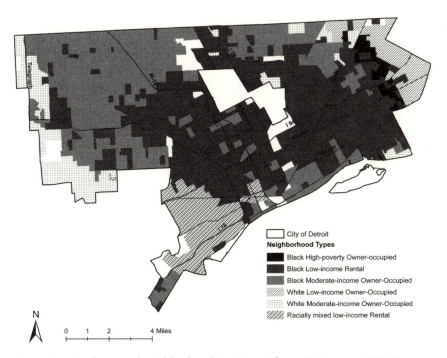

Figure 2.1. Six clusters of neighborhoods in Detroit from 1990 census. U.S. Census Bureau, Census 2000 TIGER/Line Files.

are labeled as either low income or moderate income. As Figure 2.1 shows, two neighborhood types dominated in Detroit in 1990: neighborhoods of black low-income renters and neighborhoods occupied by black moderate-income homeowners. About 80 percent of the city's census block groups fell into these two categories. The homogeneity among Detroit's neighborhoods reflects the city's experience of white flight and economic decline. The analysis also shows that, in identifying the comparison group for the LIHTC neighborhoods, controlling for their socioeconomic characteristics is not enough in Detroit, since neighborhoods with similar characteristics were spread across a large area. I thus limit the comparison group to neighborhoods in the same cluster and also in the same zip code to control for location. Finally, Figure 2.1 also shows that the city had a small number of other types of neighborhoods. Neighborhoods that had a large share of non-Hispanic whites, for example, were mostly located along the city's eastern and western borders, while some racially mixed, low-income rental neighborhoods existed in southwest Detroit.[27]

Location Pattern of LIHTC Projects Built by 1999

Figure 2.2 maps the location of the LIHTC projects by project size. The 151 LIHTC projects built by 1999 (5,021 units) are located across 104 census block groups. A majority of these block groups were either black low-income rental neighborhoods or black moderate-income owner-occupied neighborhoods, the two largest clusters discussed above. While the LIHTC block groups have an average of about 48 units each, some groups accommodate hundreds of units, while others have only a few. Figure 2.2 shows that projects of different sizes have distinctly different location patterns, with smaller projects more dispersed than larger projects. Single-unit rehabilitation projects have spread across the city's west and northeast side and are mainly located in neighborhoods with a large single-family housing stock. By contrast, larger projects, including all new construction projects, are mostly located either close to the city's central corridor or in the lower eastside, especially next to the riverfront. As Figure 2.2 shows, LIHTC projects and units are most concentrated in three places: the Midtown area, the Elmwood Park neighborhood, and the Jefferson-Chalmers district. Together, these contain almost half of the LIHTC housing units produced. The three

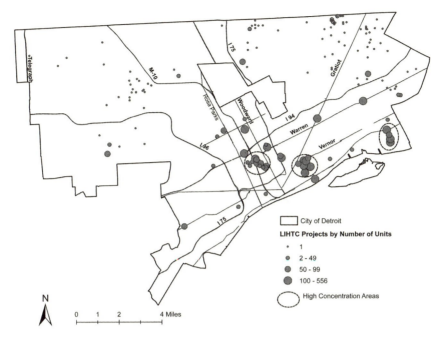

Figure 2.2. LIHTC projects built by 1999 in Detroit. U.S. Department of Housing and Urban Development, LIHTC Database, 2010; U.S. Census Bureau, Census 2000 TIGER/Line Files. Geocoded by the author.

areas are circled in Figure 2.2. Table 2.4 presents a list of the LIHTC projects built in those areas.

The first area, Midtown, surrounds Wayne State University and runs south toward downtown. The area is also proximate to the city's cultural center and medical center. With major institutions and hospitals nearby, Midtown is now one of the most vibrant places in the city and has a large number of apartment and condo developments. The cluster analysis identifies all block groups in this area as black, low-income rental neighborhoods in 1990. A total of ten LIHTC projects and 575 units were built by 1999. Except for one mixed-income development, the LIHTC projects were 100 percent affordable. Units were almost equally split between rehabilitation and new construction.

The second area with a large concentration of LIHTC projects is Elmwood Park, east of downtown. Federally funded urban renewal projects

Table 2.4. LIHTC Projects in the Three Most Concentrated Places, 1990–1999

Neighborhood location	LIHTC project name	Total units	Low-income units	Year[a]	Type[b]	Sponsor status
Midtown Area	Calumet Townhomes	104	104	1992	A&R	Nonprofit
	Coronado Apartments	24	24	1992	A&R	Nonprofit
	Algonquin Apartments	12	12	1993	A&R	For profit
	Mt. Vernon Apartments	46	45	1995	A&R	Nonprofit
	Westwill Apartments	60	60	1999	A&R	For profit
	Casgrain Hall	82	81	1999	A&R	For profit
	University Club Apartments	120	36	1993	NC	For profit
	University Meadows	52	52	1993	NC	For profit
	Architects Building	51	51	1999	Both	For profit
	Mildred Smith Manor II	24	24	1999	NC	For profit
	Total	*575*	*489*			
Elmwood Park	Prince Hall Place Apartments	556	31	1991	NC	Missing
	Circle Drive Commons	129	26	1991	NC	For profit
	Circle Drive Commons II	112	36	1993	NC	For profit
	Helen Odean Butler Apartments	97	96	1996	NC	For profit
	Noel Village	128	26	1990	NC	Missing
	Ida Young Gardens	56	56	1998	NC	For profit
	McDonald Square	180	180	1991	A&R	Nonprofit
	Elmwood Towers Apartments	168	168	1993	A&R	For profit
	Total	*1426*	*619*			
Jefferson-Chalmers	Grayhaven	190	38	1990	NC	For profit
	Jefferson Meadows	83	83	1991	NC	For profit
	Jefferson Square	180	180	1991	A&R	Nonprofit
	Total	*453*	*301*			

Source: U.S. Department of Housing and Urban Development, LIHTC Database, 2010.

[a]Year project was placed in service.

[b]A&R: acquisition and rehabilitation; NC: new construction; Both: both A&R and NC.

created both Elmwood Park and the adjacent Lafayette Park. Both were well-planned, middle-class communities with a mix of income groups and housing styles.[28] Elmwood Park was, in particular, known for its success in integrating federally assisted low-income housing with middle-class housing.[29] According to the cluster analysis, both neighborhoods were moderate-income communities with predominantly black homeowners in 1990. Eight LIHTC projects, with a total of 1,426 units, were built in two adjacent block groups in Elmwood Park. Two were rehabilitation projects, and the other six were new construction, adding over 1,000 units to the neighborhood. While both rehabilitation projects were 100 percent affordable, four out of the six new construction projects were mixed-income developments. Only about 20 percent of the new construction units were low-income housing, consistent with the neighborhood's historically mixed-income character.

The third area, Jefferson-Chalmers, is located along the Detroit River on the far east side of the city. Since the area is next to the wealthy suburb of Grosse Pointe Park, it has a mixed housing and demographic profile with a significant non-Hispanic white population. The cluster analysis shows that neighborhoods in this area fell into three categories: black low-income rental neighborhoods, black moderate-income owner-occupied neighborhoods, and white moderate-income owner-occupied neighborhoods. The area has long been part of the city's riverfront development strategy.[30] One notable development in this area is Victoria Park, built in the early 1990s, the city's first new single-family subdivision in thirty years.[31] The area also saw several large-scale multifamily housing developments, including three LIHTC projects. Two of them were new construction, and the third was a rehabilitation project. From 1990 through 1999, they added 453 units, with 301 low-income units.

The recent concentration of LIHTC investment in these places is one part of cumulative efforts to redevelop these areas. All three areas have a history of neighborhood redevelopment that dates to the urban renewal era of the 1950s and 1960s.[32] For several decades, the City of Detroit has pursued a downtown/riverfront development strategy and channeled many resources to the central business district (CBD), the riverfront on either side of the CBD, and the corridor between the CBD and the Wayne State University/Medical Center area.[33] All three places fall into these targeted areas. Each was a designated urban renewal area, and for many years, each had an advisory citizens' district council to address redevelopment in the area.[34] For example, in the 1980s, under Coleman Young's administration, these designated renewal areas received a large amount of CDBG funds for neighborhood redevelopment.[35]

The concentration of investment may also reflect MSHDA's allocation preferences. MSHDA's LIHTC Qualified Allocation Plans (QAP) show that MSHDA has rewarded projects located in areas that have a neighborhood revitalization plan or are the targeted investment areas of other public programs, hoping to generate synergy for revitalization. Given their redevelopment history and MSHDA's application scoring system, MSHDA may have favored such places over other parts of the city.

Despite the state's allocation preferences, private developers generally initiate LIHTC projects. Since for-profit developers conducted most of the LIHTC projects in these places, the concentration of LIHTC projects also reflected the private sector's efforts to capture market opportunities at these prime locations. As Table 2.4 shows, several LIHTC mixed-income developments have produced a large number of unsubsidized units for middle- and higher-income families. Even most of the subsidized housing units targeted households making 50 or 60 percent of AMI. Together these projects may help retain the city's working-class population.

Concentrating resources at these core locations is controversial. As Detroit's redevelopment history shows, critics have long worried that doing so would sacrifice the needs of the more disadvantaged and the neighborhoods where they live.[36] The allocation of LIHTC has to some degree addressed this concern. As Figure 2.2 shows, developers built LIHTC projects throughout the city, in places other than the three core locations above. Some projects were fairly large, but no clear pattern of clustering emerges. Moreover, projects outside the core areas were also more likely to be nonprofit developments. The nature of nonprofits may have motivated them to undertake difficult projects in resource-poor environments.[37] A critical issue this study addresses is whether these efforts have generated positive effects on neighborhoods.

Measuring Changes in LIHTC Neighborhoods

In this section, I examine how each LIHTC neighborhood has changed between the 1990 and 2000 census in relation to a comparison group consisting of all the non-LIHTC neighborhoods in the same clusters within the same zip code. I examine neighborhood changes on four indicators: change in poverty rate, change in neighborhood median household income, change in median gross rent, and change in median housing values. I used the Geo-lytics Neighborhood Change database to measure changes on these four indi-cators because this database adjusts 1990 census data to fit the 2000 census boundaries, thus allowing me to measure neighborhood changes for the same geographic areas. I chose the four indicators to describe the characteristics that a LIHTC development most likely would affect, given that such a develop-ment would build or rehabilitate housing units and bring additional residents to the neighborhood. Together, these indicators can offer useful information on how a LIHTC neighborhood's socioeconomic status changed relative to its comparison group. Yet neighborhood changes have numerous dimensions, and these changes may also affect different groups in different ways. As a re-sult, the four indicators considered in this study do not capture the complex-ity of neighborhood changes or their impacts on neighborhood residents.

With this caveat in mind, for each LIHTC neighborhood, I compare changes in this neighborhood with the distribution of changes experienced by its comparison group and calculate a Z-score of change for each indica-tor. I use Z-scores because they provide standardized measurements and, thus, can be summarized across the different indicators.[38] For example, an LIHTC neighborhood with a Z-score of one on median household income experienced an increase in median household income that is one standard deviation above the mean change experienced by non-LIHTC neighbor-hoods in the comparison group. I then summarize the Z-score across all four indicators and calculate an average Z-score per indicator.[39] If the aver-age Z-score is positive, it shows that the LIHTC neighborhood experienced more improvement in its socioeconomic status than its comparison group. On the other hand, if the average Z-score is negative, it shows that the LIHTC neighborhood experienced a decline in its socioeconomic status, lagging be-hind the comparison group.

Table 2.5 tabulates the distribution of LIHTC projects and units according to the type of changes their neighborhoods experienced. Among the 104 cen-sus block groups with LIHTC projects, 46 experienced more improvement in socioeconomic status than their comparison groups, and 49 experienced less. Half the LIHTC projects were located in each type of census block group. However, developers built more units in neighborhoods experiencing socio-economic improvement than in neighborhoods that fell behind (56 percent versus 21 percent). Table 2.5 also reveals a large difference between total units and number of low-income units in LIHTC neighborhoods experiencing im-provement, indicating mixed-income developments in those neighborhoods.

Table 2.5. Distribution of LIHTC Projects and Units by Neighborhood Change Types, 1990–2000

Classification	No. of LIHTC block groups	Total LIHTC projects	Percent of LIHTC projects	Total units	Percent of total units	Low-income units	Percent of low-income units
LIHTC neighborhoods with improvement in socioeconomic status	46	69	46	2,809	56	1,645	48
LIHTC neighborhoods with decline in socioeconomic status	49	69	46	1,061	21	1,060	31
Neighborhoods whose changes could not be measured[a]	9	13	8	1,151	23	754	22
Total	104	151	100	5,021	100	3,459	100

Sources: U.S. Department of Housing and Urban Development, LIHTC Database, 2010; U.S. Census Bureau, Census 1990 and 2000 Summary File 3.

[a]Includes five census block groups that did not report owner-occupied housing values and four census block groups for which comparison groups did not exist in the same zip code area.

Since mixed-income developments often added higher-income families and more expensive housing units to the neighborhoods, they may have contributed to the improvement in neighborhood socioeconomic status.

Did the LIHTC projects cause the observed neighborhood changes? This analysis cannot establish causality. For example, a neighborhood might have experienced development activities or events other than the LIHTC developments over the decade. As a result, neighborhood changes may not come about solely from the LIHTC developments. On the other hand, examining the general pattern of the changes in LIHTC neighborhoods can provide some useful lessons about the most effective ways to invest limited resources.

Figure 2.3 presents the spatial distribution of LIHTC neighborhoods experiencing the two types of changes. To highlight the role of the LIHTC projects, Figure 2.3 includes only the 34 block groups with more than 10 LIHTC units.[40] It excludes many of the neighborhoods with single-unit rehabilitation projects, since these very small projects likely did not play a significant role in shaping neighborhood changes. Figure 2.3 reveals a striking contrast in the spatial pattern of LIHTC neighborhoods experiencing the different types of neighborhood changes. LIHTC neighborhoods experiencing a decline in their socioeconomic status were largely dispersed in the city, while LIHTC neighborhoods experiencing improvement were located along the city's central corridor and riverfront areas. Neighborhoods in the two places that have the largest concentration of LIHTC projects, Midtown and Elmwood Park, all experienced more improvement than similar neighborhoods in the surrounding areas. Other LIHTC neighborhoods that improved include three census block groups in the Rivertown area to the south of Elmwood Park, which have several LIHTC rehabilitation projects.[41] As discussed above, all these neighborhoods, including the Rivertown area, have been the focus of the city's redevelopment efforts for several decades and have received a significant amount of public and private investment, of which LIHTC is part. The infusion of resources facilitated some notable improvement in these areas during the study period.

Unlike Midtown or Elmwood Park, the third place with a large concentration of LIHTC projects, Jefferson-Chalmers, had a mixed pattern of neighborhood changes. Three census block groups in this area contain LIHTC developments. One of them, located along the riverfront, was identified as a white moderate-income owner-occupied neighborhood. Since it was the only neighborhood of this type, no comparison group existed in its zip code area. As a result, neighborhood change in this block group was not measured. The

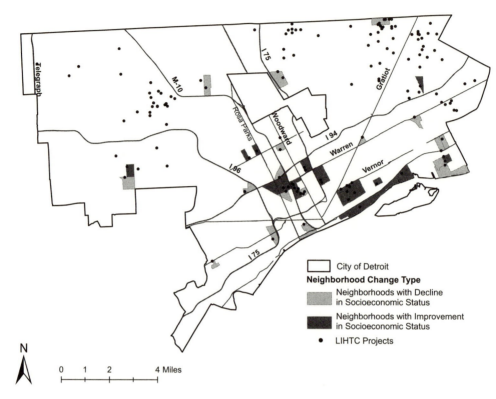

Figure 2.3. Distribution of LIHTC neighborhood changes, 1990–2000, for neighborhoods with over 10 LIHTC units. U.S. Department of Housing and Urban Development, LIHTC Database, 2010; U.S. Census Bureau, Census 2000 TIGER/ Line Files. Geocoded by the author.

other two block groups, adjacent to each other, were identified as black low-income rental neighborhoods. While the block group on the east side experienced more improvement than its comparison group, the other one declined in socioeconomic status. The first block group improved so dramatically that it had the highest Z-score (3.78), which shows that it far outperformed other neighborhoods in the nearby area. For example, according to the 1990 and 2000 censuses, the poverty rate in this block group declined from 38 to 4 percent, while median household income jumped from $14,248 to $69,844.

How did this dramatic transformation happen? An examination of the development activities in this neighborhood shows that the changes were largely due to the development of Victoria Park, the expensive single-family housing subdivision mentioned before. Since 1992 when homes built in the first phase were sold, the Victoria Park project has produced 157 detached single-family housing units for this neighborhood. The units initially sold at about $160,000 and more, but high demand drove the price up to $300,000, far higher than the prevailing market price in Detroit.[42] By bringing in middle- and upper-income families, Victoria Park has significantly changed the neighborhood's socioeconomic profile. In contrast, the LIHTC project located in this block group, Jefferson Meadows, was an 83-unit rental housing development targeting senior households making less than 60 percent of AMI. Thus, while Jefferson Meadows may have also contributed to the observed neighborhood changes, Victoria Park drove much of the dramatic transformation.

Despite its impacts on its own neighborhood, Victoria Park did not appear to generate many spillover effects. Because the surrounding housing was still severely decayed, builders of Victoria Park homes physically isolated their units from the surroundings, with very limited access from the outside.[43] The other LIHTC block group adjacent to this development experienced a decline in its socioeconomic status relative to its comparison group. Measured in absolute terms, this other block group—which has a 180-unit rehabilitation LIHTC project—saw a decline in poverty rate and an increase in median household income over the ten-year period. But these changes were more modest than those of the comparison group.[44] Thus, this LIHTC block group, historically the poorest neighborhood in the Jefferson-Chalmers area, continued to lag behind other neighborhoods in the area. According to the 1990 and 2000 censuses, although the block group's poverty rate fell from 53 percent to 30 percent, it remained a high-poverty neighborhood as of 2000. The differences in neighborhood changes experienced by the two adjacent block groups may also reflect the incompatibility of efforts to build middle-class, single-family homes and efforts to provide affordable housing for low-income families. Due to their differences in both physical characteristics and socioeconomic profiles, these projects were largely isolated from each other, which may have limited their potential to generate synergy effects. The development of Victoria Park, perhaps even more heavily subsidized than the LIHTC development, might have had more positive effects on the surrounding area if it had been integrated with other redevelopment efforts.

Finally, Figure 2.3 also shows that most LIHTC neighborhoods experiencing a relative decline in socioeconomic status were located outside the core areas and tended to be dispersed. These neighborhoods often contain only one or two LIHTC projects. A review of the city's redevelopment history shows that these neighborhoods were rarely among the city's focused redevelopment areas.[45] Lack of improvement in these neighborhoods may reflect ineffectiveness of the LIHTC investment; however, it also reflects the historic lack of public investment in these areas, as well as weak demand for housing as the city's population declined. As a result, these LIHTC projects could not have singlehandedly turned around their neighborhoods.[46]

Conclusion

For cities like Detroit that have long suffered from disinvestment and abandonment, building subsidized affordable housing offers one of few opportunities to channel resources into neighborhoods. In Detroit, for example, the LIHTC funding supported the rehabilitation of over 6,000 housing units from 1990 to 2007. Moreover, the program also helped produce over 5,000 new housing units, about half the new housing stock the city added during the same period. The significance of the LIHTC program in Detroit illustrates the importance of government subsidies in inducing development activities in cities suffering from abandonment. For-profit developers built a majority of the LIHTC projects in Detroit; Detroit's nonprofits have faced both capacity constraints and practical barriers that have limited their participation in LIHTC developments.

   LIHTC developments in the 1990s took place in neighborhoods that experienced varied changes between 1990 and 2000. Half the LIHTC neighborhoods experienced more improvement in their socioeconomic status than their comparison groups, while the other half lagged behind. The spatial distribution of these neighborhoods reveals a strong relationship between the concentration of LIHTC investment and the changes in their neighborhoods. For example, while LIHTC projects concentrate in the city's central corridors and riverfront areas, most of the neighborhood improvement also occurred there. These neighborhoods have long been at the center of the city's redevelopment efforts. While the LIHTC developments did not necessarily cause the observed neighborhood changes, this finding suggests the importance of resource concentration and long-term commitment in neighborhood revitalization, especially in a city that has lost over half its population. On the other hand, the mixed pattern of neighborhood changes in the Jefferson-Chalmers area shows that concentrating resources may not be enough to promote neighborhood redevelopment. Instead, the different types of redevelopment efforts should be integrated so that their effects can reinforce each other.

What lessons do LIHTC neighborhoods provide about socioeconomic decline from 1990 to 2000? The LIHTC developments cannot take the blame for such changes, given the weak housing market and the historic neglect of public investment. Nevertheless, the decline in these neighborhoods raises questions about the effectiveness of the LIHTC investment in influencing neighborhood conditions, given the geographic isolation of such investment. Considering the limited resources the city has, could the LIHTC be better invested somewhere else if the goal is to promote neighborhood redevelopment? This is a challenge facing MSHDA, the state housing finance agency that allocates tax credits among projects. The program does not involve local governments in the LIHTC allocation decisions. However, in other jurisdictions, for example, Santa Clara County in California, local governments have offered gap financing or other incentives such as density bonuses to direct LIHTC projects to strategic locations that fit local development plans. This is not the case in Detroit. Except for the downtown and riverfront areas, the city of Detroit has neither the resources nor the planning capacity to influence LIHTC developments, even though these developments have become an essential part of local redevelopment efforts. Better coordination between state and city authorities could help improve LIHTC's impacts on neighborhood redevelopment. As of 2010, MSHDA encouraged projects to seek local support, for example, by awarding extra points for projects that received tax abatements or other subsidies from local governments. However, the limited number of extra points cannot shape the LIHTC development patterns, given MSHDA's many other criteria for allocating LIHTC. Besides increasing the weight on local support for projects in proposal evaluation, MSHDA could communicate directly with local planning and development authorities on how to invest the LIHTC to serve local redevelopment goals. On the other hand, given the large amount of tax credits Detroit receives each year, the city government should become more involved in the LIHTC development decisions. While it may not provide much financial support, the city government can influence the LIHTC development pattern either through land use decisions or the process of selling city-owned land. Together, these efforts can help ensure that affordable housing developments become part of a conscious plan to promote neighborhood redevelopment, not just build houses.

CHAPTER 3

Detroit Art City: Urban Decline, Aesthetic Production, Public Interest

Andrew Herscher

As Detroit has attracted growing attention as an exemplar of North American postindustrial urban decline, it has also attracted growing attention from artists and architects interested in the material, spatial, cultural, and social conditions of a city marked by depopulation, disinvestment, and decay. This latter interest has yielded projects ranging from documentations of ruined buildings and urban grasslands, through installations on vacant properties, to the introduction of participatory art platforms, artists' residencies and collectives to "communities in need" and to "distressed" neighborhoods—a cross-section of artistic responses to "community," "site," "social relations," "collaboration," and "the public."

Contemporary North American public culture approaches these practices from two prevailing positions. One perspective, drawing on the work of urban theorist Richard Florida, literalizes this artistic "investment" as a motor of economic development and, thus, urban renewal.[1] For example, according to Rocco Landesman, chairman of the National Endowment for the Arts, "When you bring artists into a town, it changes the character, attracts economic development, makes it more attractive to live in and renews the economics of that town . . . there are ways to draw artists into the center of things that will attract other people."[2] Scholars have analyzed the relation between artistic work and economic development by studying, for example, the way that the arts help generate new "social networks," encourage "innovation" and "creativity," and spur "civic engagement."[3]

In the guise of politically neutral concepts of both art and development, many arguments in support of art as a driver of economic development rely on neoliberal principles of economic growth and social organization. In conditions of urban decline, civic boosters may outsource urban redevelopment to its lowest-cost producers, members of what Florida has termed a "creative class," attracted by the cheap living and working space and the dynamic urban culture of postindustrial cities. As first-stage gentrifiers, artists and other creative workers can improve properties, stimulate retail and service businesses, and effect potential rises in real estate values. When the gap between the existing capitalization of property and the potential return on investment in that property becomes wide enough to allow property development to become profitable, redevelopment becomes attractive to investors.[4] Through this redevelopment, a neighborhood becomes "renewed," at least from the perspective of this renewal's beneficiaries.[5] "Renewal" is much more likely to take place in prosperous cities with strong demand for land than in cities with extensive abandonment, such as Detroit. Critics of such "renewals" point, moreover, to the many displaced or disenfranchised by redevelopment, such as the urban poor and working class, immigrant communities, and even the artistic members of the "creative class" whose labor encouraged redevelopment in the first place.[6]

Another, second position draws on a modernist tradition of art as an autonomous aesthetic activity, defined by its separation from other domains of social life. Here, adherents view urban decline not as an object of amelioration, economic or otherwise, but as a resource for artistic production.[7] Thus, novelist and former advertising copywriter Toby Barlow has opined that

> Detroit right now is just this vast, enormous canvas where anything imaginable can be accomplished. From Tyree Guyton's Heidelberg Project (think of a neighborhood covered in shoes and stuffed animals and you're close) to Matthew Barney's "Ancient Evenings" project (think Egyptian gods reincarnated as Ford Mustangs and you're kind of close), local and international artists are already leveraging Detroit's complex textures and landscapes to their own surreal ends. In a way, a strange, new American dream can be found here, amid the crumbling, semi-majestic ruins of a half-century's industrial decline. The good news is that, almost magically, dreamers are already showing up.[8]

While this position hearkens back to—and simplifies—modernist notions of art for art's sake (artists "leveraging Detroit's complex textures and
landscapes to their own surreal ends"), it also comprises the historical ante-
cedent for the first position, in which municipalities leverage art's complex
textures and landscapes to their own economic ends. Yet, both positions
mirror each other in their institution of parallel separations between artistic
practice, on the one hand, and social dynamics, on the other. That is, to posit
art as mere economic driver is to nullify art's aesthetic dimension, while to
posit art as an autonomous aesthetic practice is to nullify its social dimensions. These positions thus fit neatly together. If neoliberal descriptions of
art as economic driver posit the social in wholly economic terms, then modernist descriptions of art as autonomous aesthetic practice extract art from
the constellation of other practices that determine socioeconomic development, leaving the neoliberal modeling of that development almost wholly
intact. At the same time, "leveraging Detroit's complex textures and landscapes to their own surreal ends" describes the first phase of a process through
which artists process the raw material of urban decline into aesthetically
and economically valuable forms—the process of commodification that can,
for neoliberalism, "renew the economics" of distressed cities.

Both received positions—the neoliberal position of artist-entrepreneurs
driving economic development and the modernist position of artist-dreamers
producing aesthetically innovative art—therefore neglect the complicated
relationship between artistic production and social effect. Recent art theory
has analyzed these relationships through such terms as "relational aesthetics," "public art," "community-based art," "site-specific art," "dialogic art,"
"participatory art," "collaborative art," and "littoral art," among many others.[9]
While significant differences exist within and between these terms, they may
be unified by their common suspicion of neoliberal models of economic
growth and modernist models of autonomous aesthetic practice and by
their common insistence on linkages between the social and the aesthetic,
albeit in complex ways.

A key concept in this discussion—as reference and as target—is "relational aesthetics," coined by art theorist and curator Nicolas Bourriaud.[10]
Bourriaud defines "relational aesthetics" as aesthetics "where the substrate
(of art) is formed by intersubjectivity, and which takes being-together as a
central theme . . . and the collective elaboration of meaning."[11] In other
words, relational art focuses not on *objects*, but on *relationships*, particularly
those between artist and audience, each forming part of a collective rather

than an assemblage of individuals. Bourriaud also provides a concrete mission for this art of relationships to fulfill: "the role of artworks is no longer to form imaginary and utopian realities, but to actually be ways of living and models of action within the existing real, whatever the scale chosen by the artist. . . . It seems more pressing to invent possible relations with our neighbors in the present than to bet on happier tomorrows."[12] Here, the collaborative form of relational art allows artists to invent new forms of social praxis ("ways of living and models of action") specified both in terms of their physical locus and their intentional scope (inventing "relations with our neighbors in the present" rather than utopian futures). Of relevance to what follows, Bourriaud stages relational art as an outcome of the *"urbanization* of the artistic experiment": the way the experience of the city as a "system of intensive encounters" infiltrates the imagination, formation, and experience of art.[13]

In response to such ideas, some theorists and critics have argued that "some of the most challenging new collaborative art projects are located on a continuum with forms of cultural activism, rather than being defined in hard and fast opposition to them."[14] For other theorists and critics, however, locating art on this continuum implies an extraction of art "from the 'useless' domain of the aesthetic," a peremptory and unfounded extraction because "the aesthetic does not need to be sacrificed at the altar of social change, as it already inherently contains this ameliorative promise."[15] Based on these differences, discussions of socially engaged art revolve around the status of the artist (whether a privileged bearer of pedagogical or creative insights or a facilitator of collaboration), the audience (a preexisting collective or a product of a social relationship formed by an art work), the work of art itself (a fundamentally aesthetic form or a potentially ethical practice), and many other issues.

In the following, rather than analyzing the theorization of socially engaged art, I will discuss four recent and contemporary art projects (the Heidelberg Project, Object Orange, Motor City Blight Busters' Artist Village, and the Power House) that exemplify different forms of urban engagement in Detroit. These projects represent examples of the wide range of artistic engagements with Detroit, facilitated by the city's vast repository of abandoned buildings and vacant lots; city government's inability to police or regulate use of urban territory; and depopulated neighborhoods, where few neighbors remain who might protest artistic interventions. I intend to shift attention from the particular status of these projects as *art* to their status as *urban interventions* that assume a certain urban condition and propose a certain urban transformation.[16] Thus, rather than regarding the city as an objective presence (a "system of intensive encounters," for example) that generically structures contemporary art, I will explore the way that contemporary art in Detroit at once imagines and intervenes in the city—the way that the city is incorporated into this art as site, material, medium, and content. While drawing on discourse in art theory, which has provided rigorous concepts of community, collaboration, participation, and related terms, I will focus on how art projects read the urban present and project the urban future through deployments of aesthetic strategies. I will argue that the capacity of art to critique urban conditions seems to relate inversely to its capacity to enlist the collaboration and participation of urban collectives; urban critique and urban engagement appear difficult to pursue simultaneously in artistic practice.

Detroit, Decline, Demolition

Detroit's decline has registered in the city's rapid decrease in population, investment, tax base, and other indicators of urban development since World War II.[17] This decline left many large buildings in Detroit's downtown vacant and uncared for. In addition, tens of thousands of detached single-family houses that make up the primary form of residence in Detroit and occupy vast tracts of land outside the city's downtown were abandoned, creating an extended landscape of empty buildings and vacant land.

Since at least the 1990s, successive municipal administrations have responded to Detroit's physical decline by eliminating that decline's architectural residue, along with building new architecture.[18] Amid building campaigns, that is, both city leaders and citizens have called the city's derelict, abandoned buildings a threat to public safety and security, a locus for illicit and criminal activities, an obstacle to economic development, and an unaesthetic urban form. The demolition of vacant, unsecured, and derelict houses, in particular, has comprised both a political desideratum and a putative urban survival strategy in Detroit. Mayoral candidates pledge to demolish vacant, dangerous buildings if elected, and mayors have promised to carry out these demolitions during their terms in office. Their efforts responded to citizens' complaints about degraded structures in their neighborhoods. As Dennis Archer said in 1997, "When you say you're going to tear down abandoned houses, to be able to say you're going to start on it and tear them all down, I think it creates an enormous pride in the entire city."[19]

The city government's demolition program reflects its inability to manage decline. First, demolition deals with an effect of decline, rather than a cause. Demolishing abandoned buildings has little impact on the structural forces responsible for Detroit's decline, nor does it open new possibilities for the city's citizens to deal with decline, beyond that of removing evidence that may undermine confidence that investments in upkeep are worthwhile. Second, city officials were never able to achieve planned levels of demolitions.[20] Nevertheless, city government and property owners demolished around 38,000 houses between 1995 and 2010, with ten times more demolition permits than building permits given during this period.[21]

The pronouncements of Dave Bing, elected mayor in 2009, are typical: "Abandoned and dilapidated buildings are hotspots for crime and a living reminder of a time when the City of Detroit turned a blind eye to owners who neglected their properties."[22] Thus, among Mayor Bing's urban development programs in 2010 was a plan to demolish the most degraded 10,000 of the city's estimated 33,000 vacant houses by using newly available federal funds.[23] In a departure from past administrations, he conceived of this demolition agenda in the context of a plan to "downsize" or "rightsize" Detroit by clearing sparsely populated or "dilapidated" neighborhoods and relocating the few residents of those neighborhoods to "healthy" neighborhoods where the city can maintain the provision of services and infrastructure.[24] In such a plan, the strategy of housing demolition as management of urban security joins with its proposition as an enhancement of social welfare—an operation in which a program for spatial control is posed as a program for urban revitalization.

Abandoned commercial buildings in the city's downtown have also been subject to demolition throughout the postwar decades. Almost 40 percent of the block frontage in Detroit's 1896 downtown no longer existed in 2002, transformed mostly between 1950 and 1970 in response to "slum clearance" or other forms of urban renewal.[25] Some of this destruction led to the fabrication of new parcels of "developable size" to sell to investors; some led to public investment in privately owned property, transforming devalued buildings into more profitable parking lots.[26] The *Detroit Free Press* and *Detroit News* have supported this demolition by labeling vacant downtown buildings "towers of neglect" or visible signs of the city's decline.[27] This narration has provided an aesthetic rationale for demolition often driven by profit for private developers and their public facilitators, as well as occasional concerns for public safety.

Yet precisely what the city leadership and media of Detroit have targeted as signs and forms of blight to eradicate has also become a site for unsanctioned occupation—licit and illicit, hidden and revealed, culturally innovative and economically survivalist. Property that has lost economic value has acquired other values—cultural, social, and political—as a result of that loss.[28] Dan Pitera, director of the University of Detroit Mercy's Detroit Collaborative Design Center, has evoked this movement of devalued real estate from the bottom of the market economy into other structures of value: "The residue itself—the 'gap,' the vacancy, the abandonment—has become the space of social, cultural, and environmental actions, interactions, and reactions. What is seen as void of culture is actually culturally rich. Through time, neglect, and abandonment, the space of speculative development—the urban single family home—has been revealed as a possible alternative urban public space."[29]

Some of this movement has occurred via the labor of artists. Pitera has acknowledged, however, that not all this movement yields real "alternatives" to given spaces, ideologies, and structures of value. For example, many Detroit-based artists have simply apprehended devalued property as cheap living and/or working space. Here, users adapt devalued spaces as locations to produce goods to reenter the market economy, a process that involves no opposition to that economy. Yet other artists have engaged Detroit in more active and critical terms, in parallel with a number of art theories and practices that emphasize collective relationships, social activism, and public interest.

Many of these engagements deal with abandoned or devalued houses, not simply as affordable living or working space but as sites and subjects of artistic exploration. In their work, artists position art in relation to public interest in very different and often highly mediated ways. The City of Detroit thus has become one point within a global geography of sites of artist-led resistance to hegemonic systems of economic development, social organization, and political imagination. At the same time, the return to the local, particular, and site-specific that motivates much socially engaged art in Detroit is itself part of a global and non-site-specific turn in contemporary art practice—an alterglobalization rather than an escape or retreat from globalization, as some of the creators of this work claim. Therefore, artistic engagements with the local, particular, and site-specific are not themselves marks of critical, alternative, or counterhegemonic practices. As David Harvey has written, "The problem for oppositional movements is to use the validation of particularity, uniqueness, authenticity, culture and aesthetic meanings in ways that open up new possibilities and alternatives rather than to allow them to be used to create a more fertile terrain from which monopoly rents can be extracted by those who have both the power and compulsive inclination to do so."[30]

In my assessment of the following four projects, I am interested in art's relationship to social critique and participatory engagement. The Heidelberg Project and Object Orange, the first two of the four projects I will discuss, connect least directly to citizen engagement in creation of the art, although they offer trenchant critiques of urban problems. The Motor City Blight Busters' Artists Village and the Power House, the second two projects, allow for citizen engagement but surrender critical perspectives in their effort to enhance participation.

Heidelberg Project

The Heidelberg Project, the best-known public art work in Detroit, was initiated by the artist Tyree Guyton in 1986; over the course of the 1990s and 2000s, the project evolved from a target of municipal demolition to a cultural landmark (see Figure 3.1). The project comprises open-air installations of found objects, discarded mass-produced goods, and paintings on appropriated property that encompassed vacant lots and abandoned houses around a block of Heidelberg Street, on Detroit's east side. The abandoned houses and vacant lots on Heidelberg Street themselves reflect larger contexts of poverty, disempowerment, and depopulation in the surrounding neighborhood, which has been in decline since the 1960s.[31]

Many of Guyton's assemblages comprise arrays of such objects as tires, vacuum cleaners, suitcases, shoes, telephones, car hoods, and dolls, sometimes complemented by painted circles, lines, faces, or words. On and around Heidelberg Street, objects and paintings occupy surfaces and spaces on abandoned homes, vacant lots, trees, sidewalks, parked cars, and the street itself. Guyton originally appropriated these spaces with regard not to their ownership status but rather to their physical availability. This extended a practice of appropriating vacant space for licit and illicit uses that was common in neighborhoods like that around Heidelberg Street, where both property owners and city government had left much urban space uninhabited and unmanaged.

Figure 3.1. The Heidelberg Project. Andrew Herscher.

Some of the spaces used by Guyton on Heidelberg Street were government owned, having reverted to the city after their owners had failed to pay
property taxes. Yet other residents also occupied Heidelberg Street, many of
whom complained about Guyton's work as an eyesore and as an attraction
that brought unwanted attention to the street.[32] In 1991 and 1999, in response to neighbors' protests, city officials bulldozed the lots the city owned
on Heidelberg Street, destroying large parts of the Heidelberg Project. During the same time, however, Guyton also received the Spirit of Detroit
Award from Detroit's City Council (1989), was named a "Michiganian of the
Year" by the *Detroit News* (1991), and received a grant (later rescinded) from
Detroit's Cultural Affairs Department to develop a café and welcome center
(1997). This bifurcated recognition of the author of the Heidelberg Project as
both urban threat and urban supporter reflected a similar bifurcation in
perception of the project as both sign of urban decline, as many neighborhood residents saw it, and potential instrument of urban recovery, as some
municipal institutions saw it.

These ambivalent responses to the Heidelberg Project express the challenge it posed to imagining what art and urban space could look like in Detroit. Especially before its institutionalization as a nonprofit corporation in the late 1990s, the project appropriated houses, spaces, and objects not so much to revalue or refunctionalize them but to foreground their abandonment. Referring to a contemporary architectural strategy, John Beardsley has termed the Heidelberg Project a form of "adaptive reuse," a means of converting the uses that urban spaces and properties support.[33] More precisely, however, the project reframed the abandonment of its spaces and properties, rendering that abandonment visible in a new way; the project comprised a material address to an urban audience that otherwise would pay no attention to abandonment or accept it as a regrettable but unremarkable feature of Detroit's landscape. These spaces and properties thus became what Jerry Herron has termed "visible tokens of a humiliated history."[34] The architecture, spaces, and objects of the Heidelberg Project became part of a performance of mourning—one whose relation to urban futures was at once actual but enigmatic and unscripted. At the same time, the project transformed the urban present from a time not only of decline and suffering but also of disconcerting aesthetic encounters, posing this present not simply as the prehistory to a time of recovery but also as a moment with its own values and possibilities. These were decidedly not the values and possibilities of neoliberal urban redevelopment, but rather of the city as a repository of disparate and small-scale enclaves of cultural production.

The Heidelberg Project can be placed in a genealogy of outsider-art appropriations of urban space to facilitate the construction and display of architectural-scale assemblages; its contested reception is typical. Often, artists can secure such projects only on the basis of expert declarations of their status as "art." The lawsuit that Guyton brought against the City of Detroit in 1999 revolved around the artistic status of his project. And yet, "art" itself is a complex and highly differentiated category, contested intensively both from without and within. The history of the Heidelberg Project as a self-declared work of art thereby forces a reconsideration of prevailing ideas about the social vocation of the artist, the relationship of the artist and audience, and the proper artistic commitment to urban transformation. Here, critical discourse about public art can become enmeshed with the object it seemingly describes from a distance, serving to legitimize that object or endow it with cultural value.

For example, in a 2007 edited volume celebrating the Heidelberg Project, *Connecting the Dots*, Marion Jackson described the Project as an example of what Grant H. Kester has called "dialogic art," or art premised not on the production of an object but on an event in which artist and audience engage in a collaborative exchange that opens each to new perceptions of themselves, each other, and the larger world.[35] Kester was describing new forms of social engagement that contemporary art has been striving to formulate. Yet while "collaborative exchanges" might emerge from the encounters of visitors to the Heidelberg Project with Tyree Guyton, who often works on Heidelberg Street, these encounters are not essential to the project; the project is based on a particular strategy of assembling and reassembling abandoned buildings, spaces, and objects. In the Heidelberg Project, in other words, artist and audience exist in their traditional places; the innovative aspect of the project lies in its reformulation of objects and spaces associated with failed attempts at urban survival as a critical reflection on contemporary urban conditions in Detroit.

In another essay in *Connecting the Dots*, Michael H. Hodges writes that "twenty years on, it's fair to ask whether the Heidelberg Project has improved the neighborhood and helped its community."[36] This is a "fair" question, however, only if one presumes that the vocation of art in conditions of urban decline is to "improve the neighborhood" and "help the community." What if "neighborhoods" and "communities" are not so much contexts that preexist and stand outside attempts to engage them, in art or otherwise, but are inextricably enmeshed with those attempts? That is, the Heidelberg Project might not simply engage its neighborhood or community as already constituted entities and might not presume to give these entities what their self-declared representatives want. Who or what speaks on behalf of a neighborhood and community? Can art *transform* the public interest instead of merely *satisfying* it? Can an artist serve the public interest by creating an aesthetic composed of the residue of urban decline instead of or as well as attempting to overcome that decline? These questions are also "fair" if urban engagement includes a wider spectrum of possibilities than those encompassed by humanitarian assistance.

Object Orange

Object Orange, a project carried out in 2005 and 2006, undertook a site-specific intervention as a critical reflection on Detroit's decline. Organized

Figure 3.2. An Object Orange house. Andrew Herscher.

by four recent graduates of the Cranbrook Academy of Art in the Detroit suburb of Bloomfield Hills, the project was to paint a series of abandoned houses in Detroit bright orange (see Figure 3.2). After four of these houses were painted, the group (under its original name, "Detroit Demolition Disneyland") sent a manifesto to the online publication *The Detroiter* explaining the project as follows: "The artistic move is simple, cover the front in Tiggeriffic Orange—a color from the Mickey Mouse series, easily purchased from Home Depot. Every board, every door, every window, is caked in Tiggeriffic Orange. We paint the facades of abandoned houses whose most striking feature are [sic] their derelict appearance.... Rallying around these elements of decay, we seek to accentuate something that has wrongfully become part of the everyday landscape."[37]

As in Tyree Guyton's Heidelberg Project, which the group's manifesto referenced, this project appropriated a residue of Detroit's decline as a resource for aesthetic production. The monochromatic painting of abandoned houses cast those houses not only as residues of decline but also as objects of visual interest and aesthetic pleasure. At the same time, and unlike the

Heidelberg Project, the authors explicitly framed this treatment of the abandoned house as social critique. Through an object where "every detail is accentuated through the application of color," Object Orange sought to repurpose the abandoned house from a mere *effect* of urban decline to a conspicuous *sign* of that decline.[38] The abandoned house is not only a medium of the Object Orange project; it is also a subject of that project, to be understood in a new way.

The official municipal response to the Object Orange project mirrored the predominant response to the Heidelberg Project. According to James Canning, communications coordinator for Mayor Kwame Kilpatrick, "They may believe they are making artistic statements but they are just trespassing and adding to the blight of the buildings."[39] Canning's statement marginalized "blight" as unworthy of "artistic statements," with the image of the city presumably to be confined to recognizable signs of urban prosperity, such as, for example, the new houses and public buildings built on cleared property. If nothing else, this response confirmed the force of Object Orange's gesture of revelation—a gesture aimed at exposing precisely what was to be disregarded according to an official regime of urban vision.

Indeed, according to Object Orange's manifesto, the group intended the project to defamiliarize urban decline and render it visible in a new, striking manner: "Our goal is to make everyone look at not only these houses, but all the buildings rooted in decay and corrosion. If we can get people to look for our orange while driving through the city, then they will at the same time, be looking at all the decaying buildings they come across. This brings awareness. And as we have already seen, awareness brings action."[40] Here, the project supplements the "awareness" it aims to produce with an "action" intended to follow and realize that awareness. This action is a collective painting of abandoned buildings: "If you see a house that you would like to see painted orange, paint it. . . . Take action. Pick up a roller. Pick up a brush. Apply orange."[41] "Action," thus, becomes a mimesis of the artists' original move; the project posits the collective as a passive interpreter of the meaning that the artists inscribed in their work, rather than an active cocreator of these works. This approach rejects the possibilities of collaboration and participation, at least according to theories of such collaboration in art discourse. The force of the Object Orange project, that is, is enmeshed with its specified end (recognition of/response to Detroit's decline). The gesture of exposure, with Object Orange presuming that its audience would be surprised, disturbed, or educated by its architectural revelation of Detroit's decline, "is assigned a crucial operative power."[42] Aimed at this exposure, the project intends its audience to decipher and reproduce its objects, rather than to interact with and transform those objects in a way that engages the audience in the process.

Motor City Blight Busters' Artist Village

Collaboration and participation are explicit foci of the second two projects I will discuss. The first of these projects, Motor City Blight Busters, is a non-profit organization in northwest Detroit dedicated to "stabilizing and revitalizing neighborhoods."[43] Part of the Blight Busters' work is dedicated to fulfilling the city's demolition program, with the organization employing workers from both Michigan's prison-to-work program and Detroit's summer youth program in order to demolish government-owned houses in bad condition.[44] This strategy is a "collaboration" with municipal institutions; it is also a symptom of municipal incapacity, with volunteer organizations assuming the responsibility of public authorities to either carry out demolition or require property owners to do so. The Blight Busters explain the demolition they carry out along the same lines as Detroit's municipal authorities; according to John George, founder and director of the organization, when derelict structures are demolished, "crime goes down, property values go up and community spirit soars."[45]

Another part of the organization's work involves the renovation and building of new homes, again with the assistance of volunteers, including many from summer youth programs. According to the Blight Busters' website, between 1988 and 2011, Motor City Blight Busters employed 12,000 volunteers in demolition of 113 abandoned homes, renovation of 176 homes, and construction of 114 new homes.[46] The organization achieves a wide "participation," albeit in the frame of realizing the city's given projects of demolition and construction; again, the strategy blurs the boundary between economic outsourcing and social community building.

Among the urban renewal projects that Blight Busters has carried out is an "Artist Village" in the Old Redford neighborhood in northwest Detroit.[47] The organization has focused on this neighborhood, site of its headquarters, and has assisted several business start-ups in the area.[48] The Artist Village is located in a series of adjacent buildings acquired by the Blight Busters; the organization converted spaces in these buildings into a gallery, café, theater,

Figure 3.3. Plywood butterflies painted in Chazz Miller's workshop for Motor City Blight Busters. Andrew Herscher.

and artist studio. The intention was "to provide a space for artists to nurture and develop their creative spirit . . . while also providing a community gathering place where residents of the area could come together to enjoy arts, music and entertainment."[49] The artist studio in the village was occupied in 2010 by Chazz Miller, who has painted murals over the exterior walls of the complex of buildings, as well as on several other buildings in the neighborhood. Miller also leads workshops where volunteers, including many youth in after-school programs, paint large plywood cutouts shaped like butterflies, which Miller then places on walls throughout the surrounding neighborhood, including on abandoned buildings that Blight Busters has boarded up (see Figure 3.3). The Blight Busters claim this as a form of "urban beautification," a claim often repeated in media reporting about the work of the organization: "melding commerce and creativity, [Chazz Miller] uses larger-than-life art to pull investments into some of the city's most blighted blocks. Art is not just for museums anymore—it's a way to redevelop and redefine a city by changing its visual landscape."[50]

Here, proponents yoke the most conventional form of art ("beautification") to a development agenda that is at once community based and neoliberal—an outsourcing of urban renewal to the private sector, which murals and butterflies putatively orient toward spaces of potential investment. On one level, this is magical thinking, as the mere presence of art neither produces nor signals the gap between actual real estate values and potential returns that prompt investment in real estate development; on another level, this thinking is not magical enough, as it renders art a mere instrument of real estate marketing and the public merely passive admirers of this instrument. The Motor City Blight Busters adeptly involve volunteers in the production of art, just as in housing demolition and construction; but, in so doing, art becomes but one more activity, one more form of urban renewal, with no distinguishing characteristics or possibilities. Art is therefore entered into the city's sanctioned development processes.

Power House

The Power House, imagined by the artist Mitch Cope and the architect Gina Reichert in the frame of their two-person group, Design 99, explicitly focuses on collaboration and participation as central goals. The Power House is located in the north of Hamtramck, a city of 25,000 surrounded by Detroit. Its neighborhood functions, as does much of Hamtramck, as a destination for new immigrants, particularly those from Bangladesh and the former Yugoslavia. Though Design 99 posits this area as "challenging," its demographics, relative to Detroit as a whole, are those of a relatively intact and functional neighborhood.[51] Nevertheless, the Power House project poses this neighborhood as a site of ameliorative community building.

The Power House comprises one of several properties that Design 99 has purchased with the intention of forming a neighborhood infrastructure for artistic and cultural activity (see Figure 3.4).[52] In the words of Design 99, the Power House is a "social art project" intended to become "a platform for communication between members of the community."[53] Its authors describe the content of this communication in terms of "ideas, knowledge and expertise about the fundamentals of neighborhood living, i.e., gardening, house work, new technologies, safety and so on."[54] Numerous institutions and projects in Detroit have taken on the tasks of community building and knowledge sharing; Power House's novel approach is to conceive of these tasks as those of art.

Figure 3.4. Power House. Andrew Herscher.

At the same time, its proponents also pose the Power House as a pedagogical object, teaching neighbors about novel and sustainable forms of architecture:

> Each move we make to the house is meant to be a kind of crude per-
> formance in that the house is situated in a highly visible location
> and has no trouble in attracting an audience and help from the im-
> mediate neighbors. Each action is an unusual and complex move,
> not within the norm of what is a familiar way to build, renovate or
> garden. This is intentional for two reasons: [1] We are attempting to
> develop a way of renovating with as little money as possible, because
> we have none, by using resources that are unique to our contempo-
> rary life such as the internet, cheap renewable energy, an old pick
> up truck and help from local skilled and unskilled workers. [2] We
> would like to prove that you can renovate old Detroit houses cheaply,
> but with even more quality, efficiency and functional as well as aes-
> thetic design than if you simply bought all the raw materials from

a big box store, hired a professional crew and finished the project in a week.[55]

The Power House project thus poses its Hamtramck neighborhood, and Detroit more generally, as a space for social and economic improvement. Part of this improvement is directed at derelict houses, with the Power House intended as a model of architectural renovation. Yet proponents also pose physical renovation as a facilitator of social interaction, with the Power House inspiring dialogue between its artist/architect and neighborhood audience, becoming "a symbol for creativity, new beginnings and social interaction within the neighborhood."

Yet who, exactly, are "members of the community" that these proponents address? In the terms of the project, they are people concerned with "gardening, house work, new technologies, safety and so on"—people who either own property or have access to property. Here, the "public" that concerns the Power House is circumscribed and, in the context of Detroit, rather entitled; the purpose of the project is to consolidate the property relations of this public, rather than to transform these relations more generally or more radically.

Moreover, though proponents describe the Power House in interactive terms ("social art project," "platform for communication," "interactive site," and so on), Design 99 positions itself in the traditional role of an artist broadcasting to an audience, as well as a participant in an exchange where both artist and audience have capacities to speak, listen, learn from another, and transform one another. In what directions can "communication" facilitated by the Power House move? From Design 99's description, artists primarily communicate know-how on low-cost house renovation to their audience, while this audience provides "help" in response. Design 99 posits this audience first as "immediate neighbors," with the performance of the Power House's renovation intended to function within the boundaries of the building's neighborhood context. If the neighborhood has an immediate spatial identity, its other identities—the ethnic, religious, socioeconomic, legal identities of a community of recent immigrants to the United States—are here minimized or bracketed. On the basis of this bracketing, Design 99 and its neighbors can become members of the same neighborhood "community."

The wide circulation of the ideas of Power House, in its still unfinished form, in discourse about contemporary art in Detroit, testifies to the extraneous nature of collaboration and participation in the project.[56] While some theorists posit "conversation [as] . . . an integral part of the work itself," in the case of community-based art, the Power House is already functioning as an (imagined) work without such conversation.[57] One commentator on the Power House, Charles Esche, director of the Van Abbe Museum in Eindhoven, the Netherlands, has described the project as located "at the intersection of relational art practices and site-specific art."[58] Esche's description of the Power House acknowledged the project's intentions toward interaction and dialogic exchange but also smoothed over the tension between the project's status as a site-specific *object* and as a relational *occasion* for communication between artist and audience. That is, the Power House is intended both as a pedagogic object, a model house where artists can display useful techniques of renovation to their urban audience, but also as a communicative occasion between artists and audience.

When and how do artists switch from being authors of "crude performances" to serving as an audience receptive to their own audience's performances? How does the "social interaction" that the Power House intends to facilitate relate to the neighborhoods' other social interactions, now defined in terms of ethnic identity and religious affiliation? To whom, finally, accrues the value—economic and cultural—that the Power House is intended to produce? Esche writes that, to Design 99, "it is about finding a way to live in the existing condition of their communities, with its existing problems."[59] While this statement may be true, it poses the project as a way for contemporary artists to "keep it real" in Detroit, rather than to contribute anything to residents whose inhabitation of Detroit may be the result of social or economic necessity instead of artistic freedom. Here, the artist's experience of "community" serves as proxy for the neighbors' experience of and interaction with an artist.

Conclusion: Detroit Art City

The Heidelberg Project and Object Orange serve not as "solutions" to urban decline, but rather as critiques of and reflections on given solutions and, in the case of the Heidelberg Project, on the very categorization of Detroit as a problem to solve. The Heidelberg Project and Object Orange open up thought about and imagination of urban futures in Detroit, beyond those currently on offer. Each project leverages artistic practice to reconsider the identity and development of the city; each project, thus, poses art in conflict with the city as an object of normative political, social, and economic practices. Opponents have forced the Heidelberg Project, with its ongoing occupation of an urban site, to resolve the conflict between its conceptual status of critique and spatial status as appropriation of property. Object Orange, by contrast, was a series of one-time property appropriations whose spatial residues were left available for subsequent appropriations, a form of performance whose meanings the project manifesto attempted to determine.

Promoters offer the Artist Village and Power House as solutions to decline, deputizing artistic practice in service of urban development. These projects offer a putative rapprochement between art and the city, surrendering critical perspectives on one or the other phenomenon in the service of social effect, use, or outcome. The Artist Village and Power House may extend particular futures already on offer, futures premised on neighborhood-based collectivity and participation in sanctioned forms of urban development. At the Artist Village, the artist accepts the traditional role of art as beautification; the project is thus more of interest as "urban intervention" than as "art." At the Power House, the artists take on tasks (building neighborhood identity and interaction) that other urban actors have already imagined and attempted; the project is thus more of interest as "art" than as "urban intervention."

In Detroit, then, the capacity of art to engage critically in the city relates inversely to its capacity to enlist collaboration and participation of urban collectives. Projects that suggest critical reformulations of the urban present and future exist as site-specific objects, like the Heidelberg Project, while projects that allow wide participation also accommodate the development agendas the city has outsourced, like the Artist Village. The possibilities for an art project to engage a neighborhood's residents or a city's citizens in a critical reformulation of the city and of the project itself remain untested. Kester asks, "What does it mean for the artist to surrender the security of self-expression for the risk of inter-subjective engagement?"[60] This question, in Detroit, remains open, along with the possibilities for rethinking the city's decline and future.

PART II

What Makes a Difference in
What Cities Become
After Abandonment?

CHAPTER 4

Decline-Oriented Urban Governance in Youngstown, Ohio

Laura Schatz

Population decline presents numerous challenges for municipal officials: vacant properties, infrastructure overcapacity, shrinking municipal revenues, and high crime rates. Policies to address these challenges typically focus on attracting outside investment to "grow" the local economy and population. "Going for growth," however, has been largely unsuccessful.[1] In recent years, shrinking cities researchers have called for a new approach to planning and policy making: decline-oriented planning.[2] Decline-oriented planning leaves behind the assumption of the likelihood and need for population growth. Instead, it urges planners and policy makers to "rightsize" the city to current population levels (by, for instance, removing infrastructure) and plan for future population decline while maintaining good quality of life for remaining residents.

Adopting a decline-oriented approach will not be easy, especially in North America where growth-oriented planning is entrenched.[3] The fixation on growth has deep roots in the boosterism that accompanied the settlement of the West and the industrial revolution. Growing North American cities "are the 'successful,' desirable, and admired ones, while residents of Nowheresville struggle with a diminished sense of self-worth."[4] Convincing local policy makers and planners to accept future population decline and plan for it will require a paradigm shift. In addition, another layer of complexity exists: in the process of urban policy making and implementation, local officials depend on the expertise and resources of a wide range of actors (including private, civil, and intergovernmental sector actors) to make and implement policy. Even if planners and policy makers shift their mind-set away from growth-oriented planning, they cannot "go it alone" to create and implement successful decline-oriented policies. They will need a strong "supporting cast" also willing to make this shift.

In this chapter I examine the constellation of actors—including local government, external planning consultants, the university, and local residents and community groups—involved in the creation of the *Youngstown 2010 Plan* for Youngstown, Ohio. Youngstown was one of the first cities in the United States to adopt a decline-oriented approach to planning in its citywide plan.[5] My goal is to contribute to understanding what might facilitate the adoption of decline-oriented planning. The *Youngstown 2010 Plan* was created through the fortuitous coming together of several key actors—in other words, through the process of *governance*—each of whom was eager to "do something different." Using Minnery's concept of "stars and their supporting cast,"[6] I conclude that leadership from public sector and non-profit sector "stars," including a new generation of city officials, Youngstown State University (YSU) administrators and City Council members; the relegation of the private business sector into a small supporting role; and the rise of the local residents and community groups (whose participation was facilitated by outside planning consultants) as key supporting actors enabled the adoption of a decline-oriented approach. While some have criticized the *Youngstown 2010 Plan* as overly ambitious about what city officials and others could implement, its focus on rightsizing the city represented a break from traditional growth-oriented planning but inspired little opposition.

The Urban Governance Perspective

The urban governance perspective provides a useful lens through which to examine local policy making and implementation.[7] According to urban governance researchers, declining financial resources and growing responsibilities for service delivery have led officials in both growing and shrinking cities to change how they govern. Minnery explains that governance is "an approach to public policy making and implementation that specifically incorporates the roles of formal government, the market and civil society. The change from 'government' to 'governance' illustrates a change from an expectation that public policy making is the sole responsibility of formal governments to an expectation that public policy making also incorporates a role for the private sector and the community sector."[8] Local policies are no longer created and implemented solely by local *government*, but by various local actors through the "messy" process of local *governance* in a particular context.[9] State and federal structures and policies define the functions and scope of local governance, such as the capacity of local government to raise revenue.[10] However, local actors play a critical role in shaping and responding to that context.[11]

In an era of globalization where communities face a multitude of complex issues, local governments have become more dependent on the expertise and resources of private, voluntary, and civil sector actors. As Stoker states, "No single actor, public or private, has the knowledge and resource capacity to tackle problems unilaterally."[12] Needing policy innovation and creativity, local governments must draw on the expertise of a range of actors.[13] One of the key tasks of local government officials in policy making is to encourage public participation, "to facilitate network governance, to mobilise citizens through public meetings or the media and in other ways work for more inclusion."[14] Not only does drawing on local knowledge and varied expertise lead to more creative solutions,[15] involving actors outside government results in more efficient implementation: "if consensus has been reached around a public policy, its implementation is smooth, since the policy is either passively accepted or, most likely, actively endorsed by the citizenry."[16] But involving other actors may lead to outcomes at odds with policy intentions. The nature of governance "implies a greater willingness to cope with uncertainty and open-endedness on the part of policy-framers."[17]

The urban governance perspective assists in studying policy making in shrinking cities. Not only do these local governments face the fiscal cutbacks and growing responsibilities imposed on all cities, they also must deal with the challenge of a declining tax base, which hampers the capacity of local government leaders to cope with the issues that arise from population decline (including infrastructure overcapacity and vacant properties).[18] Therefore, planners and policy makers in shrinking cities need to draw on other sources of expertise and other resources. What is more, since traditional growth-oriented policies have proven ineffective in reversing population and job loss, leaders need innovative policies. However, local officials in many shrinking cities cannot develop new solutions because of strong ties within networks of "old" local actors unreceptive to new, innovative approaches.[19] Matthiesen argues that the "wrong" constellation of actors can inhibit creativity.[20] On the other hand, the right constellation of actors can lead to creative governance.

What constellation of actors, then, contributes to decline-oriented planning? Urban governance literature identifies the major parties as the public sector, the private sector, the community (including residents and community groups such as neighborhood groups and churches), and the voluntary sector (including nonprofit organizations).[21] Each comprises parties with some connection to the locality, either through location in the place (neighborhood groups, local businesses) or through political/economic/social ties (county, state, and federal governments; globalized private interests). They do not play an equal role. According to Minnery, in any urban governance relationship, one party plays a "starring" role and the others play "supporting" roles.[22]

The makeup of the "cast" will affect the outcome.[23] Where business interests dominate—what Pierre has termed "progrowth governance"—local officials may not work in the interest of the broader public.[24] Where local residents and community groups dominate—in what can be called "welfare governance"—officials may overlook the potential role of the private sector.[25] Policies created through each type of urban governance (be it progrowth, welfare, managerial—where the role of government is to manage the delivery of services—or corporatist—where government tends to the interests of organized labor and business sectors) reflect the overarching norms, values, and political objectives of the "star." Most often, the local government functions as "star," which, according to Minnery, means its role may range from dominating the policy-making process and outcomes to simply being the center of attention.[26]

Overview of the *Youngstown 2010 Plan*

Youngstown[27] is a former steel town located in the Mahoning Valley of northeastern Ohio. Like other cities in this industrial heartland, Youngstown's fortunes have grown and declined with the fortunes of the industry, steel, on which it depended.[28] The first steel mill appeared in the Mahoning Valley in the late 1800s when Youngstown was a village of 3,000. By the 1930s, Youngstown reached its peak population of 170,000.[29] In a short period of time beginning in September 1977 with the announcement of the impending closure of Youngstown Sheet and Tube's Campbell works and the layoff of 5,000 workers, Youngstown lost about 50,000 manufacturing jobs.[30] The loss of these jobs, together with suburban flight starting in the 1950s, led to population decline to just under 67,000 in 2010.[31] A Youngstown economic development official (and native) noted that "You went from a community you felt had prosperity and a future to a community that had a 20 percent unemployment rate and there are lines for people to get jobs at McDonald's. I mean, it was just a collapse of almost the American Dream."[32]

At the turn of the millennium, after years of unsuccessful efforts to return Youngstown to its former population (mostly through attempts to attract large-scale developments including, according to one local official, a blimp factory), city officials embarked on creating a new plan. The last comprehensive plan was written in the early 1950s and updated in 1974. Planners in the thriving city had expected the population to grow.[33] The city set aside large amounts of land for residential, commercial, and industrial expansion. After the collapse of the steel industry, the lack of appropriate vision and guidance resulted in failed "knee jerk reactions to events outside of the city's control."[34] At the time of the new planning process, city officials faced demographic, physical, economic, social, and environmental challenges unanticipated in 1951. After losing more than half its population, the city had excess infrastructure (roads, sewers, and water lines) to maintain with tax revenues from a shrinking number of taxpayers whose property had lost taxable value.[35] Dealing proactively with the physical effects of population decline became the primary focus of the planning process and the *Youngstown 2010 Plan*.

The two main components of *Youngstown 2010* are the Vision and the Citywide Plan. Urban Strategies (a Canadian planning consulting firm) crafted the Vision after extensive public consultation. A team made up of city planners; and Youngstown State University staff wrote the Plan based on the Vision and further public consultation. The four principles of the Vision are

Accepting that we are a smaller city: Youngstown should strive to be a model of a sustainable mid-sized city;
Defining Youngstown's role in the new regional economy: Youngstown must align itself with the realities of the new regional economy;
Improving Youngstown's image and enhancing quality of life: Making Youngstown a healthier and better place to live and work; and
A call to action: An achievable and practical action-oriented plan to make things happen.[36]

The acceptance of Youngstown as a smaller city led the media to describe the Plan as "unusual," an "exception," "a monumental step in the face of the US growth paradigm," "haltingly honest," a "big psychological shift," and a "radical experiment."[37] The implication was that Youngstown could not depend on future population growth. Consequently, the city must downsize the built environment to meet current population levels.

The Plan contains such decline-oriented policies as consolidating infrastructure, directing development into stable neighborhoods, and converting abandoned spaces into green space. The general theme is that vacant land can be a good thing; city officials can be "generous" with urban land and can explore "new options for the city's neighborhoods and open space systems."[38] The downsized city can become "cleaner and greener" and offer a better quality of life for residents. Officials in other shrinking cities, such as Wheeling, West Virginia, and Dayton, Ohio, noticed and sent representatives to Youngstown to determine whether this new approach might work in their cities.[39] As a Cleveland publication stated, "the buzz has left others wishing aloud that Cleveland would follow the lead of, yes, *Youngstown*."[40] What constellation of actors contributed to the adoption of this innovative approach?

Starring and Supporting Roles in the *Youngstown 2010* Planning Process

The Stars: City Officials, Youngstown City Council, and Youngstown State University Administrators

Key public sector and nonprofit actors played a strong leadership role by initiating and guiding the *Youngstown 2010* planning process. They did so with the intent of finding a new approach because the old approach—waiting for a "white knight" that would "save" Youngstown, as several participants described it—was not working. In 2001, the Youngstown City Council, motivated in part by a Harwood Group report commissioned by the C. S. Mott Foundation in 1999 that found that Youngstown had assets but was "waiting for leadership," decided to allocate $300,000 in Community Development Block Grants for the planning process.[41] One participant (a YSU administrator with experience planning in another declining city) commented that, for allocating this funding (and for later adopting the *Youngstown 2010* Plan), the City Council "deserves an enormous amount of credit. [The council] played a . . . quite heroic role in all of this."[42] In his previous experience in another shrinking city, the council was not as supportive.

Significantly, the City Council made this decision during a period of change in local politics characterized by removal of the "old guard" (key members of the business community and local politicians) and the election and hiring of a younger generation of politicians and planners. In the 1990s, law enforcement cracked down on organized crime and political corruption in Youngstown. Particularly important was the indictment, conviction, and imprisonment of U.S. representative James A. Traficant, Jr., for corruption. Many residents and officials viewed the jailing of Traficant "as a turning point for the community. It offered an opportunity to focus on new beginnings."[43] A Youngstown State University administrator explained that Congressman Traficant "was sort of the last of the machine politicians. . . . there was a long, long history of a few key actors in the business community and the unions and the political world calling the shots. So you had a power vacuum that emerged when he was sort of the last of the bosses."[44]

New leaders filled this power vacuum. They were able to leave behind old approaches in search of a new idea. The younger leadership included Jay Williams, director of Youngstown's community development agency at the start of the *Youngstown 2010* planning process, elected mayor in 2003 at age thirty-four (the first African-American and the youngest mayor of Youngstown); Anthony Kobak, twenty-nine when he took over as chief planner; and Bill D'Avignon, who became planning director in his mid-thirties.[45] They had only known Youngstown in decline, not as a thriving steel town. A high-ranking city official explained: "I was born in 1971, and certainly the steel mills were still going. Youngstown still had a significant population, so it hadn't crashed yet. But the Youngstown I remember growing up is pretty much the Youngstown we have now. . . . My parents did not work in the steel mills. My grandparents did, but my immediate family members had already understood that there was going to be change in their jobs and in their careers. So I think generational influences certainly played a lot in [the willingness to find a new approach]."[46]

Another YSU administrator agreed that a generational shift precipitated interest in a new approach for Youngstown: "We had 27 miles of mills from Newton to Newcastle, Pennsylvania, and all of them are gone, so for a long time the buildings were still there, and I think a big change in the attitude here came when the buildings finally disappeared [in the 1990s]. . . . [A]s long as those buildings were standing there, the people who had worked in the mills all thought, 'well there's still a chance.' We have a generation now that never saw the mills, and so their attitudes are completely different."[47]

This new generation of public sector actors recognized that, with only two staff planners, they needed outside help in crafting the new plan. Thus, local officials sought out the expertise of a key nonprofit sector actor: Youngstown State University. City officials and YSU administrators formed a partnership to make the university a key "costar" in the planning process. As one YSU administrator explained, "The city and the university did it together, and that was kind of serendipity."[48] Traditionally, both entities looked inward and had not coordinated efforts.[49] By the late 1990s, each had independently decided to update its comprehensive plans, with YSU looking for ways to clean up the areas surrounding the campus. Both city and university leadership "realized the status quo was only going to lead to further decline and that the future of both institutions was in doubt. The demise of one would lead eventually to the demise of the other."[50]

Particularly instrumental in the partnership from the university were YSU president David Sweet, Hunter Morrison, and Tom Finnerty. Sweet, who became president in 2000, had a background in planning and "set in motion plans to connect the university's future with the city's future. The university realized it was hard to sell on-campus residency if nearby neighborhoods were in a state of disrepair."[51] Sweet was interested in halting the decline of enrollment numbers by improving curb appeal, in particular through addressing "trashed lots and boarded-up windows on nearby streets."[52] Morrison had been Cleveland planning director for twenty years and became director of YSU's Center for Urban and Regional Studies in 2002. Morrison lent his expertise (in a self-described role as "senior advisor") in both the visioning and planning process. Morrison had been one of the prime architects of the 2000 Cleveland Civic Visioning Process. Finnerty, associate director of YSU's Center for Urban and Regional Studies and a Youngstown native, also lent his planning expertise and extensive knowledge of the city.

Partnering with YSU proved to be a pivotal marketing decision: "The well-regarded institution provided staff expertise and resources, as well as something less tangible."[53] In effect, this "unusual town-gown partnership" gave credibility to the Plan that it would not have had if city officials had produced it alone.[54] The small planning staff also received much needed "expertise that [was] available in the Center for Urban and Regional Studies," said one YSU administrator. These public and nonprofit sector actors came together with the expectation of taking a different approach. The city's young leadership, supported by City Council and aided by YSU administrators with strong planning backgrounds, together constituted the "stars" in the *Youngstown 2010* planning process. In addition to setting the plan in motion, these stars, with the help of external planning consultants, encouraged Youngstown residents and community groups (such as neighborhood groups and churches) to play a large role as a "strong supporting actor" in crafting the *Youngstown 2010* Vision and Plan.

Strong Supporting Actors: Residents, Community Groups, and Outside Planning Consultants

A key task for the city/YSU planning team was setting the framework for community participation and finding a consulting firm to facilitate the visioning process. The "stars" sought extensive, meaningful community participation. Finnerty describes the 2010 planning effort as a "unique collaborative planning process."[55] More than 5,000 residents participated in one way or another; indeed, the amount of public interest was unexpected and surprising.[56] As recognition for the team's efforts to encourage community participation, the *Youngstown 2010* Plan received the American Planning Association's 2007 National Planning Excellence Award for Public Outreach.[57] According to a Cleveland-based urban designer who has consulted in Youngstown: "I think Youngstown's major strength is the level of civic engagement that they've been able to achieve as a result of having this open dialogue . . . [P]eople have *embraced* it. Anthony Kobak tells me that when he goes down to a community meeting and talks about development, people raise their hand and go, 'Excuse me, but I thought this process was about shrinking!' The fact that [city officials] have been forthright about what's happening and what the potential of the city could be, people have embraced it in a way that if they stood up and had this rhetoric about growth, people would have been inherently skeptical of it, with good reason."[58]

Through this process of community engagement, the idea of accepting decline and planning to rightsize the city emerged. According to one team member, "We weren't admitting decline or shrinkage [prior to the visioning process]. We were just admitting—we needed to have a vision, we needed to have a plan and direction. . . . [F]rom all the comments, these four platforms [the four parts of the vision] kind of rose up . . . The only thing we did was paint the picture of the history, the trend, where we're at right now and the importance of planning."[59] After being asked where the idea of accepting decline came from, another team member responded: "It was not a planner's idea imposed on people. It really came out of listening to folks and listening to what they had to say. You cannot impose this."[60]

So, how did the city obtain community input? After Youngstown's City Council allocated money for the planning process in 2001, city officials issued a Request for Proposals (RFP) for Phase 1—the Vision. YSU officials had also issued an RFP for YSU's plan update. As Finnerty explained, "As a first step in building collaboration, YSU's Center for Urban and Regional Studies had a staff member on both search committees."[61] When city officials chose Urban Strategies, Inc., of Toronto to facilitate the visioning process in late 2001, YSU leaders delayed their search to participate fully in the city process. According to one member of the planning team, choosing a Canadian consulting firm lent a fresh perspective to the visioning process: "Quite frankly by inviting Urban Strategies of Toronto to come in, [the search committee] did something really quite remarkable. One of the advantages that Canadian firms have in dealing with the situation in America like this is [they] can speak as a second cousin. [They]'re not really part of the family. [They] don't have quite the self-censoring aspects because it's slightly a different culture that's 10 or 15 degrees off. So [they]'ll say things differently and in a slightly different language that will cause people to say, 'Oh yeah, I hadn't thought of that.'"[62] Soon after its selection, the Urban Strategies team—partners George Dark and Frank Lewinberg, project manager and associate Pino Di Mascio, planner Oliver Jerschow, and urban designer Eric Turcotte—performed a reconnaissance of the city (using the expertise of the city and YSU planners) and then began the visioning process.

To start the process, Urban Strategies engaged 250 community "influentials" in 40 to 50 focus group and one-on-one interview sessions. These influentials were people who "held some say among their peers."[63] They included representatives from government, neighborhood watch programs, social agencies, banks, high schools, religious organizations, and businesses. With respect to the focus groups, one planning consultant commented, "[There were] about 15 to 20 people at each [focus group meeting], and what we told them at each of the sessions, you have to mix everyone . . . We don't want all the university people in one. We don't want all the church people [in one] . . . because all you're going to have is people talking about the same issues. . . . In Youngstown, it really was kind of the first time people had been engaged at this level and had quite a bit to say so we got into quite interesting discussions."[64] Urban Strategies distilled the results of these sessions into key issues and then held six workshops where these influentials conducted an analysis of the city's strengths and weaknesses and of the opportunities and threats from conditions outside city control. In essence, "This influential group of citizens became the vision's creators and champions."[65]

Between June and December 2002, Urban Strategies staff summarized the input into four Vision principles that they brought back to the 250 community influentials for comment and criticism. They then crafted the final Vision to present to the public. Urban Strategies progressively brought in more and more people to talk to each other about the issues in an "ever-widening circle of participation."[66] The process culminated with a public meeting in December 2002 in the 2,500-seat Stambaugh Auditorium. The planning team did not anticipate high attendance because "public meetings concerning planning in Youngstown have never been well attended."[67] However, 1,200 to 1,400 people attended, a "pleasant shock to city and planning professionals alike."[68] One planning consultant stated, "I saw the auditorium ahead of time and said, well, this is going to feel pretty empty when we're in here. They had a newspaper ad. They had the local radio station talk about it too, so that got people out. But not only was it the *number* of people, but how *positive*. . . . by the end of it, it really felt like, 'This is great.' "[69]

During the meeting, members of the audience made oral and written comments, and 100 people volunteered to participate in the planning process. In general, audience members expressed wide agreement on the Vision principles (including the notion of accepting Youngstown as a smaller city). One participant noted: "I hate to make it sound so wonderful and euphoric and just a great process here with little opposition but there really wasn't much negativity. I mean at that time, all of the comments [were positive], nearly all . . . I mean I can count [the negative comments] on one hand . . . someone saying oh, Youngstown should have done this 20 years ago, and it's too late now. But truly I mean, [other than] four or five people making some [negative] comments at the meeting, it was all supportive."[70]

Key to the success of the visioning process (and later the planning process) was the fact that the city/YSU planning team involved the local media "as *participants* rather than observers and critics on the sidelines. As a result, the process garnered well-informed and supportive coverage."[71] The *Vindicator* (Youngstown's local newspaper) ran a four-part series laying out the principles of the Vision; leading up to the public meeting, the paper ran editorials emphasizing the importance of public participation in planning: "Hundreds of Youngstown's residents responded to the publicity by emailing and phoning their comments and checking the *Youngstown 2010* website for details."[72] As a high-ranking city official stated, "the media really got on board, which I think helped."[73] Another city official explained that "what made [our approach] successful (not so much for decline but it has to do with maybe apathy and obviously if you're talking about decline, there's usually some apathy thrown in there) . . . is the marketing effort. We marketed truly like a company markets its products. [We also had a] really unique partnership with PBS, and even the public radio station would rebroadcast stuff. I think [marketing is essential] if you're going to talk about decline or just planning in general, but even decline because people's attitudes can be really down."[74]

After the planning team presented the Vision to the public, the City Council adopted it unanimously. At the same time, the council enacted other recommendations from Urban Strategies that would facilitate the creation of the more technical Citywide Plan. For instance, the council formed a technical committee consisting of city planning and YSU staff to oversee the creation of a steering committee of residents who had volunteered during the visioning process. In addition, the council created working groups for each of the four Vision principles. Residents then volunteered to assess neighborhood conditions; in 2004, the planning team targeted eleven neighborhood clusters for resident input into the Plan, and more than 800 residents participated in this process. In January 2005, more than 1,300 residents attended a public meeting where the planning team formally presented the Citywide Plan.[75]

The city/YSU planning team created a "strong supporting actor" role for the local residents and community groups in the *Youngstown 2010* planning process, facilitated by consultants. In the spirit of finding a new vision, the team set in motion and guided a process that ultimately resulted in articulation and broad acceptance of the notion that Youngstown had to be a smaller city. The supporting role of the residents and community groups did not end with the Plan's completion; city leaders continued to encourage residents and community groups (such as neighborhood groups) to play a role in implementing the Plan. A high-ranking official noted that: "Our planning department is woefully understaffed as we go out and do the neighborhood-level planning. . . . Now, the people who we have there are phenomenal and proficient at what they do. In fact, as far as I'm concerned, they're all geniuses, but the resources just aren't there and that's where the collaboration becomes much more important. . . . [T]he community has a lot of involvement and there's reliance on the community."[76]

Indeed, residents and community groups have begun to take action. A shrinking cities researcher who has consulted in Youngstown explained: "people of the city are beginning to implement [the Plan] . . . [O]ne of the churches has begun acquiring vacant properties, and there are lots of them in the area around it, and they've planted corn and they had this big event this summer where you could come out and eat corn. I know it might sound silly, but I really think that corn-eating may save Youngstown in the end. There's a day care center in Youngstown that's adopting a similar strategy." According to that same participant, in Youngstown, the implementation process "may be about enabling rather than about actually doing."[77]

Several community organizations have formed to undertake projects designed to implement the Plan's principles. The *Youngstown 2010* website lists fifteen neighborhood groups in the South Side District as involved in implementing the *Youngstown 2010 Plan*. One organization in particular— the Idora Neighborhood Association (INA) —has set up a website with the stated mission "to revitalize the neighborhood and carry out the strategies laid forth in the neighborhood plan." Together with residents of the Idora neighborhood and geographic information system (GIS) experts from YSU, Karen Perkins (a zoning officer with the City of Youngstown) and Ian Benis-ton (of Ohio State University) comanaged the creation of a neighborhood plan for Idora. The neighborhood plan aims to convert vacant land into community gardens, parks, or side yards. In March 2008, the City Council recognized the Idora plan as reflecting the *Youngstown 2010 Plan*.[78] According-ing to a city official involved in the process, "It was a *huge* success because [the residents are] now taking over their own neighborhood. They don't wait for the city to come in and suggest that you need to do this or that."[79]

The revitalization of Wick Park is another example of how planners in Youngstown have enabled residents and community organizations to assume implementation of the principles of the *Youngstown 2010 Plan*. Several community organizations, led by Defend Youngstown and Youngstown CityScape, undertook the Wick Park Revitalization Project.[80] The group en-listed the services of Terry Schwarz, from the Urban Design Center of North-east Ohio (now the Cleveland Urban Design Collaborative). While a city planner attended the meetings, members of the group initiated and carried out this project, with city planners facilitating. The planner explained that, while the group asked him to be on the steering committee for this project "with being so busy, I just said, 'No, you guys look like you're going in the right direction.' I offered comments, and I just kind of watch how things are going and offer advice that way."[81] Certainly, local government is the key body implementing the *Youngstown 2010 Plan*, but as in the planning process, residents and community groups are playing a "strong supporting role."

Weak Supporting Actor: Private Businesses

Participants did not identify businesses as playing a key role in the *Youngstown 2010* planning process, beyond the participation of local businesses and the Youngstown Business Incubator in the focus groups and subsequent public meetings. Indeed, the lack of strong private sector participation in the *Youngstown 2010* process may have contributed to the Plan's focus on land use planning issues (for instance, excess infrastructure) and the social issues associated with them (such as the rise in crime in neighborhoods with vacant homes), rather than traditional "going for growth" economic development strategies. The lack of a strong business push for development that could raise land values especially downtown is perhaps one reason participants in the *Youngstown 2010* process were able to reach a consensus on a decline-oriented approach.

The Vision and the Plan do discuss economic development issues. One of the four principles of the Vision is that Youngstown needs to determine how to play a role in the "new regional economy." Policies in this respect include supporting the university and health care sectors and nurturing innovative start-up high-tech businesses in the downtown core. However, the major focus of *Youngstown 2010* is adjusting land use to meet current population levels and consolidating infrastructure. While the Vision deals with economic, social, and environmental issues to varying degrees, the Plan itself deals almost exclusively with issues of physical regeneration. The "meat" of the Plan is the detailed analysis of the physical conditions of each of the planning districts and strategies for improving those conditions. The Plan addresses economic development issues by implication; physical regeneration can help accomplish the economic development goals in the Vision. Greening the city and developing more outdoor recreational opportunities will help attract high-tech businesses whose workers value quality of life. The primary purpose of strategies such as these, however, is to improve the quality of life of existing residents, not to meet the needs of businesses.

Not all local officials agreed with the approach to economic development taken in the Plan. One finance official was particularly adamant that the way to address Youngstown's economic issues was to attract large multinational corporations that would create a large number of jobs. To him, while nurturing small high-tech businesses is a good idea, it is not the answer. After describing the Youngstown Business Incubator's efforts to nurture local startups as "nice," he pointed out that the city's finance office will do one or two "deals" (involving, for instance, tax incentives, grants, and infrastructure provision) with large corporations that will equal the incubator's activities on an annual basis. He further stated, "I applaud [the incubator's] efforts. I want them to do well. I want them to continue to succeed. I want them to be downtown, but at the same time, I think as an overall redevelopment strategy for the area that we have to 'cookie cutter' [continuously replicate] [larger-scale economic development strategies aimed to attract large multinational corporations]. We have to do a lot and we need to do it fast."[82]

This frustrated one high-ranking proponent of the 2010 Plan, who expressed the hope that this official would eventually "buy-in" to the critical importance of smaller-scale initiatives like the startups in the Youngstown Business Incubator: "He's sort of critical of the incubator because this is a guy who's put together deals, taking old steel mill sites and done wonderful things. The incubator is sort of a different animal. A lot of money has been thrown into that thing, [and as a recent local newspaper article reported], one of the [incubator] companies is the seventh fastest growing [small and medium sized] company in the country [and it is] headquartered two minutes from here. And that company's acquiring and going global. So it's different than what [the finance official] has been fighting for 20 years."[83]

Thus, in addition to the business interests not playing a large role in the *Youngstown 2010* planning process, a lack of consensus remains among public sector actors as to what will most aid economic development efforts. The weak role of business interests and lack of consensus on economic development strategies may have made embracing decline-oriented planning easier.

Conclusion

In adopting decline-oriented planning in Youngstown, key public sector and nonprofit "stars" played a leadership role. These included the City Council that allocated funds for the planning process and provided support by adopting the Vision and implementing the recommendations of Urban Strategies about the planning process; key local officials who saw the need for a new approach and who initiated and guided the process of extensive public participation; and YSU administrators who contributed planning expertise and local knowledge. In seeking extensive community participation, city officials cast residents and community groups in the role of "strong supporting actor," aided by Canadian consultants who brought "fresh eyes" to the process. In their role as supporting actor, residents and community leaders generated the idea of accepting Youngstown as a smaller city—an idea that, according to the planning team, they could not have imposed on residents. The business sector was a "weak supporting actor," and this weak role likely contributed to the lack of opposition to the adoption of a decline-oriented approach. Urban governance is not always a collaborative process;[84] where only two parties assert their interests, the likelihood of agreement is enhanced.

This case of the *Youngstown 2010* planning process supports Bernt's assertion that new forms of governance are emerging in shrinking cities that differ from the "growth machine."[85] It suggests that decline-oriented governance is possible where public sector actors are receptive to a new approach, draw on local knowledge and expertise from key nonprofit actors and residents, and act with less influence from business interests. Certainly, serendipity played a large role in bringing together this particular constellation of actors at this particular time. Matthiesen similarly found luck to be a "crucial ingredient" for generating creative governance options in shrinking post-socialist cities; in his case studies, he found success in generating creative solutions in the context of shrinkage was partly a result of "a 'lucky' constellation between a small number of creative individuals . . . the right constellation of time, place and persons."[86] In the case of Youngstown, the desire of new public and nonprofit sector leaders to try something different insured that the "lucky" constellation of actors resulted in an innovative approach.

Whether the decline-oriented approach of the *Youngstown 2010* Plan will be successfully implemented remains to be seen. The Plan does not contain an economic development strategy. How "downsizing" the built environment might lead to stabilization or even growth of the local economy has not been addressed. Some who worked on the Plan in Youngstown—including one city planner and one urban design consultant—expressed concern that the Plan is "too ambitious," that some ideas "should have been reserved for a *Youngstown 2020* Plan," and that implementation thus far [2009] has been "almost non-existent."[87] While the Vision will likely guide any successor plan, some are concerned that city officials' slow progress in implementing some of the Plan's policies means that city officials have taken on too much. One participant expressed concern that the slow implementation may lead to residents' disillusionment.

In addition, encouraging residents to play a significant role in implementing the ambitious plan raises questions of legitimacy. As Minnery asks, by incorporating nongovernment actors into policy making and implementation, "Do we also move beyond the traditional mechanisms of authority, legitimacy and accountability that are part of the very nature of government? And perhaps more importantly, what happens to the role of government as the only legitimate user of coercive power? Can these issues be properly addressed in the new and fluid arrangements?"[88] Is local government in Youngstown further unburdening itself of responsibility while overburdening its citizens? Minnery refers to this as the "dark side" of community participation in urban governance.[89] Whether these issues arise and how they will be dealt with by the "stars" and "supporting cast" of decline-oriented urban governance in Youngstown bears watching. Breaking free from the "planning for growth" paradigm, while a laudable accomplishment, will likely be an uncertain process of trial and error in the already "messy" world of urban governance.

CHAPTER 5

Targeting Neighborhoods, Stimulating Markets: The Role of Political, Institutional, and Technical Factors in Three Cities

Dale E. Thomson

Cities experiencing abandonment face complex community development demands with diminishing resources. This challenge requires city leaders to allocate resources strategically. Countering their inclination to assist all areas with need, officials in many cities have determined that targeting resources to a limited number of geographic areas may enhance the impact of their community development investments. In some cases, this includes targeting resources to "middle neighborhoods" that possess a mix of socioeconomic characteristics and have less need for assistance than high-poverty neighborhoods.

This chapter examines geographically targeted interventions in three cities with high levels of abandonment—Baltimore, Cleveland, and Detroit. In each city, influential nongovernmental community development funders altered their approach to resource allocation and neighborhood intervention. Rooted in rationality and embracing an allocation model that excluded many areas, these targeted initiatives exposed their backers to potential opposition from those excluded. The inclusion of middle neighborhoods escalated the potential for opposition from those concerned about diverting resources from the neediest areas. In each city, government leaders endorsed the initiatives, committed city resources to them, and used them as a vehicle for allocating substantial, new federal funding to improve housing markets. Yet their resource commitments, adherence to targeting principles, commitment to strategic geographic targeting as an allocation framework, and willingness to target funding to middle neighborhoods varied.

These targeting initiatives demonstrate that strategic geographically targeted approaches appeal to community development funders for their potential to enhance impact; however, political, institutional, and technical factors hinder their use as an overriding allocation framework. These factors also hinder city officials' ability to emphasize market indicators when selecting target areas or target middle neighborhoods at a scale to alter outcomes significantly.

Overview of Strategic Geographic Targeting

Although geographic targeting is not new—urban renewal, Model Cities, and Empowerment Zones all embraced targeting—today's targeting differs from past approaches.[1] During the early 2000s, initiatives emerged from within cities, rather than the federal government. They are often initiated and funded by nongovernmental organizations, rather than being government driven. They are typically asset driven, rather than exclusively targeting areas with advanced decline. Whether attempting to capitalize on the presence of anchor institutions; solidify areas surrounding development projects; or invigorate promising, but stagnant, housing markets, nongovernmental entities and city officials often adopt these strategies expecting that concentrated investments in small areas with market assets will stimulate greater investment and long-term stability than investments in areas without them.

Since these initiatives' designers consider geographic targeting essential to accomplishing program goals, I refer to these initiatives as "strategic geographic targeting." Community development funders typically adopt this approach to increase the impact per dollar invested or to serve the areas with greatest need.[2] When the former is the goal, I consider targeting to be efficiency based. Efficiency-based strategic geographic targeting can enhance program impact by capitalizing on cost savings, as well as multiplier, interaction, focus, and neighborhood threshold effects. This approach aims to stimulate investment and recognizes that neighborhoods differ in their appeal to homeowners, businesses, and other investors.

Neighborhoods that have endured years of outmigration from the city but face significant challenges to maintaining stability are probable targets for efficiency-based strategic geographic targeting. These "middle neighborhoods" include a mix of incomes, of which middle-income households form an essential component. Yet low- and moderate-income households are also prominent, and backers of these initiatives seek to engage all households to enhance the viability of the community development interventions and increase the households' gains from the neighborhood's improvements. Several general criteria characterize middle neighborhoods. A mix of incomes and market indicators—homeownership rates, sales, values, vacancies, and foreclosures—that show the neighborhood to have a viable, but threatened, housing market are critical. Indicators of other important phenomena related to neighborhood stability, such as crime, school quality, or social cohesion, can also be considered. Criteria and their values vary across cities, as they do for the three cities in this study, but market indicators are central.

Middle neighborhood targeting embodies two principles. First, without assistance, housing markets in these places will reach a tipping point leading to substantial disinvestment. Second, the presence of a significant number of homeowners with resources to invest increases the probability that institutional investment will stimulate household investment. These neighborhoods may have historically stable markets or markets that are stabilizing after decline. Strengthening such markets can benefit the city as a whole by preventing disinvestment, strengthening the city's tax base, and enhancing the city's overall investment appeal.[3] Such outcomes help city officials address high-need areas by increasing public resources for service delivery and community development and stimulating market forces to aid recovery. A middle-neighborhood approach to targeting can especially benefit weak market cities where stable middle- and working-class neighborhoods can quickly decline, particularly as large numbers of mortgage foreclosures threaten neighborhoods' stability and recovery.

Few evaluations of efficiency-based strategic geographic targeting exist, but investigations of the property value effects of concentrated investment demonstrate its potential for improving development outcomes.[4] How much of a city's overall community development strategy should or can be dedicated to targeting remains unanswered. Where nongovernmental funders are prominent, city government need not lead such strategies. Given local government's role in land use regulation and resource allocation, city officials' engagement in this kind of targeting as a framework for guiding community development policy enhances the impact of such a strategy, even though it may be only one element of a broad set of community development interventions.

Efficiency-based targeting recalls 1970s proposals for urban triage, which advocated increasing government spending to sustain stable neighborhoods at risk of serious decline while decreasing spending in cities' most deteriorated neighborhoods. Though rationally based, urban triage encountered political opposition.[5] Proponents were left to pursue strategies that, at most, implicitly adopted some triage principles, which reduced the potential for accomplishing triage's goals. Efficiency-based targeting applies to only a portion of community development funding and is more consistent with Anthony Downs's moderate version of triage (which provided for reduced, but continued, targeted funding to highly deteriorated neighborhoods) than with William Baer's call for abandonment of areas not targeted. Nevertheless, funders that adopt efficiency-based strategic geographic targeting expose themselves to potential opposition from advocates for areas not targeted, especially high-need neighborhoods.

Such funders also face challenges in aligning actions of multiple actors in a complex institutional environment, adhering to technical attributes of program design, and accessing resources that are sufficiently flexible for such programs. Thus, three categories of factors—political, institutional, and technical—affect strategic geographic targeting. Political factors relate to the people involved, their interests, and the power they possess and are willing to exert in pursuit of their interests. Institutional factors reflect the prevailing intra- and interorganizational characteristics of the community development network. Technical factors cover programmatic aspects of targeting—how to do it and the tools and systems for implementing it.

Examining Cases of Strategic Geographic Targeting

Through the case studies of Baltimore, Cleveland, and Detroit, I sought to identify the factors that facilitate or hinder strategic geographic targeting. I also wanted to determine, in cities where strategic geographic targeting was adopted, what share of governmental and nongovernmental resources were allocated through this approach and whether the targeting was efficiency based, market based, and focused on middle neighborhoods. Finally, I wanted to know if the factors affecting use of efficiency-based strategic geographic targeting to middle neighborhoods differed from those affecting need-based targeting. Answers to these questions enabled me to empirically assess the potential for cities with high levels of abandonment to adopt this strategy widely.

I examined the validity of several propositions. First, community development funders increasingly accept strategic geographic targeting as a means to improve program impact. Second, nongovernmental funders are more supportive of strategic geographic targeting as an overriding allocation strategy than are city governments, especially when it is market based, efficiency based, and targets middle neighborhoods. Third, opposition from low- and moderate-income households, organizations that serve such households, and politicians who represent those households or organizations hinders city governments' use of efficiency-based strategic geographic targeting. Fourth, program regulations that constrain the use of funding outside low- and moderate-income neighborhoods hinder government targeting of middle neighborhoods. Finally, the implementation of strategic geographic targeting and efficiency-based targeting, in particular, depends on their consistency with cultural norms within the organizations that control community development funding. Collectively, these propositions suggest that strategic geographic targeting can become more common but will not become a dominant strategy among cities with high poverty and abandonment. Targeting will most likely direct resources to high-need neighborhoods, even when they do not offer the potential for strengthening housing markets as envisioned by the efficiency-based targeting model.

Case studies are effective for understanding the factors affecting community development strategies because they enable researchers to investigate "a contemporary phenomenon in its real-life context, especially when the boundaries between phenomenon and context are not clearly evident."[6] The cases must provide data that answer core research questions and assess the accuracy of research propositions.[7] The cases reviewed here satisfy this criterion because, in each city, a nongovernmental resource provider adopted strategic geographic targeting that included efficiency-based targeting that the city eventually used as a basis for allocating resources. Each case is a Rust Belt, weak-market city with a large number of low-income households, significant levels of abandonment, and a long history of city government-sponsored community development.[8] These shared characteristics enabled me to generalize the findings to propositions related to cities possessing such characteristics. Yet differences in the targeting initiatives and city government's participation therein across the cases enabled me to examine reasons for those differences, such as the structure and power of city council, the historical emphasis of community development interventions, and the structure and cohesiveness of the community development network.

More than 70 semistructured interviews with elected, appointed, and career government officials; community development corporation (CDC) directors, consultants, and senior management; and foundations' and community development intermediaries' staff provided the core data for these case studies. I selected interviewees using a purposive, snowball sampling technique. Analysis of program documents and evaluations; intra- and interorganizational communications; external studies of community development organizations, institutions, and initiatives in each city; and newspaper articles provided additional data. Financial data from nonprofits' annual reports, the U.S. Department of Housing and Urban Development (HUD), cities' Consolidated Plans and Action Plans for community development spending, city budgets, cities' and nonprofits' internal financial documents, and Internal Revenue Service (IRS) 990 forms enabled me to construct financial measures. Participant observations from four years of advising the Detroit City Planning Commission and City Council on community development, five years of membership on the board of a Detroit CDC, and participation in various facets of Baltimore community development during the 1990s further informed the analysis.

I begin with an overview of each city's nongovernmental targeting initiative, highlighting its origin, key rationale, and main program elements. Next, I discuss the city government's involvement in the initiative and answer the research questions about the nature of the targeting initiative. After describing each city's targeting initiatives, I examine the political, institutional, and technical factors that helped or hindered targeting across the cases.

Baltimore—Healthy Neighborhoods Initiative

Baltimore's Healthy Neighborhoods Initiative emerged through the collaboration of individuals from various community development funding and advocacy groups. The efforts of Cheryl Casciani, executive director of the Citizens Planning and Housing Association (CPHA), were central to this collaboration. Many of the city's government and civic leaders in the post-World War II period were affiliated with CPHA, which had a track record of successful civic advocacy that gave it credibility and connections in the city and state networks of policy makers and resource providers.

CPHA was interested in land use, social conditions, and community building across the region. By the late 1990s, Casciani and her colleagues from nongovernmental funders and community organizations believed that inadequate support from community development funders threatened the viability of some of the city's middle neighborhoods. They had witnessed continued city investment along the waterfront, as well as heavy city and foundation investment in revitalizing high-poverty neighborhoods through public housing revitalization, the federal Empowerment Zone program, and the failed multimillion-dollar partnership with the Enterprise Foundation and other institutional partners in the west side neighborhood of Sandtown-Winchester. They felt city officials should turn their attention to middle neighborhoods. Through her connections, Casciani garnered commitments from local foundations to target significant resources to these neighborhoods through the Healthy Neighborhoods Initiative (HNI).

Securing foundation support for HNI required deliberate construction of institutions and opportunities for shared learning to build policy knowledge and a shared perspective. Casciani and representatives from nonprofits serving middle neighborhoods formed an informal group, the Healthy Neighborhoods Alliance (HNA), to help frame and advocate for policies that promoted middle neighborhood investment. HNA lobbied city and state leaders for government funding. Simultaneously, Casciani and David Boehlke, a consultant who convinced Casciani to promote a middle neighborhood strategy based on a successful program he ran in Battle Creek, Michigan, met with foundation representatives to convince them of the value of a new, targeted investment strategy. The Baltimore Neighborhood Collaborative (BNC), a forum created in the mid-1990s for pooling foundation and corporate resources to support and enhance awareness of community development activities, furthered understanding of this approach. HNA and foundation representatives traveled to Battle Creek in 1998 to observe the impact of the city's strategy and returned resolved to craft a pilot initiative to test the approach in Baltimore.[9]

Casciani, Boehlke, and key stakeholders built the pilot around the Healthy Neighborhoods model, a specific type of efficiency-based strategic geographic targeting that emphasized stimulating neighborhood housing markets by improving physical conditions and social connections in small target areas to increase homeownership and property owners' investment.

While many community development interventions intentionally avoid perceptions that they aim to increase property values, the Healthy Neighborhoods model made this an explicit goal. Healthy Neighborhoods aimed to get at the heart of why people move into, invest in, and stay in neighborhoods. It assumed neighborhood investment was determined by individuals' investment of money and time, as well as emotion and energy to address neighborhood issues together.[10]

Healthy Neighborhoods recognized that city neighborhoods compete with neighborhoods throughout the region for investment, and to win that competition they must instill confidence in the neighborhood's future real estate market and residential characteristics.[11] Healthy Neighborhoods sought to create neighborhoods of choice by ensuring that the housing stock, public spaces, and other components of neighborhoods' physical plants were attractive and well maintained, building social connections, creating a sense of place, and marketing the positive image of the neighborhood broadly. Healthy Neighborhoods initiatives selected places where investment in the neighborhoods' built environment occurred with care, focusing on projects that had a high probability for stimulating "spillover" investment from property owners in reaction to the project investment. Healthy Neighborhoods initiatives also supported community-building activities, such as block parties and neighborhood patrols to build social networks or mobilize residents to address important neighborhood issues collectively.

Healthy Neighborhoods was a neighborhood preservation strategy rather than a redevelopment strategy that reconfigures the physical or socioeconomic conditions in the neighborhood. Although many of its conceptual foundations could inform community-development interventions in high-poverty neighborhoods, Healthy Neighborhoods did not aim to transform high-poverty, high-need neighborhoods. Nor did supporters of Healthy Neighborhoods adopt the strategy to cause gentrification or channel resources to upper-income neighborhoods with strong demand for housing. Rather, the Healthy Neighborhoods model aimed to address market needs in neighborhoods between these two extremes, neighborhoods that face threatening environmental forces but have sufficient assets, market activity, and resident commitment to warrant optimism for market growth.

In 2000, the Goldseker and Abell Foundations, in partnership with the Baltimore Community Foundation (BCF) and CPHA, sponsored the Healthy Neighborhoods Initiative pilot. The foundations provided funding to six community-based organizations for home purchase and rehabilitation loans on targeted blocks, marketing the neighborhood, and supporting small block projects to foster connections among residents while improving physical conditions.[12] A $1 million appropriation from Maryland's General Assembly and a federal earmark aided the pilot.[13] After two years, 93 housing rehabilitation and purchase/rehabilitation loans for $3.8 million were closed or in the pipeline, and home prices had increased by 10 percent in one target area.[14]

In 2004, BCF incorporated Healthy Neighborhoods, Inc., to institutionalize the HNI approach. In 2007, Healthy Neighborhoods, Inc., added a second group of neighborhoods to HNI. By 2008, 15 organizations representing 37 different city neighborhoods, mostly middle neighborhoods, were part of HNI.[15] Foundations continued to fund participating CDCs to implement the types of interventions developed in the pilot. From 2000 through 2009, the Goldseker, Abell, Baltimore Community, and France-Merrick foundations provided over $12 million to Healthy Neighborhoods, Inc., and its participating CDCs for staff, technical assistance, marketing, and the small block projects.[16] More critical was a $40 million loan pool that provided loans from private lenders that were guaranteed by the Maryland Department of Housing and Community Development and foundations. This pool provided below-market, home purchase, purchase-renovation, and refinance-renovation loans to owners in target blocks selected by each Healthy Neighborhoods CDC, as well as home renovation loans available to all residents in the broader HNI target community. Each renovation loan required visible improvement to the exterior of the home to increase the probability of spillover investment; matching grants increased the amount of renovation that could be done. The HNI loans imposed no income limit for borrowers. By July 2009, lenders participating in the loan pool had originated 114 loans for $21.4 million, with $6.8 million more in the pipeline.[17] Healthy Neighborhoods, Inc., developed and administered this loan pool, provided technical assistance, coordinated with government officials, administered block project funding, solicited external funding, and oversaw the overall program.

City Government's Role in Targeting

City support of HNI came in three phases. In HNI's formative phase, recognizing the city's role in service delivery and distributing community development resources, HNI leaders tried to engage the city government as a partner. They called HNI the "Mayor's Healthy Neighborhoods Initiative" to give the mayor credit and a sense of ownership, briefed city officials on program design and implementation, and allowed the mayor and housing commissioner to suggest alterations to the list of HNI pilot neighborhoods. The mayor promoted HNI in public forums, yet the city government did not provide expected financial support. City officials committed $400,000 to HNI for street improvements and supported projects in HNI target areas, but these did not always align with HNI interventions.[18]

The second phase emerged as HNI became institutionalized. With Healthy Neighborhoods, Inc., managing HNI, a large loan pool and foundation support, and more target areas, Mark Sissman, director of Healthy Neighborhoods, Inc., continued to work with city officials. A strong supporter in City Council helped secure annual funding of $750,000 to $1,500,000 from 2006 through 2011 for a matching grant program for HNI borrowers. Total city funding to HNI through Fiscal Year (FY) 2011 came to $6.65 million, with additional annual commitments of $700,000 to $750,000 planned for future years through the city's capital plan.

The third phase occurred as HNI matured and substantial new federal resources came to the city. The financial crisis of 2008 decreased the resources available from foundations and banks and, along with increased mortgage foreclosures, created new challenges for Baltimore neighborhoods. Healthy Neighborhoods, Inc., searched for new funding, which arrived with the federal Neighborhood Stabilization Program (NSP) authorized in the Housing and Economic Recovery Act of 2008. Neighborhood Stabilization Program funding could finance acquisition, rehabilitation and resale, or demolition of vacant and foreclosed properties. The City of Baltimore targeted most of its $5.8 million in NSP (NSP1) funding to support homeownership in 11 HNI neighborhoods.[19] Healthy Neighborhoods, Inc., successfully competed for $26 million from the second round of NSP (NSP2), which it targeted to seven census tracts. Five of the tracts had HNI target areas; the other two were adjacent to HNI areas. Figure 5.1 shows the areas targeted under HNI and NSP. All shaded areas were HNI target areas. The darker shading indicates overlap of HNI and NSP areas.

The city of Baltimore eventually directed some of its own funding to HNI; however, city officials did not adopt strategic geographic targeting as an overarching strategy for allocating community development resources prior to NSP. With new funding through NSP, the city accepted HNI as the de facto city program for promoting reinvestment in areas that did not have

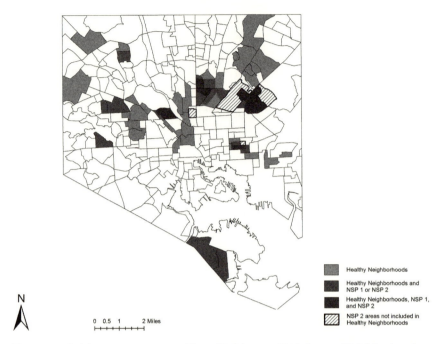

Figure 5.1. Baltimore target areas. City of Baltimore, 2010 Census Neighborhoods database; Live Baltimore, "City Living Resource Guide 2011," 36; Housing Authority of Baltimore City, "Baltimore City Consolidated Plan Substantial Amendment for the Use of Federal Neighborhood Stabilization Program Funds," May 2010, http:// static.baltimorehousing.org/pdf/nsp_amendedapplication.pdf, 8; Healthy Neighbor-hoods, "Healthy Neighborhoods NSP 2 Application," Baltimore, July 2009, http:// www.healthyneighborhoods.org/buyandrenovate/NSP2_Application_Final.pdf.

extremely high need. Rather than submitting their own application for NSP2 funding, city officials encouraged HNI to do so and joined as a consortium member in HNI's application. To the extent that city funding aligned with HNI, city officials have adopted an efficiency- and market-based strategy targeting middle neighborhoods. However, the vast majority of city commu-nity development funding is not allocated under this framework.

Cleveland—Strategic Investment Initiative

Cleveland's Strategic Investment Initiative (SII) emerged through the joint efforts of Neighborhood Progress, Inc. (NPI), and its funders, most notably the Cleveland and George Gund Foundations. NPI is a community development intermediary with more than $26 million in assets and more than twenty years of experience providing financing and technical assistance to CDCs and convening community development stakeholders to craft interventions.

From 1999 to 2004, NPI provided an average of $62,000 annually in operating support to an average of 16 CDCs.[20] Average CDC operating funding from NPI increased significantly by 2003 to about $87,000 and was an important, reliable funding stream. NPI also provided project financing, yet Cleveland's neighborhoods continued to experience challenges, and NPI's funding never could push the CDCs to a new level of neighborhood impact. By the mid-2000s, the Cleveland and George Gund Foundations, NPI's creators and primary funders, sought to change this result. They sponsored analyses suggesting that concentrating resources in a limited number of geographic areas could more effectively stimulate neighborhood change.[21] In 2004, the foundations made their more than $7 million in three-year funding contingent on NPI's adopting a more targeted approach; NPI developed the Strategic Investment Initiative in response.

NPI's assistance to SII CDCs came in two forms. Most notably, the six SII CDCs received more of NPI's funding for operations and marketing and special consideration for project funding from NPI's subsidiary, Village Capital Corporation.[22] From 2005 to 2009, average annual operating funding provided to the SII CDCs increased by an average of almost 300 percent compared to pre-SII funding. SII CDCs received an average of $257,000, while the non-SII CDCs received an average of $76,500. In FY 2006, Village Capital Corporation committed 50 percent ($2.4 million) of its loans to SII projects.[23] In 2010, NPI's commitment to targeting intensified when it devoted almost all its CDC funding to nine CDCs, including the six original SII CDCs, through a second round of SII. Most of the non-SII CDCs received modest tie-off grants to aid their weaning from NPI funding. Four received sustainability grants to deal with specific issues, like foreclosures.

NPI also provided enhanced technical assistance to SII CDCs. Initially, this assistance focused on finalizing plans for completing anchor projects and stimulating housing in Model Blocks surrounding those projects. A land assembly team helped CDCs obtain site control. As the foreclosure crisis grew, the technical assistance moved to helping with blight removal and stabilizing neighborhood housing markets.

SII promised another important change for NPI's interactions with CDCs. NPI replaced its previous measure of impact—housing units—with an emphasis on broad market outcomes. This meant attention to interventions that improved the demand for housing, rather than just completing projects.

Like HNI, SII was an efficiency- and market-based effort. SII concentrated resources for physical improvements in limited geographic areas where market data or significant neighborhood assets suggested that market stabilization or recovery was possible. However, NPI did not believe that this required limiting investment to areas that could be classified as middle neighborhoods based on market indicators.[24] Although NPI had funded CDCs serving middle neighborhoods in the past, only three SII areas—Detroit Shoreway, Ohio City, and Tremont—had significant portions of a target area that would be considered middle neighborhoods. A portion of a fourth SII neighborhood—Burton Bell Carr—could be considered middle, but it was not a focus area for the SII intervention in that neighborhood. These areas emerged from the competition as viable targets because of the capacity of the CDCs, their long experience with NPI, and the amount of investment/market activity taking place.

City Government's Role in Targeting

The city government's support for SII grew over time. In 2008, as mortgage foreclosures erased the demand for new housing development and threatened to overwhelm gains from recently completed projects, NPI changed SII's emphasis to foreclosure prevention and acquisition and reuse of vacant properties. In collaboration with the city government, Cleveland Housing Network, and CDCs, NPI created Opportunity Homes, which resulted in the city's first commitment to target significant resources to SII: $1 million per year to demolish 100 homes, plus $600,000 per year to rehabilitate up to 50 units.

This commitment complemented earlier steps taken by the Department of Community Development to integrate strategic geographic targeting into city programming. In 2006, the department classified each neighborhood according to its housing market conditions through the Cleveland Neighborhood Market Typology. City officials used the classifications to guide neighborhood interventions and encouraged other community development participants to do the same. The following year, the department initiated a Model Block program to concentrate up to $120,000 in housing improvements in small target areas identified by CDCs to stimulate increased sales, resident pride, and investor confidence. In 2010, the department required CDCs applying for its Competitive Grant Program, a program funded with federal Community Development Block Grant (CDBG) dollars, to use the funding for "strategic initiatives" in a maximum of three "focused geographic areas."[25] The CDCs determined target area size, but the department prioritized funding for programs targeting small areas for demonstrable impact.

Although the city devoted significant money to targeting and aligned much of it with SII, the commitment was modest compared to total community development funding. Targeted funds accounted for an estimated $8.6 million through FY11.[26] This equaled about 9 percent of Cleveland's CDBG and HOME Investment Partnerships Program (HOME) dollars from FY09 through FY11.[27] SII areas received commitments of $5.5 million, 64 percent of this total.[28]

By advocating strategic approaches to investing and adopting market-based, efficiency-based strategic geographic targeting for some community development resources, city officials nudged investment toward neighborhoods where data suggested that market stabilization and recovery were feasible and refocused investments in distressed areas toward adaptation of vacant properties to nonresidential uses. This strategy targeted investments within neighborhoods, rather than limiting the number of areas where the city would invest. The Department of Community Development took a laissez-faire approach to selecting target areas; it established funding priorities and provided analysis to aid targeting decisions but relied on CDCs to select target areas. Like NPI, city officials did not focus on middle neighborhoods. Slightly more than one-third of the Model Blocks funded by the city were identified in the Cleveland Neighborhood Market Typology as transitional markets, a middle neighborhood classification. Almost all the others were "distressed" or "fragile" in the typology.

The arrival of more than $53 million in federal NSP funding significantly increased the city's commitment to targeting, though the targeting was not immediate or dominant. HUD awarded Cleveland $16.1 million under NSP1 in 2008. Most of the city was eligible for funding under HUD regulations, and the city's spending plan kept options open. The Department of Community Development plan, approved by the mayor and City Council, based interventions on each area's market conditions but did not

explicitly limit the areas where the city could spend money. The city government ratcheted up its commitment to strategic geographic targeting and
alignment with SII with the $9.4 million received through the State of Ohio's
NSP1 allocation. Cleveland included portions of SII areas in five of the ten
"market recovery investment target areas" eligible for state NSP1 investments. However, the commitment to SII areas was limited because the city
committed less than 30 percent of the total state NSP allocation to market
recovery investment; ten areas were eligible, and two non-SII areas were

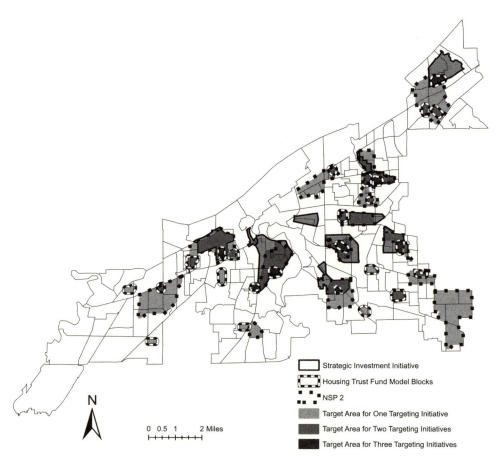

Figure 5.2. Cleveland target areas. Center on Urban Poverty and Community
Development, Mandel School of Applied Social Sciences, Case Western Reserve
University.

identified as the highest priorities. Despite the absence of explicit targeting, significant dollars went to SII areas. By 2011, city officials estimated $3.2 million in NSP1 funding was allocated to housing rehabilitation in SII areas through Opportunity Homes. The city also used NSP dollars to increase acquisition and rehabilitation funding for Model Blocks.

In 2009, a consortium that included the City of Cleveland secured $40,841,390 from NSP2. About $21 million went to 15 target areas in the city, Model Block areas with expanded boundaries to accommodate the greater funding.[29] All six of the original SII areas were targeted, as were portions of two SII areas added in 2010. The allocation plan again emphasized interventions that responded to market conditions and the potential for strengthening demand for housing. By February 2011, the amount of money allocated to SII areas was still uncertain; however, given their prominence among the NSP2 areas, they were likely to receive considerable funding. Cleveland was awarded $6.8 million from NSP3 in 2010, most of which was to be spent on demolition and rehabilitation or construction of rental housing citywide. These funds were not targeted to specific areas, but the plan was to invest them according to market typology classifications—demolition in distressed areas, very low-income rental housing in regional choice or stable areas, and low/moderate/middle-income rentals in transitional and fragile markets. Figure 5.2 shows the SII, Model Block, and NSP target areas for Cleveland, demonstrating the size, distribution, and overlap of the areas.

Detroit—Strategic Investment Areas

Detroit's targeting program was initiated by the Local Initiatives Support Corporation (LISC), a national intermediary that channels corporate, government, and philanthropic contributions to CDCs through loans and grants. From 1990 through 2004, the LISC Detroit office raised over $67 million for community development and leveraged an estimated $282 million.[30] In 2004, driven by calls from CDCs and other community development stakeholders for greater support for CDCs with proven track records and more comprehensive approaches to community development, a desire to increase impact on neighborhoods, and the need to create appeal for a new capital campaign, Detroit LISC leaders initiated the Strategic Investment Areas (SIA) initiative.

Modeled after a highly acclaimed New Communities Program run by the Chicago LISC office, SIA promised to alter LISC's investment in two ways. First, LISC would broaden its investment beyond real estate development projects to include public safety, education, workforce development, social services, and related efforts to support comprehensive community development strategies developed through community-based planning processes. Second, whereas LISC historically invested in projects throughout the city, it would now limit most investment to four SIAs.

Within a couple of years, LISC was allocating 75 to 90 percent of its funding to SIAs. In 2008, it invested $30.5 million in the city, leveraging an estimated $211 million.[31] About 97 percent of this investment occurred in SIAs. Yet investment varied greatly across SIAs. Ninety-one percent ($27.7 million) of LISC's total 2008 investment and 93 percent of its 2008 SIA investments went to the Central Woodward and Southwest SIAs. This included $12.5 million in New Markets Tax Credits for one building in the Central Woodward SIA and $4.2 million in Low Income Housing Tax Credits for two structures in the Southwest SIA. Detroit LISC officials acknowledged that SIA aided LISC's capital campaign, but LISC was unable to get other major funders to commit investment to their SIAs as hoped. Not counting federal and state tax credits, LISC reported an investment of $1.5 million of its own resources in the Central Woodward SIA, but foundations had committed less than $1 million beyond what was committed to LISC in its capital campaign. Much of this funding went to social service and youth programming; investment for physical development was limited. Several major CDCs operating in SIAs voiced frustration with the program, and by 2008, two SIAs existed in name only. In 2006, Anika Goss-Foster, LISC's senior program director who created SIA, left LISC to work as the City of Detroit's director of philanthropic affairs. In 2010, the national LISC office replaced Goss-Foster's successor and pushed the office to adopt a Building Sustainable Communities initiative, which retained the comprehensive and collaborative focus of SIA but targeted three new areas.

The Strategic Investment Areas initiative was one of several targeting initiatives adopted by nongovernmental funders in Detroit during the same period. In 2005, the Skillman Foundation, one of the largest foundations in Michigan, began its Good Neighborhoods Initiative, a plan to invest $100 million over ten years in six target areas to improve the lives of children. In 2006, the Community Foundation for Southeast Michigan began the Detroit Neighborhood Fund, which dedicated approximately $15 million from the Kresge and Ford Foundations to an 11-square mile section of the city that extended east from downtown to encourage riverfront redevelopment to spill over into neighborhoods north of the river. Two years later, the Hudson-Webber Foundation announced its 15x15 Strategy, which called for the foundation to target its approximately $5 million in annual funding to the greater downtown area to attract 15,000 new, young, and talented workers to live and work in the area by 2015. The goal of concentrating resources to achieve specific neighborhood goals drove these targeting initiatives, which represented a commitment of about $150 million to strategic geographic targeting beyond LISC's funds. The initiatives varied in the extent to which they addressed community development, but each added a dimension to the increasingly complex milieu of efforts to revitalize Detroit neighborhoods.

City Government's Role in Targeting

Late in 2006, while LISC and its SIA partners were drafting intervention plans and Skillman and the Community Foundation were implementing their targeted initiatives, the mayor of Detroit announced the Next Detroit Neighborhoods Initiative (NDNI) to target $225 million in city, foundation, and corporate funding to six Detroit areas.[32] Like SIA, NDNI's interventions were to be comprehensive and driven by neighborhood plans created through a collaborative process. Backed by the mayor and incorporated as a nonprofit to act on behalf of the city and receive foundation funds, NDNI staff worked closely with target area groups and city agencies to implement plans and secure external funding. A scandal leading to the mayor's imprisonment consumed city officials for much of 2008, and NDNI suffered. Foundations and corporations had committed $8,000,000 to NDNI by mid-2008, but commitments stopped when the scandal broke. The NDNI's director resigned, and NDNI's future was uncertain. Although the new mayor pledged support for NDNI, by 2011, support had yet to emerge as the city's Planning and Development Department (P&DD) implemented NSP and the Detroit Works Project, an effort to develop a strategic framework to realign the city's population, land use, and public services.

The Detroit city government did not adopt strategic geographic targeting as an overriding strategy, and NDNI did not select areas based on factors that were critical to program success. A comparison of the NDNI and

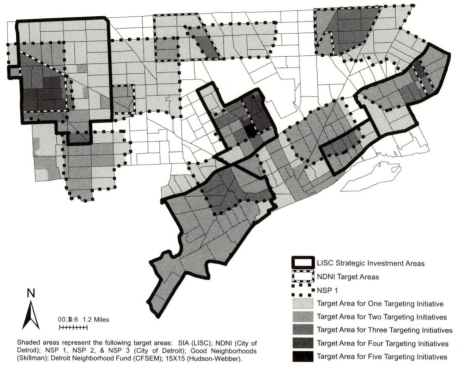

Figure 5.3. Detroit target areas. "Neighborhood Stabilization Program Plan,"
January 2009, City of Detroit Planning & Development Department database.

SIA target areas shows some overlap, but this was more fortuitous than the
result of a collaborative effort to ensure alignment. City officials chose areas
independently, based on departmental priorities and politics.[33]

The NSP provided Detroit's most significant commitment to targeting
community development resources, though target areas were much larger
than models for strategic geographic targeting recommend. Detroit targeted
its $47 million in NSP1 funding to nine target areas, its $41 million in NSP2
to six different areas, and its $22 million from NSP3 to six new target areas.
City officials aligned several of its target areas with areas targeted by other
funders. The foundations and intermediaries had taken the lead on targeting and, when forced to prioritize areas for NSP spending, city officials relied on what already existed. Significant differences between SIA and NSP
target areas remained, the result of the city's efforts to align with founda-

tions' targeting programs, focus on areas where the city government had already invested significant funding, and meet HUD's regulations. Figure 5.3 maps all the targeting initiatives mentioned for Detroit, highlighting SIA, NDNI, and NSP1 target areas. The map shows that more parts of the city were targeted than not; many of the target areas were very large; and many of the target areas did not overlap significantly. The result was great potential for diluting the effects of targeting.

The designers of SIA, NDNI, and NSP framed their strategies in terms of concentrating resources and leveraging investments. In this broad sense, these initiatives were efficiency based. They touted the value of building off assets, which made them broadly market based. But the details of each initiative show that none fit these classifications well. Some SIA areas had physical assets that might serve as market stimulants, but the assets varied considerably, and emphasis on social service programs weighted the initiative toward needs. City officials selected NSP areas primarily by need, focusing on areas the foreclosure crisis hit hardest. Data on the market viability of the areas did not influence selection of target areas or design of interventions.[34] All three programs emphasized assets in a needs-based framework. Inclusion of middle neighborhoods was incidental to the core programs.[35]

Factors Enabling or Hindering Targeting

Political, institutional, and technical factors determined the degree of strategic geographic targeting to middle neighborhoods in the three cities. I explain how they did so in this section, drawing on the case studies.

Political Factors

Strategic geographic targeting appears easiest to initiate when its supporters have *legitimate power* (formal authority) over resources to be targeted.[36] The extent to which the nongovernmental entities that initiated strategic geographic targeting had legitimate power varied. It was most evident in Cleveland, where funders directed NPI to target. It was least evident in Baltimore, and Detroit fell in between. In these cities, *referent* (derived from personal identification and attraction), *connection* (from relationships with those who possess power), and/or *expert power* (from experience and knowledge) were used to convince those with legitimate power of the value of strategic geographic targeting.[37]

In Baltimore, Casciani had developed strong relationships built on trust and respect with leaders of the foundations that supported HNI. These relationships, combined with her legitimacy as an advocate derived from her position at CPHA, made foundation leaders willing to listen to her arguments for HNI. Casciani's ties with program staff who lobbied for HNI from within the foundations complemented her access to foundation leaders. In making the case for HNI, advocates relied on the expertise of David Boehlke, who had established a national reputation for implementing Healthy Neighborhoods in Battle Creek, and Paul Brophy, a consultant to the Goldseker Foundation with years of experience with foundations and governmental agencies involved in community development.

In Detroit, Goss-Foster needed to get the buy-in of the national office, which she secured by basing her model on the experience of Chicago LISC. Her expertise in fund-raising led her to recognize the appeal of the comprehensive, neighborhood-based approach to her funders, and her connections to funders who supported LISC gave her access to make the request and predisposed the funders to comply.

Convincing elected officials accountable to areas not targeted was a greater challenge for targeting advocates. Detroit mayor Kwame Kilpatrick demonstrated support for targeting when he pushed NDNI, yet NDNI became politically driven, which diverted it from strategic geographic targeting, diminished support from funders, and inhibited alignment with LISC's SIA.[38]

Alignment of mayoral support with the nongovernmental targeting initiative was most obvious in Cleveland where mayor Frank G. Jackson's arrival in 2006 brought a new director of community development, Daryl Rush, who served on NPI's Board of Trustees and helped design and implement SII as NPI senior vice president of programs. He embraced the asset-based, targeted approach that emphasized market stabilization and growth. The mayor's chief of regional development—whose extensive history in Cleveland community development included founding one of the SII CDCs, directing the city Department of Community Development, and handling market-based investments as president of Shorebank Enterprise Group and director of economic development for the city—supported Rush's approach from above. Rush's assistant director had roots in the CDC and business communities and supported strategic, market-based interventions from below.

The 19-member, district-based Cleveland City Council offset the administration's push to target. City Council controlled the Neighborhood Development Activities (NDA) fund that provided each council member an even share of federal CDBG funding to distribute among CDCs in his or her district. In FY11, NDA accounted for $8.5 million, roughly 34 percent of all CDBG and HOME dollars allocated to housing and community development.[39] The NDA fund was a key vehicle for constituent services, and members resisted efforts to alter distribution of this funding.

Council authority over all other community development spending further constrained targeting. Council members screened proposed expenditures to ensure they included spending in their districts that was consistent with their interests. This magnified the administration's sensitivity to geographic spread and placed an implicit, though undefined, upper limit on the administration's targeting efforts. Conversely, council control shielded the administration and NPI from potential targeting critics. Since most of Cleveland's CDCs still received operating support through NDA, their outcry was muted.

In Baltimore, support from elected officials evolved over time. Mayor Martin O'Malley took office as HNI moved into pilot phase. He aimed to revamp city government, which he considered poorly managed, misdirected, or corrupt. He spoke frequently about the need for the city government to build from strength and make decisions strategically. In his first term, his planning and housing departments crafted the Baltimore Housing Market Typology, which Cleveland used as a model. He also created a high-profile Mayor's Council on City Living that included holding "at least two more rounds of the Mayor's Healthy Neighborhoods Initiative" as its top recommendation for actions to "ensure that Baltimore [was] well positioned to retain and attract a diverse group of homeowners and renters who are excited and confident about city living."[40] O'Malley's interests and the Healthy Neighborhoods model coalesced, yet HNI was not a high priority. He had no background in community development and little knowledge of asset-based approaches. He focused on public safety and the implementation of Citistats, a management system to enable data-driven decision making in city government. Not until O'Malley was in the heat of a successful governor's race in 2006 did City Council member Stephanie Rawlings-Blake, herself running for City Council president, secure the first $1 million for the city's matching grant program with HNI. Her support as council president and later mayor was critical to continued city funding.

Institutional Factors

Cleveland's experience showed that city agency leaders who understand and support targeting can enable the strategy. Detroit's experience showed that the absence of a supportive agency culture can undermine targeting, even when the mayor supports it. Without a powerful leader pushing for adherence to the technical integrity of efficiency-based strategic geographic targeting, agency officials used their historical emphasis on need, departmental interests, and prior spending patterns when selecting target areas, rather than examining indicators to identify areas where strengthening housing demand and stimulating spillover investment were most likely.[41]

In Baltimore, agency leaders and culture were also influential. Had HNI backers secured support from the housing commissioner, they likely could have secured funding from the city. Casciani had power from connections with O'Malley's first housing commissioner, Patricia Payne. Payne, who previously served as Maryland's secretary of housing and community development, had pushed for an initiative similar to HNI with the mayor, and she quickly aided Casciani's and HNA's efforts to secure state funding. However, Payne left the administration in its first year after a falling-out with O'Malley. Paul Graziano, former head of the New York City Housing Authority succeeded Payne and was less supportive of HNI. Graziano had a background in public housing. The priorities of Baltimore Housing, an agency that comprised the Housing Authority and the Department of Housing and Community Development, soon reflected Graziano's emphasis. Lawsuits against the agency influenced this, but even where development was a priority, the focus was on major redevelopment projects, particularly the massive project on Baltimore's east side to expand the Johns Hopkins Hospital. No one expressed animosity toward HNI, but no high-level advocacy emerged. During the 1990s, the agency's culture changed to emphasize social programming over community development. Institutional support within Baltimore Housing has grown, but few changes have resulted.

Cities' community development agencies fall within a broad network of community development organizations. The cohesion, interaction, and capacity of the funders, intermediaries, advocates, and CDCs that compose the nongovernmental component of that network also affected targeting. The BNC helped institutionalize Baltimore's community development network by enhancing collaboration, building capacity of community organizations, and increasing the understanding of community development, including the

special needs of middle neighborhoods, among foundation and bank partners. BNC assisted several HNI areas; this built support for HNI among participating funders. The Baltimore Homeownership Preservation Coalition
(BHPC) emerged from BNC to help neighborhoods deal with mortgage foreclosures. Baltimore Housing turned to BHPC to develop a strategy for spending NSP dollars. The BHPC used a data-driven process for selecting target
areas; the HNI areas emerged as top candidates. BNC was less influential
with city allocations prior to NSP, mainly because city participation in BNC
responded to specific requests for assistance and city officials did not join
the ongoing dialogue to identify collaborative opportunities. The NSP provided a specific reason for city officials and BHPC to ally.

In Cleveland, the community development network was even more developed. CDCs were firmly implanted as network partners, and the city
government consistently engaged with nongovernmental network participants. This network created complex interdependencies. Many individuals
in leadership positions within government, CDCs, foundations, and funding intermediaries had worked in community development for many years,
and many had moved from one type of community development institution
to another. Participants developed many shared values through shared experiences and gave colleagues the benefit of the doubt on key policy decisions. The NPI reputation as a responsible, thoughtful partner that helped
strengthen the community development network predisposed others to
view NPI's targeting strategy as legitimate. Even CDCs that lost out in the
SII competition acknowledged that efficiency-based strategic geographic
targeting was legitimate and NPI was implementing it in a responsible,
open manner. While the strength of this network enabled targeting for NPI,
it hampered city targeting. Community development corporations had grown
accustomed to receiving NDA funding and project assistance through CDBG,
HOME, and other sources. Both City Council and the administration knew
that proposals to limit a substantial share of community development funding to specific places would meet opposition.

Detroit's network of CDCs was organized more loosely, and its members
varied in capacity. The absence of a well-organized CDC network limited the
ability to mobilize opposition to SIA and other targeting efforts. However, the
lack of integration of CDCs, city government, and nongovernmental funders
in the community development network also limited the ability of CDCs that
supported strategic geographic targeting to push funders to adopt it.[42] CDCs'
influence on targeting decisions was limited to CDC-specific successes in

capitalizing on their mobilizing ability or contacts within funding organizations. For instance, city officials added the NSP2 target area in southwest Detroit in response to protests from residents and community leaders when it was excluded from NSP1, and the Central Woodward area was added to SIA only after Donna Williams, executive director of one of the area's CDCs and chair of the trade organization for Detroit CDCs, lobbied LISC leadership.

The wide array of Detroit targeting initiatives and their limited alignment reflects this disjointed network. The relationships among foundations were positive and cooperative for the most part; however, the composition, leadership, and programmatic foci of Detroit's nongovernmental community development funders changed significantly during the time of these targeted initiatives. The creation of the Detroit Neighborhood Forum, which brought funders of neighborhood interventions together to share information and collaborate and the Detroit Vacant Property Campaign (a collaboration of LISC, Community Legal Resources, and university faculty to push for policies that addressed vacant property) strengthened this network. Yet considerable room for progress remained, especially in aligning city and nongovernment funder strategies.

Technical Factors

The source of funding, which determines which groups feel entitled to receive funds and the flexibility in funding allocation and use, was a critical technical factor in all three cities. The strategic geographic targeting initiatives relied primarily on private financing, far easier to target than government funds, since foundations and banks need not answer to the general public regarding investment decisions. In contrast, elected officials are sensitive to the political implications of government funding decisions. Traditional sources for community development funding, such as CDBG, have funded a somewhat stable set of activities and organizations, and groups that are cut out of this funding often challenge such decisions. This led government officials in each city to rely on new or general purpose funds—general obligation bonds, general funds, and NSP—when targeting government dollars. No group or purpose had a specific claim on these funds; thus, potential funding recipients were less likely to view targeting as reallocating dollars from one group of neighborhoods to another.

Funding source also determined flexibility in use. While the bulk of federal community-development funding came with income restrictions, general fund and general obligation bonds did not. This proved important for HNI in Baltimore. Even though the program served low- and moderate-income households, the initiative leaders preferred the flexibility of funding without income restrictions or other regulations that complicated its use. Although NSP dollars had restrictions on income of those who would benefit, they were higher (up to 120 percent of Area Median Income, AMI[43]) than typical federal dollars (80 percent of AMI for CDBG, for example), which made them more attractive to HNI.

Similar conditions existed in Cleveland and Detroit. Cleveland's largest and earliest commitment to SII targeting came through general obligation bonds for demolition. The NSP served as an even larger source. Mayor Kilpatrick planned to fund most of NDNI with bonds, and much of the city funding initially allocated to NDNI came from reallocations of agency budgets, supported mostly by the general fund or bonds. Again, NSP provided the largest source of funding that city officials targeted.

In all three cities, the fact that the targeted funds amounted to a small portion of the cities' annual funding for community development prior to NSP also aided targeting. Baltimore's commitment of $6.65 million in general fund and bond money to HNI equaled less than 2 percent of its community development funding through CDBG and HOME from FY01 through FY11. Cleveland's commitment to targeting and SII specifically equaled about 9 percent and 6 percent of total CDBG/HOME dollars over the period of targeting.[44] Total funds committed to NDNI by the City of Detroit were not available, but estimates show that prior to NSP they accounted for a smaller share of city community development funding than in Baltimore or Cleveland. The NSP greatly increased each city's commitment to strategic geographic targeting.

The share of total funding committed to targeting also enabled nongovernmental targeting in each city. Although HNI, NPI, and LISC targeted nearly 100 percent of their funding, the foundations that financed the interventions committed a small share of total funding. In Baltimore, Abell's and BCF's contributions to HNI accounted for an average of 2 percent and 4 percent of their total annual grants.[45] Goldseker's contributions accounted for an average of 16 percent. The percentages increase to 19 percent and 50 percent for Abell and Goldseker if only grants for community development are considered, but still less than 10 percent of BCF's discretionary grants. In Cleveland, the George Gund and Cleveland Foundations contributed 7 percent and 4 percent of their grant dollars to NPI from 2004 to 2010. Foundations' commitments to Detroit LISC also accounted for a small share of their total grants.

Even with enabling factors in place, supporters of nongovernmental targeting initiatives had to structure the programs carefully to minimize opposition. In Baltimore and Cleveland, an open selection process driven by criteria that led to diverse areas aided this effort. In Detroit, LISC's closed, unclear selection process hampered support for SIA. Creators of HNI and SII selected target areas using a competitive process with specific, programmatically relevant criteria. Review committees evaluated proposals, and the initiatives' funders made final decisions. The selection processes were politically astute but not politically driven. Participants understood the need to have defensible selections to minimize opposition. The top-ranked proposals demonstrated adherence to selection criteria and produced a fortuitous geographic spread and socioeconomic and racial diversity.[46] In Baltimore, HNI supporters even allowed the housing commissioner and mayor to review the list. Neither attempted to alter the list, despite the fears of HNI supporters.

In Cleveland, adherence to programmatic selection criteria was evident in the exclusion of the Bellaire-Puritas Development Corporation (BPDC), which had consistently received NPI funding, from SII designation. BPDC was the primary CDC serving the district of City Council President Martin Sweeney, who worked closely with BPDC to ensure his constituents received services. Sweeney took his district's exclusion from SII as a personal offense, since NPI representatives told him of the decision while he was collaborating with NPI and the CDC trade organization to restructure the way that City Council awarded CDBG funding to CDCs. Sweeney had considerable influence on spending, and excluding BPDC made NPI and the CDCs it supported politically vulnerable.

In Detroit, LISC publicized 13 criteria for assessing neighborhood conditions and worked closely with P&DD to map those criteria by census tract. Ultimately, however, LISC's primary criteria seemed to be the presence of at least one economic engine and an organization that had received significant LISC funding previously. LISC then drew boundaries to expand the reach of these organizations to areas that had no organization with sufficient capacity to implement comprehensive community development. Logic underlay the selection—fund organizations with demonstrated capacity, target areas where LISC could leverage prior investments and extend the success of established CDCs to areas otherwise unlikely to experience community development investment. Yet LISC handled the selection process internally, and the CDCs that were supposed to lead SIA implementation were largely unaware of their role until LISC told them it would target their areas.

LISC's intervention model further hampered SIA because the approach called for the lead CDCs in each target area ("initiating" CDCs) to pull together other organizations in the target area to create a new nonprofit that would represent the collaborative, develop a plan for the SIA, and serve as the lead body for implementation. This element generated considerable opposition among the initiating CDCs in most of the target areas. In two of the areas, those CDCs backed out of the SIA or submitted alternative proposals that LISC rejected. In a third, the initiating CDCs challenged LISC to drop this aspect of their model. After heated arguments that included a threat from LISC to withhold funding, the initiating CDCs complied with LISC's demands. However, even in the SIAs that LISC touted as successes, this collaboration took a great deal of time to become workable or never evolved as planned.

Conclusion

The experiences of Baltimore, Cleveland, and Detroit show that nongovernmental and governmental resource providers view efficiency-based strategic geographic targeting as an important community development strategy. However, a variety of political, institutional, and technical factors complicate city governments' adoption of the approach as a primary strategy, particularly when it targets middle neighborhoods. Efficiency-based strategic geographic targeting is more likely to emerge from nongovernmental funders. Such initiatives are more likely to be sustained when developed collaboratively with others in the community development network who control implementation resources or have supportive relationships with those who do than if they are developed unilaterally.

City governments' support for efficiency-based strategic geographic targeting is likely to arise gradually through occasional opportunities to align flexible funds, rather than from a commitment to adopt this type of targeting as an overriding allocation strategy, even for a small share of community development funding. This is true even in cities where residents and CDCs lack the capacity to forge an organized protest against such targeting because government leaders operate under an implicit limit on the amount of resources they can target. The financial commitment is likely to be helpful but modest. So, nongovernmental leaders must construct efficiency-based strategic geographic targeting initiatives to enable sustainability without major financial support from city government, but they also need to maintain close connections with city government throughout implementation. Funders that can achieve this mix are more likely to capitalize on occasional opportunities to receive city funding, especially when substantial new funding becomes available for community development interventions, as with NSP.

The ability of efficiency-based strategic geographic targeting advocates to align their initiatives with governmental resources apparently depends on the interplay of clear support and direction from the city's top elected leaders and support from leaders of the implementing agency who understand the factors that make such targeting effective and are committed to implementing programs that adhere to those factors. The latter can be especially challenging in older, weak-market cities where the culturally embedded service priority of community development agencies is to serve the highest need without regard for potential to strengthen housing demand. Nongovernmental resource providers that show a sustained commitment to such targeting can help city agency personnel learn what makes such strategies successful. Realizing this potential depends on the extent to which the nongovernmental initiative adheres to the technical principles of efficiency-based strategic geographic targeting, demonstrates results, and enhances the capacity of the network participants in the initiative. It also depends on the readiness of agency personnel to learn.

CHAPTER 6

Recovery in a Shrinking City: Challenges to Rightsizing Post-Katrina New Orleans

Renia Ehrenfeucht and Marla Nelson

Five years after the 2005 hurricanes Katrina and Rita, vacant property remained a daunting challenge for New Orleans. With 47,738 vacant housing units in 2010, its 25 percent vacancy rate was among the highest in the nation.[1] In addition to posing serious safety hazards, blighted structures and unmaintained lots threatened to undermine fragile neighborhood recovery efforts and deter future investment.

New Orleans had experienced derelict land resulting from population loss long before Katrina. In the hurricane's aftermath, however, planners, redevelopment professionals, and commentators from around the country framed the massive destruction as an "opportunity" to address the city's long-standing problems comprehensively.[2] Many observers thought that the scale of the disaster would enable city officials to "rightsize" the city or shrink its footprint. In this context, to "rightsize" meant to defer development in and thereby clear less populated areas and to cluster redevelopment. The intent would be to create more densely populated neighborhoods in a smaller area and leave undeveloped land with fewer services and utilities.

The flooding had created an urgency that was accompanied by federal and philanthropic resources to fund citywide planning initiatives. Despite three recovery planning processes and widespread attention to derelict buildings and unmaintained lots, New Orleans did not develop a citywide strategy to guide redevelopment in a way that addressed pre- and post-Katrina population loss and the accompanying abandoned property. Instead, the city initiated many parcel-scale programs and targeted revitalization strategies. The recent trauma and historic inequities made envisioning a fair resettlement plan difficult. Absent a citywide strategy that included neighborhoods with weaker real estate markets, however, post-Katrina redevelopment patterns could exacerbate inequities among neighborhoods and residents.

This chapter examines the difficulties that New Orleans officials and residents faced when trying to determine a way to plan a recovery that might differ from 2005 settlement patterns. We begin by analyzing recovery across New Orleans neighborhoods within the context of decades-long population loss and disinvestment. We then explain the challenges to rightsizing New Orleans. Finally, we examine the possibilities and limitations of parcel and neighborhood-scale strategies.

Our analysis drew on reports, public documents, agency records, and secondary sources that addressed storm damage and recovery, vacancy, and poverty rates by neighborhood. We evaluated three citywide recovery plans and participated in dozens of recovery planning meetings. We attended board meetings of the New Orleans Redevelopment Authority (NORA), a state agency with bonding and expropriation powers and the city's key blight remediation entity; reviewed its programmatic information and board meeting minutes; and interviewed staff members.

The New Orleans Context: Recovery in a Shrinking City

Eighty percent of New Orleans flooded in 2005 when the federal hurricane protection system failed. Water and wind damaged 134,000 housing units, roughly 70 percent of the occupied housing stock.[3] The damage, nevertheless, varied greatly by neighborhood. The high ground along the Mississippi River, which includes the central business district and the city's main tourist centers, escaped major flood damage, as did neighborhoods on the lakefront and the river's west bank. Other areas were submerged by up to 15 feet of water for days or weeks.

New Orleans had 73 officially designated "neighborhoods" organized into 13 planning districts (see Figures 6.1 and 6.2). Estimated percentages of residents residing in damaged areas within each neighborhood and district, listed in Table 6.1, illustrate the differential impacts of Katrina.[4] Virtually all residents were affected in the hardest hit planning districts—Mid-City, Village de l'Est, New Orleans East, Gentilly, Lower Ninth Ward, and Lakeview.

Table 6.1. Characteristics of Neighborhoods and Planning Districts in New Orleans

Planning district/ neighborhood	Percent of residents residing in damaged areas[a]	2010 population as percent of 2000 population[b]	Vacancy rate (2010)[c]	Poverty rate (2000)[d]
Mid-City	100.0	60.4	31.3	44.4
B.W. Cooper Project	100.0	18.6	23.0	69.2
Bayou St. John	100.0	72.6	24.7	32.0
Fairgrounds/Broad	100.0	79.0	22.1	16.9
Gert Town/Zion City	100.0	76.1	29.3	48.6
Iberville Project	100.0	48.7	44.3	84.2
Mid-City	100.0	73.5	25.7	32.1
Seventh Ward	100.0	60.1	38.3	38.0
St. Bernard Area/Project	100.0	15.2	41.4	66.0
Tremé/Lafitte	100.0	46.9	37.0	56.9
Tulane/Gravier	100.0	86.2	34.9	56.2
Village de l'Est Total	100.0	62.0	14.9	7.8
New Orleans East	99.2	68.4	23.4	18.9
Pines Village	100.0	67.0	24.5	18.3
West Lake Forest	100.0	41.8	27.0	27.2
Plum Orchard	99.3	56.4	22.7	33.2
Read Boulevard East	99.3	88.4	18.5	11.2
Edgelake/Little Woods	99.0	71.5	23.6	17.4
Read Boulevard West	98.8	75.7	25.6	10.5
Gentilly	96.5	69.1	23.7	15.3
Dillard	100.0	67.6	24.1	20.6
Fillmore	100.0	60.5	29.7	11.6
Gentilly Terrace	100.0	77.9	21.7	16.1
Gentilly Woods	100.0	64.2	20.2	14.4
Milneburg	100.0	60.4	26.0	14.4
St. Anthony	100.0	66.0	29.8	20.6
Pontchartrain Park	99.9	56.3	24.4	10.2
Lake Terrace/Lake Oaks	29.1	114.0	4.9	1.9
Lower Ninth Ward	92.6	28.5	44.8	34.4
Lower Ninth Ward	99.9	20.3	48.0	36.4
Holy Cross	74.0	49.3	41.1	29.4
Lakeview	89.8	75.8	20.1	6.3
City Park	100.0	96.3	12.4	12.3
Lakeview	100.0	64.7	21.4	4.9
Lakewood	100.0	83.7	18.4	1.3
Navarre	100.0	79.0	19.0	8.5
West End	87.2	66.6	30.9	9.1
Lakeshore/Lake Vista	43.8	95.5	12.0	2.7

(continued)

Table 6.1. (continued)

Planning district/ neighborhood	Percent of residents residing in damaged areas[a]	2010 population as percent of 2000 population[b]	Vacancy rate (2010)[c]	Poverty rate (2000)[d]
Bywater	85.4	56.1	33.3	38.7
Desire Project	100.0	na	na	62.5
Florida Area	100.0	41.1	38.2	36.2
Florida Project	10.0	0.4	33.3	79.6
St. Roch	100.0	55.4	37.7	37.1
Desire Area	99.8	45.0	25.6	35.7
St. Claude	94.8	58.2	39.0	39.0
Bywater	43.6	65.5	29.4	38.6
Marigny	19.4	94.5	20.3	24.1
Viavant/Venetian Isles	N/A	47.5	27.2	N/A
Viavant/Venetian Isles	78.6	44.6	26.3	33.1
Lake Catherine	N/A	50.7	28.0	10.7
Uptown-Carrollton	60.9	86.2	19.5	24.3
Broadmoor	100.0	74.4	30.8	31.8
Dixon	100.0	71.7	28.6	31.1
Freret	100.0	70.1	30.6	33.5
Hollygrove	100.0	63.3	32.9	28.4
Marlyville/Fontainbleau	100.0	85.3	18.0	12.9
Leonidas/West Carrollton	70.5	75.6	25.9	31.5
Audubon/University	40.8	106.5	10.4	17.9
East Carrollton	30.0	95.8	12.1	24.5
Uptown	29.1	89.6	15.9	23.9
West Riverside	1.2	90.7	13.3	18.1
Black Pearl	0.0	97.9	12.5	26.4
Central City/Garden District	46.8	74.6	27.0	39.7
Milan	96.9	70.7	29.2	28.6
Central City Area (includes CJ Peete Project)	79.8	59.0	39.5	49.8
Lower Garden District	2.0	104.0	21.5	28.5
St. Thomas Project	0.4	73.1	14.5	69.1
Touro	0.1	92.5	14.8	15.5
East Riverside	0.0	83.8	18.1	36.9
Garden District	0.0	97.8	12.9	11.3
Irish Channel	0.0	79.0	16.4	41.1
French Quarter/CBD	12.2	102.0	39.2	16.9
Central Business District	37.9	126.9	29.3	32.3
Vieux Carré (French Quarter)	1.1	91.3	43.0	10.8

(continued)

Table 6.1. (continued)

Planning district/ neighborhood	Percent of residents residing in damaged areas[a]	2010 population as percent of 2000 population[b]	Vacancy rate (2010)[c]	Poverty rate (2000)[d]
Algiers	1.2	92.0	18.2	24.1
Whitney	7.1	90.8	19.9	29.3
Algiers Naval Station	2.0	76.0	19.1	21.8
Tall Timbers/Brechtel	1.2	97.8	17.6	19.4
Old Aurora	0.9	106.2	12.7	9.9
Algiers Point	0.7	103.1	18.8	17.3
Behrman	0.7	77.3	24.8	33.4
Fischer Project	0.0	41.7	18.0	88.2
McDonogh	0.0	86.3	30.2	48.3
New Aurora/English Turn	1.1	101.7	12.5	24.8
Total New Orleans	73.0	70.9	25.1	27.9

[a]*Source:* John R. Logan, "The Impact of Katrina," report for American Communities Project, Brown University, Providence, R.I., 2006, http://www.s4.brown.edu/katrina/report.pdf.

[b]*Source:* Allison Plyer and Elaine Ortiz, "The Loss of Children from New Orleans Neighborhoods," Greater New Orleans Community Data Center, April 15, 2011, http://www.gnocdc.org/LossOfChildrenInNew-OrleansNeighborhoods/index.html.

[c]*Source:* Allison Plyer, "Population Loss and Vacant Housing in New Orleans Neighborhoods," Greater New Orleans Community Data Center, April 15, 2011, http://www.gnocdc.org/PopulationLossAndVacantHousing/index.html.

[d]*Source:* U.S. Census Bureau, "Poverty Status in 1999 by Age," Census 2000 Summary File 3, Table P87.

In contrast, the Algiers and New Aurora/English Turn districts, located on the Mississippi River's west bank, suffered little damage. The Uptown/Carrolton and Central City/Garden District areas had less damage than average but contained hard-hit neighborhoods. Analyses of damaged areas indicate that Katrina took a disproportionate toll on African Americans, renters and poor residents.[5]

Prior to the mandatory evacuation and flooding, New Orleans had experienced decades-long population loss. The city's estimated 2005 population, 452,170, was down from 627,525 in 1960.[6] The rapid rebound in the years following the storm earned New Orleans the title of the nation's fastest growing city in 2008.[7] Yet repopulation rates slowed, and no post-flood projections anticipated that New Orleans would return to its peak population. The 2010 census count (343,829) amounted to approximately 76 percent of its 2005 estimate but only 55 percent of its historic high.[8]

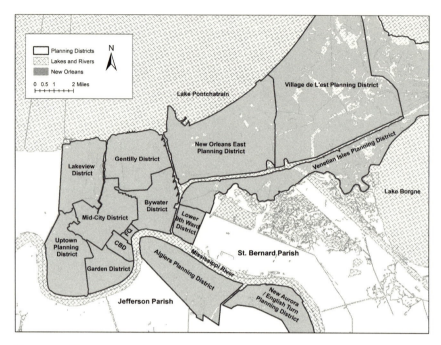

Figure 6.1. New Orleans planning districts. Greater New Orleans Community Data Center database; ESRI, Census 2000 TIGER/Line Files. Map by Robert Linn, 2011.

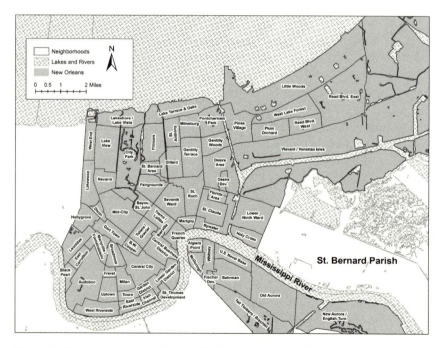

Figure 6.2. Neighborhoods in Orleans Parish. Greater New Orleans Community Data Center database; ESRI, Census 2000 TIGER/Line Files. Map by Robert Linn, 2011.

Additionally, city and parish population estimates—useful indicators in tracking overall recovery—provided little insight into neighborhood dynamics. The 2010 census showed uneven recovery (Table 6.1). Many neighborhoods had rebounded strongly, in some cases even exceeding the number of pre-Katrina households.[9] Yet in 31 of the city's 73 neighborhoods, the number of residents dropped by 30 percent or more between 2000 and 2010. On the whole, heavily damaged districts and neighborhoods rebuilt more slowly than those that experienced lower levels of damage.[10] Five of the neighborhoods with slow return rates contained public housing sites that were demolished to make way for new mixed-income developments (B. W. Cooper Project, Central City Area, Florida Project, Tremé/Lafitte, St. Bernard Area/Project).[11]

For many observers, the repopulation of New Orleans in 2010 exceeded expectations and testified to the resiliency of the city and its residents.[12] Examining the repopulation rates in conjunction with pre-Katrina vacancies provided a more sobering view. Many New Orleans neighborhoods experienced disinvestment as damaging as the flooding. Nearly two-thirds of the city's overall population loss happened before the levees failed.[13] Some New Orleanians left the city for the suburbs and beyond, while others moved into suburbs within the city. The amount of developable land nearly doubled from 36.8 square miles in 1960 to 66.7 square miles in 2000, and much new development occurred in low-lying areas.[14] Between 1960 and 1990, population density decreased dramatically, and the percentage of vacant housing units rose from 6 to 20 percent.[15] Nearly half (16,000) of the 37,000 vacant housing units in 1990 were blighted.[16]

In the 1990s, the city embarked on an anti-blight initiative demolishing over 10,000 houses.[17] Despite these efforts derelict property plagued the city. Just months before Hurricane Katrina struck, Mayor C. Ray Nagin unveiled an ambitious program modeled on Philadelphia's Neighborhood Transformation Initiative to revitalize the city's most distressed neighborhoods.[18] City officials never implemented the program.

In March 2010, New Orleans had 50,076 blighted residential addresses and empty lots and 5,214 blighted commercial buildings. Another 7,409 residential addresses were habitable but vacant.[19] The 2010 census found 25 percent of residential units unoccupied. New Orleans lacked a database of number, type, and location of vacant land and abandoned buildings, preventing systematic examination of vacancies and abandonment by neighborhood. Repopulation rates coupled with vacancy data from the 2010 census illuminate two situations about recovery in a shrinking city.[20]

First, rates of residential recovery mask pre-Katrina disinvestment. The neighborhood referred to as Central City had a moderate population recovery with approximately 60 percent of the 2000 population returning and a 40 percent vacancy rate in 2010. This obscures the fact that the vacancy rate had been high at 21 percent in 2000 and empty lots and derelict structures peppered the neighborhood.[21] Katrina's floodwaters accelerated deterioration in neighborhoods such as the Lower Ninth Ward, Desire, Florida, St. Claude, and St. Roch. For instance, the Florida area had a vacancy rate of 17.5 percent before the storm and almost 60 percent fewer residents in 2010 than in 2000 (Table 6.1).

Second, derelict properties and vacant parcels became significant problems in areas such as New Orleans East, Lakeview, and Gentilly, which before Katrina had low vacancy rates. Blight permeated virtually all neighborhoods post-Katrina.[22] Some areas recovered most of or more than their pre-Katrina population but still faced high vacancies: Algiers Point, Old Aurora, and Tall Timbers in the Algiers planning district; the Lower Garden District neighborhood in Central City; and Marigny in the Bywater (Table 6.1). Unflooded neighborhoods that added units after Katrina faced increased vacancies as population growth slowed.[23]

The Challenges to Rightsizing New Orleans

City leaders and residents can choose how they respond to population loss: "ignore it, accommodate it, combat it, or embrace it."[24] Most often, city leaders attempt to counter depopulation by pursuing growth-oriented strategies. Alternatively, they can develop strategies to adapt the built environment in an attempt to manage and guide depopulation and disinvestment. Conventional market-based policies to induce reinvestment will neither reverse widespread depopulation nor the accompanying disinvestment.[25] How cities should respond to these challenges, a question first raised in the 1970s during the urban fiscal crisis,[26] gained renewed interest in the shrinking cities scholarship.[27]

One land management strategy, referred to as "planned shrinkage," "clustering and clearing," or "neighborhood consolidation,"[28] calls for consolidating population and investments into the most "viable" nodes of the city while clearing and land banking others to bring the level of infrastructure and housing in line with a smaller population. Strategically consolidating development can potentially create a more livable city for remaining residents.[29]

In New Orleans, the devastation from Hurricane Katrina seemed to provide an opportunity that other shrinking cities did not have.[30] In many observers' eyes, New Orleans appeared to be a "blank slate," and therefore they suggested strategies to shrink the city's footprint to reduce risk from future flooding, mitigate blight, and sustain key services for a smaller population. New Orleans also appeared uniquely poised to implement such strategies given the resources that would be available and the redevelopment that had to occur.

In eighteen months following the hurricanes, New Orleans engaged in three recovery planning processes. The first began in September 2005, less than a month after the flooding, when Mayor Nagin initiated the Bring New Orleans Back Commission (BNOBC). Drawing on recommendations from the Urban Land Institute, the BNOBC Land Use Committee proposed residential consolidation with accompanying "urban reserves"—temporarily underutilized land not immediately reoccupied.[31] The plan also proposed converting select residential parcels to open space that could be integrated into the city's stormwater management system. As a first step, the committee recommended a four-month moratorium on building in flood-affected areas and an accompanying neighborhood planning process in which residents would prove the viability of their neighborhoods and demonstrate that a significant proportion of residents intended to return.

BNOBC committee members were responding to uncertainty about residents' return and the fact that the city's population had at least temporarily fallen drastically. Planners and redevelopment professionals expressed concerns that partial rebuilding throughout the city would result in a "jack-o-lantern" effect, a haphazard patchwork of redevelopment surrounded by vacant lots and blighted buildings. Advocates of restricting immediate redevelopment of particular areas argued that allowing residents to rebuild in heavily damaged neighborhoods that might or might not recover was irresponsible. Rather than empowering residents, it "denies them the fundamental assurances needed for rational investment" and merely "extends the period of uncertainty."[32]

The BNOBC committee presented its plan in January 2006, when most residents remained evacuated or had just returned to the city. Many residents first learned of the proposals through a graphic in the *Times-Picayune*, the local newspaper, that showed additional parks inserted in low-lying areas for surface water management. The graphic depicting neighborhoods covered in green became an infamous "green dot" map that came to symbolize forced displacement. Hundreds of enraged residents and advocates for residents who had not returned—such as the local office of Association of Community Organizations for Reform Now (ACORN)—opposed the BNOBC proposals. The mayor, facing a tough reelection campaign, denounced the commission's land use recommendations and allowed rebuilding throughout the city.[33] The land use recommendations in the plan were not further developed.

Planners might have anticipated that residents would react strongly when their neighborhood attachments became mapped abstractions and levels of elevation or levee protection suddenly determined whether they could rebuild. Yet, planners did not present the impact of inconsistent rates of return and explore viable alternatives to the BNOBC proposals in a deliberative process. Although BNOBC committee meetings were open to the public, the process was not designed to engage neighborhood residents. This would have been difficult in any case, because the meetings occurred when most residents, particularly those hardest hit by the flooding, had not yet returned to the city, and commission members developed the strategies in only three months.

BNOBC Land Use Committee members also failed to recognize that their proposals would exacerbate the disparate impacts of the flooding. African Americans were nearly 70 percent of the pre-Katrina population and disproportionately affected by the devastation. Two heavily flooded areas that immediately appeared more vulnerable to a slower return and future flooding were the Lower Ninth Ward and Eastern New Orleans, both predominantly African American parts of the city. With no proposed resettlement plan for those to be displaced, "shrinking the footprint" became a euphemism for denying African American residents the right to return.[34] Because high-income African American and white neighborhoods were flooded, along with middle-class and lower-income areas with white, African American, and Vietnamese American residents, opposition to selective redevelopment had a broad base.

On the heels of the BNOBC, the New Orleans City Council established a neighborhood planning process for flooded areas called the New Orleans Neighborhoods Rebuilding Plan (NONRP). The City Council consists of members elected by district and two at-large members. Council members from the four badly flooded districts were wary of proposals to consolidate development. Unlike the BNOBC's proposed neighborhood planning process, this plan was not intended to identify which neighborhoods would be viable. Instead, the council structured the process so that residents could help assess damage and convey what they wanted in their neighborhoods. The City Council proposed this planning process prior to the BNOBC January meeting because the mayoral administration and City Council were not working collaboratively.

The neighborhood planning meetings became an opportunity to talk through what had happened. Because of the focus on the traumatic events, some derisively called the meetings "therapy sessions." The meetings, however, were needed as a communal way to grieve and develop ways to move forward. Residents believed their neighborhoods could be what they were before the storms but better, and that became the objective of neighborhood plans.[35] The City Council process assumed all neighborhoods would be rebuilt as they had been. Residents, nevertheless, raised pre-Katrina concerns about abandoned residential, commercial, and public property.[36]

Philanthropic sources, rather than the Mayor's Office or City Council, funded the third and final recovery planning process called the Unified New Orleans Plan (UNOP). The process was associated with the predominantly white philanthropic elite rather than the predominantly African American City Council. Residents' opinions varied concerning which of the plans, if any, aligned with their interests.[37] UNOP planners proposed clustering households and businesses in each neighborhood in areas with higher population levels and less flood risk.[38] While clustered development represented a compromise between untenable consolidation strategies proposed by the BNOBC and unguided rebuilding throughout the city, the plan articulated the concept vaguely. While the formal processes occurred, neighborhood residents also met and planned independently. The City Council and Louisiana Recovery Authority eventually adopted all three plans along with two community plans—without reconciling their differences—as the official recovery plan.

Could city officials and residents have developed a citywide restructuring plan in these circumstances? BNOBC Land Use Committee members had rational reasons to propose restricted redevelopment. The strategic shrinkage would allow the city to guide redevelopment, target limited resources, maintain or increase density, and potentially reduce public service costs.[39] Planners and redevelopment officials in shrinking cities nevertheless pay little attention to the political, social, and logistical challenges of rightsizing initiatives.[40] This was the case in New Orleans.

Consolidation efforts, no matter how sensible from a land use management standpoint, are difficult to implement,[41] in part because the very process of selecting some neighborhoods for preservation while excluding others constitutes "a form of public redlining and could become . . . a self-fulfilling prophecy."[42] No one knows whether all residents who returned to heavily flooded neighborhoods would have come back if their neighborhoods faced deferred development. Proponents in the past have, nevertheless, argued that neighborhood consolidation, coupled with relocation assistance for residents to move to more stable neighborhoods, would be better than irregular repopulation.[43]

In New Orleans, the situation was further complicated because planners and city administration failed to realize that residents needed to come to terms with their losses and potential changes. Significant societal changes such as those in New Orleans lead to a "profound loss of meaning" that evokes grief.[44] Because people need continuity, when familiar patterns are broken, they must go through a process of making sense of events, reestablishing meaning, and determining how to move forward.

Acknowledging the process of bereavement could have led to a different course of action, but rapid citywide reorganization still would have been unlikely. Prior to Katrina, planning efforts had not begun to address population loss.[45] In 2005 and 2006, New Orleanians needed time to grieve and reorganize their options, as they contemplated unexpected but inevitable changes in their neighborhoods, social networks, and city. In these circumstances, residents accepted neither proposals to shrink the city's footprint nor decisions others made for them.

Even if restructuring proposals had garnered public and political support, limited organizational capacity hindered large-scale land use changes. The disaster decimated city government capacity. Soon after the floodwaters receded, the city had to lay off roughly half its 6,000 employees,[46] and the New Orleans Redevelopment Authority faced an uncertain future. In 2005, just prior to the levee failures, NORA had a reputation as an underfunded and ineffective agency that instigated individual blight expropriations on requests of interested parties. When Katrina hit, NORA had only three staff, with no clear source of future funding.[47] In the early months after Katrina, the Planning Department and other agencies such as the Sewer and Water Board were also ill equipped to reconfigure physical form. In the years following, NORA's staff expanded to 40 by 2010, and the agency received title to over 10,000 properties and tens of millions of dollars in state and federal grants. The Planning Department and other involved agencies also hired staff, although not at NORA's rate.

In addition, planners and city agencies lacked the tools and resources needed to develop and implement restructuring proposals.[48] Shrinking cities have few mechanisms to facilitate relocation.[49] Although the federal government obligated billions of dollars to the recovery and redevelopment of New Orleans, these funds only slowly filtered down to local government; city agencies faced strict restrictions on the use of funds, and the funds were insufficient to address the damage given that 80 percent of the city had been affected. Given these obstacles and the lack of models from other cities, neither policies nor programs to help households or businesses relocate within the city accompanied any of the original proposals. The city's Office of Recovery Management (later Office of Recovery and Development Administration and subsequently dissolved) under the direction of nationally known planner Edward Blakely unsuccessfully attempted to develop a land swap program—a program that would allow a property owner to trade a property for a similar property in another area regardless of land value differences or demand for the original property—to support clustering put forth in the UNOP proposal. Subsequently, NORA proposed a limited house swap program for the sole occupants on a block or in a townhouse. Yet no one knew how such a program might function, and the city developed no options for residents in sparsely populated areas who might want to move elsewhere in the city. In total, rather than developing workable strategies for citywide restructuring, the planning processes and the subsequent plans and initiatives developed by the city's recovery office and NORA generated parcel- and neighborhood-level strategies.

Opportunities and Limitations of Parcel- and Neighborhood-Level Initiatives

Despite the public backlash against BNOBC proposals, vacant land and blight were foremost concerns on residents' minds. Residents told the planners in detail about unused property in their neighborhoods, its ownership, and the history of efforts to maintain and reuse it. Residents also compiled lists of problem properties.

In response to these concerns, the City Council NONRP process led to a "Lot Next Door" program. The Lot Next Door program intended to give owner occupants the opportunity to purchase abutting properties that had been conveyed to the state as part of the Road Home program. The federally funded housing recovery Road Home program gave grants to owner occupants to repair their properties. Alternatively, homeowners could transfer properties to the state (referred to as "LLT [Louisiana Land Trust] Properties").[50] The Lot Next Door became the primary method of returning properties to neighborhood residents. NORA expanded the program from its initial scope of offering the state-acquired LLT properties to include all properties that NORA obtained. NORA also broadened participation by developing a program that allowed any individual to purchase a property if that person or a family member would live there.[51]

For property owners, the Lot Next Door program had many benefits. It provided the opportunity to buy property that might become blighted or be converted to a rental unit; for some residents, both were threatening. In many neighborhoods, residents had maintained unkempt properties before the storm, so the Lot Next Door program also formalized those relationships. Other residents spoke of the opportunity to acquire properties for family members who needed housing. From NORA's perspective, the program cut the cost of maintaining vacant properties.[52]

The transfer of vacant and abandoned properties to neighborhood residents can have notable benefits. For instance, programs in Flint, Michigan, that transferred tax-reverted property to abutting property owners found those properties more likely to be used and less likely to go into subsequent tax foreclosure than properties sold at auction.[53] Nevertheless, resident-based programs can reduce potential blight more effectively in some areas than others. Neighborhoods with high rates of owner occupancy better absorb vacant and abandoned properties than do areas with more rental units.[54] As a result, neighborhoods with high rates of rental properties and the residents within them benefit less from transfer programs. Before the flooding, rental housing accounted for more than half (54 percent) of the city's occupied housing units.[55]

The Lot Next Door program also affected only a small percentage of the city's vacant and abandoned property. As of August 2010, 2,585 of the almost 5,000 LLT properties conveyed to NORA were Lot Next Door eligible. Of these, 391 were under a purchase agreement and 238 had gone to closing.[56] By June 2011, NORA announced its thousandth closing.[57]

Because the LLT properties were all owner occupied prior to Katrina, preliminary data on the Lot Next Door program indicate that a disproportionate share of eligible properties (46.5 percent) existed in heavily flood-damaged neighborhoods with homeownership rates above the city average. More than a third (38.1 percent) of all eligible properties were concentrated in four neighborhoods: the Lower Ninth Ward, Little Woods, Lakeview, and Filmore. Whereas the Lower Ninth Ward and Little Woods were mixed-tenure neighborhoods before Katrina, with homeownership rates at 59.0 and 51.4 percent respectively, homeownership dominated the more affluent neighborhoods of Lakeview and Filmore, where 69.5 and 85.6 percent of units were owner occupied.

The Lot Next Door program had more impact in higher-income neighborhoods where residents were more likely to have the means to acquire an additional lot. Through late 2010, a disproportionate number of properties were transferred to Lakeview and Filmore residents. Together these two neighborhoods accounted for 11 percent of eligible properties but 30 percent of properties sold or under purchase agreements. In contrast, nearly 19 percent of eligible properties were in the Lower Ninth Ward, but the neighborhood had only 10 percent of properties sold or under purchase agreements. In Little Woods, the figures were 8.3 percent versus 3.9 percent. To make property available to more homeowners, NORA credited documented "sweat equity" and abutting property owners' specific improvements toward the selling price.

For-profit and nonprofit housing developers could purchase properties that were not sold to residents through neighborhood-specific Request for Proposals (RFPs). To encourage concentrated redevelopment, NORA bundled available properties in given areas. These could include blighted properties that NORA expropriated, LLT properties, and properties that NORA obtained through other processes. Neighborhood organizations also approached NORA with lists of problematic properties for possible expropriation. NORA then worked collaboratively with neighborhood organizations in crafting the RFPs. While community-driven acquisition and reuse plans can build trust and result in better redevelopment outcomes,[58] in many of these collaborations, the RFPs reflected fear of rental housing and preference for homeownership. NORA also sometimes transferred properties for community-oriented development projects identified in neighborhood plans, such as for community health centers, small grocers, or public facility expansions.

Although the properties offered through NORA's RFP process came with strict redevelopment requirements, the properties' development ultimately depended on local demand for housing and services. The unflooded Irish Channel became the first neighborhood to establish an agreement with NORA. Adjacent to a pre-Katrina HOPE VI redevelopment project, the Irish Channel was a transitional neighborhood with an active homeowner-dominated neighborhood association. Given increasing land values in the neighborhood both pre- and post-Katrina, many developers expressed interest in the RFP. By comparison, few established developers responded to an RFP issued for a particularly distressed section of Central City, the area with the lowest pre-Katrina land values and poverty rates at 50 percent.[59]

NORA officials acknowledged the difficulties in disposing of properties in the most blighted neighborhoods. In neighborhoods with weak demand for land, NORA attempted to target investments around anchor institutions including schools, commercial corridors, and parks to accompany blight remediation efforts.[60] Significant public resource investment in a geographically focused and sustained way can spur localized improvements, increase property values in and around targeted areas, and even alter a neighborhood's trajectory.[61]

NORA differentiated among neighborhoods that suffered from legacy blight but had generally stable real estate markets, storm-damaged properties in formerly stable markets, and concentrated blight in areas with historic disinvestment.[62] NORA's participation in the second phase of the federal Neighborhood Stabilization Program (NSP2) illustrated how the agency leveraged investment in areas that had much storm-damaged property but generally stable markets. NORA received a highly competitive $29.8 million NSP2 award from the U.S. Department of Housing and Urban Development in 2010 to work with 11 partner organizations to shore up 21 census tracts in nine areas that suffered from abandoned and foreclosed properties. Because the NSP2 program dictated which census tracts would qualify and its focus was the mortgage foreclosure crisis, it affected areas that had not previously been targeted. NORA and its partners, nevertheless, took the opportunity to concentrate funds strategically in these areas to increase redevelopment. NORA was to provide gap financing to spur construction, assist its partners in acquiring and rehabilitating blighted homes, and provide resources to facilitate affordable housing construction.[63]

NORA also took a targeted approach to redevelopment in commercial corridors that included investments in commercial buildings, efforts to rebuild nearby housing, and collaboration with other city agencies to make street improvements. In 2010, the Mayor's Office authorized NORA to invest over $10 million of Community Development Block Grant money in several commercial corridors. NORA allocated $2 million to commercial projects on Oretha Castle Haley Boulevard, a historic corridor in Central City close to downtown. Through a gap financing program, NORA provided financing for 14 commercial projects along the boulevard, including a 20,000 square foot building where NORA planned to relocate its offices. NORA also worked with its NSP2 partners to develop over 50 single-family houses and 70 rental units for seniors on currently blighted property in the residential areas around the corridor.[64] Numerous other residential and commercial projects had been constructed in the vicinity by mid-2011, and the city was to make $300,000 in street improvements.[65]

Given limited resources, city officials may see the most results from investing resources strategically,[66] and in some circumstances, targeting can change local market dynamics and strengthen stable but threatened neighborhoods. However, in cities like New Orleans with extensive blight and disinvestment, areas outside targeted recovery zones could experience further deterioration. Planners and other officials must concurrently develop strategies to stabilize untargeted neighborhoods. While financially and logistically difficult, ignoring untargeted New Orleans neighborhoods became no better than proposing to shrink the footprint. Neither gave residents options through which to assess and address their situations.

NORA's focus on neighborhood initiatives and its partnerships with neighborhood and community-based organizations represented a fundamental shift from the organization's pre-Katrina activities. However, while residents engaged in the city's recovery efforts in unprecedented numbers, participation was uneven across neighborhoods. As a result, if NORA directed its resources toward active organizations and neighborhoods, NORA could exacerbate inequities among neighborhoods.[67]

Conclusion

Five years after Hurricane Katrina, New Orleans had rebuilt substantially. Yet uneven repopulation and blight weighed on recovery. For those who supported proposals for a smaller New Orleans, widespread blight was a predictable outcome of the missed opportunity. Planning for large-scale change such as citywide restructuring, however, became impossible. The proposed consolidation, like the flooding, would have disproportionately affected

African American residents as well as those with lower incomes. Because planners developed no resettlement plans for displaced residents, rightsizing would have exacerbated the already disparate impacts of the devastation. Furthermore, discussions about shrinking the footprint failed to acknowledge the loss residents experienced. During the mid-twentieth century, governmental entities ignored residents' responses to large-scale urban renewal schemes. The substantial neighborhood disruption and social upheavals these projects caused have made large-scale change difficult to accomplish.[68] No matter how "rational" consolidation proposals appeared, residents needed time to experience their loss and construct new possibilities.

Even if a clustered redevelopment strategy had gained citywide support, New Orleans lacked the staff, financial resources, and tools to restructure the built environment. City staff could not, for instance, quickly structure land swaps or relocation programs. New Orleans received significant resources, but these could not pay for rebuilding the city, relocating residents, and removing buildings. Additionally, many agencies would have had to coordinate, just when they were trying to assess damage and make immediate repairs to resume operations.

Nevertheless, Katrina created an urgency that catalyzed discussion and policy action around population loss and abandonment. In 2010, city officials were developing the capacity to address blight strategically. Mayor Mitch Landrieu created an executive position on blight and neighborhood revitalization, and NORA's capacity continued to increase. However, the parcel- and neighborhood-level strategies implemented by 2010, while essential, remained inadequate. At that time, city agencies still needed strategies for the weak market neighborhoods that were unlikely to benefit from lot-level initiatives and fell outside targeted recovery zones. To overlook these neighborhoods would be an injustice to the residents who had struggled to return.

CHAPTER 7

Missing New Orleans: Lessons from the CDC Sector on Vacancy, Abandonment, and Reconstructing the Crescent City

Jeffrey S. Lowe and Lisa K. Bates

As in many other major U.S. cities with shrinking populations, the New Orleans experience with vacant and abandoned properties has constituted a significant long-term problem where community development corporations (CDCs) sought to respond. "Vacant and abandoned" properties—including those temporarily unoccupied (vacant) as well as permanently empty dwellings and lots where owners have walked away (abandoned) and that often appear unkempt or dilapidated—made up over 12 percent of the housing stock in 2000.[1] After Hurricane Katrina, the chronic problem became a catastrophe. New Orleans sustained 57 percent of all damages in Louisiana.[2] Approximately 80 percent of the city flooded, reportedly damaging 134,344 homes; and one in six (105,155) occupied units sustained severe damages.[3] In all, 200,000 New Orleanians were displaced, residential damages totaled $14 billion, and an estimated 27,284 units lay vacant, including 13,113 "other" vacant, likely abandoned, properties.[4] As of 2008, New Orleans led seven comparison cities in vacancy, including Detroit, Flint, Baltimore, and Pittsburgh, with over one in three residential properties unoccupied.[5]

Given such an environment, this chapter explains why the New Orleans CDC sector did not play a major role in remaking the city after catastrophic vacancy and abandonment in the five years post-Katrina. Whereas in some places CDCs have contributed considerably to neighborhood redevelopment, New Orleans serves as a case of the CDC sector's minimal role due to barriers to building capacity and empowerment before Hurricane Katrina hit the city in 2005. New Orleans lacked a CDC sector with significant capacity and voice representative of those most in need. Further, the frail community development system—the network of foundations and local public, private, and nonprofit entities including a community development partnership along with the CDCs—was too weak to build that capacity. This situation offers lessons for planners, policy makers, and others concerned with the participation of low-income residents in the transition from vacancy and abandonment after catastrophe, as well as in situations of chronic vacancy and abandonment.

This chapter first briefly reviews the literature on CDC involvement in community revitalization and explains the methods for case analysis. To lay a foundation for understanding the current context, the second section describes the pre-Katrina status of vacancy and abandonment and the evolution of the community development system and CDC capacity. The third section assesses the community development system and CDC activities to deal with abandoned properties in the post–Katrina era. The chapter concludes with recommendations for broadening community development outcomes in New Orleans to include the participation and empowerment of indigenously rooted CDCs that could influence the choice of activities slated for vacant and abandoned properties.

Conceptual Framework and Methods

CDCs and supporters have helped to revitalize neighborhoods by transforming vacant and abandoned properties into affordable housing in many cities.[6] At the same time, CDCs have not transformed the structural conditions that limit the ability of low-wealth communities to achieve a better quality of life for their residents.[7] As frontline organizations with paid staff that serve and represent the interests of residents, CDCs struggle with sustaining core operating support.[8] Neighborhood needs often call for a balance in focus on rebuilding physical structures and empowering both individuals and organizations such as CDCs to increase their capacities.[9] CDCs rarely act alone in this process of rebuilding and empowerment. The actions of other participants in the community development system influence what they can do.

Beginning in the 1980s, many major U.S. cities experienced a rise in community development systems. Alliances between local and nonlocal funders seeking to enhance local CDCs strengthened community development systems. As part of that process, funders often helped to establish local community development partnerships that would provide sustained core operating support and technical assistance.[10] Local funders typically included foundations, businesses, and municipal administrations. Nonlocal funders tended to be national foundations (sometimes through national intermediaries) and federal and state governments. The goal in establishing local community development systems was to set standards for CDCs and relieve CDCs from the constant challenge of securing operating support, thereby helping stabilize and expand CDC capacity in production of affordable housing and in neighborhood revitalization.[11]

By the 1990s, efforts to strengthen the community development system and establish a community development partnership were underway. These endeavors aimed to build capacity beyond real property development and advance empowerment to improve the quality of life among residents of lower-income neighborhoods. However, the efforts lacked sustainability, and resulting CDC capacity and resident empowerment could have little impact on vacancy and abandonment after Hurricane Katrina.

To explain this outcome, we investigated the capabilities of the CDC sector and CDCs' response to vacancy and abandonment pre-Katrina through newspaper articles, reports, books, scholarly publications, and interviews undertaken in 2000 with CDC staff and others involved with major sources of CDC support. Next, with attention focused on post-Katrina agenda setting for property redevelopment, we examined planning documents, meeting minutes, and news accounts. We inspected documents from the New Orleans Redevelopment Authority (NORA) to shed light on the involvement of CDCs. We interviewed NORA staff in 2007 and 2010 and CDC leaders from 2005 through 2010. Thus, the analysis considers the CDC sector and also examines the influence of the community development system on CDCs' ability to advance resident empowerment and to affect vacancy and abandonment post-Hurricane Katrina.

CDC Sector Pre-Katrina

Contextualizing the local CDC sector prior to Hurricane Katrina provides insight into organizations' ability to respond to vacancy and abandonment. New Orleans CDCs emerged in the 1990s out of heightened awareness of and support for transforming massive vacancy and abandonment. Historically, New Orleans maintained a dense development pattern more typical of northern urban areas because much of the city lay below sea level. This pattern changed after World War II. With drainage of the surrounding swamplands and completion of Interstate 10, the Lake Pontchartrain Bridge, and the Veterans Memorial Highway, the suburbs grew, and by the mid-1970s over 40 percent of the New Orleans metropolitan population, characteristically middle- and upper-income with medium to high educational attainment, resided outside the city.[12] In the city, African Americans and the poor tended to occupy the lowest-lying areas.[13] Suburbanization and the permanent elimination of jobs after the oil bust of the 1980s had yet to receive attention for causing increases in vacancy and abandoned properties.

Throughout the 1980s, city officials did not give priority to resolving the mounting problem of vacancy and abandonment, and virtually no community-based organizations engaged in real estate development.[14] By the beginning of the 1990s, the vacancy rate had almost doubled from 9 percent in 1980 to nearly 17 percent, or over 37,000 housing units.[15] Around the same time, in 1991, the national intermediary Local Initiatives Support Corporation (LISC) established a New Orleans affiliate as one of the three localities in its National Demonstration Program.

New Orleans LISC's mission was to implement the National Demonstration Program, an initiative testing the effectiveness of consensus organizing, to (1) build community capacity by fostering relationships between residents of low-income neighborhoods and metropolitan-wide resources and (2) form new CDCs (where well-seasoned ones did not exist) that would sustain resident volunteers on CDC boards and committees and increase local support for housing development.[16] Subsequently, New Orleans LISC stimulated the creation of six new CDCs.

With more than 37,000 vacant and abandoned housing units,[17] the state of housing finally gained local recognition as a significant problem and became a major issue in the mayoral campaign in 1993.[18] Subsequently, the new mayor, Marc Morial, dissolved the troubled Office of Housing and Urban Affairs and established the Division of Housing and Neighborhood Development. The new administration desired CDCs to play a leading role in rehabilitating abandoned properties and promised public funds to assist them in the undertaking.[19]

The Morial administration's choice of CDCs to participate in addressing the vacancy and abandonment problem produced two reactions. First, the number of new CDCs increased. Second, with the rising number of CDCs, concerns arose about how to deepen and expand their long-term support beyond public funding. In response, the Greater New Orleans Foundation (GNOF) facilitated a year-long planning process involving representatives from the public, private, nonprofit, and philanthropic sectors that culminated in the establishment of a community development partnership, New Orleans Neighborhood Development Collaborative (NONDC), in 1995. With support from the Ford Foundation and GNOF, NONDC leveraged additional support from local and regional philanthropies, businesses, and banks that enabled the partnership to provide funding and technical assistance to 9 of the 28 CDCs. NONDC deemed these CDCs most likely to engage successfully in real estate development. In addition to encouraging CDCs' real estate development, NONDC planned to expand CDC organizational capacity so that they could better represent those most in need and advance resident and community empowerment.

The majority of these CDCs worked in the lowest-income neighborhoods, with poverty rates exceeding the city's average of 31.6 percent in 1990. Also, these neighborhoods sustained high levels of vacant and abandoned properties. NONDC believed that building the human capital of these CDCs' staff and board members would translate into stronger organizations that would produce more physical development, increased interactions with businesses and government, and greater influence over neighborhood development.[20]

The Community Development System's Influence on CDC Capacity

Unlike cities with a longer history in community development, New Orleans had many organizations that had not engaged in community development before responding to the call of the Morial administration for greater participation in rehabilitating vacant and abandoned properties. Hence, New Orleans's nascent, small community development system that provided support to CDCs consisted of technical assistance providers, organizations focused on community organizing, providers of operating support, and private financial investors.

The Center for Non-Profit Resources and New Orleans LISC provided most of the technical assistance, including workshops and training on topics such as grant writing, nonprofit management, and strategic planning.

Meanwhile, New Orleans LISC rendered technical assistance tailored specifically to the six CDCs receiving its support.

Three primary organizations provided support for organizing. Two faith-based umbrella community organizing entities, All Congregations Together (ACT) and the Jeremiah Group, included CDCs as members. Training for ACT came from the Pacific Institute for Community Organization (PICO), while the Industrial Areas Foundation (IAF) prepared the Jeremiah Group.[21] Both ACT and the Jeremiah Group instructed emerging leaders and built grassroots support through issue-based organizing among its member organizations, with some success. For example, because of pressure from ACT, city officials allocated additional funding for demolishing abandoned housing.[22] The New Orleans affiliate of the Association of Community Organizations for Reform Now (ACORN), the oldest of the three community organizations, advocated for giving abandoned homes to low-income people.[23] ACORN expanded beyond advocacy and community organizing and formed a housing development arm (ACORN Housing Corporation) in New Orleans.

The primary sources of operating support, which went almost entirely to organizations rehabilitating abandoned properties, came from the Division of Housing and Neighborhood Development and NONDC. NORA remained dormant, playing virtually no role. The lead public agency fostering community development, the Division of Housing and Neighborhood Development, administered operating support to most CDCs from federal Community Development Block Grant (CDBG) funds and project-specific support through federal Home Ownership Made Easy (HOME) funds. While NONDC invited all CDCs to participate in seminars and workshops, the organization supplied three-year operating support, technical assistance and training, and organizational assessments to nine CDCs.[24]

Banks supplied most of the private financial investment, providing equity investments and establishing limited partnerships with some CDCs, at the urging of the Morial administration.[25] To limit the exposure of banks to risky home loans, the administration initiated the "Mayor's Challenge Fund" to leverage additional private funds from other investors for rehabilitation-related activities, including city purchase of homes that did not sell within a designated time period.[26]

Consensus did not exist within the community development system for long-term commitment to building CDC capacity, due to a clash of values. Some, particularly nonprofits, supported CDC efforts at individual and community empowerment. Others, especially those with private sector connections, placed greater emphasis on efficient housing rehabilitation. Initially, NONDC recognized that, while the organization expanded capacity for rehabilitating vacant and abandoned properties, building CDCs' capacity to empower individuals and community organizations was just as important.[27]

The NONDC board determined at the outset that, along with creating safe and affordable housing, the organization would increase individual and organizational empowerment in the neighborhoods.[28] At the same time, the community development system lacked the internal relationships and the understanding of community development necessary to achieve these outcomes. Therefore, NONDC staff began educating their board, representatives from CDCs, and the public and private sectors about community development. At board meetings, nationally recognized experts often presented best practices and illuminated the lessons from these. The board also relied heavily on the NONDC executive director, a native New Orleanian with over twenty years of experience and a former leader in the Chicago community development system.[29]

By the end of the 1990s, the resources available to CDCs had expanded due to the flow of funds from national and community foundations disbursed through NONDC. Also, NONDC provided opportunities for interaction and networking among CDCs and funders. Conversations began about starting a CDC association with the 28 CDCs as members. Moreover, CDCs showed expanded organizational and production capacity.

CDCs, no longer totally dependent on volunteers, employed an average of two paid staff including the director. Also, many CDCs had undertaken their first real estate ventures, with most rehabilitating at least three abandoned homes annually. Prior to NONDC, CDCs produced virtually no housing. By 2000, the nine NONDC-assisted CDCs had renovated 625 housing units, with 15 percent owner-occupied.[30] Some CDC staff and board members indicated the usefulness of NONDC-funded organizational assessments, consultancies, and other tools in helping their organizations further community cohesion and empowerment. For example, one CDC, Community Resource Partnership, participated in a process that led to planning, organizing, and establishing a consortium of like-minded community groups.[31]

Some members of the community development system considered this expansion of human resource and production capacities among CDCs impressive. Others considered it an inefficient use of time and resources and insufficient in scale for curbing vacancy and abandonment. Over the next five years, significant changes within the community development system impeded CDC capacity to address vacancy, abandonment, blight, and neighborhood revitalization. First, the National Demonstration Program ended and New Orleans LISC closed. Second, the Ford Foundation changed the focus of its community development activities and substantially lessened support for community development partnerships such as NONDC. New Orleans corporations did not increase support for CDCs to compensate for the withdrawal of national funders. Meanwhile, the new Nagin administration appeared ambivalent toward addressing vacancy and abandonment and did not prioritize the involvement of CDCs through the Division of Housing and Neighborhood Development or NORA.

With sudden deaths and other changes among key staff and board members during the early 2000s, NONDC intensified the focus on efficiency and, to the detriment of CDC capacity, transitioned from a community development partnership to a property developer, concentrating its efforts on the revitalization of the Central City neighborhood.[32] On the eve of Hurricane Katrina, without a community development partnership to convene influential actors, shape policy, and aggregate resources, CDC capacity to transform abandoned properties and empower communities was exceptionally low.

In 2000, New Orleans sustained a 12.5 percent housing vacancy rate; 5 percent (10,714) of housing units lay apparently abandoned.[33] After Katrina, the housing stock decreased by 53 percent. Of the 114,426 units in 2008, one of every four was vacant, and noticeably abandoned properties made up 11.5 percent (13,113) of housing units.[34] With a quarter of the housing stock vacant or abandoned, the absence of strong action from the CDC sector may help to explain the lack of more positive results. The section that follows highlights the workings of the community development system and the capacity of CDCs to help deal with vacancy and abandonment within the first five years after Katrina.

CDC Sector Post-Katrina

Immediately after Katrina, vacant properties—some vacant lots and many flood-damaged homes—became a critical component of redeveloping the city. With tens of thousands of pre-Katrina vacant and abandoned properties and thousands more newly vacant and damaged houses, NORA saw nonprofit developers as key participants in moving properties into service. However, even before Katrina, the community development system did not have the capacity to assume that role. This section describes the evolution of New Orleans's CDC sector and community development system from the immediate aftermath of Katrina through activities under the federal Neighborhood Stabilization Program (NSP) that started in 2009. We pay particular attention to the capacity of CDCs to engage in redevelopment, given the vision in NORA's 2007 plan of "an active nonprofit and subsidized development community."[35] Two critical barriers existed for CDCs' property redevelopment after the storm: (1) underdeveloped public sector institutions and policies for property transfers and (2) the high costs of property development in conjunction with a weak community development system to build CDC capacity. The result was a bifurcated CDC sector: pre-Katrina indigenously rooted organizations that struggled to work with NORA and engage in development and externally endowed organizations that tapped into post-Katrina networks and included new CDCs having greater programmatic capacity than others.

Public Entities and Clogs in the Vacant Property Pipeline

One challenge for CDCs attempting partnership in the reconstruction of the city emerged from the underdeveloped nature of public institutions responsible for vacant properties. Different public and private entities prepared several versions of post-Katrina recovery plans, so CDC leaders and neighborhood residents alike had difficulty knowing how state and city officials would allocate rebuilding resources.[36] Several iterations of recovery plans, including the United New Orleans Plan, adopted in late spring 2007, included a targeted recovery strategy that would not rebuild all infrastructure. The idea of focusing public subsidies and projects in only some neighborhoods proved unpopular, but its persistence made individuals and organizations uncertain about moving forward with reconstruction in some heavily damaged areas. Additionally, efficient and effective public sector mechanisms and legal processes for distributing vacant properties to developers did not exist. NORA, emerging from dormancy, lacked staff capacity, procedures, and a sufficient budget to handle the scope of the vacant property problem.[37] As NORA became active, the organization had to develop a plan to receive thousands of flood-damaged properties that owners sold to the state. The evolution of the legal and policy framework for moving vacant properties into the hands of developers to meet recovery plan priorities continued with the development of the plan to use federal NSP funds for 2009 through 2011.

The legal environment for redevelopment in Louisiana was complex, and lack of clarity and delineation of roles interfered with creating a framework for community development post-Katrina. The pipeline of properties potentially available for redevelopment included two streams: properties that the city could expropriate due to tax adjudication or blight (almost all predating Katrina)[38] and flood-damaged properties that their owners sold to the Louisiana Land Trust as part of the Road Home program.[39] Louisiana had complex statutes and constitutional amendments that addressed the seizure and transfer of vacant, blighted, and tax-delinquent property.[40] These processes changed after Katrina with new state constitutional amendments.

As of June 2006, the city's rolls included approximately 6,000 tax-adjudicated properties and 20,000 blighted properties designated as such before Katrina.[41] At first, due to the lack of staff and process at NORA, Mayor Nagin's office implemented a program to move pre-Katrina properties into the development pipeline. Due to clouded titles, these properties could not be fully under the city's control until completion of a potentially lengthy and costly expropriation process and the mayor's signoff on each property's transfer to the city.[42] In August 2006, the mayor announced that the city attorney would make 2,500 tax-adjudicated properties available to developers at no cost, after owners received a chance to redeem their properties by paying the taxes and fees owed. Developers, including 11 nonprofits, were to pay for the legal process to transfer title from the original owner to themselves in order to begin construction. Without clean title, many developers could not proceed with projects.

The mayor's first post-storm disposition of tax-adjudicated vacant properties considered the capacity to build at scale as a critical factor in approving a developer's request for properties.[43] The mayor's initial program awarded 11 CDCs between 100 and 300 properties each in some of the city's most devastated neighborhoods and expected these CDCs to complete housing repair or new construction within 24 months.[44] Walker's 2002 national census of CDCs found that nearly half produced fewer than 10 units per year and only 1.8 percent produced more than 200 units annually, so meeting these targets would require an unusual level of development capacity for a CDC.[45] In New Orleans, CDC production was even more limited before

Katrina. The storm brought additional challenges in technical issues with flood damage, historic status, and elevation requirements, as well as in shortages in construction labor. Due to financing problems, the majority of these properties had never been developed, and according to NORA staff, some with standing structures faced repossession for failing to address blight conditions.

While NORA existed before Katrina, the agency did not have a legal role in the transfer of vacant, blighted, or adjudicated properties from owners to the city and on to buyers. NORA officials struggled through 2006 and 2007 to develop the agency's policies and procedures as the city designated it to receive properties sold to the Louisiana Land Trust (LLT) under the Road Home program's relocation options. The LLT's requirement for parish property disposition plans pushed NORA to define its development priorities, including the role of nonprofits.[46] As of the writing of the parish plan in 2007, NORA anticipated receiving 4,000 properties in the first year and another 3,000 to 4,000 properties over the life of the Road Home program.[47] The first post-storm disposition of tax-adjudicated vacant properties considered the capacity to build at a large scale as a critical factor in approving a developer's request for properties.[48] NORA staff quickly realized that a developer's ability to complete construction on large numbers of properties was not as important as the ability to access financing to complete quality construction, even of small numbers of properties. By spring 2008, NORA had held community meetings to present plans to require nonprofit developers to demonstrate the ability to complete five or more units in order to purchase properties that NORA staff attorneys had fully expropriated.[49]

The failures of Mayor Nagin's program to work with tax-adjudicated properties, among other constraints, led NORA to focus on LLT properties, where title transfer occurred in the course of the Road Home program at no cost to the agency or the developer. NORA disposed of few tax-adjudicated and blighted properties due to the high costs of expropriation, except where they were in revitalization target locations. NORA's main focus turned to the disposition of properties within the Recovery Zones designated by the Office of Recovery Management. As NORA received LLT properties, the agency created strategies for the Recovery Zones and made redevelopment area compacts to guide development plans with community input. In 2009, NORA applied for federal NSP funds to move more properties into service and received $30 million. Also, the NSP proposal created a consortium of nonprofit developers that NORA considered its high-capacity CDC partners.

The strategy focused attention on neighborhoods with large numbers of LLT properties and some demand for housing. This strategy, seeking to stabilize and build on market activity, shifted attention from the pre-Katrina CDCs' activities in the neighborhoods with the most poverty and abandonment toward a range of neighborhood types.

Financial Problems for Developing Properties

CDCs, as partners for affordable development, faced severe financial constraints. In order to obtain vacant and abandoned properties for redevelopment from NORA, an organization had to demonstrate access to financing to complete the project, including letters of credit or proof of funds raised via partners. Organizations that were not credit worthy had difficulty obtaining sufficient upfront money to pay for lots and construction, as well as bridging the gap between purchase price and development cost. A CDC needed either very sound financial health or a partner developer who could access financing and put up the large amounts of collateral necessary in a constrained credit market. NORA staffers explained that many CDCs needed flexible underwriting to qualify for construction loans, due to the extreme difficulty of preselling units or prequalifying buyers. NORA had neither funding for CDCs nor the staff capacity to offer assistance for CDCs with insufficient financial pro formas but could refer CDCs to foundations to seek resources.

Barriers for redevelopment of adjudicated properties included the costs associated with the legal procedures for the city's property seizure and the complicated property histories. Because tax-adjudicated properties had to be legally expropriated from their owners, developers needed to pay title abstracters and attorneys to clear the properties' titles before asking the mayor's approval of the transfer. Costs for clearing title could exceed $2,000 per property. The complicated process left many CDCs unable to clear titles to take possession of vacant property due to tangled legal histories and decades without sales; both increased the cost of abstracting. Some properties "in heirship" had multiple legal owners because low-income families frequently did not complete "succession" to pass ownership to the next generation after a death.[50] One CDC that received nearly 400 properties in the mayor's disposition in 2006 had a staff experienced with rehabilitation and affordable development, including internal financial expertise and a dedicated construction crew. By February 2007, this CDC had completed two model homes in the Lower Ninth Ward for residents who had received Road Home grants to rebuild. According to development plans, they anticipated completing 75 units by the end of the year. Instead, by August 2007, the CDC had not been able to finance the cost of the title transfers, which required legal fees, abstracting and title clearance, notification ads, and recording fees, for a total of $2,250 for each transferred property. In order for the CDC to take ownership of the nearly 400 properties it had been awarded, it needed at least $900,000 in predevelopment funds, even though the properties themselves were "free." In February 2008, GNOF granted the CDC $200,000 for these predevelopment costs, with a likely renewal of the funding over the next two years.[51] With this level of upfront costs and the delays of the title transfer process, CDCs receiving properties from the adjudicated lists had little success in completing construction.

Once NORA received LLT properties, the agency shifted disposition priorities to these houses and lots, where the Road Home program cleared the titles. CDCs no longer needed to find money for the legal transfer but still needed to purchase parcels. NORA did not give properties to CDCs. A CDC seeking to develop vacant properties had to pay fair market value, between $15,000 and $30,000 per lot, unless the CDC had an agreement to pay only transaction costs based on the CDC's ability to produce 30 to 40 houses per quarter.

Significant gaps in the development pro forma also existed due to the low purchasing power of potential homebuyers. As the first developments launched, NORA officials realized that, in the post-Katrina context, building was more costly than originally anticipated, and they revised estimates for construction costs and the prices of homes affordable to potential homebuyers. NORA staff recognized that significant deficits existed between construction costs and sales price for any housing development that aimed to serve low- and moderate-income residents. At the writing of the Orleans Parish LLT Plan in 2007, NORA estimated the financial gap for homeowner unit development at $20,000 to $30,000 per unit.[52] By the writing of the NSP proposal in 2009, based on experience with the length of time to complete development and a realistic sense of buyer purchasing power, NORA reestimated the gap as $40,000–80,000 per unit to serve households at 50 percent of area median income—a priority population for many CDCs.

National philanthropic organizations invested hundreds of millions of dollars in post-Katrina recovery, sponsored development professionals as fellows in organizations, and imported technical expertise to work on local projects. At the same time, New Orleans CDCs remained in a nascent state because little sustained funding existed to build capacity. For example, national intermediaries and foundations had funding available for development, but they did not always target these funds to the particular challenges of development. LISC and Enterprise created the Louisiana Loan Fund (LLF) for predevelopment finance, but the fund had made few loans by the end of 2010. The loans could only be used for predevelopment and acquisition and had to be repaid out of equity or new loans before construction could start.[53] A nonprofit developer had to show the full financing for project completion to be eligible for LLF funds.[54] Accessing this fund depended on the ability to access much greater levels of financing to close the gap between construction costs and selling prices. The program's efficacy was limited because predevelopment costs were not the main financial problem for housing developers. When subsidies for homebuyers were not confirmed until later in the development process, a significant funding gap remained initially. The difference between construction costs and the affordable sale price of the home could not be closed upfront in order to meet underwriting criteria for this predevelopment loan fund. This barrier was addressed for NORA-NSP consortium developers by providing the deep subsidy needed upfront to complete construction—a riskier use of funds, but one that NORA staff argued was the only way to get projects underway. For CDCs that did not have financing in place to access the LLF and other stringently underwritten debt financing, launching construction was very difficult, even for those with experience in housing development.

The CDC Sector: Fragile and Bifurcated

Perhaps the most telling indicator of the state of CDCs as of late 2010 was their lack of visibility and participation in neighborhood redevelopment more generally. Because CDCs had limited impact on housing and revitalization before Katrina, philanthropic organizations did not necessarily view CDCs as a potential major partner in post-Katrina reconstruction. In December 2006, Carey Shea, at the time with the Rockefeller Foundation, assessed the city's environment as not conducive to CDC activity due to limited government and philanthropic support but told the *Times-Picayune*, "I do think that in the post-Katrina era, a few strong CDCs are going to emerge."[55] A few strong CDCs with high levels of capacity to redevelop vacant property did emerge, though they were not the indigenously rooted organizations NONDC supported pre-Katrina. The biggest players were post-Katrina externally endowed organizations that included resource partners from outside New Orleans. Indigenously rooted CDCs remained less fully formed.

In areas outside Recovery Zones and where blight designation or tax adjudication was the main source of properties, NORA gave limited attention to property disposition. NORA did not work to build CDC capacity; in the words of NORA staff, CDCs must be "shovel ready" to acquire properties. Those CDCs that since Katrina demonstrated success in development in targeted areas were part of the NSP consortium, with influence and involvement in major strategic investments. Consortium CDCs—grassroots grown or not—had high capacity. On the other hand, locally based CDCs, neighborhood-based groups without significant resources, and those outside the revitalization target areas struggled to have input on plans for development.

COMMUNITY-BASED ORGANIZATIONS IMMEDIATELY AFTER THE STORM

After Katrina, the challenges for community-based organizations (CBOs, including CDCs, advocacy/organizing groups, and neighborhood-based hurricane relief organizations) were enormous. The Unitarian Universalist Service Committee (UUSC) produced a series of reports on community-based organization capacity in 2006, assessing the strength of a variety of neighborhood and citywide organizations. At that time, many CBOs listed staff as their most immediate and pressing need.[56] Organizations serving flooded neighborhoods also needed to relocate when conditions did not permit reoccupancy.[57] Many organizational leaders wanted not only funds but more time—explaining that the challenges of the unprecedented situation delayed spending while they retooled programs, created new programs to respond to the disaster (for example, ramping up large-scale house gutting), and prepared for redevelopment planning.[58]

Leaders of indigenously rooted organizations voiced concerns about the large amounts of money flowing into the region from national philanthropic organizations without local direction, the expectations of funders, and the long-term prospect for community-based organizations' programming. Eisenberg, a scholar-advocate for responsible philanthropy, used the term "deplorable" to describe the choices of foundations like Ford, Packard, and Rockefeller.[59] These foundations funneled significant funds through local foundations (such as the GNOF and the Baton Rouge Area Foundation) that had no significant history of funding grassroots organizations, particularly those that served communities of color and low-income residents. One local organization director asked why the large foundations would not commit to work in New Orleans until they had completed extensive assessments— "What's wrong with the 501c3 structure that everyone could come down for a five day tour but no one could come to actually do the work for a month? . . . What's wrong with the foundation world that they have to produce 207 fancy glossy interview reports to their board in order to shuffle a few thousand dollars our way?"[60] Many funders were "obsessed" with accountability,[61] pressing organizations for plans and results at a time when the organizations were still determining the best course of action. The unpredictability of population return, the lack of clarity of federal and state policies and local plans, and the lack of institutions and systems for moving redevelopment forward meant CBOs, including CDCs, had trouble providing tangible, "bricks and mortar" evidence of progress.

Furthermore, CBOs had trouble making longer-term strategic plans for programming, given their uncertainty about future funding beyond the emergency of Katrina recovery. Should organizations continue their prestorm programming, shift to relief for returning residents or move into redevelopment? While new needs emerged with the disaster, long-standing problems for low-income neighborhoods persisted. The UUSC report highlighted two housing organization leaders' views. One leader argued that CDCs needed self-generating money, rather than depending on outside grants, in order to set long-term program goals.[62] A second CDC leader suggested that given the historically "fleeting nature" of funding in New Orleans, rather than direct resources, local organizations needed to build networking capacity—for "relationship building and . . . strategic planning sessions to ensure fiscal sustainability, even after philanthropic attention shifts elsewhere."[63]

TWO TIERS OF CDCs

The ability of CDCs to assume a major role in reconstructing the city—not only physically but socially, economically, and politically—was in question post-Katrina. Many CDCs operated in crisis mode due to storm damage, staff shortages, and a need to address immediate needs of residents (including the displaced) for housing and other necessities. The lack of local government capacity compounded the challenge of strategizing, aligning resources across organizations and with philanthropic partners, and addressing emerging community needs. In a changing system of rules and programs,

CDCs faced additional difficulties in development, and philanthropic attention turned to creating plans and institutions for redevelopment.

During the 1990s, national supporters of community development provided core operating support, technical assistance, and organizational development to nascent CDCs in New Orleans, particularly through LISC and NONDC. This role shifted after Katrina, with the focus of national organizations turning to policy making and strategy setting more than to building CDCs as implementers of an antiabandonment plan. The National Vacant Properties Campaign (NVPC) was no longer a strong presence as a national organization; in 2009, NVPC presented best practices for developers that explained property acquisition but was in transition to becoming part of the Center for Community Progress. NVPC also created a blight strategy for New Orleans mayor Mitch Landrieu in 2010, which focused on the city's role in building the infrastructure for property disposition.[64] NONDC became a nonprofit developer in collaboration with Enterprise-founded Gulf Coast Housing Partners working with the Housing Authority of New Orleans on HOPE VI redevelopment projects, rather than acting as a capacity builder for other organizations. Local philanthropies focused on housing development, not a broader community development mission of empowering grassroots organizations to play a part in determining how to rebuild the city. GNOF's community reinvestment funds went largely to post-Katrina-established, externally endowed CDCs with demonstrated programmatic capacity, not to new, emerging, or less experienced indigenous organizations or those that focused on grassroots participation along with physical redevelopment. For example, GNOF funded development by the Pontchartrain Park CDC, the Broadmoor Improvement Association, and the Jericho Road CDC; all these funds went toward deepening the resource capacity of well-positioned organizations, rather than to CBOs seeking to become development organizations.[65]

NORA planned to use federal NSP money to close financing gaps for organizations in the NORA consortium of developers—CDCs that had proven their programmatic, financial, and organizational capacity to develop properties. These organizations achieved physical redevelopment, but many did not incorporate broader community development goals of grassroots participation in shaping the future of neighborhoods and the city.

This group of CDCs had a considerable role in redevelopment in the city, focused on target neighborhoods. Still, the total numbers of properties developed by 2009 was a small percentage of the number of vacant and blighted properties in the city. According to NORA's NSP application, the consortium had site control for 20 percent of the city's vacant properties. In addition, about 200 newly constructed single-family houses and 260 rehabilitated units were completed along with approximately 1,000 new rental units (most in partnership with HOPE VI redevelopment of public housing).

The consortium was a decidedly post-Katrina network. Of the twelve nonprofit entities (not including NORA) that made up the NSP consortium of developers in 2010, only four existed prior to Hurricane Katrina. These four—NONDC, Jericho Road, Rebuilding Together New Orleans, and UNITY of Greater New Orleans—developed new partnerships after 2006 with entities from outside New Orleans providing financial resources and technical assistance (Enterprise Community Partners' Gulf Coast Housing Partnership, Rebuilding Together Inc., and Common Ground Institute). Two neighborhood-based CDCs emerged post-Katrina to become more than residents' associations. Pontchartrain Park CDC was tied to actor Wendell Pierce. Reared in this historic middle-class black neighborhood, Pierce brought on board private developers and consultants to create a neighborhood plan and purchase NORA properties soon after Katrina, and Pontchartrain Park CDC became a NeighborWorks partner.[66] Broadmoor Development Corporation branched off from the Broadmoor Improvement Association and connected with Harvard's Graduate School of Design shortly after Katrina, receiving extensive technical assistance and organizational capacity building.[67] These two CDCs became early NORA partners via the neighborhood redevelopment compacts. External interests founded additional consortium members post-Katrina. These organizations—Brad Pitt's Make It Right organization and Project Home Again, which was capitalized by the founder of Barnes & Noble—brought funding and developers to New Orleans, without necessarily working with grassroots organizations. While Make It Right focused on housing for the low-income residents of the Lower Ninth Ward, some questioned its focus on cutting-edge modernist design as demonstration projects. Project Home Again developed in Gentilly, a middle-income neighborhood. Prior to the NSP consortium, it worked strictly with private capital, so did not partner with the public sector or align with plans developed with broader resident participation.[68]

While these consortium groups increased the numbers of housing and commercial buildings produced, they did not develop capacity of indigenous CDCs. Without robust participation by indigenous CDCs, broader community development goals of accountability and community empowerment in the redevelopment process are not a priority of consortium members.

Some community-based organizations did not meet NORA's criteria for development capacity but wished to participate in vacant and abandoned property redevelopment. Many neighborhood organizations applied to NORA for properties but also sought funds or technical assistance, neither of which NORA provided.[69] For these nascent CDCs, NORA staff suggested partnering with NSP consortium members or other established developers to meet the capacity criteria for purchasing property. NORA partner nonprofits and/or experienced and creditworthy developers could access funds, borrow, and manage the extensive reporting processes for multiple sources of financing. For fledgling indigenous CDCs, little assistance existed for building organizational and resource capacity. The Neighborhood Partnership Network provided a "Community Capacity College," a series of seminars including organizational structure and strategic planning, "City Hall 101,"and other basic topics. However, sufficient support did not exist for community-based organizations seeking to strengthen their capacity as development organizations to meet NORA's criteria.

NORA plans targeted the NSP resources to neighborhoods with greater demand for housing and the possibility of sparking revitalization.[70] While NORA produced plans for the LLT parish plan requirement and for the NSP application, these were more strategic programs than policy-setting documents. NORA continued to function as an "implementation agency" rather than a "planning agency."[71] No mechanism existed for CBOs/CDCs to participate in NORA strategy setting outside the NSP consortium. Furthermore, since NORA and the NSP consortium focused on particular neighborhoods with potential housing demand, some neighborhoods and their CDCs received almost no attention in dealing with vacant and abandoned properties.

Lessons

By the time Hurricane Katrina hit New Orleans, the CDC sector had almost disappeared. The absence of CDCs with significant capacity and the lack of an effectual community development system to support CDCs contributed to limitations in policy alternatives and actions. This case suggests three lessons for community development goals in the context of addressing vacancy and abandonment.

1. *The New Orleans CDCs could not play a viable role in dealing with the catastrophe of vacancy and abandonment when no viable community development system existed to build their capacity to do so.*
Without a strong community development system, CDCs lacked the capacity to take a strong role in tackling vacancy and abandonment. CDCs that maintained production capacity tended to have non-New Orleanians as directors and did not have the community roots that create accountability to their neighborhoods' residents. Some CDCs maintained their grassroots connections by having long-term residents as staff and remained accountable to residents, but these CDCs had low capacity and support. CDCs needed sustained long-term funding to expand their capacity for participation in transforming vacant and abandoned properties. The small corporate sector and local philanthropies and public agencies did not provide concentrated support; the traditional funders of the community development system elsewhere were absent. Without a support system, the capacity of CDCs will remain low, and locally based CDCs will continue to be fringe players in dealing with vacancy and abandonment.

2. *Outside funders offered an immediate response to post-Katrina vacancy and abandonment. However, they did not build the capacity of indigenous CDCs and other CBOs to redevelop properties.*
Outside funders made important contributions to post-Katrina rebuilding efforts, but they had not made a perpetual commitment to the city. They did not use collaborations and networks that built CDC-sector capacity and did not fill the void once occupied by traditional funders whose approach was to partner to build a support system that would enable CDCs to become long-term players in the process of comprehensive community development.

3. *Although NORA affiliated with some CDCs to tackle adjudicated and blighted properties in neighborhoods, NORA and other public agencies did not build the capacity of CDCs to enhance city government-led revitalization activities.*
NORA expected partner organizations, private and nonprofit developers, to have the capacity to carry out rehabilitation and/or new construction. Without a community development capacity-building component in post-Katrina rebuilding policy and programs, many CDCs could not participate in the

revitalization of real property. Other benefits of CDCs—adding community perspectives to development partnerships, representing resident interests in the formation of public policies affecting their neighborhoods, and obtaining resources for meeting community needs—could not come to fruition.

NORA focused on implementing strategies for properties in the Recovery Zones, mostly neighborhoods with severe flood damage rather than those with long-term blight conditions (with the exception of the Lower Ninth Ward). NORA estimated that bringing LLT properties back to productive use would take nearly a decade.[72] Due to costs of expropriation, the extremely poor condition of pre-Katrina blighted buildings, and the weakness of demand in areas with pre-Katrina blighted properties, staff expected to make little headway on blighted and adjudicated property that dated from before 2005. As of late 2010, no entity dealt strategically with the 30,000 vacant and abandoned properties outside the Recovery Zones. Outside of its geographically targeted NSP consortium efforts, NORA did not engage in planning that could involve CDCs in complementary strategies to lessen vacancy, abandonment, and blight throughout the city. NORA's capacity was limited; however, the lack of a strategy for neighborhoods outside the target zones left much of the city without a plan for dealing with abandonment, and without CDCs to address their needs.

Conclusion

New Orleans CDCs remained fragile in 2010. Lacking the capacity to play a primary role in tackling the challenges of vacancy and abandonment prior to the storm, the city's CDCs had even less capacity after Katrina. Virtually no organizations existed to constitute a local community development system to provide resources for CDC capacity building.

The CDCs that participated in tackling the vacancy and abandonment catastrophe were established post-Katrina and maintained networks outside New Orleans. This network capacity enabled a few CDCs to enhance their organizational and production capacities primarily from non-New Orleanian financial and human resources. Hence, a bifurcation developed within the CDC sector: those organizations indigenous to New Orleans that existed before the storm and those externally endowed organizations established after the storm.

As of 2010, prospects looked grim for the restoration of a local community development system that was stronger than before Hurricane Katrina. For indigenous CDCs, their survival and ability to increase empowerment were at stake. For externally endowed CDCs, more concerned about production capacity than empowerment, the question concerned sustainability of the model. Therefore, the CDC sector was likely to remain ineffective in addressing vacancy and abandonment due to the lack of support for building resident capacity and empowerment.

What does the minor role of CDCs mean for what the city may become? Who will benefit from these outcomes? These queries remained important as five years after the storm the population stood at three-fourths of the pre-Katrina level and about one-fourth of residents lived in poverty in 2009.[73] One-fourth of properties were vacant or abandoned with the majority of these in the lowest areas of the city, predominately African American and lower-income neighborhoods.[74]

The need existed for a vibrant CDC sector, given CDCs' commitment to a comprehensive approach to community development that empowers people most in need. However, much of the work that higher capacity CDCs undertook addressed the housing needs of middle-income neighborhoods. Also, some higher-capacity CDCs demonstrated sustainable housing innovations in lower-income neighborhoods, yet the building occurred neither at the scale nor in a manner that met the shelter and human capital needs of low-wealth residents. The innovators, external benefactors, and middle-income households, not lower-income neighborhoods, benefited most.

Indigenously rooted CDCs provided value to the city, although they did not carry out large-scale real property reuse and restoration. A CDC's long-term connection to a neighborhood, both in the past and for the future, can be a critical factor in creating a city where residents influence the direction of redevelopment.

The vision for planning should extend to making the city better than it was before Katrina. To accomplish this feat, New Orleans needs a community development system to advance a model for nonprofit community development that will last beyond postdisaster recovery funding. Further, the CDC sector should pursue relationships between groups in lower-income neighborhoods and outside supporters for funding and other resources that expand the capacity of indigenous CDCs to organize community interests and to influence political and policy-making agendas.

In general, building CDC capacity is costly, time consuming, and challenging. In New Orleans, this effort was complicated by the complexities of establishing a viable community development system with virtually no private sector commitment and historically limited public sector and philanthropic roles. CDCs need support to become high-capacity, self-sustaining, community-based development organizations accountable to lower-income residents. If this happens, then CDCs will more likely engage in the political advocacy essential to asserting the rights of marginalized African American and lower-income residents, as well as gain the capacity to contribute to overcoming the catastrophe of vacancy and abandonment. To do otherwise may result in (responding to the question raised in the song first performed by Louis Armstrong and Billie Holiday) truly experiencing what it means to miss New Orleans.[75]

What Helps or Hinders Nonprofit Developers in Reusing Vacant, Abandoned, and Contaminated Property?

Margaret Dewar

Where vacant, abandoned, and contaminated properties concentrate, community development corporations (CDCs) operate as the major developers along with other nonprofit developers such as Habitat for Humanity. CDCs, committed to place, remain while for-profit developers seek higher returns on investment in areas with stronger demand for housing.[1] Other nonprofit developers, committed to housing people who would otherwise be homeless or to providing decent housing for everyone, also work in these areas. In these roles, they function as key actors in remaking cities after abandonment. When they do their jobs well, their projects improve the quality of life for residents who remain. Their work can demonstrate projects' financial viability and therefore attract other development that would not occur without corrections in investors' assessments of high risk in disinvested areas. Further, nonprofit developers can create markets where individuals and businesses will invest in their own properties when the nonprofits' projects make places attractive for living and working.[2]

Because nonprofit developers play such an important role in remaking abandoned areas of cities, they also have a major role in the reuse of vacant, abandoned, and contaminated property. Factors that help or hinder that reuse in part determine what such developers can accomplish and what disinvested areas of cities become. This chapter investigates what causes nonprofit developers to succeed or fail in reusing this land.

No consistent data exist on the extent of vacant, abandoned, and con-taminated properties in cities that have experienced extensive population loss and property disinvestment, but fragmentary information indicates ex-tensive property of this type, especially in the Northeast and Midwest.[3] Baltimore had 12,700 housing units that the city had judged unfit for habitation by the early 2000s; the city had nearly 14,000 vacant lots. As of 2000, Philadelphia had 26,000 vacant houses and 31,000 vacant lots. In 2001, between 10 and 11 percent of Cleveland's properties were vacant. In Detroit, about 90,000 properties, including residential, commercial, and in-dustrial, had no structures in 2001, about 18 percent of the city's land area.[4]

Data on contaminated sites and on brownfields (abandoned, idled, or underused sites with contamination or possible contamination) are just as uncertain because local governments use different definitions in their counts and because no one knows which untested sites have contamination. In 1996, the Urban Land Institute estimated that about 150,000 acres of abandoned or underused industrial land existed in major U. S. cities. Responding to a sur-vey of the U.S. Conference of Mayors, city officials made widely varying esti-mates. Cleveland officials reported the city had 14,000 acres of brownfields, while Newark, New Jersey, officials estimated 203 acres. Efforts to count all brownfields show very large numbers. In Flint, Michigan, a historically in-dustrial city with a population of slightly over 102,000 in 2010, for instance, about 5,000 brownfield properties existed in 2005.[5]

The next section of this chapter explains the research design. The sec-tions that follow discuss findings on reuse of land by nonprofit developers in Cleveland and Detroit and the reasons for the differences in the two cities' experiences.

Design of the Research

This study compares the experiences of nonprofit developers in Detroit and Cleveland, a useful comparison because the two cities had nearly identical indicators of demand for land (changes in population and employment, in-come levels) in the time period of the study, from the late 1980s through about 2007, but nonprofit developers' reuse of property differed consider-ably. In Cleveland a visitor would see many new housing structures in ar-eas that had lost most of their original housing; in Detroit, a visitor would observe much less new housing. The two cities had lost close to half their

Table 8.1. Indicators of Demand for Land

	Detroit	Cleveland
Percent population change, 1950–2000	−48.6	−47.7
Percent manufacturing employment change, 1947–92	−81.6	−73.4
Percent retail employment change, 1948–92	−71.0	−56.6
Poverty rate, 1999	26.1	26.3
Median household income, 1999	$29,526	$25,928
Per capita income, 1999	$14,717	$14,291
Housing vacancy rate, 2000	10.3	11.7

Sources: U.S. Census Bureau, *Census of Manufactures 1947*, vol. 3, *Statistics by State* (Washington, D.C.: GPO, 1950); U.S. Census Bureau, *Census of Business 1948*, vol. 3, *Retail Trade-Area Statistics* (Washington, D.C.: GPO, 1951); U.S. Census Bureau, *Census of Retail Trade 1992*, Geographic Area Series, http://www.census.gov/prod/1/bus/retail/92area/92ret. html; U.S. Census Bureau, *Census of Manufactures 1992*, Geographic Area Series, http:// www.census.gov/prod/1/manmin/92area/92manufa.htm; U.S. Census Bureau, "Poverty Status in 1999 by Age," "Median Household Income in 1999," "Per Capita Income in 1999," Census 2000 Summary File 3, Tables P87, P53, P82; U.S. Census Bureau, "Occupancy Status," Census 2000 Summary File 1, Table H3; D. Andriot, *Population Abstract of the United States* (McLean, Va.: Documents Index, Inc., 1993).

peak population by 2000 and had the same poverty rates. Detroit's median household income stood somewhat higher than Cleveland's in 1999, but per capita income in the two cities was virtually identical. Both cities had lost large shares of their manufacturing and retail employment by the early 1990s, although Detroit had lost more. Housing vacancy rates stood somewhat higher in Cleveland (see Table 8.1). Because market conditions cannot explain the differences, the experiences of reuse of property in the two cities can reveal institutional, legal, political, and social factors that affect reuse.

To learn about the differences in nonprofit developers' reuse of vacant, abandoned, and contaminated property, I first derived lists of nonprofit developers' purchases of publicly owned land from the Cleveland Land Bank, Detroit Planning and Development Department, and State of Michigan.[6] Nonprofit developers reported that all projects involved purchase of city-owned land and, in Detroit, often depended almost entirely on publicly owned, tax-reverted property. For these properties, I determined from 2005 aerial photos whether reuse had occurred.[7]

In each city, I took a random sample of thirty nonprofits engaged in development. They included CDCs, faith-based development organizations, nonprofit housing corporations, developers of supportive housing, and city-wide organizations focused on community-oriented development in low-income areas.[8]

To assess the prior condition of land the sampled nonprofit developers had reused, for Detroit, I used 2005 aerial photos to determine the boundaries of projects and the total amount of land reused.[9] For scattered-site housing, Detroit organizations used only property purchased from the city or state. In Cleveland, Northeast Ohio Community and Neighborhood Data for Organizing (NEO CANDO) collected data on the properties nonprofit developers handled through early 2004;[10] I added the redeveloped properties to the list of those I had already identified in Cleveland from land bank sales. I researched the prior condition of the properties nonprofit developers had reused to determine whether the land had been vacant, abandoned, or contaminated. "Vacant" meant vacant land, determined from aerial photos shortly before reuse.[11] "Abandoned" was defined as property previously owned by the city or state due to property tax foreclosure.[12] Properties were "contaminated" when Sanborn maps from the 1970s showed land uses likely to contaminate and/or when properties had received a Baseline Environmental Assessment in Michigan or participated in the Voluntary Action Program in Ohio.[13]

After determining the differences in the two cities' nonprofit developers' reuse of land, I interviewed 22 individuals in each city who had perspectives on their city's nonprofit development industry beyond their own organization. In Detroit, I also relied on my observations of numerous meetings of nonprofit developers and my previous research.[14]

Nonprofit Developers' Reuse of Vacant, Abandoned, and Contaminated Property

When nonprofit developers purchased property from the Cleveland Land Bank or the Detroit Planning and Development Department, they intended to reuse or redevelop the land.[15] Therefore, analysis of nonprofit developers' purchase and reuse of city-owned land aids in understanding the development experience in each city.

Detroit nonprofit developers purchased less city-owned property for development than those in Cleveland. Cleveland nonprofit developers bought more property in total—about 640 properties more—from the city's land bank than Detroit nonprofit developers purchased from the city department

Table 8.2. Nonprofit Developers' Reuse of City-Owned Land Purchased for Development

	Detroit (1983–May 2006)	Cleveland (1988–May 2005)
Number of city-owned properties purchased for development	2,756	3,393
Per 10,000 parcels of city property	71.2	208.2
Per 10,000 city residents	29.0	70.9
Percent of properties remaining unused	29.2	27.3
Percent of properties reused for building	68.5	71.4
Percent of properties purchased before 2004 remaining unused	22.5	4.6
Percent of developers reusing at least 95 percent of properties purchased before 2004	36.4	78.8
Percent of developers reusing none of properties purchased before 2004	28.1	0.0

Sources: Calculations based on City of Detroit Planning and Development Department, "Detroit City Property Inventory and Geographic Property Files" (data files, 2006); Aerial photos of Detroit, 2005, Southeast Michigan Council of Governments; City of Cleveland, City Record, 1988–2005; City of Cleveland City Planning Commission,"Geographic Shape Files for Cleveland" (data file, 2003); U.S. Census Bureau, "Total Population," Census 2000 Summary File 1, Table P1; Aerial photos of Detroit and Cleveland, 2007, maps.live.com, and maps.google.com.

(see Table 8.2). In comparison to the cities' populations or to the cities' total numbers of land parcels, the cities' nonprofit developers' volume of purchases contrasts sharply. Cleveland nonprofit developers bought nearly three times as many properties for reuse in proportion to the cities' total properties and nearly two-and-one-half times as many in proportion to the cities' populations as did Detroit nonprofit developers. This result needs explanation. Why did Cleveland nonprofit developers purchase so much more city-owned property for development than did Detroit nonprofit developers?

In Detroit, a slightly higher percent of properties purchased from the city office remained unused in 2005; Cleveland developers had built or rehabilitated buildings on a slightly larger percent of properties than had Detroit developers. More notably, Detroit nonprofit developers had failed to reuse a much larger share of properties purchased before 2004. Because nonprofit developers typically purchase property just before development, these figures suggest that more projects fell through in Detroit than in Cleveland.

Substantially more Cleveland nonprofit developers than Detroit ones had reused all the property they purchased before 2004. Close to 80 percent of the nonprofit developers in Cleveland had reused at least 95 percent of the land they bought before 2004. In contrast, less than half that proportion, about 36 percent, of Detroit nonprofit developers had done so. Furthermore, nearly 30 percent of Detroit nonprofit developers had reused none of the property they purchased before 2004, while all Cleveland developers had reused at least some of the property they bought. These results raise a second question: why were Cleveland nonprofit developers more successful in carrying out development plans?

The timing of nonprofit developers' activities differed in the two cities. From 1988 through the mid-1990s, Cleveland nonprofit developers increased their purchases of city-owned property and their development activity. By 1992, they were purchasing approximately 120 to 420 properties per year from the Cleveland Land Bank. Detroit nonprofit developers' purchases and development activities began to increase later than in Cleveland, around 1998. They bought substantial amounts of property from the Detroit Planning and Development Department through 2006. The commonly held view among Detroit nonprofit developers was that the Cleveland industry had "matured" earlier. Why did Cleveland nonprofit developers purchase city-owned property for development so much earlier than those in Detroit?

The prior use of properties reused by a sample of nonprofit developers showed similarities and differences between the cities' experiences. Close to 85 percent of reused properties in both cities were vacant when nonprofit developers acquired them, although this amounted to a smaller share of the reused acreage in Cleveland than in Detroit. Detroit nonprofit developers depended more heavily on abandoned property than did Cleveland developers. In both cities, nonprofit developers reused little contaminated land; contaminated properties made up a smaller share of properties for Cleveland nonprofit developers than for Detroit ones but constituted about the same share of acreage. One nonprofit's redevelopment of the large site of a closed mental hospital skewed numbers for Cleveland nonprofit developers. Excluding that site, nonprofit developers in both cities reused about the same amount of property that was not vacant, not abandoned, and not contaminated (see Table 8.3). A fourth question these results raise is why nonprofit developers in both cities apparently reused so little contaminated property.

The first three questions—explaining Cleveland CDCs' greater purchase of city-owned land, greater success in reusing the land they purchased, and

Table 8.3. Percent of Vacant, Abandoned, and Contaminated Properties
Reused by Sampled Nonprofit Developers in Detroit and Cleveland

Type of property	Detroit	Cleveland	Cleveland, excluding state hospital site
Vacant lots			
Percent of properties vacant	84.8	83.1	83.1
Percent of area vacant	83.6	65.9	78.6
Abandoned			
Percent of properties abandoned	75.9	57.5	57.5
Percent of area abandoned	75.4	40.2	48.0
Contaminated			
Percent of properties contaminated	3.7	0.6	0.6
Percent of area contaminated	6.4	5.6	6.7
Not vacant, abandoned, or contaminated			
Percent of properties with none of these characteristics	6.4	8.9	8.8
Percent of area with none of these characteristics	6.2	22.9	8.0

Sources: Calculations based on City of Detroit Planning and Development Department, "Detroit City Property Inventory and Geographic Property Files" (data files, 2006); Sanborn, Detroit maps, 1977–78; Revitalife, "Records of Sale of State-Owned Tax-Reverted Property in Detroit" (data file, 2007); Aerial photos of Detroit, 1998, Michigan State Center for Geographic Information; Aerial photos of Detroit, 2005, SEMCOG; Michigan Department of Environmental Quality, Contamination Data, 2007; City of Cleveland, City Record, 1988–2005; City of Cleveland City Planning Commission, "Geographic Shape Files for Cleveland" (data file, 2003); Aerial photos of Cleveland, 1991, U.S. Geologic Survey; Digital orthophoto quadrangle for Cleveland, 1994 and 2000, U.S. Geologic Survey; NEO CANDO, "Properties of Community Development Corporations Through 2003" (data file, 2007); Sanborn, Cleveland maps, 1968–72; Ohio Environmental Protection Agency, Contamination Data, 2007; Interviews with nonprofit developers; Aerial photos of Detroit and Cleveland, 2007, maps.live.com and maps.google.com.

earlier purchases of properties—have similar answers so are addressed together below. The question about reuse of contaminated property is addressed separately.

Explaining the Differences in Nonprofit Developers' Reuse of Properties

The differences between Cleveland and Detroit nonprofit developers' reuse of vacant, abandoned, and contaminated property are due to the differences in the capacity of these organizations. Analyses of community development corporations emphasize the organizations themselves. According to Glickman and Servon, CDCs' capacity depends on the ability to increase, manage, and sustain funding; the depth, skills, and experience of directors, board members, and staff; skills related to a variety of program directions; the ability to build relationships with other organizations; and political strength with city officials and with residents and others from the neighborhoods served.[16] Their conclusions are consistent with other studies. Vidal cited the importance of the size of the organization's budget and staff, priority setting, experience with programs and projects, leadership stability, and clarity of strategies.[17] Gittell and Wilder pointed to the importance of mission, political capital, leadership and management skills, and funding.[18] When CDCs failed, they often did not diversify their activity enough to adjust to change, relied too much on a single funding source, had internal management problems, lacked expertise in the board and staff, experienced difficulties in communication, and lacked strong support from the constituents in the area served.[19]

These explanations for differences in community development corporations' capacity do not answer the question of the difference between Detroit and Cleveland nonprofit developers. Variations among organizations do not necessarily aid in understanding why nonprofit developers as a group have greater success in one city than in another in reusing property under the same market conditions. Cleveland nonprofit developers had more capacity than Detroit nonprofit developers. A larger number of nonprofit developers in Cleveland reused more property and operated longer than Detroit nonprofit developers. No data exist to allow comparisons of staffing and funding levels, leadership stability, or other possible measures of organizational capacity over the last two decades. However, walking into the offices of numerous nonprofit developers offers a strikingly different experience in the two cities. Cleveland nonprofit developers have more office space, crowded with more staff. The question remains *why* Cleveland nonprofit developers have more capacity than those in Detroit.

This chapter, therefore, looks at the community development system in the two cities. The system includes CDCs and other nonprofit developers but also the numerous other institutions that interact with nonprofit developers in community development—the political structure of the city, institutions that support or deter nonprofit development, and relationships necessary for achieving goals.[20] As Keyes and others pointed out, nonprofit developers' success in "stitching together the patchwork financing of development deals" depends on an "institutional support network" that includes numerous other public, private, and nonprofit organizations.[21] An evaluation of the National Community Development Initiative (NCDI), which aimed to increase CDC capacity through funding and strengthening ties to other community and citywide institutions, concluded, "New local collaborations to supply project funding and core operating support are the institutional revolution of the 1990s for CDCs. These alliances attract new funders, provide a more coordinated approach to decision making, stabilize potentially fickle public policies, help to introduce better practice, and raise the visibility of the community development field."[22]

Walker pointed to the emergence of "community development systems" as key to understanding increases in CDC activity.[23] Community development partnerships (intermediaries that attract resources from a range of sources and distribute them strategically to CDCs) increase CDC capacity in numerous areas.[24] City governments also play a key role in community development systems. City government "best practices" in community development systems include goals for housing that rely on analysis of market conditions, financial support for CDC operations and capacity building, gap financing for projects, effective provision of city-owned land, efficient administration for processing projects, positive relationships between city government and CDCs, recognition of CDCs' key role in providing affordable housing, effective institutional support for affordable housing, and administrative capacity to assess and improve practices and relationships.[25] Figure 8.1 provides a simple diagram of a community development system.

Major differences in politics, institutions, and working relationships exist in community development in the two cities, although both benefited from national programs to strengthen CDCs, such as the NCDI. The differences underline the importance of the local system's particular characteristics in enabling nonprofit developers to reuse land. In Cleveland, community development corporations and associated institutions have developed into an industry with a complex web of supportive relationships.[26] Interviews with leaders of nonprofit development organizations about what enabled them to reuse land became complex discussions of laws and regulations, political leadership, citywide institutions, and personal relationships. In contrast, in Detroit, the network of community development corporations still was peripheral to much of land development interest in the city. Interviews with nonprofit developers in Detroit portrayed a changeable and unpredict-

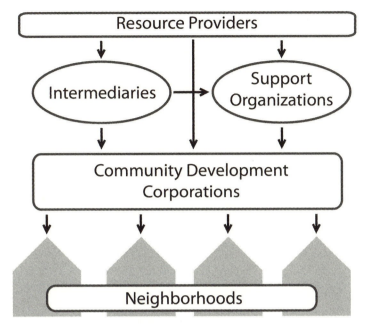

Figure 8.1. Structure of a city's community development system. Adapted from Avis Vidal, sketch on a blackboard during a presentation to a class, University of Michigan, Ann Arbor, January 2009.

able environment with important institutional challenges unresolved. The discussion below lays out the major differences and similarities that help to account for the divergent records in reuse of vacant, abandoned, and contaminated land. This analysis demonstrates the vital importance of a strong community development system in supporting nonprofit developers' work.

The Focus of City Council and Mayoral Administrations

In Cleveland, community development corporations received substantial funding from the city government. As of 2008, the Department of Community Development supported 28 community development corporations through the Cleveland competitive grants program, from Community Development Block Grants (CDBG). In the early 1980s, members of City Council gained the right to allocate large amounts of the city's CDBG funds. The 21 council members each disbursed about $400,000 in CDBG dollars in their wards annually as of 2009, and they used much of these funds for non-profit developers. This funding meant that about 25 percent of the city's CDBG funds went to nonprofit developers for expenses including operating costs, according to staff in the Department of Community Development. This assured stable staffing and program continuity. The result was that to-tal funding for nonprofit developers averaged nearly $225,000 per organiza-tion in program year 2005–6, although the range between lowest and highest allocations was quite large.[27] As a result of this funding, nonprofit develop-ers had close connections with council members, a "critical" relationship, as one CDC director said. At least one nonprofit developer was so close to the council member that the member answered the organization office phone and was the person to whom staff referred requests for interviews.

In Detroit, in contrast, no one kept track regularly of CDBG funding going to nonprofit developers, although nonprofit developers considered CDBG funding important to their survival and submitted the complex ap-plication each year. The nine members of the Detroit City Council were elected at large and allocated CDBG funding in small amounts among many organizations across the city, with no geographic constituency.[28] In 2006, 6 percent of the CDBG budget went to community-based organizations for new home construction, public improvements, substantial housing rehabili-tation, economic development, and commercial district improvement.[29] In 2008–9, 8 percent of CDBG allocations went to nonprofit developers.[30] The Detroit nonprofit development sector was, therefore, less financially stable than Cleveland's.

In both cities, members of the City Council considered the allocation of CDBG funds important. In Detroit, council members exercised more con-trol over this part of the city budget than any other.[31] The differences in City Council allocations of CDBG funds reflected in part the differences in their electoral systems. Cleveland elected 21 council members from small wards. Detroit, twice the size of Cleveland, elected nine council members, all at large. Cleveland's council members took care to serve the interests of the areas they represented and valued the visible, physical improvements that nonprofit developers produced. In contrast, the Detroit council members paid much less attention to the specific problems of particular neighbor-hoods, given their citywide constituency, and they had weak connections with nonprofit developers.[32] Frustrated residents and nonprofit developers said they could not get council members to attend to blighting conditions that harmed neighborhoods.

In Cleveland, Mayor Michael White, previously a City Council member involved in community development, made new housing construction a goal of his administration after he took office in early 1990. A leader in Cleveland's affordable housing development remembered White as saying, "I'm going to create a building boom in Cleveland." White used financial support for nonprofit developers and subsidies for homeowners to encourage housing development. The city government offered tax abatements, reduced-interest mortgages, and reduced down payments for homebuyers, construction financing, and infrastructure improvements in collaboration with banks and foundations.[33] The next two mayoral administrations continued White's emphasis on building new housing in neighborhoods.

In contrast, Detroit mayors did not focus on neighborhood development. Mayor Coleman Young, in office from 1974 through 1993, focused his efforts on large-scale projects such as the new General Motors and Chrysler assembly plants and the downtown riverfront.[34] Mayor Dennis Archer, whose term extended from 1994 through 2001, focused his development attention on downtown—in particular casinos, stadiums, and the theater district.[35] Both Young and Archer supported major new housing developments undertaken by private developers that involved the use of eminent domain to assemble land; clearance of old, often derelict housing; and construction of new neighborhoods.[36] However, they did not seek to strengthen nonprofit developers as agents of neighborhood improvement or widespread affordable housing construction. In 2007, Mayor Kwame Kilpatrick announced the Next Detroit Neighborhood Initiative, a program to target certain neighborhoods for strengthening with an emphasis on city service delivery, the first time that a mayor had focused to such an extent on neighborhoods. The program, however, did not emphasize strengthening nonprofit developers and accomplished little before Kilpatrick resigned following his perjury conviction.[37]

The interest of the City Council and the Mayor's Office in Cleveland meant that city administrative offices also attended to neighborhood issues. The directors and assistant directors of the city's Department of Community Development had often worked for years in community development organizations. The comparable office in Detroit, the Neighborhood Support

Services Division of the Department of Planning and Development, also in charge of handling CDBG funds, never gained the prominence or leadership in community development that the Cleveland department did. Leaders of community development corporations tended to view the staff of this office as obstructionist and unresponsive.

One of the most important city government institutions for facilitating nonprofit developers' reuse of vacant and abandoned land was the system for selling tax-reverted, city-owned land. These differed greatly between the two cities. In Cleveland, the land bank aimed to sell land for new construction or for use that would enhance established development with parking or open space, for instance. In contrast, in Detroit, where the Planning and Development Department sold city-owned property, officials prioritized raising revenue from the sale of land rather than seeking longer-term benefit from redevelopment. The system for selling land worked much better in Cleveland than in Detroit. In Cleveland, the land bank sold vacant land with clear title, while the Detroit Planning and Development Department offered land and buildings for sale without guarantees of clear title. The Cleveland Land Bank provided accurate information about property in its inventory to anyone who wanted it. The Detroit Planning and Development Department had poor records about what land the city government held, and nonprofit developers described occasions when the department sold the same property through two different offices to different purchasers. The Cleveland Land Bank could hold land for nonprofits to redevelop. In Detroit, the Planning and Development Department could also hold property for a prospective project, but poor property records meant that the department might inadvertently sell the property anyway or might hold property long after a planned project had died. Cleveland's land bank offered property at low, predictable prices, saying land previous owners had abandoned had very low market value. The Detroit department set much higher prices for land in unpredictable ways, aiming to find fair market value for land that previous owners had abandoned and no one had expressed interest in purchasing for many years.[38]

Although both cities had experienced substantial losses of tax revenues and severe fiscal problems, they evolved quite differently in their capacity to respond to constituents and deliver services. As reflected in the differences in the way city officials handled sales of city-owned land, Cleveland had a policy-oriented government culture where city officials expected systems to work and where systems were transparent, but Detroit had a government culture where constituents needed to cultivate personal relationships to get attention to their needs. In the Archer administration, this culture seemed initially due to lack of technology; offices operated without desktop computers as of 1994 and could not respond quickly or efficiently. Lack of responsiveness often seemed to cover up staff's inability to provide answers or deliver services. The Archer administration put some systems in place to improve services and increased the transparency of government processes. However, the Kilpatrick administration dismantled many of the systems, and leaders of CDCs reported that, to accomplish work with the city, they needed to depend on particular contacts that they established. In discussions in the community developers' trade association in the late 2000s about how to improve city systems that CDCs needed, directors of CDCs themselves resisted change because it would disrupt the personal relationships they depended on to get their work done.[39]

Intermediaries

Intermediaries have filled important roles in encouraging nonprofit developers' projects in both cities, but these have functioned differently. Intermediaries operate between community development corporations and funders such as foundations and provide financial and other types of assistance to advance a city's community development. In a national assessment, Walker called the creation or strengthening of intermediaries "the number one accomplishment of the community development leadership system in the 1990s."[40] National intermediaries—both the Local Initiatives Support Corporation (LISC) and Enterprise—operated in Cleveland. Both worked closely with local organizations to invest heavily in Cleveland CDCs beginning in the early 1980s, bringing national foundations' and federal government dollars.[41]

The locally created intermediary, Neighborhood Progress, Inc. (NPI), played an even larger role in Cleveland. NPI became especially important in the late 1980s in encouraging reuse of vacant, abandoned, and contaminated property. Foundation and corporate leaders founded NPI in 1989 with Ford Foundation support.[42] They aimed to increase investment in CDCs and to increase the scale and pace of neighborhood physical development. NPI's programs have evolved since its beginnings, but the organization consistently worked to revitalize neighborhoods through physical development with an emphasis on strengthening CDCs as the agents of development. NPI focused on investing in "catalytic" projects that could increase the interest of private developers in neighborhoods. They promoted mixed-income housing and attraction of moderate-income homebuyers. NPI became a major conduit for foundation and corporate support for CDCs. As of the late 1990s, NPI had assisted more than twenty-five CDCs and was providing multiyear operating support to fourteen. The six most productive CDCs were receiving multiyear operating funds that averaged about $260,000 annually and preferential access to other resources. By the late 2000s, NPI was implementing the Strategic Investment Initiative that focused on six neighborhoods with "plans for stimulating market recovery and improving the quality of life to create neighborhoods of choice," according to NPI's president.[43] Besides the Strategic Investment Initiative, NPI offered competitive grants, worked on vacant property and land assembly, established the New Village Corporation to work with nonprofit developers to make complex real estate deals succeed, and was the home of the Village Capital Corporation that invested in development projects that could have major impacts on neighborhoods. In the past, NPI also offered training and technical assistance around organizational development and human resources and operated the Brownfield Redevelopment Initiative to assist CDCs and businesses in reusing contaminated land. By 2009, NPI had had a role in the development of thousands of units of housing and hundreds of thousands of square feet of commercial space.[44]

Although directors of CDCs in Cleveland tended not to articulate this, the differing priorities of City Council members and NPI could create tensions for organizations seeking resources from both. City Council members expected delivery of varied kinds of projects and services in the ward, while NPI applied technocratic criteria to judge an organization's capacity and productivity.[45] NPI's criteria often reflected the latest thinking and research in community development nationally.

In Detroit, no institution like NPI existed. The most important intermediary in Detroit was LISC, which opened its Detroit office in 1990. Detroit area foundations principally worked through Detroit LISC to support neighborhood development, and, as in Cleveland, LISC brought access to national foundation funds and to specific federal funds. Major Detroit area corporations were not involved. Beginning in the mid-1990s, a new LISC program titled the Funders' Collaborative provided operating support and training to selected community development corporations.[46] The program moved nonprofit developers to a new level, in the words of one director of a CDC. By the early to mid-2000s, however, LISC's emphasis had shifted, and the Funders' Collaborative program ended. Beginning in 2004, Detroit LISC emphasized funding to the organizations that worked in targeted areas.[47] Nonprofit developers lamented the change.

Other programs complemented the Funders' Collaborative program in Detroit. The City Council launched training programs for CDCs, for instance. The director of the Planning and Development Department under Mayor Archer worked to clear clouded title on city-owned land and established clearer systems for the purchase of land.[48]

In sum, intermediaries in Cleveland provided more support, sustained more consistently over time, than did intermediaries in Detroit. The homegrown intermediary in Cleveland, NPI, provided the most extensive support to community development corporations and the basis for a community development industry that could reuse more vacant, abandoned, and contaminated property in Cleveland than in Detroit.

Other Networks and Support Organizations

In 1981, five neighborhood organizations and Famicos (a well-established housing rehabilitation and development organization in Cleveland's Hough area), all of which had rehabilitated housing for low-income households through lease-purchase agreements, founded the Cleveland Housing Network (CHN). The goal was to "stabilize neighborhoods by saving existing housing and creating affordable home ownership opportunities and to promote neighborhood controlled development."[49] Additional CDCs affiliated with CHN, and, as of 2008, 15 worked with the organization with territories that covered much of the city.[50] CHN functioned as the developer in arranging the financing and carrying out the development of housing but worked in partnership with the CDCs in making decisions about what projects to undertake, where to build housing, and what type of housing to build. CDCs managed the properties after they were built. As of 2006, the housing network had produced 2,400 lease-purchase homes, 1,350 for-sale homes, and 300 multifamily units and had completed 71,000 energy conservation and home repair jobs. Ninety percent of families involved in lease-purchase homes took title at the end of the fifteen-year lease period.[51] CHN directly purchased almost 20 percent of the properties that the Cleveland Land Bank sold to nonprofit developers and had a role in the development of many more of the properties that CDCs purchased. The Cleveland Housing Network operated at a scale that managed risk, staff stated in interviews; if some projects failed, others' success compensated. Housing that did not sell quickly could move into the lease-purchase program. CHN's large scale, about $60 million of housing development per year, enabled the organization to package complex financing and to employ staff with a high level of skills in affordable housing development.[52]

Thus, CHN operated somewhat as an intermediary in bringing housing financing and technical skills to the development of affordable housing at a scale that small CDCs could not achieve. At the same time, CHN remained committed to the member CDCs' goals. In the words of CHN's first director, CHN's approach "eschews the monolithic solutions of government in favor of community-devised and controlled programs."[53] By the mid-2000s, CHN operated as a major regional developer of affordable housing, distinguished, along with a small group of other large-scale housing partnerships in the nation, as making major contributions to the development, financing, and management of the nation's stock of affordable housing.[54]

Numerous other support organizations existed in Cleveland. For instance, the Cleveland Neighborhood Development Coalition (CNDC, a trade association for CDCs) supported CDCs through networking, training, technical assistance, and advocacy.[55] NEO CANDO, based at Case Western Reserve University, provided extensive data for nonprofit developers' use.[56]

In Detroit, a distinguishing feature of the nonprofit development industry was its collaborative organizations. Community development corporations, nonprofit housing corporations, and comprehensive housing development organizations created nonprofit associations to work on issues of common concern. The Detroit Eastside Community Collaborative began in 1992, for instance, to advance nonprofit development efforts on the large east side of the city, in the belief that by working together nonprofit developers could strengthen their capacity to plan and implement economic development.[57] The Gateway Development Collaborative in Southwest Detroit formed "to enhance the growth of Southwest Detroit as an ethnically and economically diverse community and promote its image as an exciting place to live, work, shop and play."[58] A trade association, Community Development Advocates of Detroit (CDAD), formed in 1997 to enhance the capacity and effectiveness of Detroit CDCs.[59] CDAD sought to provide a citywide CDC voice in improving policies and systems such as the CDBG subrecipient system and a Detroit land bank. CDAD, and to a lesser extent other collaboratives, however, suffered from members' lack of a sense of individual benefit from collective action and seemed to have little impact on city procedures.

Detroit had no institution that resembled CHN to support nonprofit development of affordable housing. This helped explain why the scale of affordable housing development remained low, as each CDC needed to build capacity for development on its own.

Foundations

Cleveland foundations supported NPI, CHN, CNDC, and CDCs and had played leadership roles in the creation of NPI. In 2007, the three large foundations that provided the most support for community development allocated about 13 percent of their funding to Cleveland intermediaries and CDCs.[60] Foundation leaders articulated their commitment to Cleveland neighborhoods: "The highest priority is given to initiatives that bolster the impact of Foundation-supported intermediary organizations working to improve the competitiveness of Cleveland's neighborhoods and its metropolitan region," stated the Gund Foundation website, for instance.[61]

In Detroit, in contrast, the principal foundations making grants for community development allocated 7 to 8 percent of their funding to CDCs and to Detroit LISC in the mid-2000s. The total amount for the five foundations making community development grants in Detroit was less than that by the three principal foundations making grants for community development in Cleveland, although Detroit had about twice Cleveland's population.[62]

In sum, the support for CDCs and other nonprofit developers in Cleveland was much stronger than in Detroit and became institutionalized into a community development system much earlier. These institutions were essential in enabling nonprofit developers to carry out housing development and to reuse land in Cleveland.

Working Relationships

Working relationships among city officials and community leaders involved in reusing land differed considerably between the two cities. In Cleveland, individuals moved among jobs in city departments, intermediaries, elected positions, and community-based organizations during their careers. This enabled them to understand the perspective of others with whom they needed to work, according to several of those working in nonprofit development. The leaders of community-based development in Cleveland had worked together for decades by the early 2000s. A newcomer who became director of a CDC in Cleveland said he quickly realized he was an anomaly.

Long-time working relationships can be difficult rather than smooth, but, in Cleveland, the norm was cooperation. The key to success in handling vacant properties, said one central actor, was the cooperation and communication among many people over long periods of time. An observer noted, "The collective story . . . is one of relationships and outcomes getting better because of cooperation and a shared vision. . . . [T]he tradition of working together, expanding the pie, not worrying about turf, has become part of the common language in Cleveland."[63]

In Detroit, in contrast, only a few leaders in community development moved into city administration or moved between community development organizations and intermediaries or foundations. A "strong culture of distrust"[64] of the city administration was evident in meetings of coalitions of community development leaders, a legacy, in the view of some, of the Young administration's pursuit of business investment and neglect of neighborhood development.[65] Indeed, as Cleveland's community development system became very strong in the late 1980s, community development advocates in Detroit and their City Council allies engaged in conflict with Mayor Young over the CDBG budget and other issues that would allocate more resources to neighborhood development.[66] Most striking to a newcomer in the mid- to late 1990s was the paranoia among community development leaders about what city officials were doing and a general attribution of malice rather than lack of capacity to respond when city decisions were unfavorable or staff failed to follow through. City administrators, in turn, acted leery about inviting community development leaders into discussions about change in the way city departments operated or about possible development projects. Distrust between "the community-based organizations and city government and between the community-based organizations and Detroit's large institutional organizations . . . was the underlying issue for much of the debate"[67] around the governance of the Empowerment Zone in the mid-1990s.

In Detroit, in addition, the leaders of community development corporations included many whites, most of whom had always lived in Detroit, but who filled far more than their proportion of the staff positions in CDCs in the predominantly African American city and in the heavily African American neighborhoods where the CDCs worked. African Americans filled the staff positions of faith-based development organizations in numbers close to their share of the population. In the context of a region with poor race relations where elected officials used racial conflict to political advantage, the racial differences seemed to add to the difficulties of the leaders of community development corporations in working cooperatively with city officials.[68] Although Cleveland, too, had a history of poor race relations, African Americans and whites seemed to have reached an easier accommodation than they had in Detroit.

The Problem of Contaminated Property

The discussion above suggests explanations for the differences between nonprofit developers' reuse of vacant and abandoned land in Cleveland and Detroit. In both cities, however, nonprofit developers reused little contaminated property. Why have nonprofit developers reused so little contaminated property?

Uncontaminated land is plentiful in both cities. "Why would we use contaminated land when so much other land is available?" asked a staff member of a nonprofit developer in Cleveland. Integrating contaminated properties into a project caused delays and uncertainty that could jeopardize the financial viability of the project, nonprofit developers explained. Study of old Sanborn maps showed that nonprofit developers frequently acquired and reused almost all properties in an area except those likely to be contaminated. In Cleveland, most vacant properties had had residential uses in the past and were unlikely to be contaminated (although one nonprofit staff member stated that all were contaminated with lead and asbestos). Between 10 and 11 percent of the city's properties were vacant. In Detroit as well, most vacant properties had been residential and were unlikely to have severe contamination, although a demolition contractor had used fill contaminated with industrial waste after removing houses on many properties. Nearly 23 percent of all Detroit's properties were vacant in 2001. About 27 percent of residential properties were vacant in 2009.[69]

When nonprofit developers reused contaminated properties, they did so primarily because the property had an important place in their vision for the future of their area. Their ideas about transforming an area had more influence on their decisions than the drive to get developer fees from larger-scale development. They often initially took on a project without appreciating the complexities ahead but afterward said that they had learned that they did not need to fear such properties and would take on another. "We sort of backed into going after brownfield dollars," the director of a Cleveland nonprofit developer said, because specific properties they wanted to reuse could benefit from those.

Part of the reason that the analysis above shows that nonprofit developers have reused so little contaminated property is that the data include only land that passed through nonprofit developers' ownership. Nonprofit developers frequently work to reuse contaminated sites without becoming owners and developers of the site. They facilitate reuse of contaminated sites by bringing considerable knowledge of real estate development, community organizing, and brownfield reuse to a project.[70] Cleveland's Slavic Village CDC, for instance, had an instrumental role in finding ways to clean up and reuse a long-empty industrial facility without ever taking ownership.

Conclusion

This chapter considers the extent of nonprofit developers' reuse of vacant, abandoned, and contaminated property in Cleveland and Detroit and offers explanations for Cleveland developers' much greater activity in the reuse of land and for the low rates of reuse of contaminated land in both. Cleveland's institutions and working relationships have facilitated nonprofit developers' reuse of property much more successfully than Detroit's have. What could have made such a difference in the way their community development systems evolved? Both cities' economies had historically depended on jobs and income from heavy manufacturing, and both had lost most of those jobs. Therefore, both had a legacy of labor-management conflict and class divisions. Both had experienced the migration of large numbers of people from Europe and the South who sought better jobs. Both had racial divisions and high levels of residential racial segregation, although one Cleveland observer opined that racial antagonism was less prevalent in Cleveland. "Never underestimate the importance of key leaders at the right time," a long-time scholar of Cleveland said, pointing especially to the way the Cleveland Housing Network came into existence. Nevertheless, no explanations for the differences in the way the community development systems developed feel complete.

Addressing the challenges in community development systems need not depend on an explanation. Rather, in Detroit, for instance, new leaders in city government, LISC, foundations, CDCs, and other nonprofit organizations can address numerous issues that hinder Detroit's nonprofit developers' reuse of vacant, abandoned, and contaminated property, if they want to enable nonprofit developers to do more to remake the city in disinvested areas. Some of the possible ways to pursue such a direction include reform of Detroit's system of Community Development Block Grants to enable recipients to use the funds more effectively;[71] discussion of the need and possible role for a local intermediary to work with LISC in strengthening community development; discussion of the need for a regional, large-scale affordable housing developer that could work in the city as well as in inner-ring suburbs in partnership with community-based organizations; and work on building trust among government officials, foundation leaders, nonprofit developers, and other community-based organizations. Nevertheless, the differences in working relationships and in the responsiveness of city government officials to community development issues suggest historically determined sociopolitical relationships that, in turn, determined what institutions exist and will have major influence on what can exist in the future.

The differences in the two cities exist in a context of continuing loss of population and abandonment of property. Detroit lost a quarter of its residents between 2000 and 2010, 61 percent of its population since 1950. By 2010, Cleveland had lost 57 percent of its 1950 peak population. They remained the poorest big cities in the nation. In 2009, 36.4 percent of Detroit's population lived in poverty, compared to Cleveland's 35 percent. Detroit and Cleveland had the highest mortgage foreclosure rates among all cities in the country in fall 2007, a fact that contributed to degradation of neighborhoods in both cities. The high rate of mortgage foreclosures and the recession reduced community-based developers' capacity to produce affordable housing in both cities, and the loss of developer fees threatened the survival of many. In 2010, Detroit's housing vacancy rate stood at almost 23 percent and Cleveland's at 19 percent. Detroit had 20 percent less occupied housing in 2010 than in 2000; Cleveland had 12 percent less in 2010.[72]

Nevertheless, even in the context of weak demand for land resulting from continuing population loss, this research shows that different ways of structuring systems of community development lead to quite different outcomes in the reuse of vacant, abandoned, and contaminated property. Different systems lead to different outcomes in what cities can become after abandonment, regardless of market forces.

CHAPTER 9

Targeting Strategies of
Three Detroit CDCs

June Manning Thomas

In considering what happens to cities after abandonment, and why, it's essential to note that CDCs have played a major role in helping to fill in the gaps left literally by the demolition of abandoned buildings and economically by the decline in private investment. Yet we know very little about how CDCs choose to invest housing development dollars in the context of vacancy and reduced market demand and why they use some patterns of land use as opposed to others. Such knowledge is important if we expect CDCs in distressed environments to play a role in neighborhood redevelopment, in a way that has identifiable impact. This study explores what factors appear to influence CDC decisions to target their use of land in areas that have experienced abandonment and in a city experiencing population loss.

CDCs carry out de facto land use strategies through their selection of which local projects to undertake and where to invest in resources such as playgrounds, housing rehabilitation, or housing construction. I look in particular at how CDCs have chosen to locate the housing they have built, choosing to target certain blocks or not. I examine three CDCs in Detroit, Michigan, using a case study approach to assess rationales, benefits, and drawbacks of different ways of targeting: modified dispersion, infill housing, or closely targeted development.

Targeting is just one issue related to the effectiveness of CDC activities. Local governments may have more effect on community development if they target certain areas of their cities.[1] Yet, as a research question, CDC targeting has received little attention, with a few exceptions that focused on neighborhood spillovers due to nonprofit housing or related issues such as land acquisition or new urbanism strategies.[2] Because CDCs are major investors in lower-income neighborhoods and aim to strengthen them, any efforts they make to have greater effects with their resources call for examination.

Key questions for this research were whether the three case study CDCs did target their investments spatially and why or why not. One might assume a priori the need for CDCs to target limited housing construction dollars, so as to create critical mass capable of changing market perception about an area, but this study suggests that, even when CDCs attempt to target investment, a number of factors may interfere, such as lack of organizational capacity, a weak local demographic profile, or the role of government at several levels.

CDCs and Targeted Housing

A bigger question is whether financial investment in housing and community development matters in efforts to improve central-city neighborhoods. At least a couple of examples suggest that it does. Schill et al. studied the nation's largest neighborhood improvement program, launched in 1985 in New York City, involving an investment of over $5 billion in close to 100 different programs.[3] Many affected New York neighborhoods saw new housing and businesses filling vacant and empty lots, but this initiative may not be replicable; it was a massive investment in a multidimensional effort coordinated by a strong city government with more than adequate financial resources.

A smaller city that implemented a successful strategy for neighborhood revitalization, in part using housing investment, was Richmond, Virginia.[4] The city chose to invest its Community Development Block Grant (CDBG) and other funds in seven neighborhoods with high levels of poverty and housing vacancy; six of those neighborhoods had housing vacancy levels of at least 18 percent, more than twice the city's average rate, and one-third of the housing was vacant in one of those areas.[5] After expenditure of funds, researchers looked for the threshold level of investment necessary to raise surrounding housing prices and identified this level as $30,000 per block over five years or $6,000 per year. The findings suggest targeting resources yielded increased values in nearby properties, but many conditions existed in Richmond that would not easily transfer elsewhere, such as substantial investments by the Local Initiatives Support Corporation (LISC) and the federal HOME[6] housing construction program, in addition to investment by the City of Richmond, focusing of city services in target areas, committed city leadership and staff, and a well-functioning community development industry.

Other studies have shown some evidence that housing production leads to increases in housing values for nearby properties, suggesting spillover effects.[7] Studies that measure impacts such as increases in housing value have offered insight into just one dimension of effects, however; the value of neighborhood improvement could include other possible benefits, such as increased resident satisfaction or enhanced social capital, which would not necessarily lead to higher housing value.

Even if targeting a small area for housing improvement does lead to neighborhood improvement, such efforts may be a difficult route to success. Neighborhood housing markets are subject to numerous external as well as internal dynamics.[8] The strongest external dynamics are metropolitan, a level out of reach for CDCs to influence; little done at the local or neighborhood level within a core central city will change trends strongly tilted toward suburbanization. At the micro scale, such as within a few blocks, a possible CDC target area, homeowners make decisions about whether to improve their own housing and whether to stay in a particular neighborhood, based in part on their perception as to other homeowners' investments and commitment. Sense of commitment, in turn, depends somewhat on the demographic profile of remaining residents, particularly in situations characterized by ethnic or racial prejudice or metropolitan-area segregation. A critical mass of investment would need to offer apparent improvements on a specific block in order to see tangible results.[9]

Although many issues are important besides whether a city or CDC invests in a limited geographic area, focusing investments on certain neighborhoods and blocks still makes sense. Resources are never sufficient to allow for wide geographic dispersion of public and nonprofit investment dollars, unless physical conditions of concern are minor and relatively scattered. In many "legacy" cities—defined here as cities with major cultural and historical attributes but difficulties adjusting to a postindustrial economy[10]—conditions of physical deterioration are not minor, but major, and cover many blocks and census tracts. A CDC in such circumstances would probably need to frame its actions carefully to make a visible impact.[11] The organization would need to target specific blocks for construction, in order to create critical mass to influence others' investment decisions. Under certain distressed conditions, the level of investment would have to be fairly intense, much higher than the threshold amounts of money—$6,000 per block per year for five years—indicated in the Richmond study.

Studying Three CDCs

I chose Detroit as a venue to study the issue of targeting by CDCs because of accessibility, the availability of myriad background materials on Detroit, and my familiarity with related rejuvenation activities.[12] Some previous research suggested that CDC efforts had not been as effective in Detroit as in other comparable cities, in part because of a flawed community development system but also because of land acquisition problems.[13] A study of thirty Detroit CDCs, approximately half of the total number of known CDCs at the time of the study, revealed great variation in these organizations' ability to use land for development purposes. The present study looks in more detail at the fact that several Detroit CDCs appeared not to target in their new housing development strategies and explains why they did not do so.

Because the study aimed to explore a "why" question related to organizational behavior, undertaking case study analysis is the most appropriate approach. The selection of cases depends on examining variation in the conditions of most interest;[14] I chose three case-study CDCs in Detroit that had records of new housing production but varied approaches to targeting specific blocks for building housing within their service areas. Figure 9.1 shows their location within Detroit. Case study analysis methods guided the organization of the study, including the development of protocol formats for interviews and review of all documents and iterative revision of research propositions.

I selected the case CDCs by examining records of thirty CDCs in Detroit, material lent to us by above-cited researcher Dewar; consultation with a university outreach person who works closely with many CDCs in Detroit; and my personal knowledge of various CDCs in the city. I aimed to sample the spectrum of approaches, from targeting investments on one or two streets to a more dispersed strategy. Primary sources of information included interviews with sixteen respondents, including all staff members with programmatic responsibility in the three CDCs, as well as informed neighborhood board members, residents, and city staff, most of whom earlier respondents

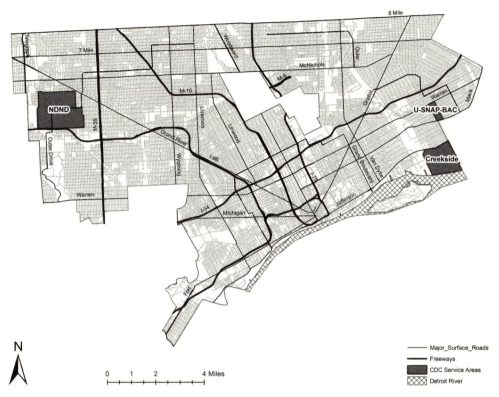

Figure 9.1. Target areas of the three Detroit CDCs. ESRI, Census 2000 TIGER/Line Files. Map by Robert Linn, 2011.

recommended. Some CDC staff and two well-informed citizen activists were interviewed twice. Data gathering from individuals took the form of taped qualitative interviews usually forty-five to ninety minutes in length, conducted from fall 2009 through spring 2010. I also closely examined all neighborhood plans associated with the three CDCs and other documents such as city plans and Low Income Housing Tax Credit (LIHTC) allocation standards and records for the State of Michigan. The research team conducted site visits to all three CDCs and created maps of their housing construction activities to reveal targeting patterns. Data gathering for the two CDCs that did not target as visibly as the third was more exhaustive than for the third; study of the third CDC benefited from a previous case study on the organization's land acquisition.[15]

The following propositions frame the reporting of results. The wording of these propositions evolved during the course of the study, as recommended by Stake:[16]

1. Demographics/market factors and changes affect a CDC's ability to pursue an effective targeting strategy (a human ecology/economic model).
2. Organizational and neighborhood relation factors, such as lack of a viable neighborhood plan, nonstrategic acquisition of land, or lack of programmatic capacity, affect a CDC's ability to target its housing development to specific geographic areas (an organizational model).
3. Federal, state, and local policies have flaws or unintended consequences that lead to problematic use of land and construction of housing for some CDCs (a policy model).

The first case study CDC, Northwest Detroit Neighborhood Development (NDND), founded in 1989, serves an area of northwest Detroit known as Brightmoor. The city's master plan designates Brightmoor as a recognized "neighborhood," which typically includes a few census tracts. NDND has constructed over three hundred units of housing, a remarkable achievement among Detroit CDCs. At the outset, NDND focused on housing construction and rehabilitation, first through infill housing concentrated in a 15-block area, but after a few years in several other areas of Brightmoor, which covers four square miles. In total, NDND built housing in at least five different target areas in Brightmoor. This CDC's pattern of housing construction is more dispersed than the pattern for the other two CDCs; see Figure 9.2, which suggests several nodes of construction activity in a mixture of targeting and dispersion—"modified dispersion."

The second CDC, Creekside, is located in Detroit's far southeastern corner in an area popularly known as Jefferson-Chalmers but designated in the city's master plan as the East Riverfront neighborhood. Creekside began as an environmental activist group, focusing on park development, tree plantings, and waterfront improvement. Using largely LIHTC and partnership with a national development group, the CDC also constructed 45 units of low-income housing. Its housing investments target a much smaller geographic area than NDND's. Most Creekside CDC housing concentrates on four streets, interspersed with numerous older housing, other new housing, and vacant lots in the northwest section of Jefferson-Chalmers (Figure 9.3)—a

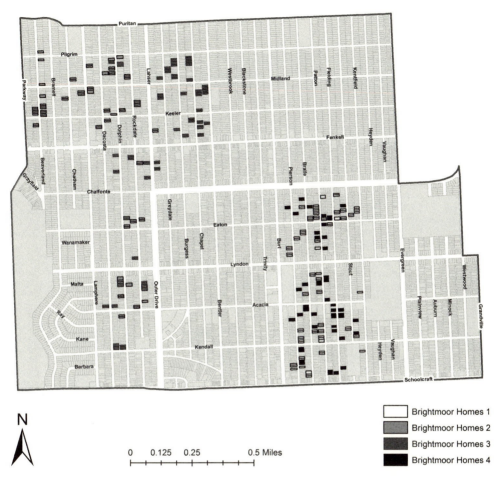

Brightmoor Homes 1
Brightmoor Homes 2
Brightmoor Homes 3
Brightmoor Homes 4

0   0.125   0.25   0.5 Miles

N

Figure 9.2. Housing construction by Northwest Detroit Neighborhood Development CDC, 1999–2010. Building Permit Data, City of Detroit. Map by Robert Linn, 2011.

pattern of "targeted infill." The entire Jefferson-Chalmers neighborhood area has benefited from urban renewal and subsequent related development projects, outside the CDC's target area for housing construction.

United Streets Networking and Planning Building a Community (U-SNAP-BAC) aimed to improve a few targeted blocks for contiguous new construction as well as associated rehabilitation. This organization began in 1987 as a coalition of seven neighborhood organizations and four business associations. After a period of considerable effort, in large part because the

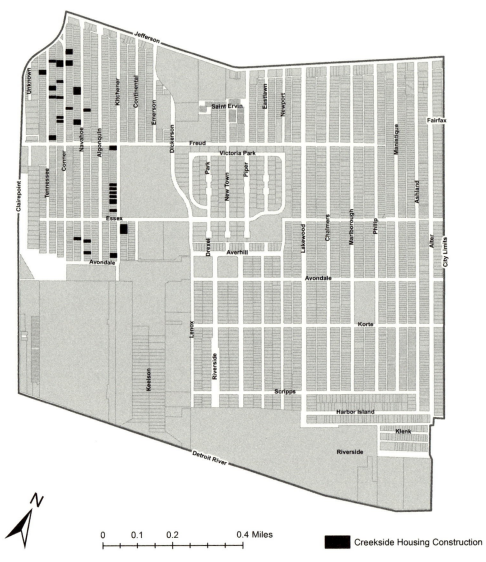

Figure 9.3. Creekside CDC housing production, 2004–10. Building Permit Data, City of Detroit; windshield survey by Scott Pitera, 2010. Map by Robert Linn, 2011.

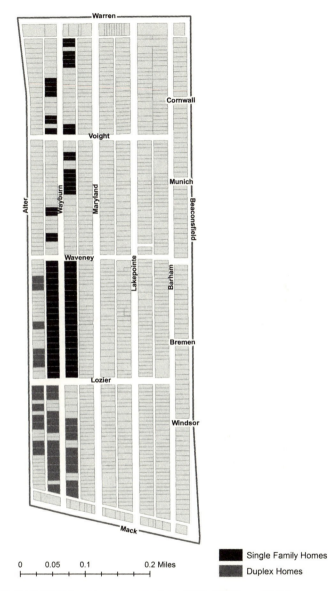

Figure 9.4. U-SNAP-BAC CDC housing construction, 1998–2005, as of 2010. Building Permit Data, City of Detroit; windshield survey by Scott Pitera, 2010. Map by Robert Linn, 2011.

City of Detroit's land acquisition policies were difficult to navigate,[17] the CDC has built MorningSide Commons, with phases I, II, and III located in the same small target area for a total of 131 units, using a "closely targeted" strategy (Figure 9.4). This development area includes 67 single-family homes built and sold and 64 townhouses built and leased, all on the western edge of the historic MorningSide residential area. In addition, U-SNAP-BAC has taken over a 30-unit apartment building and carried out other activities such as support for homeowners and renters and for a nearby commercial district. The city's master plan has designated the larger official neighborhood that includes MorningSide as Finney; the U-SNAP-BAC housing target area is located on the far western edge of Finney.

Table 9.1 shows basic information about new housing developed in the three organizations' service areas and lists the projects for which each CDC, and other developers, received LIHTC funding during the specified time period. State records suggested that NDND and U-SNAP-BAC were the only major builders of LIHTC housing in their service areas, but several developers carried out low- and mixed-income projects in the Jefferson-Chalmers neighborhood, which the Creekside CDC served. This table also reveals that NDND launched many separate LIHTC projects over a number of years.

LIHTC were not the only sources of funds for these organizations. For example, U-SNAP-BAC built MorningSide Commons with LIHTC funds, but for an earlier phase used several sources including federal HOME funds.[18] The other two CDCs, however, used mostly LIHTC, supplemented by Habitat for Humanity construction efforts.

None of the three CDCs may survive in the long term because of the uncommon difficulties associated with the economic downturn and the housing crisis, with particularly depressed economic conditions in Michigan and in the City of Detroit. As of late 2010, two of the CDCs no longer had paid staff.

The CDC that managed several noncontiguous target areas in a "modified-dispersion" pattern, NDND, apparently did not receive Neighborhood Stabilization Program (NSP) funding and possibly other funding in part because the perception had grown among city staff and funders such as LISC either that its housing strategy was too scattered or that no housing demand existed in its area of service. The small area of Brightmoor that observers identified as possibly the "most successful" in appearing to be a viable neighborhood with minimal property abandonment was NDND's first

Table 9.1. Housing Units by CDCs and Others, Funded by Low Income Housing Tax Credits, 1989–2009

CDC neighborhoods (City of Detroit "neighborhood")	Project allocation year, name	Development type, CDC developer in study	Dwelling units allocated
Brightmoor (Brightmoor)	1999 Brightmoor Scattered I	Scattered site sf[a], NDND CDC	5
	1999 Brightmoor Scattered II	Scattered site sf, NDND CDC	45
	2002 Brightmoor Homes II	Scattered site sf, NDND CDC	50
	2003 Brightmoor Homes III	Scattered site sf, NDND CDC	50
	2005, 2006 Hope Park Homes	Scattered site sf, NDND CDC	36
	2006 Brightmoor Homes IV	Scattered site sf, NDND CDC	45
Jefferson-Chalmers (East Riverside)	1989 Jefferson Meadows	Apartments	82[b]
	1991 Grayhaven Manor	Multifamily	190 (38 LIHTC)
	1991 Jefferson Square	Multifamily	180
	2004 Creekside Homes	Scattered Site sf, Creekside CDC	45
	2007 Jefferson Square Apt.	Apartments	180
	2008 Chalmers Square	Apartments	49 (38 LIHTC)
MorningSide[c] (Finney)	2001 MorningSide Commons Multifamily	Duplexes/sf, on four target blocks, U-SNAP-BAC CDC	64

Sources: Web-based records of State of Michigan; Michigan State Housing Development Authority, http://www.michigan.gov/mshda/0,1607,7-141 -5587_5601-37847-,00.html.

[a] Single-family housing.

[b] According to federal records (Deng, Table 2.4 of this volume), the amount eventually built was 83 units. However the state of Michigan lists this 1989 allocation as 82 units.

[c] U-SNAP-BAC by-laws indicate a huge service area, but this chapter concentrates on MorningSide, which includes the CDC's target area for housing development.

target area, in the southeast section of Brightmoor, where additional construction by Habitat for Humanity (which built as well in the other two CDC
areas) supported NDND's efforts, but even there gaps exist in the form of a
few vacant lots and boarded-up homes. Driving down other streets of Brightmoor reveals newly constructed CDC housing standing next to vacant lots
and burned-out or vacant, boarded-up houses. Specific reasons, discussed
later, led to the organization's scattered, leapfrog strategy.

The CDC with the middle-of-the-road strategy, Creekside, released its
paid housing staff in 2010. Creekside's partnering with a national housing
construction firm that siphoned off some of the developer fees may have
played a role in its difficulties. Creekside was in the process of building the
technical skills necessary to carry out a housing construction program
without outside help, but the board chose to release staff even though monies were available to carry out housing rehabilitation programming.

U-SNAP-BAC, with its closely targeted geographic strategy, has served
as somewhat of a model CDC for the City of Detroit, albeit with a downsized
staff. In the early 2000s, funding agencies and the Mayor's Office drove visitors through the CDC's target area to show an example of a successful
CDC's work in Detroit. U-SNAP-BAC has had difficulties, as have all CDCs
dependent on developer's fees associated with housing construction, but its
reputation does not seem to have faded among city observers both inside
and outside City Hall. Its continued existence and good reputation appear
to relate at least in part to its targeting strategy, which enabled anyone to
drive down one street and see nothing but its new, occupied housing.[19]

The leadership of each CDC was aware of the concept of targeting. The
staff of each CDC used at least one neighborhood plan in making decisions about where to construct new housing, and those plans recommended specific areas for housing development. For NDND, a consultant
created a plan that the organization relied on,[20] and other plans were important as well. Creekside CDC's Jefferson-Chalmers neighborhood benefited from a number of redevelopment efforts because of the neighborhood's
status as an urban renewal site, with one crucial plan important because
of its official city standing.[21] U-SNAP-BAC also used neighborhood planning documents for MorningSide Commons.[22] But the housing market,
demographic trends, and the economy may have overridden the desire to
target investments.

Demographic/Market Considerations

The demographics of U.S. metropolitan areas make central-city development very difficult, especially in a city such as Detroit that has experienced housing disinvestment for decades. The city has a predominately African American and low-income population after decades of first white and later black middle-class flight. The metropolitan dissimilarity index between non-Hispanic whites and African Americans, one measure of racial segregation, was the largest in the country in 2000, compared to other large metropolitan areas.[23] Continuing loss of population, as in Detroit, would mean that a central-city housing development strategy would struggle against conditions that pull households away from the central city. Although all CDCs in the city faced this situation, each of the three case-study CDCs faced different circumstances in the strength of housing demand within the regional housing market.

The housing market was undoubtedly weakest for Brightmoor, where the CDC began to build low-income housing in 1999 because historic development built very small, poorly constructed houses designed for blue-collar workers.[24] Although sections of Brightmoor contained better quality housing and although Brightmoor bordered middle-class Detroit neighborhoods, many of its small neighborhood areas struggled against the forces of decay. Not only did Brightmoor have low household incomes, it also bordered Detroit's western edge, meaning that it competed for residents with the nearby suburb of Redford Township as well as more prosperous nearby Detroit neighborhoods. According to its 2001 plan, 94 percent of the houses within one mile of the geographic center of the neighborhood were over thirty years old. In one rectangular central portion of the neighborhood, 20 percent of the residential parcels were city owned, signaling abandonment.[25] Brightmoor's total population was predominately black or African American "only," about 80 percent in 2000, about the same as the city as a whole. The white population[26] was 14.7 percent of the total. Only 8.4 percent of its households made $75,000 or more, demonstrating fewer higher-middle-income households compared to the two other neighborhoods (Table 9.2). This could have implications for home ownership or for a household's ability to maintain a house. By 2008, household density in the neighborhood's central portion was only 1.5 to 2.4 households per acre,[27] and other parts of the neighborhood suffered from high vacancy as well.[28]

Table 9.2. Selected Demographics for Three City of Detroit "Neighborhood" Areas, 2000

City of Detroit designated "neighborhood"	Population	Percent change population (1990–2000)	Percent change housing units (1990–2000)	Percent households less than $10,000	Percent households $75,000 or more	Percent "white only" population[a]
Brightmoor	19,837	–16.6	–16.9	20.7	8.4	14.7
East Riverside	8,647	–17.2	–8.7	21.8	12.8	11.1
Finney	32,232	3.3	–1.3	10.0	23.4	24.6
City of Detroit	951,270	–7.5	–8.5	19.1	13.3	12.4

Source: City of Detroit, Master Plan, 2009, citing 2000 U.S. Census.

[a]I use "white only" because whites are the numerical minority in Detroit and because the census for 2000 has overlapping categories for nonwhites. For example, people identified as "black or African American only" or "American Indian only" are separated from people of "two or more races."

In Jefferson-Chalmers, the three census tracts included handsome waterfront housing, new subdivisions, and sturdy brick bungalows in addition to more modest housing characteristic of Creekside's target area. Jefferson-Chalmers also benefited from years of urban renewal and CDBG investments, which laid the groundwork for a diverse income base for its housing. Jefferson-Chalmers bordered prosperous suburbs just over Detroit's city boundary known as the Grosse Pointes, but in addition its households' income levels varied widely. One census tract to the east and south of the west-side CDC target area had a 16.4 percent individual poverty rate in 2000, whereas the Creekside target area tract had a 27.6 percent poverty rate.[29] The entire Jefferson-Chalmers area, "East Riverside" in the city's master plan, was 11.1 percent white in 2000, and 12.8 percent of its households made $75,000 or more. This area also struggled with vacancy, long before the CDC began to build housing there, particularly but not only in the northwest segment.[30]

The third larger "neighborhood" area, Finney, had more substantial housing than Brightmoor but not the history of redevelopment projects of Jefferson-Chalmers. When U-SNAP-BAC began to construct housing, the organization was working with nearby neighborhood associations whose areas contained few vacant houses or vacant lots. The first target area that the CDC chose as Phase I contained 60 parcels, but 55 were vacant, and the city owned 40 of those.[31] Vacancy made it a very reasonable site but marketable; the condition of several strong nearby neighborhoods suggested that the demand for housing was still strong to the east of those targeted streets. Finney was 24.6 percent white in 2000, with 23.4 percent of households making $75,000 or more a year, close to three times the proportion of households in this higher-income category in Brightmoor. Finney benefited as well from less housing-unit loss from 1990 to 2000 than the other areas, as Table 9.2 reveals.

All three organizations built housing in high-poverty areas. Seventeen percent of the households in the immediate area of the MorningSide Commons target area earned less than $10,000 a year and only 14.5 percent earned $75,000, according to the 2000 census. Thus, the demographics for U-SNAP-BAC's target area did not differ from those of CDC target areas in Brightmoor and in East Riverside; in fact, all tracts the three CDCs chose as target areas had QCT (Qualified Census Tract) designation, qualifying them for special consideration for LIHTC applications.[32] However, NDND was targeting sections of five of Brightmoor's census tracts with few households earning at least $75,000 a year. U-SNAP-BAC's MorningSide project had an advantage in access to nearby higher income households (Table 9.2), and Creekside's target area could benefit from nearby redevelopment projects in Jefferson-Chalmers, with fewer such advantages for NDND's Brightmoor. This suggests that NDND was playing David to a Goliath of a context in Brightmoor by trying to improve the neighborhood through construction of new rental low-income housing, without the benefit of nearby higher-income households.

Other demographic conditions mattered as well. Of the three areas, Brightmoor suffered the most from crime and drugs, especially in the 1960s and 1970s, but the neighborhood never recovered after that. Designed as a working-class community from its origins, Brightmoor lost people as the working class lost jobs in the automobile industry. This made it very difficult to attract potential renters and buyers to the neighborhood. In Jefferson-Chalmers, the CDC target area was surrounded by developments that ranged from low income to middle income, but the organization built housing on the streets that included deteriorated units and vacant lots, as well as older housing, modest structures not attractive to potential residents.

In addition, by 2009, the U.S. housing market was depressed, not just in central-city areas. As mortgage foreclosures increased, newer or more established housing in neighborhoods better served by public services became available at low prices in Detroit's nearby suburbs, undercutting what demand existed for the central-city housing these organizations were constructing. In 2009, an individual could buy a house in Detroit for $5,000 or less, and even then takers were not guaranteed. Lack of sales or rental potential for tax-credit housing when someone moved out led to housing vacancies. This situation overcame any efforts to undertake neighborhood revitalization through what was, for NDND and Creekside, a pattern of infill housing, in either several modified dispersed (NDND) or one loosely compacted (Creek-side) target area. Such a strategy could only work if the original housing near the infill sites stayed in place, which became unlikely as more units became empty and vulnerable.

Broader circumstances affected targeting strategies for all three CDCs but especially for NDND. Even in the 1990s NDND had a much more difficult situation in attracting households to Brightmoor, and could not have easily leveraged subsidized housing as a magnet for nonpoor families to enter the area, even without the subsequent economic downturn. When NDND's planning consultant sketched a 2001 plan for the neighborhood, a doughnut hole of emptiness appeared in the middle of Brightmoor because of both tax-foreclosed housing, abandoned by owners and later demolished, and social problems such as illegal activities. At that time, NDND was optimistic that Brightmoor would attract other families, so the organization and the consultant, avoiding the hole, prepared for future target areas beyond the first one. The huge void of emptiness and sparse housing in the middle, however, hindered efforts to market new housing elsewhere in Brightmoor. As the housing market floundered, even renters did not want to live in Brightmoor, and construction costs remained high even while housing prices fell. Residential blocks gradually emptied in spite of NDND's housing construction. This process gave even targeted blocks, especially those away from the first target area, the appearance of scattered housing, located at random in a sea of abandoned units, older housing, and numerous vacant lots.

Much the same process took place in Creekside's target area. This organization had taken care to build housing in the targeted infill area not so much on contiguous sites as on sites that were acceptable to immediate neighbors, a feat they accomplished in part by knocking on doors and asking if people would like to have new housing built next to them. They also attempted to buy easily obtainable lots. Despite the advantage of nearby intact housing, Creekside's dreams of building more housing to fill in the gaps also died in the face of lack of demand, even before the national housing crisis.

The MorningSide Commons units suffered less than other areas from housing or lot vacancy or from abandonment of newly constructed housing. U-SNAP-BAC, with its decision to build on contiguous sites in one grand sweep, buying up and demolishing all standing structures, created a micro-market of new housing that was attractive to buyers and renters. Nevertheless, demographics and market demand posed difficulties for U-SNAP-BAC in the streets surrounding its focused target area. Several of those streets have experienced a high degree of vacancy, whereas, when the organization began building, many nearby areas did not have enough vacant land on which to build. A planned third phase of additional new construction for Morning-Side Commons had to be scrapped when the national economy faltered.

Organizational Issues

A land use plan, aimed at the level of either the neighborhood or a target area, could help make sure that housing investment resources are strategic and cohesive. Such a plan would ideally look at such issues as community goals, existing and necessary public facilities, changing demographics, quality of existing housing stock, and phases for carrying out development or other related efforts. The best plans include meaningful community input, so that the vision of the plan meets as far as possible the needs of existing residents and businesses, to ensure support.[33] All three CDCs accomplished quite a lot in their service areas, but shortcomings in implementing a land use plan are not surprising.

Myriad conditions affect CDC performance in programs such as housing construction and rehabilitation. The history and politics surrounding an organization may be important, for example;[34] a CDC that places itself in a broader community context, grounding itself in community roots, could have a better chance of accomplishing its goals than one that becomes distant from its community base or too involved in patronage politics. Glickman and Servon would call such considerations "networking" and "political ability" skills.[35] They developed a typology of CDC capacity that included five major areas—resources, organization, networking, program ability, and political ability—and suggested that several components of each were important indications of capacity to accomplish goals. Carrying out housing production programs, a set of activities Glickman and Servon would call programmatic, is a particularly difficult enterprise.[36] Housing production by CDCs is difficult not simply because of the logistics of carrying out such tasks but also because these tasks may tax all the organization's vulnerabilities. Bratt and Rohe studied what happened when six case study CDCs went out of business, downsized, or merged.[37] Risk factors for failure included overreliance on single sources of dollars, dependence on one line of action, internal management problems, poor staff or board capacity, poor communication skills, or lack of community support. Yet many CDCs carrying out housing production may rely on limited sources of funds, lack staff or management skills necessary for housing development, suffer from poor operating support, and use single-focused strategies necessary to get tasks done for a complex endeavor. Sometimes CDCs pursue a construction-heavy course with little input or guidance from local residents, which could jeopardize neighborhood stability and cohesion. For many years the availability of LIHTC as a source of funding led CDCs into housing production as a primary or sole line of action. LIHTC provided important funding for low-income housing through sale of tax credits to investors, supported long-term rentals, and was popular as a financing tool.[38]

Each of the three organizations operated in the framework of at least one viable neighborhood plan. Carrying out their plans posed difficulties, however, in part because of organizational capacity and support systems.

First, to consider the property acquisition problem: CDCs that attempt to acquire property in some cities face major difficulties. Detroit is an extremely difficult place to acquire even city-owned property. The city's land information management system has slowly improved but still poses barriers, and knowledge about such fundamental matters as who actually owns a piece of property is often difficult to access.

A respondent commenting on the NDND situation noted that it was very difficult to buy land in large part because of clouded titles. Every address the CDC tried to acquire had a different story, requiring enormous time and energy. Therefore, to build 50 houses, NDND staff deemed it necessary to acquire approximately 130 lots. Fifty of the extra lots were needed because the typical 34-foot lot width was out of conformity with the 40-foot width required by the city's zoning ordinance for new construction, so the CDC acquired two lots to build one house, or three to build two. At least 30 extra lots served as insurance because it was quite likely they could not clear some titles even with great effort. The perceived need to acquire 130 lots to build 50 houses almost guaranteed that the houses could not be contiguous or appear to completely fill in a street blotted with vacancies. The determining factor was the availability of land, no matter how fragmented the pieces, rather than the need for cohesion and visible impact. Yet NDND steered away from constructing housing in the isolated central section of Brightmoor that contained abundant vacant land because it already seemed to be on its way to irreversible abandonment.

Creekside CDC also experienced difficulties with land acquisition, but Creekside started building when the city had some basic procedures in place. It also benefited from very active board members, who helped with the laborious tasks involved in identifying lots. The third organization, U-SNAP-BAC, encountered such numerous roadblocks when it began property acquisition in 1996 that it sought legal help from a University of Michigan law clinic. Even though the city owned 40 of 60 targeted parcels, titles for many properties were not clear enough for acquisition. At that time the City of Detroit had no written procedures in place for approving such projects or disposing of city-owned land, leading to many years of effort to improve procedures.[39] U-SNAP-BAC managed to build contiguous houses only with concerted help from the legal clinic.

This governmental policy problem contributed to the CDC, particularly NDND, organizational problem of nonstrategic acquisition of land. In reaction to the difficulties described above, NDND launched a Brightmoor land-buying spree that turned the CDC into a huge land owner. As I have already described, this CDC chose several target areas dispersed throughout Brightmoor. One reason it gave for leaving the first target area was that not enough land was available in that area to purchase the 130 vacant lots it perceived were needed once the first phase was finished. The CDC then launched a second and then a third target area, sometimes taking advantage of vacant lot sales carried out by the state of Michigan and Wayne County to dispose quickly of tax-reverted properties, avoiding construction in the most vacant central portion of Brightmoor (where the CDC did buy lots, however). As of late 2009, the NDND housing director estimated that the CDC owned about 600 properties and was years behind in taxes for those properties, with no easy way to sell them or otherwise pay their bills. Much of this dilemma was due to the fact that the market for new housing had died; nevertheless, this CDC seemed to own far more property than was warranted. The desire to continue to build related in part to the desire for a continued source of revenue from LIHTC developer fees, reflective of the organization's overdependence on one line of action and one main source of funding.

Insufficient organizational capacity to implement strategies also plagued some projects. NDND overcame a false start with its first phase—bringing in an outside developer who built a shoddy product—when it hired a competent housing director. However, implementing the necessary marketing strategy for success turned out to be very difficult. Furthermore, since NDND housing was funded by LIHTC, the housing was rental and served low-income people in possible need of social services. NDND held fast to its mission of housing, delegating to other organizations in the Brightmoor area tasks associated with social services, community organizing, support for small businesses, and other community development activities. The major exception to this mission focus was CDC assistance in protecting parkland from possible encroachment of a post office, which it did by successfully assembling an alternative building site in the neighborhood. This did help the CDC's credibility with residents but confirmed its role as a specialist in property acquisition and turnaround.

Lack of flexible capacity may also have been a major reason for Creekside's loss of paid staff. Creekside relied on a nationally known development firm that specializes in using the tax credit program but typically partners with a local CDC to gain points in the state application process. Thus, Creekside got 45 housing units built but received a small fraction of the developer and related fees. One observer referred to this as a typical pattern for this particular national developer: to pursue the CDCs with the least capacity and siphon off the lion's share of the resources generated. The comparatively modest $100,000 it allotted to Creekside was enough to hire two CDC staff people but not to keep them on salary for more than a few years. An area developer we interviewed charged that Creekside CDC never developed the organizational capacity to build its own housing and that the national development company simply photocopied plans it had used in other places around the country to replicate in Creekside.

U-SNAP-BAC had more diverse funds than NDND, pulling in resources far beyond tax credits, but did not have the level of programmatic support necessary to avoid cutting back its staff drastically once the recession hit.

Challenges related to networking and community organizing, another aspect of CDC capacity, also affected targeting. All three CDCs networked reasonably well with other organizations, particularly Habitat for Humanity. Within their communities they made attempts to reach out to various groups and organize residents, but with varying success.

For example, NDND helped form a larger coalition known as the Brightmoor Alliance that had a much broader agenda than housing. This alliance is a very good example of how a large neighborhood can pull together its institutions and groups into a networked organizational structure, but the strategy had drawbacks as well. The most obvious for this study is that it cemented within NDND the focus on a singular strategy, building housing, which reduced flexibility when that strategy no longer worked. Another major drawback was that the Brightmoor Alliance pressured NDND to build more housing in other areas of Brightmoor, away from the southeast where NDND first built, to spread benefits. This pressure may have overcome any tendency the organization might have had to stay in one targeted area.

Networking for Creekside in the Jefferson-Chalmers neighborhood was somewhat difficult because so many other organizations existed in that area, and these groups were sometimes at odds. These included the city government-appointed citizens' district council, a holdover from the urban renewal era, which was designed to insure citizen input into redevelopment projects but which sometimes pressed for different priorities from those of the CDC and the Jefferson East Business Association, a separate organization devoted to commercial viability on Jefferson Avenue. These, along with a homeowners' association, made for a very crowded collection of community-based organizations that were not always pulling in concert. This complicated network may have contributed to the organization's inability to continue to target because of loss of housing staff; possibly community resources were too slim to support staff for both the business association and Creekside.

In contrast to the other two CDCs, U-SNAP-BAC benefited from its grassroots, fairly unified origins, so it did not have to court other organizations serving the same neighborhood area, as did Creekside, or to cleave to a fairly narrow mission and avoid turf battles, as did NDND. U-SNAP-BAC was the offspring of preexisting community-based organizations; diverse neighborhood organizations came together to create that CDC, and its active and involved board members included representation from these groups, so it was in that sense better networked. Several homeowner and business associations played a part in helping to select the target area and support it, which enhanced its ability to target a cohesive portion of its service area and stay with that area through several years and with varying funding sources. In terms of external networks, as we have already mentioned, this area served as a drive-through model neighborhood for city officials, which buttressed its credibility for subsequent targeted efforts.

The Policy Dilemma

Policy difficulties had major effects on the CDCs' actions. The most important of these was trouble in land acquisition and transfer, which continued to be a problem even after some of the most grievous shortcomings were addressed.[40] The zoning ordinance required minimum lot sizes for new construction, which posed an obvious barrier, and in many cases city officials did not know whether the city government owned a property. In addition, working with City of Detroit staff was difficult, due in part to the existence of two official planning offices, one serving the council and the other in the executive branch,[41] but also due to staff shortages or bureaucratic inefficiency. Signature pages for property transfers were typically a page long, and all transfers of city-owned land had to go to City Council for approval. This context led NDND to buy too much property, ahead of actual need, to protect itself from difficult city government land transfers.

In addition, state policies concerning tax-reverted property hindered strategic land acquisition. A short-lived state program, Revitalife, distributed quite a bit of tax-reverted property to CDCs, but this created another opportunity for NDND to buy too much dispersed land, avoiding the labyrinthine process to buy city-owned land and preparing for future phases.

A related but separate issue was the city's lack of encouragement for neighborhood organizations to abide by neighborhood plans that included strategic action or targeted areas. Although the city's official master plan was out of date until 2009, with the city depending on a 1992 officially adopted policy plan that did not include strong neighborhood strategies, Detroit did adopt some official project area plans for selected areas, such as Jefferson-Chalmers. City officials functioned throughout the mid-2000s with draft master plans that delineated recognized neighborhood areas in the city's ten clusters[42] and that offered maps of potential land use for each cluster and its several neighborhoods.[43] But its framework for strong neighborhood or target area planning within smaller areas such as specific census tracts was weak, particularly during the long years that City Council did not formally adopt the draft master plans. The city's plans were inadequate at any rate for the purposes of creating new housing developments such as these CDCs were trying to do. At one point, the executive-branch Planning and Development Department assigned staff planners to one or two of the city's ten clusters, which had 60,000 to 120,000 people each in 2000, but most of these planners had too many responsibilities to function well. Every CDC respondent, asked whether he or she received encouragement from the city to work in specific areas of service, to target CDC resources to specific blocks, or to create viable neighborhood plans before constructing housing, answered no.

The Michigan Neighborhood Preservation Program (NPP) channeled funding to a required 16-block area, as a form of targeting. U-SNAP-BAC tapped such funds for small projects such as parks. However, state officials did not link the LIHTC program to NPP designation and did not require that LIHTC-funded projects fall within a designated neighborhood with a plan, as did NPP.

The federal program that emerged as most influential in CDC targeting decisions was LIHTC. Until the housing crisis began in 2007, the LIHTC program was the dominant federal vehicle for funding low-income housing, outpacing its other competitor, housing vouchers. Many CDCs carrying out housing construction projects during the 1990s and the 2000s used LIHTC to help fund those projects.

Several aspects of the LIHTC program relate to targeting and to program effectiveness. The first is that the program allocates tax credits to states depending on population rather than need. State rules could then allow construction of LIHTC units in areas without compelling needs.[44] The states set up their own rules for distributing the credits within federal guidelines, using a Qualified Allocation Plan. States varied widely in terms of such provisions as how much focus they put on high-poverty areas or whether they provided more or fewer points for projects that targeted areas undertaking neighborhood planning.[45] In Michigan, the state set aside a proportion (the legislature chose 10 percent as the statutory level) of the tax credits for projects associated with nonprofit organizations. Identifying targeted areas for the neighborhood to be served by the CDC or developer or referencing neighborhood plans, however, did not help applicants build up the volume of points necessary to submit competitive applications. See Table 9.3 for a summary of selected, relevant point allocations for Michigan, 2001–9, a reflection of state policy in response to the federal program.

Another aspect of the LIHTC program was its provision for QCTs. According to the 1986 and 1989 federal legislation, such tracts, where at least 50 percent of households had income less than 60 percent of the metropolitan Area Median Income or poverty rates were 25 percent or more, should receive 30 percent more tax credits than other tracts. This reinforced the effort to serve low-income areas. However, in no case could QCT make up more than 20 percent of metropolitan area population, a "capping" provision that placed high-poverty metropolitan areas or central cities at a disadvantage.[46] The QCT provision set up an incentive for developers to select low-income or high-poverty areas for tax credit development activities, as intended, but this created a number of other difficulties, particularly if such neighborhoods faced abandonment or lack of access to employment or public services. Another possibly unintended consequence of such provisions was that LIHTC further concentrated low-income people in high-poverty areas and dampened what private sector activity already existed. Baum-Snow and Marion found that developers favored QCT, but that the resulting LIHTC projects crowded out private development since LIHTC construction was associated with a decline in the number of recently built rental units in nearby areas.[47] The LIHTC program did locate development in disadvantaged neighborhoods, but this led to geographic concentration of low-income people,[48] reinforcement of racial segregation,[49] and relative isolation of low-income people in LIHTC developments.[50]

Table 9.3. Selected Points Awarded for Applications, Qualified Allocation Plans, State of Michigan Low-Income Housing Tax Credits

Project application characteristic	2001	2002	2003	2005–2006	2008	2009
Empowerment Zone/Enterprise Community location	20	20	20	1	1	1
Renaissance Zone location	20	20	20	1	1	1
Qualified Census Tract location (beyond set-aside)[a]					1	1
New urbanism/green communities features					15	20
Walkable communities features				8		
Area within a Community Revitalization Plan	5	5	5	5	10	
Participation of nonprofit organizations (beyond set-aside)[a]	5	5	5	5	5	5
Special needs populations to be served by housing[b]	35	25	35	5		
Contributing to an existing Community Revitalization Plan in a Qualified Census Tract or Tribal Land	5	5	5	5		
Apparent total number of possible points	318	308	326	265	303	425

Sources: Annual documents posted by Michigan State Housing Development Authority, http://www.michigan.gov/mshda/0,1607,7-141-5587_5601-31750–,00.html.

[a]The State also set aside funding for Qualified Census Tracts or eligible distressed areas and for eligible nonprofits, according to federal regulations.

[b]"Special needs" populations included handicapped, transitional, and formerly homeless people.

These federal policy provisions and state interpretations of those provisions affected the case study CDCs in two main ways. First, under these provisions, targeting was a form of purposely concentrating poverty, particularly in Brightmoor, when LIHTCs were the only new investments besides Habitat for Humanity homes. Therefore, targeting may not have, in fact, been beneficial to the viability of the neighborhood as a whole. Selecting distressed tracts was a less isolating strategy in Jefferson-Chalmers, which had some mixed-income projects nearby, and in MorningSide Commons, which mixed types of funding sources. Second, a problem associated with LIHTC for all three project areas, but particularly Brightmoor, was the limited number of units built in targeted areas. The state could choose how much tax-credit financing to support in high-poverty areas or in the City of Detroit since it spread the tax credits throughout the state, as did most states, and observed the guidelines in terms of the maximum percentage of credits allowable for QCT areas. Therefore, LIHTC projects for the state were not predominately located in its biggest city, even though it set aside 30 percent for "eligible distressed areas"[51] and funding for Detroit was higher than an equal per capita share.[52] Rengert has shown that several states, including Michigan, tended not to funnel tax credits to high-poverty census tracts.[53] This meant that the CDCs could not rely on LIHTC funds to create critical mass, even when they did attempt to target areas where they would have an impact, because the funds would have been inadequate for such a show of force.

Conclusion

The subject of CDC targeting opens up an opportunity to talk about a number of issues related to central-city redevelopment. This discussion connects with the larger context of CDC functioning, central-city challenges, and federal policy. However, looking narrowly at the issue of whether a CDC chose to target a specific, compact geographic area for housing construction reveals certain findings. First, all three case study CDCs attempted to create target areas, but the efforts differed in their effects. NDND chose one target area but went to others as it sought increasing amounts of land to develop under the LIHTC program, in a pattern of "modified dispersion." Creekside started with a well-defined target area but ended up unable to fill in enough vacancies to make a visible difference, providing a pattern of "targeted infill." U-SNAP-BAC concentrated its efforts on developing in one small "closely targeted" area using a broad swoop that left few gaps between its new housing units. So, targeting has been a part of each organization's actions but with differing results based in large part on these different approaches.

Investigating conditions helped explain what led to *not* targeting. Again, the Brightmoor neighborhood proves particularly instructive. There, modified dispersion resulted from institutional pressures from allied organizations that lobbied for an expansive housing development strategy, in combination with specific features of land acquisition in the City of Detroit, a CDC leadership strategy of buying land ahead in order to have enough for the future, and less directly lack of attention to the neighborhood context or targeting of LIHTC funds. At the other extreme, U-SNAP-BAC appeared to target more closely because the organization chose an area that was largely vacant but an anomaly with fairly strong nearby neighborhood associations supportive of U-SNAP-BAC.

Demographics and market conditions were an issue, because, even before the housing market collapsed, at least NDND struggled mightily to function in a city that was steadily emptying out, especially from historically low-income neighborhoods such as Brightmoor. U-SNAP-BAC benefited from a stronger market in areas to the east of its target area, although the other directional trends were not so positive. All three CDCs struggled because of the collapse of home ownership. But organizational shortcomings played a role as well. These included not so much lack of a viable neighborhood plan as inability to carry it out because of incomplete program capacity in the face of myriad challenges. In some cases, acquisition of land was not strategic and not all the CDCs had the technical skills to construct housing without partnering with outside firms that may have taken advantage of them, offering them a fraction of possible fees, as happened with Creekside.

Although all these factors were important, government policy played a strong role in targeting behavior. The failure of local and state governments to maintain a firm grasp of land development policies had major implications for these CDCs. The federal LIHTC program, planned as a way to support developers as well as low-income families, never was intended as a panacea for distressed central-city neighborhoods and certainly has not become that in practice. Provisions such as requiring set-asides for nonprofit organizations and targeting toward needy census tracts do not necessarily create the conditions on the ground necessary to frame the actions of CDCs.

Although this study showed that sometimes conditions were not favorable for a CDC to target its construction dollars, it does not answer the implicit question whether these CDCs *should* have targeted such investments and whether, if they had done so, the results would have been any different. In the context of vanishing demand for housing, with owners abandoning houses even as new houses rose next to these, targeting housing construction may have had limited impact at any rate. In addition, using the LIHTC program under the circumstances we describe, the CDCs may have further isolated the poor and not contributed to neighborhood stability, a possibility that U-SNAP-BAC staff raised in interviews and that hovered over the other

CDCs' target areas as well, as these groups were creating rental, low-income enclaves. What we can say with some certainty, however, is that the CDC that did target most carefully, U-SNAP-BAC, and also mixed its funding sources appropriately maintained its reputation as a capable CDC with city observers, even though it transformed only two streets.

PART III

What *Should* the City Become
After Abandonment?

CHAPTER 10

Strategic Thinking for Distressed Neighborhoods

Robert A. Beauregard

In January 2010, New York governor David Paterson announced his Sustainable Neighborhood Project. Designed to "fight urban decay and revitalize prime housing stock," his initiative was a response to the persistent population and job loss that beset upstate cities such as Buffalo, Rochester, Syracuse, Utica, and Albany. These losses had left behind large numbers of abandoned homes, as well as neighborhoods with residential densities far below those of previous decades. Leveraging existing state and local programs, Governor Paterson designed the Sustainable Neighborhood Project to rehabilitate blighted properties, demolish structures too costly to renovate, and turn fallow lots into community gardens, urban farms, and open space.[1] Paterson slated Buffalo, with its estimated 29,000 vacant residences—nearly one-fifth of its total housing stock—to be the "starting point" for this pilot project, with the city's West Side as its targeted neighborhood.[2]

If and when New York fully implements the Sustainable Neighborhood Project, Buffalo will join a small number of cities that have embarked on a new approach to neighborhood decline. Philadelphia's Neighborhood Transformation Initiative, Youngstown, Ohio's *2010* plan, and Flint, Michigan's Genesee County Land Bank are the best-known examples. Baltimore's Project 5000 has received less publicity but is equally relevant. These types of programs combine two ideas, one old and one new.

The old idea is that planners and policy makers should think strategically about how to intervene when severely distressed neighborhoods suffer from multiple problems such as high poverty rates, enduring population loss, falling property values, housing abandonment, blight, and crime. This means bundling programs and then targeting them geographically.

The new idea is that, for distressed neighborhoods in shrinking cities, the future most likely means fewer residents, lower demand for public services and diminished use of infrastructure, and much more open space. The goal is not to remediate current conditions or launch such growth-oriented initiatives as large-scale residential or industrial redevelopment projects. Rather, the best policy combines aggressive demolition of abandoned buildings with "greening" of vacant lots, all with the intent of downsizing or, as often phrased, "rightsizing" the neighborhood.

With more advocates urging city officials to think "small,"[3] this is a propitious time to consider how planners and policy makers might strategically intervene in distressed neighborhoods. This chapter reflects on current approaches by drawing on the experiences and initiatives of cities that have had long-term population and job loss and, consequently, neighborhoods with high levels of abandoned housing.[4] To ground the discussion, I focus on a model of neighborhood change and intervention proposed by the National Vacant Properties Campaign (NVPC, now part of the nonprofit Center for Community Progress), whose purpose is to "provide information, resources, tools, and assistance to support . . . vacant property revitalization efforts."[5] I am interested in the gap between a "best practices" model and adoption and implementation of that model, its use by individuals embedded in specific geographic, political, and organizational settings. What considerations have to be addressed to deploy the model effectively?

The following discussion emphasizes four issues. The first concerns neighborhoods that the model does not directly address; that is, places to which households displaced from distressed neighborhoods have already or will relocate. Second is the need to integrate this neighborhood-based approach with citywide redevelopment policies involving central business district and industrial area investments. A third issue concerns the place-orientation of such models and their tendency to focus on buildings and land rather than on the social conditions residents face. Implementation of the model requires sensitivity to the life trajectories and current needs of those occupying these neighborhoods. Last, and arguably most important,

are local politics and the organizational capacities of the municipal government and community-based organizations.

Models of Neighborhood Intervention

As a response to distressed neighborhoods, the National Vacant Properties
Campaign proposed "a holistic approach to vacant property reclamation"
that involves four strategic actions.[6] These actions, in sequence, are (1) prevention and information, (2) stabilization and abatement, (3) acquisition and
vacant property management, and (4) reuse and long-term planning. Each
contains a corresponding set of programs. Prevention and information
might include early warning information systems, code enforcement, nui-
sance abatement, and property maintenance during foreclosure proceedings.
Stabilization and abatement might entail housing renovation subsidies and
grants for repairs, emergency demolitions, and lot clean up. Acquisition and
vacant property management could involve demolitions, vacant property
registration, land banks, and streamlined tax foreclosure procedures. And
reuse might encompass side-lot property sales, "green" programs such as
community gardens, and redevelopment initiatives that provide affordable
housing. The NVPC approach intends to be comprehensive, pulling into itself all possible types of neighborhood-based interventions (see Table 10.1
for an illustrative list of strategies and programs).

The NVPC model aligns these four strategies with four stages through
which a typical neighborhood is presumed to pass: stability, transition,
distress, and rebuilding. The label for the model—the Vacant Properties
Revitalization *Cycle* (my emphasis)—signals the sequence. Two assumptions
operate. The first is that, without concerted efforts, neighborhoods go through
stages from relatively prosperous and desirable to abandonment. This is reminiscent of models of neighborhood change that pattern it after the ostensibly
"natural" life cycle of humans.[7]

The second assumption is that a correspondence exists between each
strategy—and the programs aligned with it—and the life-cycle stage of the
neighborhood. Here the model conflates two ideas. One is that, at early stages
of decline, small, nonintrusive, and inexpensive interventions can succeed.
For example, when a stable neighborhood first shows signs of deterioration,
the city could strengthen code enforcement. Code enforcement does not

Table 10.1. A Partial Listing of Activities Pertinent to Distressed Neighborhoods

Strategic actions	Programmatic activities
Prevention and information	Affordable infill housing
	Anti-flipping ordinance
	Code enforcement
	Foreclosure prevention: mortgage and tax
	Home repair grants
	Landlord and homeowner training
	Empty lot clean up
	Nuisance abatement
	Property maintenance codes
	Proactive housing courts
	Property tracking systems/vacant property registration
	Removal of abandoned automobiles
Stabilization and abatement	Home purchase subsidies
	Lot clean-up
	Renovation grants and loans
	Rental and point-of-sale code inspections
	Side-lot sales
	Slumlord prosecution
	Tax delinquency programs
Acquisition and management	Boarding up of abandoned buildings
	Demolitions: emergency and strategic
	Deconstruction (salvage)
	Land banking
	Land reserves and trusts
	Relocation grants
	Tax foreclosure and acquisition
Reuse	Reuse of vacant lots
	"Greening" initiatives
	Immigrant recruitment
	Neighborhood plans
	Sales to developers (bid solicitation)
	Sales to individuals (lotteries)

Note: programs can work with more than one strategic action depending on how they are configured, funded, and coordinated with other programs. My listing is based on a review of the literature on neighborhood abandonment and research on the eleven cities listed in endnote 4. It is meant to be suggestive, not exhaustive.

need special legislation or federal or state grants, and unless fiscally stressed, most city governments have staff to do it. When neighborhoods have become severely distressed, however, more aggressive and expensive programs (such as systematic demolition of vacant buildings) are needed.

The other idea is that, as a neighborhood devolves, the complexity of its problems demand more programs, not just programs of a particular size. At a very early stage, a monitoring system is sufficient. At a later stage, government officials must combine demolition, cleanup, "greening," mortgage foreclosure prevention, land banking, renovation subsidies, and slumlord prosecution programs among other initiatives. As the NVPC suggests, distress requires comprehensive action even to stabilize the neighborhood. The city government must match the complexity of the problem with an equally complex array of interventions. When a neighborhood has become distressed, the time has passed when a program with a single goal—no matter how well funded, targeted, or implemented—can stem population loss and property value decline.

Given that the NVPC model grew out of consultations with officials in cities experiencing extensive neighborhood disinvestment, its ideas and assumptions not surprisingly parallel the comprehensive initiatives undertaken over the last decade. Philadelphia, Flint, and Youngstown reflect, even as they informed, the NVPC approach.

In 2001, Philadelphia mayor John Street announced his Neighborhood Transformation Initiative (NTI) to address the continued shrinkage of the city's population and the unrelenting spread of abandoned homes and vacant properties.[8] For decades, the city government had demolished abandoned buildings. In the 1980s, it averaged 1,000 demolitions per year; in 1997 alone the city government took down 4,000 buildings at a cost of $14 million.[9] For decades, the government had subsidized home purchases and repairs and encouraged community gardens. Each of these programs, however, had operated relatively independently with minimal coordination. Moreover, city officials conducted spatial targeting by default rather than by design, and funding levels were low relative to the scale of the problems. In 2002, Philadelphia still had approximately 30,000 vacant lots and 26,000 vacant residential structures.[10]

In order to arrest decline and under the assumption that Philadelphia's distressed neighborhoods would have to shrink before they could grow, Mayor Street proposed a $250 million program to acquire abandoned and obsolete buildings and vacant lots, relocate property owners where necessary, demolish the structures, and prepare the land for redevelopment. The goal was a 5 percent increase in the city's population by 2010.

The NTI rested on several assumptions. First, Mayor Street and his advisors argued that only a large-scale, comprehensive, and targeted program would significantly affect the city's chronic and pervasive housing abandonment problem. Second, they recognized that such an initiative was "far beyond the capacity of any single, overburdened city department"[11] and required a separate program. Third, the designers of the NTI assumed that technical considerations would guide interventions. Specifically, the NTI would embrace a targeted approach to neighborhood selection based on an analysis of "market clusters." The analysis created six types of neighborhoods ranging from the best (Regional Choice and High Value/Appreciating) to those most in need of intervention (Stressed and Reclamation).[12] In addition, NTI rested on the premise that the problems of the most distressed neighborhoods needed to be addressed first; otherwise, conditions there would spread to adjacent, more viable neighborhoods, thereby making a manageable problem insuperable.

Of the NTI funds, Mayor Street and his advisors devoted $140 million (56 percent of the total) to acquisition and demolition of 14,000 abandoned buildings. Once that had begun, NTI turned to reuse of the vacant lots, aiming to create opportunities for redevelopment. When private developers expressed interest and financing became available, NTI launched Specific Development Projects, mainly for affordable housing. Where this did not happen, the Redevelopment Authority banked the land and encouraged "greening." This took the form of community gardens and basic landscaping of vacant lots using city resources and those of community associations and such citywide organizations as the Pennsylvania Horticultural Society.

Flint and Youngstown have established similar programs, though smaller in scale. The initiative in Flint is administered by the Genesee County Land Bank, established in 2002 with the support of the Mott Foundation.[13] As Flint experienced a near halving of its population after 1960 due to suburbanization and the collapse of the regional automotive industry, the city and adjacent suburban municipalities experienced higher residential vacancies and increased numbers of tax-foreclosed abandoned properties. The land bank was conceived to address this problem at the county level. It receives tax-foreclosed properties from the county treasurer that have not sold at auction and sells the more valuable ones (the latter usually located outside

Flint). The proceeds from these sales, augmented by governmental funds, are then used to demolish structures (mostly in Flint neighborhoods) and "green" the vacant lots with community or individual gardens and pocket parks. Demolition focuses on land bank-owned buildings in neighborhoods that can be most quickly stabilized, rather than being guided, as in the Philadelphia case, by a multifactor analysis of neighborhood distress.

Between its establishment in 2002 and 2009, the land bank sold 1,600 properties and raised $6.4 million for its programs.[14] Between 2003 and 2007, it demolished more than 800 structures, rehabilitated 90 affordable rental units and 80 single-family houses, and sold 500 lots to property owners as side lots.[15]

Youngstown's shrinking neighborhood initiative is similar in approach but lacked a countywide land bank as of 2010.[16] Like Flint, the city suffered serious population loss; 67,000 people lived there in 2010 compared to 170,000 at its 1930 peak. This loss led to extensive housing abandonment, with $1.5 million spent on demolition in 2007[17] and nearly 4,600 structures still vacant in 2009.[18] These conditions put the city government in fiscal stress. Elected officials and their planners began to consider downsizing neighborhoods in order to shrink infrastructure (for example, streets) and public services (for example, trash collection) and thereby reduce city expenditures.

The city's planners dedicated the *2010 Plan* to creating a "smaller, greener, cleaner" Youngstown, in part by undertaking targeted demolitions each year in 30 of the city's 127 neighborhoods. Property acquisition and demolition would produce vacant lots that could then become community gardens, side yards, and small parks or remain unused open space. The Youngstown Neighborhood Development Corporation was established to work with the city and the Mahoning Valley Organizing Collaborative to stabilize neighborhoods that experienced extensive demolitions. The city had fix-up programs for areas that could be kept viable, and officials urged homeowners to relocate from neighborhoods with only a few households remaining. Youngstown also drew on federal Neighborhood Stabilization Program (NSP) funds to prevent and mitigate mortgage foreclosures.[19] In addition, the city put a moratorium on tax credit-financed construction of low-income housing in the most distressed neighborhoods in order to encourage the use of existing stock and avoid rebuilding where few people chose to live.

One less publicized initiative also deserves mention: Baltimore's Project 5000.[20] Mayor Martin O'Malley instituted Baltimore's Project 5000 in 2002 with the goal of bringing 5,000 vacant properties under city ownership.[21]

Project 5000 used a housing market typology to divide the city's 271 neighborhoods into four types—preservation, stabilization, reinvestment, and redevelopment—and this typology guided property acquisition. Under this project, the city demolished buildings on the acquired properties and assembled the resultant vacant land as sites for redevelopment. By 2007, the project had exceeded its goal, and the city owned about 10,000 properties, approximately one-third of all vacant parcels in the city.[22]

Assessment

Within these various initiatives lurks an "ideal" model for the treatment of shrinking neighborhoods, one that the NVPC approach approximated. The promise is that strategic demolitions of abandoned properties in distressed neighborhoods will enable municipal governments to reconfigure residential land uses such that they can withdraw public services from now-empty areas and shut down infrastructure, thus aligning public expenditures with demand. Relocation assistance to homeowners and renters will enable strategic demolition, with these households subsequently moving voluntarily to areas where densities allow efficient service delivery. Affordable housing programs will offer an additional relocation incentive and enable the densities in areas being built up to match infrastructure capacities. In addition, homeowners in neighborhoods that municipal governments can make viable at lower densities will receive home renovation grants and low-interest loans.[23]

Municipal governments will then "green" nonfallow areas at low cost and turn vacant lots in viable areas into community gardens or small parks. With ownership by a government land bank, empty areas can either remain as open space or be marketed for development. The combination of newly reinforced neighborhoods and open space will make the city more livable and, because it no longer projects an image of abandonment, desirable. Eventually, a reputation for livability and the government's ability to manage its land and finances will attract new households and investors who will build homes, open businesses, and invest in commercial and industrial properties.

The above scenario makes sense. However, it is unlikely to unfold as imagined; the ideal is never the reality, and "models" always have to be adapted to actual settings. Philadelphia's NTI experience suggests what one might expect.[24] Ward-based City Council members resisted planners' attempts to target acquisitions and demolitions on technically selected neighborhoods;

inflation and strong housing markets in other neighborhoods pushed up purchase and demolition costs; money was unavailable for relocating households; and the resultant empty lots were scattered rather than contiguous, so that public services could not contract or large open spaces be created. Moreover, few developers were enthusiastic about investing in these neighborhoods; when they did do so, they required deep subsidies to build affordable housing.

Nevertheless, these initiatives, and the model on which they are based, have positive qualities. They (1) recognize the relationship between city shrinkage and neighborhood change, (2) are sensitive to the trajectory of neighborhoods, and (3) embody a good sense of how to think about multiple interventions.

First, the approach is premised on an understanding that the persistent decline of the city means that its distressed neighborhoods are chronically distressed. These neighborhoods will likely neither grow nor stabilize at their current population size. Consequently, the strategy accepts that they will be smaller and attempts to downsize them in a controlled manner. In short, the fortunes of the city and the region factor into thinking about neighborhoods within the city. This leads to a policy averse to the progrowth efforts common to most cities and more sensitive to the city's specific developmental trajectory.

Second, the NVPC model recognizes that, in shrinking cities, the trajectories of some neighborhoods are flat with home values and occupancy stable over time, whereas the trajectories of other neighborhoods are relentlessly downward. The planning problem, as neighborhood typology analyses imply, is to distinguish among trajectories so that interventions can be targeted most effectively. Such a targeting approach aims to use resources efficiently while assuring that distressed neighborhoods that are still viable receive high priority in the city's efforts. The latter is particularly important when dealing with the social consequences of neighborhood shrinkage. That these analyses omit the politics of implementation is a point I address below.

Last, these approaches to distressed neighborhoods reflect an understanding of the various tactics—sequencing, bundling, and targeting—that planners and policy makers have traditionally used to address interrelated problems. The NTI model acknowledges the sequencing of interventions in the parallelism between strategies and stages. Only at an early stage of neighborhood change, however, does sequencing seem appropriate. Then, the city government might intensify discretionary code enforcement and, if that fails, follow with mandatory inspections at sale or at a change in occupancy. At later stages, the NVPC model proposes multiple and simultaneous interventions; these neighborhoods have too many interrelated problems to treat them otherwise. More generally, though, sequencing of interventions is unavoidable and at the core of planning practice. Unless a public safety or health threat, buildings have to be acquired before they can be demolished, demolition has to occur before "greening," and contiguous demolitions must precede the creation of large development sites.

More explicit in the model is the bundling of programs. Planners can handle multiple interventions either by coordinating programs in multiple agencies or by grouping programs under a single initiative. Coordination across agencies often occurs through interagency task forces such as Cincinnati's cross-functional Financial Review Team that comprises representatives from the city's major departments. Another way is through such informal communications as when a health inspector informs the buildings department that a rodent-infested building looks structurally unsound. The NVPC model, though, suggests that programs will be more effective if bundled under a single entity, most often a land bank. The land bank agency becomes the pivot around which the other programs are organized. The Genesee County Land Bank is the oft-mentioned example.[25]

The NVPC model also incorporates strategic, geographical targeting either by default or via a neighborhood typology analysis. Targeting, among other assumed benefits, promises cost savings in service delivery.[26] It assumes that, while prosperity can be geographically contagious under certain conditions, in shrinking cities deterioration is diffusing from one neighborhood to the next, starting in the first distressed neighborhoods and moving outward from there.[27] The city must intervene strategically to halt this spread of decline. The next step in this line of reasoning is problematic. Given the prevalence of marginal and distressed neighborhoods, the worst-off neighborhoods might not be the best to target. Triage models give precisely this advice—ignore abandoned neighborhoods and focus resources where they can be most effective; that is, on neighborhoods at a prior stage.

Adjustments to the Model

Since it is a "model," the NVPC approach needs to adjust to the specific conditions and dynamics of the cities that will use it. In doing so, planners and policy makers must attend to four issues: (1) the complex geography of urban development and, specifically, the geographical relationships among neighborhoods within the city as they play out over time, (2) the social consequences of shrinking neighborhoods, (3) the importance of politics—electoral, bureaucratic, and neighborhood—in shaping what is feasible, and (4) the organizational capacity of government agencies and community-based organizations.

First, such a model needs to consider the implications of uneven spatial development, that is, the way that landscapes of growth and decline are functionally intertwined.[28] In its various formulations, the NVPC model acknowledges how neighborhoods are connected through the diffusion of slumlord practices, falling property values, and abandonment from distressed neighborhoods to adjacent ones. The emphasis is on the geographical spread of blight. Planners also need to consider that households move, leaving places they find increasingly uninhabitable and "filling-in" other neighborhoods.[29] These in-movers have the potential to stabilize destination neighborhoods and keep them from abandonment, a consequence implicit in discussions of the need to relocate households from distressed to denser, more stable neighborhoods.

Thinking about household relocation suggests a different approach to targeting, one that gives the quality and contribution of destination neighborhoods a status equal to that of acquisitions, demolition, and "greening" in distressed neighborhoods. The idea is to tap the insights of invasion-succession models to counteract the diffusion of blight before it occurs: in other words, to protect those neighborhoods in the path of spreading abandonment. Distressed neighborhoods need "rightsizing," but not to the detriment of neighborhoods that still have the potential for stability. The intent is to balance the elimination of blight with neighborhood stability. Because households in distressed neighborhoods are likely to be too poor to move to better neighborhoods, they will require relocation subsidies and other assistance such as help with searching for a new home.

Furthermore, incorporation of residential mobility into thinking about distressed neighborhoods can refine the "stage" approach's simple depiction of neighborhood change. In the NVPC and other models, all the decline-inducing factors such as undermaintenance, overcrowding, increase of poor households, and rising property crime operate in tandem. This produces "stages," with neighborhoods assumed to change in lock-step fashion from one steady state to another. Proponents of such models understand this as a simplification, but nonetheless a useful one analytically.

Stage simplification, though, has two consequences: (1) it discards useful evidence and, paradoxically, (2) it turns neighborhood change into a static notion. I suspect that almost all planners recognize the first issue and bring more nuanced and local knowledge to bear as they implement these models. The second is more interesting vis-à-vis strategic thinking. Neighborhoods change along multiple dimensions and do so through the spatial flows of investment capital, rents, households, shopping activity, and workforce commuting. That is, change is a matter of movements among neighborhoods, other areas of the city, and the metropolitan region.

These flows involve people making decisions so that they can live safe and decent lives, just as the diffusion of blight results from the spatial decisions of property owners, realtors, and bankers. A lack of attention to this interconnectedness of neighborhoods deemphasizes the actors who produce and experience neighborhood distress and creates a corresponding place bias.[30] The tendency is to isolate particular neighborhoods from the city and region, even as such models acknowledge the linkages among them. Overlooking actors also privileges property over social needs, a point to be considered below.

Uneven spatial development is also a temporal process and requires that a strategic model account for time. One such consideration involves the differences between housing abandonment caused by sustained job and population loss in the city and abandonment caused by temporary (even if recurring) problems of predatory lending and subsequent mortgage default. The NVPC model is geared more toward chronic rather than temporary conditions. That said, in many cities the difference has blurred due, in part, to the availability of Neighborhood Stabilization Program funding for "emergency assistance for redevelopment of abandoned and foreclosed homes and residential properties." Baltimore, Cincinnati, Detroit, and Pittsburgh, among others, used these funds to establish stabilization programs that were not easily distinguished from shrinking-neighborhood initiatives. Yet, NVPC differentiates between short-term and long-term property abandonment when it assumes that short-term abandonment at an earlier stage leads to long-term abandonment at a later stage.[31]

Abandonment caused by mortgage foreclosures, particularly in newly built neighborhoods, is arguably a different phenomenon requiring different interventions from those used in distressed neighborhoods in shrinking cities.[32] The housing stock is in better condition, infrastructure is newer, social problems are less prevalent, and future prospects are better. Even though a sequence of short-term foreclosure crises might turn temporary abandonment into chronic decline, the two situations are dissimilar, one due to overbuilding, predatory lending, and lack of demand and the other to the multidimensionality of urban decline.

Another aspect of uneven geographical development is the relationship between policies for these neighborhoods and redevelopment and economic development initiatives for other areas of the city. A strategy for distressed neighborhoods within a declining city has to be sensitive to the way that areas of a city connect to each other, as well as to the limitations on funds and organizational energies with which city governments have to contend. No one could possibly believe that the prosperity of the city's commercial districts and industrial areas is irrelevant for the fate of these neighborhoods. Jobs alone make this connection unavoidable. At the same time, no one would argue, I suspect, that concentrating more resources on distressed neighborhoods in order to rightsize the city is unrelated to the allocation of financial and organizational resources to the needs of business: that is, economic development. Mayor Street in Philadelphia and the mayors of other cities often minimize the impact of these programs on the budgets of other governmental initiatives, but they have effects. As an extreme illustration, consider Governor Paterson of New York and his Sustainable Neighborhood Project. He initially offered it with no funding except what state and local officials could find in existing programs. The governor's assumption seems to have been that government agencies were awash in slack resources. If this project was to succeed, it had to draw funds and personnel from current operations, leaving those agencies with fewer of both. In declining cities, resources are severely constrained and organizational capacity cannot easily expand. Consequently, such cities face the politically demanding task of redistributing existing, scarce resources.

A distressed neighborhood strategy requires a change in how city officials and others think about economic development and urban redevelopment initiatives.[33] To be internally consistent, such a strategy must avoid large, high-risk, deeply subsidized, ostensibly catalytic projects with narrowly focused gains. Rather, it should emphasize neighborhood development with low-risk projects that have immediate payoff and widely spread benefits. Economic development and neighborhood policy have to work together. Anything less is a half-hearted commitment and will limit the neighborhood strategy's effectiveness. And, although one can appreciate the political decision not to publicize this shift in focus, a distressed neighborhood strategy cannot succeed when citywide policy on redevelopment and economic development appropriates the bulk of local funds and organizational capacity. Despite significant problems, Youngstown, for example, still devotes monies to reviving its central business district, and Philadelphia continues to subsidize office development downtown and investments along the waterfront. The costs of such large, catalytic projects, combined with their low potential for improving the quality of life for city residents, is incompatible with a rightsizing policy and raises social justice concerns.

Second, an interest in the physical environment—whether abandoned houses, empty land to be "greened," or the downsizing of physical infrastructure—dominates this approach to distressed neighborhoods. The focus is on property and not on people who live in the property.[34] Relocation assistance, a key but mostly suppressed aspect of these initiatives, is the only acknowledgment of the social side of the problem. In implementing the "model," the social consequences of abandonment, shrinkage, and the responses to them also have to be addressed. The stabilization of property values and the alignment of infrastructure supply with demand are means to the goal of better providing for the needs of the city's residents. Yet, cities that have mounted a distressed neighborhood strategy seem to lack a corresponding relocation strategy that would enable residents to upgrade their housing and access services by moving while mitigating the disruption that relocation entails.

Third, models such as the NVPC leave politics to be addressed during implementation, itself a political act. In setting the basic strategy, analysis displaces politics, and planners and policy analysts view politically imposed modifications as distortions of the approach's rationality. Consequently, planners usually accommodate politics in an ad hoc fashion. Three political settings are important: executive and legislative, bureaucratic, and neighborhood.[35]

Because a distressed neighborhood strategy is a citywide policy decision, mayoral leadership and City Council approval determine the resources for it and, thus, its effectiveness. The programs in Philadelphia, Youngstown, and Baltimore have all involved explicit mayoral backing and, in some cases, a strong public commitment by the mayor. One can easily imagine why a mayor would do so. Aside from electoral considerations involving neighborhood political constituencies, any program that promises to reverse decades of decline and make the city more attractive to its residents and potential future residents is worthy of support. A major initiative that has a positive impact creates political capital. With few successes in the past, the possibility of federal and state grants, and the promise of a program (such as a land bank) that eventually can support itself, the benefits seem to outweigh the costs. Moreover, the approach creates immediate, positive, and visible results: fewer abandoned buildings and more community gardens and well-kept side lots.

City Council members, particularly if elected by district, seem less inclined to provide unconditional support. They tend to see these initiatives as opportunities for helping their constituents. Thus, the targeting of interventions is vulnerable to the kinds of politics characteristic of ward-based cities such as Philadelphia. Doing a technical analysis of neighborhoods, sorting them into types, and then devising an implementation plan hardly make sense without considering how this will influence Council support and, because of this, require deviation from the ideal strategy. In addition, planners need to reflect on political disagreements between City Council and the mayor, concerns about the efficacy of this approach, and resistance to creation of new agencies. All these require public debate and compromise.

Bureaucratic politics are also relevant. The issue is whether to coordinate programs from multiple agencies, bundle them in one superagency, or create a lead agency with a core function that can then coordinate interrelated programs.[36] Coordination strains the resources of existing agencies; new agencies often require that functions shift away from existing agencies, with a corresponding loss of influence for them; and any new "leader" will likely threaten the current division of responsibilities. Declining cities short on resources, moreover, often make coordination an unfunded mandate, as shown in Buffalo's Sustainable Neighborhood Project. By contrast, Philadelphia's NTI relied primarily on municipal bond revenues outside the current operating budget.

Political calculations should also extend to community-based organizations. These strategies almost always rely on advocacy groups, neighborhood associations, and other place-based entities to carry out the "greening" component. This is a particular type of partnership in which the core agency focuses on property acquisition and demolition and utilizes the bulk of the designated funds; volunteers and nonprofit organizations carry out the "greening" with minimal funding. In effect, a crucial step in the model— one of its major innovations—is marginalized financially and bureaucratically. This implies a lessened commitment. One might argue that the intent is to empower residents, thus generating much needed support, but this justification still leaves community-based organizations with less money and capacity than city agencies.

Local governments can also use community-based organizations to generate political support for the strategy, even during its development.[37] Given the goal to empty large parts of neighborhoods and thus to relocate households, current planning approaches suggest that early resident involvement is key.[38] Households that live in these areas are likely to be reluctant or unable to move. Thus, preparing residents for this possibility—not to mention providing material incentives and social support to do so—seems crucial. For the most distressed neighborhoods, without neighborhood associations, planners will have to find other community-based groups to serve this function.

Fourth, in any strategic intervention, organizational capacity is pivotal to its effectiveness[39] and needs to be incorporated into these initiatives. This applies both to local government agencies and community-based organizations. Declining cities are notorious for having weak governments.[40] Chronic fiscal stress limits both hiring and salaries and increases the difficulty of mounting human resource training to upgrade the skills of existing personnel. This is one reason why cities that undertake a distressed neighborhood strategy often create separate agencies or new programs within existing agencies. They hope to hire people with the requisite skills at decent salaries. New agencies, however, have significant start-up costs.

Similarly, the organizational capacity of community-based organizations is often problematic in cities that have experienced persistent decline.[41] They can be weak links in the chain of implementation. This is not true of all such cities; Cleveland and Pittsburgh have strong community-based organizations and local foundations. However, even where organizational capacity is high, problems that emanated from and well beyond the scale of the neighborhood often undermine their efforts.[42]

Conclusion

The NVPC model addresses housing abandonment in severely distressed neighborhoods of shrinking cities. Its focus is clear, and numerous cities around the country are adopting it—or variations—as part of decade-long efforts to eradicate slums. Implicit in the model is the privileging of quality-of-life concerns and neighborhood-based efforts over economic development initiatives in commercial and industrial areas. The overriding goal is to make the city livable rather than to expand the economic base for the sake of growth. The model embraces the notion that the city might be better off smaller and that urban neighborhoods can become less dense and remain viable, thereby becoming more desirable.

Like all models, the NVPC approach has to adapt to particular settings for implementation. Planners and policy makers need to attend to the interconnectedness of the city's neighborhoods, the diffusion of deterioration, and the mobility of households in order to target resources, a task that requires political sensitivity. Neighborhood interventions have to coordinate with ongoing redevelopment initiatives in commercial and industrial areas. In addition, the place-based, property orientation of the model has to change to include people-based programs. Overall, implementation has to account for the organizational capacities and political interests of governmental agencies and community-based organizations.

These adjustments suggest a "model" that is less focused yet more engaged with stakeholders. Organizational networks, political considerations, and community-based organizations receive greater attention from planners and policy analysts. The "model" becomes embedded in ongoing private and public initiatives, interagency relations, and local communities. In this way, it is coordinated with redevelopment efforts in the central business district and economic development in industrial areas. What the model loses in purity of intent, it gains in appropriateness, effectiveness, and political support.

At the same time, those implementing the model must resist mission drift and a corresponding erosion of goals. The intent of making life better for those living in distressed neighborhoods in cities experiencing widespread disinvestment must remain paramount. Eliminating blight, improving the environment, enhancing the fiscal health of the local government, and reshaping the public image of the city are merely means to that end.

CHAPTER 11

The Promise of Sustainability Planning for Regenerating Older Industrial Cities

Joseph Schilling and Raksha Vasudevan

Sustainability has become a critical policy and planning goal, with hundreds of cities launching sustainability initiatives to address threats of global climate change, depleted fossil fuels, and water scarcity.[1] As a conceptual framework that seeks balance among environmental, economic, and social values, sustainability offers a "multigenerational vision of community building that is green, profitable and equitable."[2] Translating its broad principles into practice is a complex but promising planning endeavor undertaken in the United States by growing cities confronting urban sprawl such as Seattle, Portland, and jurisdictions in the San Francisco Bay Area.

Sustainability's holistic vision could provide shrinking cities with a planning framework to catalyze their regeneration. These older industrial cities, primarily in the Great Lakes region, have experienced substantial population loss and property abandonment but could play a "distinctive and vital role" in a low-carbon world as they find ways of transforming vacant properties into opportunities for local agriculture, renewable energy, and compact, semirural villages.[3] Neighborhood-scale and citywide greening initiatives could rejuvenate urban ecology and reconfigure the excess built environment that remains after decades of depopulation.[4] Such green infrastructure strategies could strengthen demand for real estate by clustering remaining homes and businesses in sustainable urban designs. Despite decline, many older industrial cities and their metropolitan regions have important economic assets—top-ranked science and engineering universities, skilled manufacturing workforces, and high-tech research and development capacity—that could generate green jobs and sustainable industries.[5]

The planning challenge is devising a sustainability framework that addresses the socioeconomic, environmental, and physical conditions of older industrial, shrinking cities. Such a task will require a new breed of sustainability plan that reflects the different degrees of neighborhood change—those places with substantial levels of blight and abandonment and those transitional neighborhoods with promising assets.

Planners in such distressed cities have few models to follow—they cannot simply transplant the sustainability plan of Portland or even Chicago or Minneapolis. Sustainability plans in growing cities often focus on mitigating the environmental impacts of development while preparing to reduce carbon emissions through green buildings and transit-oriented development strategies.[6] Shrinking older industrial cities, on the other hand, confront problems such as fiscal instability, government incapacity, neighborhood deterioration, poverty, and persistent and severe economic decline, thus making the design and implementation of sustainability policies and programs difficult.

This chapter makes the case for why older industrial cities should incorporate elements of sustainability into plans. We assess whether such plans adequately address the conditions of shrinking cities by evaluating the content from four shrinking city sustainability plans (Buffalo, Cleveland, Philadelphia, and Baltimore). We then offer several ideas for strengthening current planning frameworks, such as adapting regeneration principles and policies from the United Kingdom, so sustainability plans will better integrate socioeconomic and environmental policies.

Defining Sustainability and the Parameters of Sustainable Cities

The United Nations 1987 Brundtland Report, *Our Common Future*, defined sustainable development as meeting the needs of the present without compromising the ability of future generations to meet their own needs.[7] Sustainability is based on natural science principles such as ecological carrying capacity, natural capital, and harmony of natural systems.[8] The foundation of sustainability rests on three principles: (1) *environmental* considerations must be entrenched in economic policy and development decision making; (2) *economic* and development considerations must focus on more than growth while improving the quality of life for residents; and (3) *equity* demands fair distribution and access to economic and environmental benefits that emerge from development and growth.[9]

Sustainability's broad definition leaves much room for debate and interpretation.[10] As a result, planners face a challenge in reconciling sustainability with other planning and policy approaches, such as smart growth, new urbanism, and livability.[11] The concepts of sustainable communities or cities can ground sustainability's broad framework in local practices that address the negative consequences of traditional economic development decisions and sprawl development patterns.[12] The ability of a city to become sustainable, however, depends on the nature and effectiveness of its local government regime.[13] Sustainable cities become the most relevant planning and policy scale because of local government's control over land use decisions. Sustainability policy at the city scale must also acknowledge problems of local government fragmentation as a critical policy barrier in addressing regional ecosystem problems.

The Sustainability Promise of Older Industrial Cities After Population Decline

Older industrial cities with decades of disinvestment, urban sprawl, and extensive property abandonment are prime candidates for a sustainability transformation. Existing carbon footprints of such cities are smaller compared to strong-market cities that have similar populations and acreage. Many such cities could facilitate reduction of carbon emissions and adoption of strategies for a low-carbon economy by adopting sustainability policies, such as converting vacant land and abandoned buildings into green infrastructure banks that sequester carbon and facilitate trading of carbon credits. Smaller older industrial cities have the right scale and size for facilitating renewable energy development by decentralizing the grid and devising new regional and local food distribution systems.[14] Converting surplus buildings, housing, and infrastructure presents an opportunity for reusing and repurposing vacant land and abandoned buildings. For example, the greening of vacant land could assist with stormwater retention, open space, parks, and recreational facilities.

Additionally, older industrial cities can become incubators of green business. The manufacturing legacy of such cities, in combination with the prevalence of vacant and abandoned land, strategically positions them to develop green industries in areas such as building retrofits, smart grids, energy conservation, and renewable energy.[15] Transitioning to a green economy could expand employment in construction and related sectors, increase municipal revenue, and develop a workforce knowledgeable about green industries.[16] For example, Toledo, Ohio, is home to over a dozen solar start-ups and four large solar companies, thanks to partnerships among the city, the University of Toledo, and the local community college.[17]

Finally, integrating sustainability principles into policy and comprehensive plans lays the foundation for ameliorating social inequities. Disinvestment in many neighborhoods, along with histories of inequities based on race and class, exacerbates the effects of poverty on employment, literacy, and public health. Pursuing the social component of sustainability, based on principles of equal opportunity and inclusion, can redress some of these issues.[18] For example, sustainability plans can create programs and policies that support the history and culture of older neighborhoods, buttress the capacity of community-based organizations, strategically deploy federal and state incentives, and develop networks to rebuild wealth in low-income and minority neighborhoods.[19] Civic engagement activities could also create campaigns to address issues such as literacy and improve access to parks, recreation areas, and healthy foods.[20] Training a local green workforce can generate numerous benefits for blue-collar workers.[21]

Infusing sustainability into older industrial, shrinking cities may seem at odds with their long industrial legacy. The major Rust Belt cities of the Midwest and Northeast—Cleveland, Buffalo, Detroit, and Pittsburgh—were America's manufacturing dynamos during the first half of the twentieth century. The health and vitality of these cities depended on the strength of the steel and automotive industries, while the region's rivers, lakes, and soils became the depository for industrial wastes. Given the lack of federal and state environmental regulations and rudimentary recovery systems, environmental disasters such as the burning of Cleveland's Cuyahoga River in 1969 symbolized the Rust Belt's industrial legacy. Subsequently, global shifts in manufacturing locations and technology caused many factories to shut down, leaving behind thousands of shuttered buildings and polluted properties and hundreds of thousands of displaced workers.

Many such cities have pursued traditional strategies to redevelop and revitalize, often relying on the promise of mega projects—such as convention centers, sports stadiums, and waterfront redevelopments—or investing in elaborate business attraction schemes to bring back lost manufacturing jobs.[22] While a few cities, such as Pittsburgh, have leveraged university expertise and other institutional assets to grow emerging economic sectors, these traditional economic development strategies for many older industrial cities do not address their underlying socioeconomic challenges. Instead of pursuing economic development in isolation, older industrial cities with substantial population loss should explore sustainability for repositioning economic and social strengths as part of a low-carbon economy. A handful of such cities have developed sustainability plans that blend socioeconomic with environmental policies. The next sections examine four of these.

Sustainability Planning in Older Industrial Shrinking Cities

In devising a sustainability inventory from twenty-four American cities with sustainability initiatives, Portney concluded, "Perhaps the single most important element in assessing the seriousness of a city's efforts towards achieving sustainable development is the presence of a sustainability plan."[23] Despite the early promise of sustainability planning, few older industrial cities in the United States have launched sustainability initiatives, and fewer have adopted sustainability plans. To understand current sustainability practice in shrinking cities, we first identified cities that had taken two common local government sustainability actions: (1) signing the U.S. Conference of Mayors Climate Protection Agreement to meet the 2012 Kyoto Protocol targets for greenhouse gas emissions; and (2) joining the national association devoted to sustainability and climate change—International Council for Local Environmental Initiatives (ICLEI) Local Governments for Sustainability.[24] Both signal a city's commitment to sustainability as they do not require considerable resources or local legislation. Fewer than 5 percent of the mayors that have made the U.S. Conference of Mayors climate protection pledge came from cities with population loss of 20 percent or greater.[25] Next, we identified which of these cities had lost 20 percent or more population from 1970 to 2010.[26] Of the 564 ICLEI members as of August 2011, roughly 2 percent, 12 cities, had population losses of 20 percent or more between 1970 and 2010. By 2010 only a handful of these older industrial ICLEI cities had taken steps, such as completing a greenhouse gases (GHG) inventory or adopting a climate action plan (CAP), which have become standard practice for ICLEI members.[27]

With few older industrial cities taking formal sustainability actions or making simple sustainability commitments, such cities have fewer sustainability models to emulate. Moreover, the sustainability literature often overlooks programs and projects from the Midwest[28] and instead evaluates the pioneering sustainability plans from the West and Pacific Northwest regions.[29] These leading sustainability plans say little about the issues of chronic vacant properties, continual population and job loss, and high rates of poverty and crime found in older industrial cities. Plus, city officials and even planning directors in shrinking cities may consider sustainability just another environmental program without understanding its interrelationships with economic growth and social equity.[30] Older industrial shrinking cities often lack the planning resources and capacity to tackle extensive sustainability planning endeavors. These cities have dwindling tax revenues and, thus, fewer resources to hire and maintain staff.[31] Flint, Michigan, for instance, lacks a planning department, and Youngstown, Ohio, has only two staff working on traditional planning tasks. With fewer models and less capacity, city officials do not have sufficient opportunities to learn from each other and, thus, have more difficulty in developing and diffusing sustainability plans among similar cities.[32]

Despite this shortage of relevant models and the potential barriers, more closely examining the content of existing sustainability plans among older industrial cities provides insights into current practice and offers suggestions on strengthening future sustainability planning. Thus, our next step was to identify major older industrial shrinking cities with formally adopted sustainability plans.

Only eight of the 12 ICLEI members from shrinking cities (20 percent or more population loss since 1970) have a multidimensional sustainability plan, either as a stand-alone policy plan or as part of a comprehensive land use plan:[33] Akron, Ohio; Baltimore, Maryland; Buffalo, New York;[34] Binghamton, New York; Cleveland, Ohio; New Orleans, Louisiana; Newark, New Jersey; and Philadelphia, Pennsylvania.

Four sustainability plans from this group became candidates for further analysis: Baltimore, Buffalo, Cleveland, and Philadelphia. As major cities (current populations over 250,000), these four exemplify the Rust Belt narrative of older industrial shrinking cities—each has substantial and persistent population losses, driven by suburbanization of jobs and people, racial outmigration, and later deindustrialization. The 2010 census indicates, however, that these cities are now on different trajectories, with Philadelphia

Table 11.1. City Demographic and Housing Characteristics

	Baltimore	Philadelphia	Cleveland	Buffalo
Total population, 2010	620,961	1,526,006	396,815	261,310
Percent population change, 2000–2010	−4.6	0.6	−17.1	−10.7
Total housing units, 2010	296,685	670,171	207,536	133,444
Percent vacant units	15.8	10.5	19.3	15.7
"Other" vacant as percent of vacant units	48.7	41.1	45.5	53.6
Median household income, 2009	$38,772	$37,045	$24,687	$29,285
Poverty rates, 2009 (percent)	21.0	25.0	35.0	28.8
Geographic size (square miles)	81	134	77	40

Sources: U.S. Census Bureau, 2010 Demographic Profiles, http://2010.census.gov/2010census /data/; U.S. Census Bureau, "Median Household Income in the Past 12 Months" and "Poverty Status in the Past 12 Months by Sex by Age," American Community Survey 2009 1–Year Estimates, Tables B19013, B17001; U.S. Census Bureau, State and County Quick Facts, http://quickfacts.census.gov/qfd/index.html.

gaining population and Baltimore's decline slowing since 2000, while Cleveland and Buffalo have lost more population, due in part to weaker regional economies, predatory lending, and the national foreclosure crisis (see Table 11.1). As part of the mid-Atlantic region that developed earlier than the Midwest, Baltimore and Philadelphia have especially compact urban form with row houses and narrow streets. Buffalo and Cleveland have wider streets and wooden, single-family homes that housed an influx of eastern European immigrants. The four city councils or plan commissions adopted these four sustainability plans from 2006 through 2009. Baltimore and Philadelphia adopted stand-alone policy plans; Buffalo and Cleveland have sustainability comprehensive plans.

Sustainability Policy Planning Profiles

Baltimore and Philadelphia's sustainability planning began with the 2007 adoption of their climate action plans. After their 2008 elections, Mayor Sheila Dixon (Baltimore) and Mayor Michael Nutter (Philadelphia) launched citywide initiatives to design and adopt sustainability policy plans. Mayors

Dixon and Nutter created offices of sustainability to develop the new plans and manage the process. Baltimore and Philadelphia also brought together sustainability advisory groups (the Sustainability Commission in Baltimore and Sustainability Advisory Board in Philadelphia) composed of civic, business, nonprofit, and neighborhood leaders to offer guidance and engage residents in the planning process. Their respective city councils formally adopted the resulting sustainability policy plans in 2009.[35]

Baltimore and Philadelphia's policy plans identify sustainability principles and themes supported by policy goals, measurable targets, and, in the case of Baltimore's plan, specific policy and programmatic strategies. With the vision of Baltimore as a "clean, healthy, efficient, green, mobile, aware, and invested community," the sustainability plan centers on seven sustainability principles and themes that emerged from the planning process (see Table 11.2). Twenty-nine policy goals support the seven themes by addressing issues, such as the transformation of vacant lots into assets, the creation of green jobs for city residents, and the expansion of the city's local food system. Finally, the plan lists 132 specific program and policy strategies to help achieve the policy goals. These program descriptions include timeframes, potential funding, and public and private organizations that might assist with implementation. Philadelphia's plan frames sustainability through five "lenses": energy; environment; equity; economy; and engagement; and fifteen total targets. Each of the five sustainability themes contains an overarching policy goal along with a few measurable targets set for 2015. Similar to but more general than Baltimore's plan, each target includes a laundry list of proposed programs and initiatives that could help the city reach its short-term targets and longer-range goals.

The offices of sustainability for Baltimore and Philadelphia now manage the implementation of their sustainability plans. Baltimore's Office of Sustainability oversees and coordinates sustainability programs, integrates sustainability practices into city operations, and engages in partnerships with other city offices. The office also develops educational activities for citizens, including environmental programs for youth. Baltimore's Department of Planning houses its sustainability office, while Philadelphia's Office of Sustainability reports to the mayor and his chief executive officer.[36] Philadelphia's office convenes, coordinates, and develops an array of partnerships within and outside City Hall along with educating the public about the long-term benefits of sustainability.[37] Additionally, each office monitors, measures, and publishes an annual report on the cities' progress toward the sustainability goals and targets.

Table 11.2. Sustainability Policy Plan Frameworks for Baltimore and Philadelphia

Sustainability policy plan	Sustainability principles/ themes	Sustainability policy goals/ targets	Sustainability strategies, programs, actions
The Baltimore Sustainability Plan	Cleanliness	3 goals	13 strategies
	Pollution prevention	5 goals	21 strategies
	Resource conservation	4 goals	21 strategies
	Greening	4 goals	21 strategies
	Transportation	5 goals	22 strategies
	Education and awareness	4 goals	17 strategies
	Green economy	4 goals	17 strategies
Greenworks Philadelphia	**Energy** Reduce vulnerability to rising energy prices	4 targets	39 strategies 10 actions
	Environment Reduce the city's environmental footprint	3 targets	30 strategies 24 actions
	Equity Increase equitable access to healthy neighborhoods	4 targets	38 strategies 14 actions
	Economy Create competitive advantage from sustainability	3 targets	30 strategies
	Engagement Unite as a city to build a sustainable future	1 target	5 strategies

Sources: City of Baltimore Office of Sustainability, *The Baltimore Sustainability Plan*, April 2009, http://www.dooconsulting.net/pdf/ref_bar/about/051509_BCS-001SustainabilityReport .pdf; City of Philadelphia Mayor's Office of Sustainability, *Greenworks Philadelphia*, 2009, http://www.phila.gov/green/greenworks/PDFs/GreenworksPlan002.pdf, 82–89.

Sustainability Comprehensive Plan Profiles

Cleveland's and Buffalo's plans integrate sustainability principles and elements into their most recent comprehensive plans as a means to address the particular challenges of older industrial cities. By using the comprehensive plan as the vehicle for a sustainability plan, these cities can avail themselves of the state and local legal stature afforded comprehensive plans in their respective states.[38] As a strategy to reinvent the city, the *Connecting Cleveland 2020 Citywide Plan* creates a promising vision of Cleveland as "a city of choice," where everyone will have access to a better quality of life. Buffalo's *Queen City in the 21st Century* uses a regional lens as the basis for its vision and structure. That plan creates an adaptable guide that builds on smart growth and sustainability principles to reestablish Buffalo as the center of the region (Table 11.3).

Both plans follow the traditional framework for comprehensive plans. *Connecting Cleveland* consists of eleven elements, each with a primary goal and several policy actions for implementation, and Buffalo's *Queen City* plan relies on seven guiding policies. While both plans use sustainability as a theme, only Cleveland's plan elevates sustainability to a stand-alone element with 14 specific policy actions.[39] Cleveland and Buffalo's comprehensive plans also rely on the strength of smaller neighborhood plans and initiatives. Building on the work of the Good Neighbors Planning Alliance, Buffalo's plan integrates existing plans, such as the downtown action plan (*Queen City Hub*), the Waterfront Revitalization Program, and the Olmsted Park Restoration and Management Plan. Buffalo's *Queen City* plan won the 2009 Congress for New Urbanism Charter Planning Award for its focus on urban design and neighborhoods.[40] Similarly, Cleveland's 36 neighborhood-level plans outline the land use details and serve as the building blocks for *Connecting Cleveland*.

Cleveland's City Planning Commission, responsible for developing and adopting planning policy, oversees the plan along with the Mayor's Office of Sustainability and Planning Department. Between 2009 and 2011, the commission implemented several sustainability policies, such as adopting new zoning provisions that promote urban agriculture. Now a member of Mayor Frank Jackson's cabinet, the sustainability office director focuses on initiatives that reduce the ecological footprint of city operations and save the city money. The staff advises departments on energy efficiency, green buildings, recycling, and green procurement and examines new capital projects for greening opportunities. For Buffalo, the Office of Strategic Planning oversees implementation of its comprehensive plan through the management of the Capital Improvement Program and Development Program.[41]

Comparative Plan Analysis

Together these plans offer a snapshot of the current frameworks of sustainability plans in older industrial cities. Several passages from the plans

Table 11.3. *Connecting Cleveland 2020 Citywide Plan*: Sustainability Element

Policy action	Description
Sustainable development patterns	High-density, mixed-use districts that promote walking, bicycling, and public transit
Sustainable neighborhoods	"Full life-cycle neighborhoods" that provide housing and services for all residents
Sustainable economy	Economic development, job training, and education meet national trends
Sustainable development practices	Use land in a manner that preserves/enhances open lands and protects natural habitats
High-performance/green building	Amend building and zoning codes and add financial incentives to encourage high-performance "green building" that conserves resources
Nonmotorized travel	Design and develop safe routes for walking and biking for all residents
Motorized travel	Upgrade and replace government and corporate fleets with more fuel-efficient and cleaner burning vehicles
Mass transit	Increase use of mass transit
Energy conservation	Reduce energy and water use in city facilities and fleets and encourage the same by the rest of the city
Renewable energy	Promote solar, wind, geothermal, and other renewable energy sources
Brownfield remediation	Clean and promote brownfield reuse through regulatory action and increased funding
Recycling and waste management	Reduce waste disposal through recycling programs and encourage consumers to be less wasteful
Water quality	Improve regional water quality by managing stormwater runoff, enforcing emission controls, and restoring urban water bodies
Air quality	Improve regional air quality by enforcing emission control, increasing alternative energy production, and promoting use of mass transit, nonmotorized travel, and cleaner-powered vehicles

Source: City of Cleveland City Planning Commission, *Connecting Cleveland 2020 Citywide Plan*, 2010, http://planning.city.cleveland.oh.us/cwp/contents.html.

describe sustainability policies and programs that could apply to any city, while other sections reflect the realities of older industrial shrinking cities. Therefore, a thorough review of the plans' content can offer insights for designing sustainability plans for cities facing similar conditions.

Berke and Godschalk's meta-analysis of 16 plan quality studies provides the basis for analyzing the four plans.[42] Berke and Godschalk's plan content criteria (seven internal and three external characteristics) operate as a checklist for a comprehensive plan content analysis (see Table 11.4). To assess the content of sustainability plans, we revise and reorganize their internal criteria into three groups: (1) green visions and sustainability goals and principles; (2) sustainability policies; and (3) plan integration, implementation, and indicators.

Green Visions and Sustainability Goals and Principles

Vision is a crucial component that enables plans to convey the city's needs, assets, trends, and future directions. A good planning vision identifies what residents, civic leaders, business owners, and elected officials want the city to become and supports that vision with data, policies, and strategies. Principles and goals that reflect public values and statements of future conditions underlie the vision.[43]

All four plans have strong vision statements that highlight different sustainability principles to support their planning elements. As comprehensive plans, though, Buffalo's and Cleveland's plans more closely follow Berke and Godschalk's list of internal characteristics than do Baltimore's and Philadelphia's. Buffalo's plan further offers four alternative development and growth scenarios and includes overarching passages that link sustainability with restoring the physical environment and reclaiming industrial land while improving the delivery of municipal services. The plan offers "a vision of a green, prosperous and revitalized city and a goal of reversing the long term decline in population and employment" that will be "driven by fundamental principles of sustainability, smart growth and the dual commitments to 'fix the basics' and 'build on assets.'"[44] Cleveland's plan envisions a city that is a leader in biomedical technology and the arts, with safe, healthy, and diverse neighborhoods.

The policy plans for Baltimore and Philadelphia offer stronger sustainability analysis and details, not only in the opening preambles and

Table 11.4. Meta Analysis of Plan Content

	Plan characteristics
Internal	(1) Issue identification and vision—describe and assess community needs, assets, trends, impacts along with a vision of what the community wants to be; (2) Goals—expressions of future land uses, development patterns, and community values; (3) Fact base—analysis of data covering a wide range of current conditions (population, existing land supply, future land demands, capacity, natural resources) and clear maps and tables; (4) Policies—specific strategies and actions to guide land use decisions to achieve plans' goals; (5) Implementation—commitments to carry out policy-driven actions, with timelines, sources of funding, and list of responsible organization; (6) Monitoring and evaluation—provisions for tracking change in community conditions with measureable goals/indicators, timetable for updating plan, and organizations responsible for monitoring; (7) Internal consistency—the issues, vision, goals, polices, and implementation are mutually reinforcing.
External	(1) Organization and presentation—provisions that enhance understanding to a wide range of audiences, such as executive summary, clear visuals, and supporting documents. (2) Interorganizational coordination—integration with other places or policies of public and private entities, such as vertical coordination with federal state and regional parties and horizontal coordination with plans and polices of other local parties within and outside the local jurisdiction. (3) Compliance—consistent with state planning requirements and mandates

Source: Philip Berke and David Godschalk, "Searching for the Good Plan," *Journal of Planning Literature* 23, 3 (2009): 227–40.

summaries but also under planning elements such as "engagement and education." *Greenworks Philadelphia* offers a vision to make "Philadelphia the greenest city in America."[45] Mayor Nutter's goal is to reposition and repurpose Philadelphia in response to rising energy prices, climate change, and an emerging green economy that could increase the value of its assets. Philadelphia's sustainability policy goals and targets differ from the other cities' in assuming that Philadelphia will gain 75,000 new residents by 2015. While it projects less population growth, Baltimore's vision infuses sustainability throughout the city's decision making and community engagement processes, so the city can become a "clean, healthy, efficient, green, mobile, aware, and invested community."[46] Like Philadelphia, Baltimore also frames its plan with citywide issues such as economic development through green jobs and businesses, as well as global issues such as climate change.

Sustainability Policies

Sustainability plans contain elements covering a range of sustainability policies on climate change, renewable energy, and green buildings. Plan content scholars explain that plans, as formal actions of local legislative and/or administrative bodies, are important products of the policy-making process and, thus, appropriate for assessing their symbolic content as "communicative policy acts."[47] Therefore, sustainability plans have become essential policy documents for scholars to analyze in assessing local government commitments to sustainability.[48] The current challenge for planners and plan content scholars is organizing the expanding field of sustainability policies into a planning framework with a manageable number of elements and categories. The following planning framework, based on a synthesis of more than 25 sustainability policy and comprehensive plans, organizes and classifies these green policies according to sustainability's three policy pillars: (1) environmental sustainability; (2) business and economic sustainability; and (3) social and civic sustainability. The next sections assess the range of sustainability policies in the four cities' plans, the plans' organizational framework, and the ways these policies address the challenges of older industrial cities.

ENVIRONMENTAL SUSTAINABILITY

The heart of any sustainability plan involves a discussion of environmental policies and programs. Policy goals and specific actions and strategies fall into two general categories of environmental policy—classic or contemporary.

- *Classic environmental policies* address solid and hazardous waste, recycling, water and air quality, storm water management, resource conservation, open space, habitat protection, and brownfields redevelopment. These environmental policies have become standard sustainability elements for comprehensive plans and sustainability policy plans.

- *Contemporary environmental policies* focus on newer sustainability challenges such as climate change, reduction of greenhouse gases, green buildings, renewable energy, green jobs and green infrastructure. These contemporary policies distinguish newer sustainability policy plans from other plans.

Environmental policy elements dominate the content for three of the four sustainability plans. The sustainability comprehensive plans of Buffalo and Cleveland weave comprehensive plan elements, such as transportation, housing, land use, and environment, with classic and contemporary environmental sustainability policies and actions. Cleveland more holistically blends the classic and contemporary environmental policies throughout the entire plan. For example, its housing element lists green building policies (defined as "new and renovated housing through code changes and financial incentives"[49]), and the transportation element discusses strategies for reducing greenhouse gases by developing biking and walking networks and moving the city away from car dependence. Meanwhile, Buffalo's plan does not have a comprehensive and cohesive environmental policy element but instead lists a few narrow environmental policies, such as brownfields cleanup and environmental management; thus, the plan fails to integrate environmental policies throughout—a critical strategy for creating effective sustainability plans.

With respect to the sustainability policy plans, Baltimore's environmental policy goals (pollution prevention, cleanliness, resource conversion, and urban greening) include a blend of classic and contemporary policies with support from more than 60 policy actions and strategies, such as strengthening the enforcement of dumping and litter codes, ensuring every household has a municipal trash can, improving sanitation codes, and creating a community land trust to maintain vacant lots.[50] Philadelphia's plan mentions classic environmental policy actions, but the overarching theme—to reduce the city's environmental footprint—focuses attention on contemporary policies, such as promoting energy conservation and renewable energy, reducing greenhouse gases, and improving green infrastructure. For example, the plan recommends that green infrastructure—trees, vegetation, and soil—

become the city's preferred method of managing storm water. The plan envisions that by 2015, 3,200 acres of green space and pervious surfaces will become areas for stormwater management while providing residents with parks, playgrounds, trees, and recreation areas.[51]

BUSINESS AND ECONOMIC SUSTAINABILITY

For any city to reach its sustainability potential, its plan should establish strong policies and programs around a green economy—jobs and businesses that protect and restore the environment by focusing on human capital and social investment and reducing consumption of natural resources.[52] A green economy accommodates a wide range of jobs and skills and provides workforce development opportunities for residents. Therefore, the plan should include a menu of sustainability policies for incubating regional and local green businesses. Energy efficiency initiatives may offer a first wave of jobs, many of which may be blue-collar, middle-skill occupations in the building, construction, and manufacturing industries.[53] For older industrial cities, a green business and economic development element offers opportunities for addressing chronic problems of high unemployment, job loss, and dwindling industrial tax base.

The four policy and comprehensive plans use a variety of strategies to address economic restructuring for their cities. Buffalo's comprehensive plan describes the creation of "strategic investment corridors" that would appeal to future investors because of targeted transportation and environmental (brownfields remediation, natural environment enhancement) improvements in those areas. Similarly, Cleveland's plan acknowledges the city's manufacturing history and natural resources as assets to catalyze economic development, specifically in brownfields remediation and "green building" construction.

By focusing economic development on the emerging green economy, Baltimore's policy plan seeks to establish the city as a regional center for green business through strategies such as encouraging construction companies to use "green" building practices; leveraging the city's natural amenities to maintain and attract businesses, including universities and medical centers; and creating financing strategies that would help attract and support green businesses. By rebranding Philadelphia as a city that has "gone green," its policy plan includes marketing and promotion strategies to attract jobs and business growth from the emerging green economy. Other Philadelphia strategies include creating a regional green jobs training center; improving transportation infrastructure, so that residents have access to more jobs; and tapping into the renewable energy sector and related federal investments.

SOCIAL AND CIVIC SUSTAINABILITY

Social sustainability remains the most elusive principle to define, promote, and achieve. Vancouver, British Columbia, offers a comprehensive definition of social sustainability, with a focus on improving access to basic human need and city amenities, building civic capacity, and expanding opportunities for meaningful public participation and civic engagement.[54] Sustainability plans should elevate social and civic sustainability as a separate element with policies and programs to address the needs and interests of residents and neighborhoods.

While each of the four sustainability plans contains a few programs and policies that address social issues, environmental and economic development strategies dominate. Cleveland's comprehensive plan emphasizes developing safe routes for walking and bicycling accessible to all residents, as well as creating "full life-cycle" neighborhoods that would provide residents with housing, a healthful environment, and convenient access to jobs, retail, and recreation. Buffalo's plan provides a strong context of social issues, specifically around race and ethnicity, that the city faces. The plan mentions social equity as an important decision making factor moving forward but provides few specific policy or programmatic recommendations to facilitate this change.

In Philadelphia's policy plan, many of the "equity" strategies tie more intimately to environmental policy. The only social strategy that indirectly benefits all residents is increasing local food access for over 75 percent of residents. With perhaps the strongest equity policies among the four plans, Baltimore's links social issues with specific social outcomes, such as improving public education and literacy by transforming city schools into "green schools" and improving health by eliminating litter and creating public health campaigns. Even in Baltimore's plan, however, social sustainability elements take backstage to environmental and economic development policies.

Integration, Implementation, and Indicators

A good sustainability plan must do more than restate laudable sustainability goals and organize long lists of sustainability policies; it must also have a framework that connects its sections and elements with metrics for measuring progress toward sustainability. Two policy plans (Philadelphia and Baltimore) offer specific targets and sustainability indicators for monitoring. Baltimore's section on plan accountability sets time frames, identifies resources, and outlines roles for city leaders and citizens. Portney's research found that cities with strong sustainability programs tend to have robust sustainability indicators and implementation schemes that coordinate sustainability activities across numerous government agencies, nonprofits, and business organizations.[55] As comprehensive plans, Buffalo and Cleveland's documents set goals and policies but do not list specific targets and measurements.

Tailoring Sustainability Planning for Shrinking Cities

The comparison of the four sustainability plans provides an understanding of sustainability planning practice in older industrial shrinking cities. This section offers suggestions for improving the design and diffusion of such sustainability plans. This section discusses (1) type of plan, (2) scale, and (3) linkages among policy elements.

Planners have four types of planning approaches to consider. They could (1) create a new, comprehensive plan that infuses sustainability principles and policies throughout—the Cleveland approach; (2) create a new, standalone sustainability policy plan—the Philadelphia and Baltimore approaches; (3) devise a coordinating planning and policy framework that aligns existing plans with sustainability and smart growth principles and policies—the Buffalo approach; or (4) amend existing plans, such as the city's comprehensive land use plan, by adopting a sustainability element or section.

Adopting the Cleveland approach—infusing sustainability throughout a new comprehensive plan—can strengthen plan coordination and collaboration across departments through vertical and horizontal planning integration. Plus, a sustainability comprehensive plan in states with stronger comprehensive planning laws would make the plan more enforceable and could persuade more businesses, property owners, and residents to take sustainability seriously.[56] With dwindling revenues and tight budgets, however, a full-scale comprehensive plan rewrite may not be feasible unless the city receives outside resources.

For that reason, sustainability policy plans perhaps offer a good starting point for older industrial cities wanting to elevate their sustainability initiatives and programs. State comprehensive planning law requirements do not apply to strategic policy plans, so city planners might have more flexibility with the policy plan content and the process. For example, Baltimore and Philadelphia spent less than 12 months to convene advisory groups, conduct public outreach, and design and adopt sustainability policy plans. Sustainability policy plans, composed of principles, goals, actions, often set more specific sustainability targets and offer more details on indicators and tracking overall plan performance. Later, city officials could also integrate the sustainability policy plan into the comprehensive plan, as Baltimore did in 2009.

Buffalo's plan offers yet a different approach. As a comprehensive plan, it adopts sustainability as one of its principles, but it does not contain a sustainability element, nor does it set forth a structure for organizing sustainability policies and programs. Instead, Buffalo's comprehensive plan acts as a coordinating framework for place-based development plans (e.g., the waterfront, Olmsted parks, and downtown).

Experimentation with all these different planning types can aid cities in adjusting the scale, scope, and elements to respond more effectively to local conditions, political dynamics, geographies, and markets.[57] The type of plan may seem less important than ensuring that city officials develop principles and policies that address socioeconomic challenges. The complex challenges of strengthening weak real estate markets, revitalizing blighted neighborhoods, and regaining the trust and respect of residents will take time to achieve; thus, putting a plan in place becomes essential for making decisions as planners and policy makers seek the right sustainability policy direction.

The scale of the plan is another aspect for planners and policy makers to consider. A regional framework would match the realities of regional ecosystems and markets that extend beyond the jurisdiction of one local government. Older industrial shrinking cities should ensure that their local sustainability plans coordinate with relevant regional plans and establish specific policy linkages.

Insights from the four plans also highlight the need to strengthen the linkages across the sustainability planning elements (environment, business, and social/civic), so the policies respond to the specific physical, political, fiscal, and socioeconomic challenges confronting older industrial cities. Each plan contains policies and passages that mention challenges such as vacant properties, blight, poverty, joblessness and low job skills; but the plans do not adequately link jobs with greening of vacant lots or incubation of green businesses with workforce training, literacy skills, and school reform. With respect to social equity, only Philadelphia has a stand-alone social-equity principle, but the policy actions to increase access to healthy neighborhoods focus on parks and local food and do not include business sustainability or other social equity policies, such as good schools and health care access.

Infusing Principles of Urban Regeneration

As the four plans demonstrate, planners and policy makers have not yet fully addressed or integrated social and civic sustainability policies with environmental and economic sustainability. City officials could better address socioeconomic conditions by infusing sustainability plans with principles and policies of "urban regeneration." "Urban regeneration is a comprehensive and integrated vision and action to address urban problems through a lasting improvement in the economic, physical, social, and environmental conditions in an area."[58] Adapting urban regeneration principles might strengthen sustainability plans in older industrial cities and help facilitate the stabilization and eventual revitalization of distressed neighborhoods. Urban regeneration emphasizes place-based approaches that link the physical transformation of distressed cities and neighborhoods with the social transformation of their residents.[59]

Urban regeneration encompasses a wide range of community and economic development policies and issues (such as housing, workforce training, education, and business development) at various scales—the region, the city, the neighborhood, and individual sites. Urban-regeneration policy principles from the United Kingdom seem most relevant for American shrinking cities, given similar histories and patterns of industrial decline.[60] In the 1990s, the British government adopted a portfolio of national regeneration initiatives that recalibrated urban policy by integrating physical, social, and economic strategies in placed-based, locally driven programs.[61] The UK urban regeneration policies and programs offer ideas for reshaping regional and local sustainability planning frameworks for America's older industrial cities:[62]

- *Coordinating policy across agencies*—facilitating coordination of housing, employment, transportation, education, environmental management, planning, health, and community development policies and programs at the regional and local levels.

- *Regenerating people as well as places*—connecting social policies that address problems facing low- to moderate-income residents with economic and community development policies that focus on revitalizing the physical, built environment.
- *Creating partnerships and strategic planning processes*—formulating partnerships across all levels of government and across all sectors (non-profit, business, civic, and philanthropic).
- *Building capacity*—creating institutional capacity in the public sector, especially local government leadership and management, to coordinate partnerships with regional and local leaders.
- *Engaging the community*—involving citizens in all aspects of local regeneration initiatives so that individuals and institutions have ownership of the planning process and the outcomes.

Local policy makers and planners might consider infusing some regeneration strategies into their sustainability plans or creating a separate regeneration element. In either case, city officials should articulate a set of urban regeneration principles and goals supported by general strategies and specific policies and programs. Based on recent literature on shrinking cities and vacant property reclamation,[63] we suggest two priority regeneration strategies that could expand and enhance the sustainability planning frameworks for older industrial cities: (1) physical transformation of vacant properties and (2) neighborhood transformation for social equity.

Physical Transformation of Vacant Properties

A priority for many older industrial cities' governments is addressing physical blight. Such cities need an array of vacant property reclamation policies. Common vacant property reclamation strategies include code enforcement, housing rehabilitation, land banking, community land trusts, and neighborhood-scale plans for urban greening and sustainable reuse. The most disinvested areas—those with substantial losses of population—will likely require reconfiguring and repurposing of public infrastructure and unused land. Many vacant lots may become gardens, urban farms, conservation areas, pocket parks, and trails. Therefore, regeneration elements should establish principles and processes for repurposing vacant and abandoned properties.

Like other sections of sustainability plans, the regeneration elements should identify policies and strategies for achieving physical changes, such as targeted demolition, deconstruction, rehabilitation, and land banking. The four cities' sustainability plans have some regeneration principles and policies, such as reusing vacant properties for urban agriculture (Baltimore and Philadelphia) and recognizing the importance of land assembly and the role of land banks (Cleveland).

City officials face difficulties in designing and implementing strategies that would reconfigure the city's physical footprint, since most of these cities have more land and buildings than they need to accommodate population and businesses. Devising a neighborhood or city plan can involve reducing municipal services, repurposing land as green space, and possibly relocating remaining residents. These approaches are fraught with political risk and racial tension, but they also provide opportunities for sustainable urban design to help residents and others envision future urban forms.[64]

Any regeneration element could identify locations to increase density and infill development and other locations to provide green infrastructure. Older industrial cities have the opportunity to become more sustainable through a smaller, compact development pattern that might allow more efficient delivery of city services, encourage public transportation, and provide opportunities for mixed-income housing. For instance, vacant land near parks could perhaps allow cities to enhance and expand parks and provide a network of recreational opportunities for walking and biking, thus offering health benefits for residents. Vacant land can also offer opportunities to manage storm water, increase biodiversity, restore water quality and soils, and improve air quality.

Neighborhood Transformation for Social Equity

Another hallmark of urban regeneration is a focus on neighborhood cohesion, public health and socioeconomic problems, such as poverty, substance abuse, homelessness, domestic violence, poor schools, and crime. Elements in most sustainability plans do not cover such a wide range of social or health issues, although the social conditions within many older industrial city neighborhoods demand stronger coordination and integration of these social policies with the policies that facilitate economic and environmental sustainability.

The four cities' sustainability plans still frame social and community issues predominately through the environmental policy lens. For example, when Baltimore's plan discusses schools, it suggests greening the school buildings and grounds and engaging the students as sustainability ambassadors. However, the plan does not connect the city's low graduation rates and high dropout rates to potential sustainability strategies.

Sustainability plans should establish stronger ways for environmental policies to offer opportunities for social and economic transformation. With high rates of unemployment and poverty and low educational attainment in many declining neighborhoods, a shrinking city's business and economic sustainability element should connect job training resources with entrepreneur capacity building and green venture capital. Shrinking cities can retool regional and local manufacturing strengths to encourage green industries in energy efficiency, renewable energy, and weatherization. Such green economic policies and programs could further target those resources to distressed neighborhoods.

In the UK regeneration plans include policies and programs that address social issues. For example, the East Manchester regeneration plan includes strategies that improve the learning environment of schools, expand parent involvement, and counsel families on subjects such as education, substance abuse, or parenting skills.[65] Taking such a holistic approach may seem difficult in the United States, as varied state agencies and local entities (for example, school districts and counties) have jurisdiction over these issues, such as education, social services, and public health. However, city officials should enhance the regenerative focus of their sustainability plans by making explicit connections to the plans and strategies of state agencies and local entities, such as school districts, community colleges, county social service providers, and nonprofits.

Conclusion

This analysis of sustainability plans suggests the need for flexible planning frameworks that can guide different types of sustainability plans and the growing number and variations of sustainability policies. Older industrial shrinking cities demand a more holistic planning framework that can simultaneously transform place, empower people, and rebuild institutions. By infusing urban regeneration principles and strategies, these new sustainability plans could help align environmental strategies that transform the physical environment (reclaim vacant properties, reconfigure neighborhoods, and promote sustainable reuse) with socioeconomic policies (workforce development, school reform, green businesses) that provide residents with greater economic opportunities and address the health, education, and income disparities in many older industrial cities. All these planning processes must engage residents in an honest dialogue to ensure the right mix of policy interventions and residents' support.

Sustainability offers an overarching framework for integrating a cross-section of policies and programs that can empower local policy makers, planners, and residents with effective strategies to reconcile their industrial past with the promise of a more sustainable future. By designing, adopting, and implementing sustainability plans with regeneration elements, older industrial cities could become models of the new low-carbon, green economy.

CHAPTER 12

Rightsizing Shrinking Cities: The Urban Design Dimension

Brent D. Ryan

Recently urban policy makers have begun to make "rightsizing" a watchword for the perceived mismatch between shrinking city populations, physical and infrastructural plants, and budgets. Built for a population in some cases over twice that currently within the city limits, shrinking cities now have an unmanageably large array of streets, utilities, public buildings, parks, and housing. "Rightsizing" refers to the yet-unproved process of bringing cities down to a "right" size, meaning a size proportionate to city government's ability to pay for itself. Rightsizing has thus far come to little in shrinking cities. In the United States, decades of optimistic master plans had little or no effect in reducing rates of population loss in deindustrializing cities such as Cleveland, Baltimore, or Philadelphia, all of which lost 25 to 57 percent of their populations between 1950 and 2010. Even in New Orleans, a city that had good reasons to make deliberate decisions about where residents and others should not rebuild after Hurricane Katrina, political fears and widespread citizen opposition stymied rightsizing decisions.[1] Just as suburban developers resent planners' proclaiming that they may not develop a parcel of farmland, residents of New Orleans resented that planners might transform their property or even their neighborhood into swampland.

On the surface, then, rightsizing appears difficult if not impossible for shrinking cities in the United States. The term also remains vague, as neither scholars nor practitioners have defined it exactly. What physical form and size should the city take after abandonment? What decisions should city officials make concerning which aspects of the city should survive and who should live where? How much would rightsizing cost, and who would pay? Does an ultimate vision of the city guide rightsizing, or will policy makers follow immediate imperatives?

This chapter argues that scholars and policy makers should develop an urban design-based vision, centered on a projection of the city's future built environment, to guide rightsizing. Though many shrinking cities began as industrial centers designed with monotonous speculative grids,[2] population decline and housing loss today present designers and planners with an opportunity to shape a better physical environment in concert with these cities' economic and social needs. Given that many view the visual landscape of shrinking cities as their most striking and disturbing feature,[3] urban design seems an obvious means by which planners and designers might reshape these cities after decline and explore new forms of the ideal urban neighborhood and the ideal city.

As abandonment of buildings and properties characterizes shrinking cities, an urban-design strategy for these places must contend with abandonment before all else.[4] Abandonment in shrinking cities is problematic at the scale of a single building or property, the city block, neighborhood, and city as a whole, causing different problems at different scales. This section considers these problems before describing city and neighborhood urban design strategies that might help resolve the problems of abandonment.[5]

The Physical Consequences of Abandonment

In a shrinking city, abandoned structures and lots are problems, and confronting the abandonment of individual structures often demands a substantial amount of policy maker attention. In the first decade of the 2000s, citywide demolition programs such as Philadelphia's Neighborhood Transformation Initiative and Buffalo's "5 in 5" program (5,000 housing units demolished in five years) act to clear derelict structures but use only individual dwelling criteria (structure condition) as a means of action.[6] In the absence of spatial planning for shrinking neighborhoods and cities, city officials may assess abandonment at a larger scale only when a development proposal is imminent.

Abandonment in shrinking cities is just as destructive as the policy-directed neighborhood demolition of the 1950s excoriated by Jacobs and other critics of urban renewal,[7] but it is harder for policy makers to influence because it occurs on an undirected, piecemeal basis as owners decide whether to walk away from their property. Understanding abandonment's piecemeal nature provides the basis for understanding the urban design problems these places face.

Because decline is episodic and scattered rather than neat and organized, a resident in a deteriorating neighborhood may have only partial information about when and if an adjoining property will become abandoned. Episodic abandonment confronts individual residents with a pressing problem: since the status and condition of properties adjoining a resident's house can shift, her home is vulnerable to losing value. Where owners abandon property piecemeal, blocks become unstable; once abandonment has progressed, the majority of houses will adjoin an empty house or lot. As abandonment continues, the neighborhood loses the collective benefit of more concentrated housing, and each resident's or landlord's incentive to keep investing in his or her property decreases.

As abandonment progresses, individual lots become vacant in a generally scattered fashion, but an aerial survey of a place such as Flint, Michigan, indicates that remaining houses sometimes cluster and sometimes do not. Above 50 percent vacancy, blocks assume a pattern of desolation that becomes more apparent as this percentage increases. At around 70 or 80 percent vacancy, remaining houses become islands in a sea of green. This pattern is most apparent at a large scale in places such as Detroit's east side or the northern half of St. Louis.

A scattered pattern of property abandonment with interspersed houses persists even at high levels of vacancy. In Buffalo, for example, except in blocks emptied by purposeful public clearance or through demolition of large, single-lot industrial buildings, some housing persists. At the scale of five to eight blocks, no cluster of blocks in Buffalo was more than 71 percent vacant as of 2010.[8] The persistence of inhabited housing even in mostly vacant areas helped defeat New Orleans's nascent rightsizing proposals of 2006 and also confronted efforts in Detroit in 2010.[9] Even in a 90 percent vacant area, one resident's wishing to remain in her home requires officials to condemn the property if they wish to make an entire block available for redevelopment and complicates their efforts to withdraw city services.

At a larger scale, piecemeal, house-by-house abandonment leads to patchiness, where large areas of the city may have varying levels of vacancy, while other areas have few vacancies or retain all their housing. In Buffalo, 50 percent of the city's census block groups were at least 10 percent vacant, and about 20 percent of those block groups (about 10 percent of Buffalo's census block groups total) were over 50 percent vacant in 2010.[10] Vacancy ebbed and flowed across space in a pattern that was never neat, always irregular, always shifting, and always interrupted by remaining structures. The presence of other vacant areas, stable or desirable areas of the city, historic industrial or low-income concentrations, and ethnic and racial patterns influenced vacancy patterns in Buffalo, but this relationship was not exact. Over time, piecemeal patches of abandonment grew, spreading from high-vacancy areas into some adjoining lower-vacancy areas.[11] The shift from an undifferentiated urban pattern to patchwork abandonment is evident in schematic form in Figures 12.1 and 12.2 and at a smaller scale in Figures 12.5 and 12.6.

Reconnecting Urban Design with Social Policy

Any move toward an urban design strategy for rightsizing shrinking cities will be difficult. Designers will not find a rightsizing vision in past ideals of city form such as garden or radiant cities, nor in contemporary ideals such as neotraditionalism, "smart growth," or landscape urbanism.[12] These ideals have little relationship to the novel physical condition of shrinking cities. Another challenge lies in the need for an urban design-based rightsizing strategy to reconcile differences between socially oriented planning and urban design. While theorists have argued that urban design must necessarily consider political, economic, and social function,[13] integration of these disparate elements within the field has proven problematic.

In planning, beginning with urban policy initiatives in the 1960s such as conservation, community renewal requirements, and the Model Cities program, and conceptually backed by Davidoff's advocacy strategy,[14] academics shifted toward grounding in social science research, while traditional practitioners continued to address land use and urban redevelopment. The profession distanced itself from design.[15] At the same time, architecture became divorced from social concerns as the Nixon administration canceled Great Society urban policies and as theorists questioned architecture's relevance to social problems.[16] After 1975, urban redevelopment in the United States consequently shifted from ambitious, modernist-inspired, large-scale work promoted by the state to a more modest mix of postmodern design and non-profit- or developer-driven projects.[17]

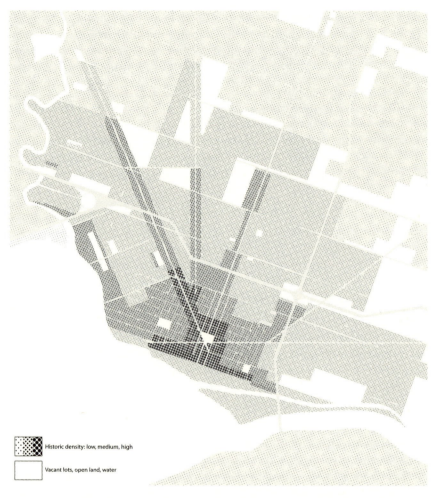

Figure 12.1. The industrial American city around 1950. Brent Ryan and Allison Hu.

Yet some links remain between innovative urban design and liberal social policies. These have persisted primarily through the works of committed practitioners and policy makers. In the 1970s, community organizing generated occasional innovative designs such as Villa Victoria in Boston's South End that linked partially abstract modernist architecture with subsidized housing while respecting the urban design of its surroundings.[18] In similar fashion, in the 1990s Philadelphia's Office of Housing comprehensively redesigned the disinvested neighborhood of Lower North Philadelphia with the

Historic density: low, medium, high

Vacant lots, open land, water

Figure 12.2. Patchwork appearance of shrinking cities. Brent Ryan and Allison Hu.

Poplar Nehemiah moderate-density, low-income housing development.[19] While design was not a signal feature of this project, Philadelphia's ambitious planning approach directly recalled accomplishments of the late modern and early postmodern eras such as the Yorktown houses constructed from 1960 to 1970 in Philadelphia[20] and the St. Lawrence development of Toronto from the 1970s.[21] Urban design studios in 2010 and 2011 for Buffalo and Baltimore replicated these combinations of innovative design and social planning.[22] The Buffalo studio showed that the city had sufficient Community

Development Block Grant funding to construct large numbers of houses if city officials chose to prioritize construction over demolition, and both studios showed that urban designers have a range of design options to relieve physical problems afflicting shrinking cities, assuming a continued demand for new housing by low- and moderate-income households.

The threads linking formally ambitious urban design to social action became thin and frayed after the end of modernism in the 1970s, but a renewed urban design agenda for rightsizing shrinking cities, if put into practice by committed policy makers and designers, might begin to regenerate these threads. I propose an *interventionist, critical, benevolent* agenda to improve on the modest and ineffective urban design strategies shrinking cities have pursued for almost forty years.

Interventionist urban design is committed to large-scale, comprehensive action across a wide area of space. Such action by and in the public interest characterized high-quality urban renewal efforts such as Yorktown in Philadelphia, but since the end of urban renewal, interventionism in shrinking cities has been limited to occasional projects such as Philadelphia's Poplar Nehemiah. Poplar's chief planner John Kromer believed that only large-scale action could demonstrate a political commitment to improving disinvested urban neighborhoods and achieve the public visibility to convince politicians of what Kromer called "neighborhood recovery."[23]

Critical urban design questions contemporary practice, such as the nostalgic bent of neotraditional urbanism, and projects innovative strategies to address social needs. Boston's Villa Victoria and other projects like Alvaro Siza's Quinta Malagueira in Evora, Portugal,[24] and the New York Urban Development Corporation's scattered-site Twin Parks Houses achieved this a decade previous.[25] Critical urban design moves beyond conventional wisdoms to project novel configurations of spaces, buildings, and activities.

Last, *benevolent* urban design acts in the interest of disempowered or underserved city residents, ranging from low-income renters to members of the middle class. Benevolent urban design recognizes the needs of the least powerful amid more powerful urban residents. At the same time, a benevolent urban design philosophy must not repeat the stigmatization of the poor by modernist, mid-twentieth-century public housing whose large-scale, *tabula rasa* developments lacked any relationship to their surroundings.[26]

A renewed urban design agenda committed to critical and benevolent interventionism is more radical than it seems. Its "benevolence" evokes the need for social justice, not always part of urban design. Fainstein's call for a more "just" urban planning identifies only new urbanism as a planning and design paradigm with potential for increased justice in the city,[27] yet its contribution to social justice is questionable. New urbanism's best-known involvement in low-income housing, the U.S. Department of Housing and Urban Development's HOPE VI program beginning in the mid-1990s, dramatically reduced the number of low-income housing units.[28] HOPE VI's new urbanist design reduced the stigma associated with the distinctive modernist towers of public housing but did so by building a substantially smaller number of units to house the very poor.

Providing for society's less privileged should be a collective mandate. Policy makers and designers should, therefore, use urban design as a vehicle to provide the rightsizing of shrinking cities with greater public visibility. Innovative spatial solutions to the problems of shrinking cities could also help renew connections between urban design and social policy.

Toward Patchwork Urbanism

Photographs from the first half of the twentieth century show industrial cities such as Detroit or Buffalo with a uniform carpet of nearly identical houses stretching toward the horizon. With the onset of population loss and housing abandonment, this homogeneous pattern (Figures 12.1 and 12.5) became a frayed and tattered urban fabric. Today, the cityscapes of shrinking cities resemble a patchwork of intact areas interspersed with areas of growing abandonment and with heavily abandoned areas (Figures 12.2 and 12.6). Contemporary rebuilding policies comprise a parallel patchwork of small-scale nonprofit-driven housing, market-rate housing in higher-income areas, and little or no new housing in those areas with very high vacancy (Figure 12.3). In other words, shrinking cities lack a comprehensive urban design strategy to shape either their continued shrinkage or their potential for areas of growth. In the early 1990s, Philadelphia's Office of Housing and Community Development recognized this problematic combination of individual building demolition, market avoidance of low-income areas, scattered nonprofit development, and lack of overall spatial planning in shrinking cities.[29]

The patchwork nature of decline with vacant areas of different sizes and housing in various states of occupancy frustrates conventional urban design approaches such as new urbanism or landscape urbanism that require large cleared areas of land. In shrinking cities, such sites are rarely available.

Figure 12.3. Conventional redevelopment strategies in shrinking cities: subsidized private development around downtown and in high-income neighborhoods, and nonprofits' scattered developments in lower-value, higher-vacancy areas. Brent Ryan and Allison Hu.

Conventional urban design also projects physical futures hardly compatible with the reality of shrinking cities. New urbanism favors restored street networks with high-density housing, but in shrinking cities, weak real estate markets prevent all but a small quantity of street and block fabric restoration. Full-scale rebuilding along new urbanist lines is also conceptually illogical, as working-class areas of industrial cities often lacked amenities such as public space and diverse housing types. A related proposal, Hollander's "reverse transect"[30] argues that regulations can guide neighborhood abandonment in an orderly progression of dedensification. But the piecemeal abandonment of shrinking cities is very far from orderly, and it is unconnected to planning regulations.

Landscape urbanism, a recent design movement with very different ideals than new urbanism, promotes the paradoxical combination of natural landscapes with precise, avant-garde design.[31] This strategy operates best in large, discrete parcels of land with few structures, such as vacant industrial sites. But the vacant areas of shrinking cities are rarely large and discrete; instead, they are more often small and scattered, with many properties, many owners, and many structures remaining. Landscape urbanism is an excellent strategy for large previously industrial areas such as Buffalo's "monumental wilderness" of empty grain elevators along the Buffalo River but not for the patchwork of vacant and settled areas that characterize most partly abandoned neighborhoods.[32] As a citywide strategy, landscape urbanism has even less traction, for any large-scale open space strategy would face skepticism from political leaders interested in increasing economic development and reluctant to alienate voters by widespread property condemnation for open space.

Shrinking cities present urban designers and planners with a physical condition that current urban design ideals do not fully address. Urban design has always projected visions of the city as a complete, idealized entity, from the symmetrical avenues of the baroque[33] to Brasilia's bird-in-flight form[34] to the picturesque new urbanist village of Seaside, Florida.[35] The opposite conditions characterize shrinking cities: their incompleteness and imperfection make the attainment of an ideal city form seem impossible. Urban designers may dislike imperfection and incompleteness, but any urban design theory for the shrinking city ideal will have to value and incorporate these attributes.

The shrinking city should become neither new urbanism's ideal restored cityscape of historicist homes nor landscape urbanism's landscape of returned nature, but rather a patchwork of differentiated areas containing settlements of varied densities and form, interspersed with open areas of various sizes, programs, and uses. At the citywide scale, a large-scale pattern of *interwoven growth and shrinkage* characterizes this "patchwork urbanism." At the neighborhood scale, interwoven growth and shrinkage comprise three smaller patterns: areas with *extensive shrinkage, growth in isolation,* and *growth in connection.* The following sections describe patchwork urbanism's patterns at the citywide and neighborhood scale (see Figures 12.4 and 12.7 for illustrations in a hypothetical city and neighborhood).

Interwoven Growth and Shrinkage

Few urban designers have acknowledged and appreciated urban incompleteness as a formal ideal. Among them is Kevin Lynch, who in 1960 described an ideal metropolitan form that he called "the polycentered net."[36] Such a net would possess both "intensive peaks" of density and "extensive regions of low density" within a "dispersed urban sheet" or urban grid. This grid would consist of streets and of "belts and tongues of open land." This pattern would "specialize and grow, perhaps in a rhythmically pulsating fashion." Lynch's recommendation captured many of the characteristics that he felt characterized the metropolis: low densities resulting from automobile use and a desire for pastoral settings, dynamism resulting in part from rapid technological and lifestyle advances, choice resulting from the desire of different types of people for different experiences at different times, and physical differentiation resulting from the presence of both historic and modern structures and urban patterns across any given area.

Lynch's polycentered net was an odd idea; he did not explore it extensively, nor has any other urban designer expanded on it. It has little resemblance to new urbanism's "transect," which offers a 1920s vision of a dense central city and low-density suburbs.[37] Fifty years later, the polycentered net remains an apt ideal for the American city, accepting both suburban sprawl and urban density with neither nostalgia nor cynicism. At a smaller scale, the polycentered net is also a helpful spatial concept to apply to shrinking cities. Historically structured around speculative grids developed with a homogenous pattern of housing and other buildings (Figure 12.1), shrinking cities have in their decline shifted toward a differentiated, unorganized pattern of lower and higher (that is, historic) building densities (Figure 12.2). The differentiated grid of shrinking cities, with some areas becoming denser and others with increasing abandonment, is analogous to the dynamic patterns of density and openness of Lynch's concept.

The fluidity and dynamism of Lynch's concepts constituted a sea change from the static urban design ideals prevalent at the time. In similar fashion, rightsizing's urban design dimension should accommodate rather than reject the shrinking city's inevitable housing loss within its established street network. Attempting to stop this shrinkage in the future is likely to be as fruitless as in the past, for individual abandonment and demolition of abandoned buildings will continue to generate piecemeal vacancies. Even if unplanned building loss continues, rebuilding decisions for abandoned areas should be deliberate and designed. Location and design should be critical elements of publicly and privately driven redevelopment of shrinking cities.

Increasing areas of lower density will continue to characterize shrinking cities as city officials and private owners demolish structures on a piecemeal basis year by year. These shrinking, increasingly empty areas will intermingle with surviving areas of historic building stock and densities. While overall shrinkage continues, urban design policy can reverse shrinkage in selected locations by constructing new large-scale, mostly residential neighborhoods that return low-density areas to higher (though not historic) densities. Government-driven redevelopment could construct these new neighborhoods, even as private developers continue to construct scattered, smaller-scale projects along major corridors (Figures 12.4 and 12.7). The overall city would continue to shrink, but certain areas of the city would grow within this declining fabric. Thus, today's pattern of patchwork shrinkage with concentrated growth in higher-income areas would shift to a more balanced pattern of shrinkage and growth across both high- and low-income areas of the city. This new growth pattern would stabilize parts of the shrinking city fabric, while allowing loss to continue elsewhere.

Extensive Shrinkage

The fate of open, vacant areas in shrinking cities constitutes much of the dialogue about shrinkage. From "blots" of vacant lots that adjoining homeowners annex in Detroit[38] to corridors of abandoned infrastructure, urban farms, and wildlife habitat, open spaces in shrinking cities provoke those who wish for regenerated historic urban fabrics and suggest promise for those who long for more nature in cities. In the absence of planning or design, open spaces in shrinking cities have grown and evolved, offering a palette for exploration and cultivation of diverse activities. Policy makers and urban designers should first see abundant vacant areas as "open territory" for whatever gestures residents or outsiders wish to make there.

Figure 12.4. Strategic interventions: new neighborhoods in "isolated" and "connected" areas. Brent Ryan and Allison Hu.

Probably the least practical transformation is to turn these areas into formal city parks. Conventional recreation equipment, maintained athletic fields, and pastoral landscapes would be expensive, and these facilities already exist in overabundance from past eras. The most practical transformations have already been occurring, such as the piecemeal, everyday annexation of empty parcels by residents who remain and who value these adjacent parcels as amenities for their homes. But "blotting" is likely to be a limited strategy and may decrease in frequency as residents of scattered homes continue to leave the city and as new developments incorporate open space into their designs. No blotting can exist without homes. By the same token, this everyday urbanism-based[39] practice holds substantial continued promise in cities with dense row houses, where outdoor private space is both absent and needed, such as Philadelphia or Baltimore. City officials should strongly encourage blotting in these cities, perhaps with low fences or walls to provide continuation of the former street wall.

The open areas of shrinking cities will eventually resemble a patchwork, a green microcosm of the city at large, with a mix of consciously designed space—maintained small blots, larger areas cultivated as urban farms, and designated natural habitat areas—and poorly maintained city- or privately owned parcels, with larger areas of land undesignated for any use. All these open areas, designed or not, will intermix with remaining homes. No single vacancy strategy is likely to dominate these areas of continued shrinkage. New development may in time occupy some open areas; if these open areas are well used, their reuse will likely engender resistance in the same way that community garden "owners" have fought redevelopment in New York and Chicago. But most new development reoccupying open areas will not encounter resistance, except from speculators. And new development will likely never occur in most open areas: given shrinking cities' weak markets and limited funding, they will remain open for the foreseeable future.

The most contentious aspect of dialogues over the fate of open areas has concerned residents in scattered houses throughout these areas. The ghost of 1960s era urban renewal's involuntary displacement haunts dialogues about rightsizing. Urban citizens who have persisted through decades of decline and abandonment and who may enjoy their isolation and spaciousness are rightly incensed at prospects that city officials may displace them simply for open space or wildlife habitat. Residents of mostly open areas who wish to remain there, surrounded by memories and a pastoral landscape, should do so. At the same time, city officials facing enormous budget shortfalls should also consider reducing city services to isolated, nearly vacant areas; city officials might officially abandon streets and their underground infrastructure where only one or two houses remain and deed maintenance responsibility for that street to the residents. Such areas are much less than those that residents of rural areas own and maintain. Residents of isolated, sparsely populated open areas will need to accept that living in abandoned areas requires them to assume additional responsibilities, as the reach of municipal services recedes to the nearest street intersection.

Growth in Isolation

In cities such as Detroit, abandonment has progressed to the point where some neighborhoods may be a mile or more from retail establishments and privately developed housing. Disinvestment has occurred for so long and to such an extent that surviving intact blocks are "isolated" by larger patches of abandonment. In Buffalo, patchwork abandonment in the city's central declining area is almost two miles in diameter.[40] Isolated areas are poor prospects for conventional, privately financed housing development. Residents or visitors unfamiliar with the areas tend to avoid them, and most city residents never see them. Since most residents are in poverty, services, police protection, and other municipal benefits are less than in other parts of the city. Many isolated areas, built in an era when cities were denser and more pedestrian oriented, are also remote from major arterials, making them inconvenient for automobile and public transportation access. The result, seen in Figure 12.3, is that isolated areas receive little redevelopment except for scattered nonprofit housing. Out of sight and out of mind to other residents of the city, isolated areas tend to remain isolated, and their decline continues.

Physical isolation imposes a cost on residents of these areas and on the city as a whole. For residents, physical isolation means disconnection from everyday amenities in denser areas, much as "social isolation" isolates residents from socioeconomic role models.[41] Large stretches of the poor neighborhoods in Newark, Camden, Detroit, Chicago, and a few other cities pictured in Camilo Jose Vergara's photos feature nary a grocery store or restaurant.[42] Other parts of the city suffer in turn from physically isolated areas' failure to redevelop, because abandonment in isolated areas and adjoining neighborhoods is related. Buffalo's growing abandonment shows this phenomenon.[43]

Creating new neighborhoods in shrinking cities' most isolated areas is, thus, an important strategy. The strongest argument in favor of new neighborhood development in such areas is based on equity; all citizens merit a decent living environment with access to public facilities, regardless of where they live. Isolated area residents' deprivation of access to amenities common in denser areas can thus reduce their civil rights, just as children citywide should have the right of access to the best available public education. New neighborhoods in isolated areas may not remove negative influences in the lives of residents, but they will increase their exposure to benefits such as new parks, streets, stable neighborhoods, improved city services, and increased public order in surrounding areas. Current shrinking city redevelopment policies that emphasize new housing in areas adjacent to high-value areas exclude residents of isolated areas from receiving spillover benefits of new development such as improved public services or police protection. An isolated-area new neighborhood strategy would be radical; recent developments like Philadelphia's Poplar Nehemiah were constructed adjacent to active areas to encourage market development and buffer healthy areas from decline. This strategy is legitimate, but the lack of development in isolated areas diminishes equity for residents of these areas.

Factors that influence private sector development in shrinking cities, particularly visibility and access from major arterial roads, should also guide selection of new neighborhood sites within isolated areas. Any new neighborhood site should adjoin at least a mid-sized arterial street to enhance auto access and increase the probability of mass transit access. A new neighborhood adjoining a mid-sized arterial offers a better market for retail development. (Figure 12.4 shows this adjacency to arterial streets.)

Urban design arguments for new neighborhoods in isolated areas are also strong. With high levels of vacancy and poor social and economic conditions, isolated areas require innovative design to reimagine neighborhood patterns. In isolated, abandoned areas, little reason exists to replicate the long-gone pattern of grids with monotonous, dense housing. New residents, many of whom long for suburban housing amenities, will desire both distinction and protection from deteriorated surroundings, as well as amenities such as private open space and off-street parking routine in new development elsewhere. Developers often provide amenities in cities through the construction of suburban-style housing providing private parking and culs-de-sac, but urban designers have a responsibility to do more than imitate suburbs.[44] Instead, they should design housing that provides expected private amenities but that also provides the activity, security, and visual and experiential interest of urban neighborhoods.

Residents of new neighborhoods in isolated areas are likely to have low or moderate incomes. Middle- and upper-income residents will likely prefer other locations, and some metropolitan-area residents' racial fears prevent them from considering a location that they consider "inner-city." However,

Parcels

Historic development

Figure 12.5. Typical neighborhood prior to decline. Brent Ryan and Allison Hu.

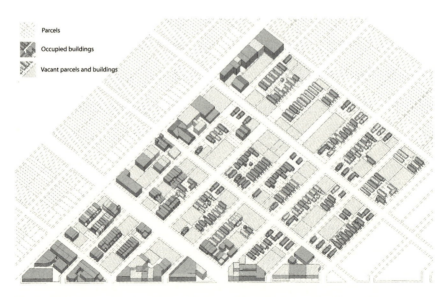

Parcels

Occupied buildings

Vacant parcels and buildings

Figure 12.6. Semi-abandoned neighborhood. Brent Ryan and Allison Hu.

Parcels

Occupied buildings

Vacant parcels and buildings

New neighborhood

Relocated houses

Figure 12.7. Reconstructing a semi-abandoned neighborhood with more open space and changed street patterns. Brent Ryan and Allison Hu.

low- and moderate-income city residents may find isolated locations desirable. Spacious homes and private space would be available at low cost, making isolated areas competitive locations for homeowners conscious of costs and tolerant of abandoned areas nearby. Such moderate-income homeowners, often African American, are the demographic that has purchased new for-sale homes in redeveloped areas of Detroit such as Victoria Park.[45] Such residents also made up the new neighborhoods of Yorktown, North Philadelphia's most stable neighborhood, as Kromer noted.[46] Lower-middle-class households may represent the best hope for preventing housing abandonment in isolated areas, but they will require well-designed new neighborhoods to attract and retain them.

Little prospect exists for private sector developer financing of new neighborhood construction in isolated areas. For-profit development in shrinking cities is risky even in the best of times and locations.[47] Only city and state governments, fiscally constrained as they are, possess the means to finance new housing in isolated locations, but they should not do so outside the framework of a spatial plan that fairly balances different neighborhoods' needs for rebuilding. Constructing new neighborhoods would be costly and would demand significant time and capacity from city agencies. Philadelphia, for example, could afford only a few sizable publicly financed new neighbor-hoods in the prosperous 1990s. But in Buffalo ten years of federal funding at the level of the early 2000s would permit construction of hundreds of new houses at densities around fifteen units per acre at a cost of up to $200,000 per unit.[48] Given low land costs in shrinking city neighborhoods, construc-tion of new neighborhoods in abandoned areas of shrinking cities would seem feasible if shrinking city agencies are up to the task.

Growth in Connection

While abandoned, isolated areas are perhaps shrinking cities' most striking and troubling environments, many areas of these cities have brighter pros-pects. Every shrinking city has healthy neighborhoods where residents choose to live, forgoing the suburbs in favor of a distinctive living experi-ence in the city (see Figure 12.5). These healthy neighborhoods differ little from their better-known cousins in "creative class" cities such as Portland, Oregon, or Boston, and their housing prices are often lower. Entrepreneurial real estate developers see these sites as excellent locations for new housing, and city administrations are willing to subsidize them.

Unlike, say, Boston or Portland, shrinking cities often possess partly abandoned neighborhoods close to these healthy areas. Buffalonians who take the short walk across Main Street from prosperous Delaware Avenue find themselves in the shrinking neighborhood of Masten Park, a low-income, African American neighborhood where half the properties are va-cant lots.[49] Buffalo, Cleveland, and other shrinking cities possess many such "connected" shrinking neighborhoods, adjacent to prosperous areas but nevertheless badly deteriorated (see Figure 12.6).

New neighborhoods in connected areas offer benefits to residents and to the city as a whole. Since these locations are adjacent to intact and higher-income residential and retail areas, residents of new neighborhoods enjoy access to these amenities. Adjacent new neighborhoods also reinforce the success of healthy areas, as additional new residents locate within a short distance of these places and can support existing retail. Proximity to active neighborhoods also gives lower-income residents access to these amenities. Development in connected neighborhoods also may attract a greater range of incomes and populations than that in isolated areas, generating increased social and income diversity. Neighborhoods adjacent to high-priced areas have risked gentrification in more prosperous cities, but risks are low in shrinking cities. Demand for housing is low, and prices are affordable even in intact neighborhoods.

At a larger scale, construction of new neighborhoods at the frontier of decline can check abandonment's spread. New neighborhoods on border-lands between intact and vacant neighborhoods indicate that "abandon-ment stops here," reduce risk to healthy neighborhoods, and help to revive at-risk shrinking neighborhoods. Helping those who are not yet beyond hope is widespread practice: medicine has triage; in crime prevention, fixing "broken windows" avoids more serious problems; and many social programs direct aid toward "at-risk" children. Constructing new neighborhoods in "at-risk," connected areas promises to arrest or stabilize decline's spread and to reverse abandonment where it has not yet taken hold, even if it offers little promise to areas elsewhere with deeper abandonment problems.

Connected areas are less extensively abandoned than isolated areas, so latitude for major urban design intervention is less. At vacancy rates below 50 percent, street, block, and settlement reconfiguration is difficult barring ex-tensive relocation of residents.[50] Urban design at moderate levels of abandon-ment is, thus, limited to small new clusters of homes, closure of occasional streets, and provision of new open spaces or community facilities on scattered sites. Since even small-scale actions may require home relocation, significant numbers of remaining houses make an infill urban design approach stronger in connected areas (see Figure 12.7). Such strategies have been pursued in moderately vacant neighborhoods such as Corktown in Detroit or Buffalo's Near West Side by private developers and nonprofit organizations like PUSH Buffalo.

Conclusion

In the 1970s, the United States abandoned the enterprise of state-driven ur-ban redevelopment in favor of decentralization and private initiative.[51] The neoliberal economics that have dominated since that time have driven plan-ning and urban design, particularly in the United States and increasingly in Europe, to follow the lead of private sector developers in rebuilding cities. Some theorists believe that such a strategy is ideal, that obeying the market's wishes is the best path forward for building cities.[52] Yet this very strategy has also cast shrinking cities adrift, leading them to spend hundreds of millions of dollars on downtown megaprojects[53] and subsidizing developers to construct housing in connected areas, while ignoring the challenge of improving conditions in the isolated, abandoned areas that grow larger as decline continues. The shrinkage of historically industrial cities represents the failure of neoliberal planning and the planners that advocate it, for shrinking cities' reliance on the market has not improved the quality of the built environment in their most abandoned areas, nor the quality of these areas' inhabitants' lives. This chapter has argued that a benevolent, interventionist, critical urban design approach can begin to undo the neglect of the laissez-faire planning of the past half century and begin to project a future for shrinking cities that goes beyond the piecemeal abandonment and demolition they currently experience.

Such an urban design approach might address each landscape of the shrinking city—areas with extensive shrinkage, new neighborhoods in isolated areas, and new neighborhoods in connected areas—with strategies that mix new construction in some areas with the acceptance of continued abandonment in others. Funds are likely to be scarce and political capacity episodic, but a robust urban design approach has the potential to transcend these constraints. Ideally, the future shrinking city would be a "patchwork city" of new, old, vanished, and vanishing neighborhoods, intermingled within the bounds of the historic city. Such cities will not be preserved historic monuments, but neither will they be ruined wastelands. Ultimately, shrinking cities might become a lively combination of different types of environments, a central-city realization of Kevin Lynch's "polycentered net."

Rightsizing will be an urban policy subject to the same challenges and opportunities as other urban policies. Political leadership in shrinking cities may be weak, and agencies have lost capacity over years of budget cuts. Federal and state funding to shrinking cities is not generous, but it can achieve substantial aims if applied in large quantities to a single site. Constructing concentrated and innovative new neighborhoods will change urban development as usual and place new demands on nonprofit and public agencies accustomed to decentralized action. But the problem of shrinking cities is too large to be left to chance, to the market, or to scattered and ineffective actors. Rightsizing shrinking cities represents a new opportunity for urban design and planning to take the lead in shaping the future of distinctive urban environments. The need to rightsize is critical, the potential to rightsize is tremendous, and the time to rightsize is now.

CHAPTER 13

Planning for Better, Smaller Places After Population Loss: Lessons from Youngstown and Flint

Margaret Dewar, Christina Kelly, and Hunter Morrison

Urban planning focuses on growth. Although many planners work in places with extensive disinvestment, they mainly focus on encouraging and responding to development projects. Much research exists on the causes of decline and abandonment but little on what planners should do when development does not occur.[1] Urban planning as a field has had little to say about what cities should become following decline—population and employment loss, property disinvestment, and property abandonment. The most recent edition of the "Green Book," a handbook of local planning, addressed ways to encourage citizen participation, reuse surplus property, and leverage assets where population has declined, nearly always with the aim of redeveloping.[2] Several chapters addressed revitalization of blighted neighborhoods but not what to do without revitalization.[3] A search of the American Planning Association's Planners' Bookstore in 2010 identified two publications that a planner working in an abandoned area of a city would find quite useful if the planner could not redevelop.[4] The American Planning Association commissioned a Planning Advisory Service report on "cities in transition" in fall 2011, which will offer another resource when complete. Nevertheless, if a planner newly arrived in a city with high levels of abandonment wanted to plan in ways consistent with major loss of population, without focusing on development, he or she could not readily find materials.

As the first chapter in this volume explains, large numbers of cities in the Northeast and Great Lakes regions have lost substantial amounts of their peak populations. Some areas of these cities experience redevelopment, but the challenge for urban planning in large sections of such cities is to find ways to manage depopulation and disinvestment in ways that achieve goals other than encouraging or managing growth. The purpose of this chapter is to bring the innovative ideas of planners working in cities with few prospects for development into urban planning discussions as one approach to integrating planning-with-decline into mainstream urban planning.

We base this chapter on Dewar's interviews of Kelly and Morrison and discussions of drafts among the authors about their efforts to plan with population loss. Hunter Morrison was one of the planners who led the development of the *Youngstown 2010* plan,[5] following twenty-one years as director of the City Planning Commission in Cleveland, Ohio; until recently he directed campus planning and community development at Youngstown State University. Christina Kelly is lead planner with the Genesee County Land Bank, which holds thousands of tax-reverted properties in Flint, Michigan. Morrison and Kelly have reframed the purpose of planners' work from redeveloping and rebuilding despite weak demand for land to creating a better city without growth and without much development, a less dense city with different distributions of land uses. Morrison and Kelly are two of the national leaders in redefining the work of planning in cities experiencing massive abandonment. Morrison has a broad view of planning in cities that have lost large amounts of population but has not needed to prioritize demolitions or make decisions about use of vacant lots; "he's the vision guy," said one of his Youngstown State colleagues. Kelly's view comes from looking for ways to handle tax-reverted properties that have almost no market value, while supporting engaged planning processes and envisioning how such decisions remake the city. She said, "Creating opportunities for people to use and care for the land improves neighborhoods and reduces maintenance costs for the Land Bank. As more residents become engaged and aware of opportunities to purchase and care for land, fewer properties are left uncared for." These complementary perspectives—the overall framework and the work of planning implementation for small areas—inform how city planning can address the challenges of places with advanced disinvestment and property abandonment where growth is unlikely.

These ideas from practice can suggest directions for further research and investigation into the efficacy of such approaches. Further, this chapter does not tackle several related issues that future research could address. The chapter does not provide a vision for what a city should become with a much smaller population. In Youngstown, the plan provided this vision for the physical place; in Flint, no citywide plan or vision existed. No one has evaluated the implementation of *Youngstown 2010* or the Genesee County Land Bank's work, and neither does this chapter evaluate what works in moving toward a vision of a smaller, better city. The chapter does not address policy changes in state land use regulation or in federal investment decisions, for instance, that could alter the fortunes of cities that have lost large shares of their populations. Finally, this discussion focuses on the built environment and not on education, safety, and other conditions that require attention to make a city experiencing large-scale disinvestment into a place where more people want to live.

The next sections explain the usefulness of Youngstown and Flint for learning about planning after substantial population loss, past research about planning in declining cities, and Morrison's and Kelly's views about how planners should work in such cities with emphasis on the differences between planning in cities with weak demand for land and in those with strong demand. Finally, the chapter points to issues that Morrison and Kelly did not discuss but that will concern planners working in cities with extensive disinvestment.

Why Youngstown and Flint?

Why choose Youngstown and Flint as the sites for considering how to plan after decline? Unlike the situation in other cities, planners in these two have worked explicitly to find ways to adjust to population loss to create a better, smaller city. Furthermore, the two cities' planners arrived at addressing population loss and property disinvestment from contrasting directions and operate in different institutional settings. Therefore, their experiences yield some of the same lessons but also quite different ones.

In Youngstown, Morrison stated, a shift in thinking about the future of the city began with a C. S. Mott Foundation-commissioned report from the Harwood Group. The report asserted that Youngstown had assets and opportunities but was "waiting for leadership" to take action.[6] The City Council decided to take leadership and put aside funds for a new plan for the city; by 2001, it had contracted with the firm Urban Strategies to carry out a participatory planning process. A "fundamental attitude shift," in Morrison's words, took place during the planning process with acceptance of the idea that Youngstown could become a "sustainable mid-sized city" no longer aspiring to return to former population levels.[7] The planning commission adopted the new plan in 2005. Cited in the *New York Times* "Year in Ideas" for "creative shrinkage," the plan won a national award for excellence in public outreach from the American Planning Association.[8] The plan provides a framework for the city's change and has guided city officials' decisions, neighborhood organizing efforts, and the actions of key institutions such as Youngstown State University.

Youngstown is an ideal place to demonstrate how to become a city with a smaller population and a better quality of life because, Morrison said, no one can continue to believe that growth will solve the city's problems. "Resizing is legitimate and important," but acceptance of becoming smaller required a generational shift. The workers who lost their jobs starting in the late 1970s hoped that growth would return, but they were also the victims who received the blame for the demise of the steel mills because they had belonged to unions, earned high wages, and lacked entrepreneurial skills. By 2005, the generation that had grown up after the mills closed no longer thought that the city could again become a major industrial center.

Accepting that Youngstown *is* a smaller city does not mean accepting that Youngstown will *continue* to lose population and employment. *Youngstown 2010* aims to reposition the city so that it can become "competitive" again.[9] The plan focuses on land use in Youngstown but emphasizes that Youngstown needs to "align itself with the present realities of the regional economy"[10] by building on its economic strengths, finding new purposes for old skills and knowledge, and making connections to the Pittsburgh and Cleveland regional economies, within commuting distance of Youngstown because of freeway connections and employment centers' sprawl to outer suburbs. The Great Lakes regional economy lagged, so Youngstown's leadership would face challenges in identifying strengths that could help Youngstown, but the decision to stop searching for answers in single large projects and revitalization of old manufacturing took the right direction.

In Flint, planning after population decline originated in a quite different way. Dan Kildee, treasurer of Genesee County, where Flint is located, saw the connection between tax foreclosure processes, land use, and planning. Kildee influenced Michigan's 1999 property tax foreclosure reform and 2004 land bank enabling legislation. Starting in 2002 when implementation of the new tax foreclosure law transferred foreclosed properties' into the county's ownership, the Genesee County Land Reutilization Council and its successor, the Genesee County Land Bank Authority, received thousands of tax-reverted properties not sold at auction. As of early 2010, the Land Bank owned 5,100 properties. Unlike previous land banks in the nation, the Genesee County Land Bank handled property proactively. As of mid-2010, the Land Bank operated a range of programs to enhance the condition of abandoned property and to sell it to responsible owners. As Kildee said, the Land Bank takes an investment approach to property reuse and avoids the "liquidation model" that dumps property on the market despite very weak demand. In 2007 the Land Bank received the national Fannie Mae Foundation Innovations Award in Affordable Housing.[11]

Taking an investment approach to abandoned property requires planning. The team of six planning and support staff

> provide input into Land Bank programs to maximize the impact of interventions in neighborhoods; . . . engage citizens in Land Bank decision-making and build support for Land Bank programs in the community; . . . coordinate with, and provide planning support to, neighborhood associations, the City of Flint and other local governments and community based partners to facilitate revitalization efforts; . . . improve the appearance of neighborhoods and engage churches and community-based groups by cleaning, greening and gardening vacant properties; . . . [and] eliminate blight, clean up blight and environmental contamination, and position brownfields for re-use to encourage neighborhood revitalization and economic development.[12]

As planners at the Land Bank worked on handling abandoned properties in ways that improved quality of life and enhanced land value, they operated without an overall plan for the city and without the presence of a city planning department. Flint had adopted its last comprehensive plan in the mid-1960s. As Robert Beckley (formerly affiliated with the Land Bank and former dean of architecture and urban planning at the University of Michigan) has pointed out, much planning took place in the intervening years.[13] Hospitals and institutions of higher education planned their centers and campuses. A few community development corporations planned their "target" areas, although without considering the city context and connections with other areas. Downtown interests made plans. Highway construction and urban renewal for an industrial park to serve General Motors were completed in the late 1970s.[14] However, no guiding principles or visions enabled these plans to complement each other in ways that could provide a shared direction. At the same time, suburbanization and white flight reduced population following World War II, and auto industry restructuring cut huge numbers of jobs from the 1970s on. These transformations had more effect on Flint than any planning.

Although Flint faces conditions similar to Youngstown's, most government officials and civic leaders have not accepted that Flint will not grow. City officials have had "embedded assumptions about what a healthy city is, and that always means growth," said Kelly. When Flint's interim mayor made a casual remark in 2009 that the city might consider "shutting down quadrants of the city where we (wouldn't) provide services" in the face of budget problems, he prompted strong concerns among residents as well, especially African Americans wary of the burdens such changes could place on them.[15]

Although the institutional and political contexts for planning differ, planners in Flint and Youngstown face similar conditions of population loss and property abandonment. Youngstown's loss of population began slowly between 1930 and 1960 and then accelerated so that the city had lost 60 percent of its peak population by 2010. Flint's population declined 48 percent from 1960 to 2010. With the fall in demand for housing, disinvestment and

Table 13.1. Population and Housing Change, Youngstown and Flint

City	Census year of peak population	Peak population (thousands)	2010 population (thousands)	Percent change
Flint	1960	196.9	102.4	−48.0
Youngstown	1930	170.0	67.0	−60.6
City	Census year of peak housing units	Peak housing units (thousands)	2010 housing units (thousands)	Percent change
Flint	1970	64.2	51.3	−20.1
Youngstown	1960	51.0	33.1	−35.0

Source: U.S. Census Bureau, "Total Population" and "Housing Units," Census 1930, 1960, 1970, 2010.

abandonment removed many units from the housing stock. Youngstown had lost about 35 percent of its housing stock and Flint 20 percent since peak years. Disinvestment in housing continues as demand remains low with continuing population loss, despite smaller household size (see Table 13.1).

As city officials and property owners demolished derelict housing, the amount of vacant land increased. The director of the Land Bank estimated that Flint had about 12,000 vacant lots in 2009, slightly more than one-fifth of the city's properties. Another 6,000 residential structures awaited demolition.[16] In Youngstown, large areas of residential property were vacant, and industrial land along the Mahoning River stood empty.[17]

What Do We Know About Planning After Decline?

In 1977, Congressman Henry Reuss assembled experts on the topic of "how cities can grow old gracefully." Cities were thinning out and becoming smaller, he said. "Contraction . . . in our largest and oldest cities seems inevitable. . . . We can begin to plan now for shrinkage . . . and actively anticipate a future in which our urban centers will be smaller but offer a quality of life for all their residents."[18] At least some urban planning scholars agreed that the field ought to turn its attention to planning without growth. Herbert Gans wrote, "Much of contemporary planning is still based on the promise of future growth, even in cities which long ago stopped growing." Indeed, he said, planning for growth could enable city leaders to "avoid dealing with the somber realities of their future." Planners needed to engage in "cutback planning," Gans argued. This meant learning how to "plan for reduced and declining capital and operating expenditures" and to "develop a viable and functioning city under conditions of decline."[19]

In the years since, urban planning scholarship has made little progress in laying a foundation for practice in addressing urban decline and the challenge of weak demand for a city's land. As the extent of vacant structures and land continued to increase in many previously industrial cities, calls for urban planning to tackle decline reappeared after 2000: "Faced with the phenomenon of shrinkage, urban planning is merely reactive because . . . it has little influence on . . . deindustrialization, demographic change, or even suburbanization. . . . We must search for new ways to intervene in urban planning" exhorted the director of the "Shrinking Cities" project of the Kulturstiftung des Bundes.[20] "Urban shrinkage is a widespread First World occurrence for which planners have little background, experience, or recourse. . . . They have to overcome their aversion . . . to the very idea of shrinkage," concluded a review of research agendas in planning.[21]

In the face of extensive population loss and property disinvestment, how can urban planning make a difference? A thin literature in urban planning suggests several directions. Thus far, the scholarship suffers from fragmentation; scholars do not engage in enough "conversations" with others' research and theory to build a cumulative body of work.

One perspective on land use planning in cities with extensive abandonment argued that remaining residents of sparsely populated areas should move to denser areas of the city.[22] City officials could guide people into clusters in a "rough checkerboard pattern," for instance.[23] Neighborhood consolidation could increase efficiency in at least two ways. For one, the rise in property values in destination neighborhoods could exceed declines in the disinvested areas that residents left; the denser areas could support retail and other local services; and city property tax revenues could increase.[24] For another, the city could deliver public services at a lower average cost in denser areas. No one has tested these assertions.

Alternatively, cities could thin out.[25] Property owners could take over adjacent vacant lots. Transforming the city to look more like suburbs, downzoning to five to ten dwellings per acre (now denser than many abandoned areas), would respond to consumer demand.[26]

Another perspective, addressing efforts to revitalize neighborhoods, argued that city officials need to target resources in a limited number of places in order to strengthen a neighborhood, especially in a city that has extensive areas of abandonment and many neighborhoods at risk of further disinvestment. The aim of targeting is to encourage confidence in the future of an area so that owners invest in their properties.[27] The common practice of sprinkling Community Development Block Grant funds across a city means that no area reaches the threshold of public and philanthropic investment needed to restore private owners' confidence. In Richmond, Virginia, evaluation of the Neighborhoods in Bloom program showed that "private investment increases significantly above a relatively low threshold of public investment," supported by a participatory planning process and infrastructure and service investments.[28]

From the late 1970s through the early 1980s, policy and planning approaches to dealing with land use in declining cities debated "triage," sorting neighborhoods into those that would prosper without help, those showing signs of blight that could suffer more disinvestment without intervention, and those with advanced property abandonment that intervention could likely not turn around. Downs articulated this view in the greatest detail. Most investment, he said, should focus on "in-between" areas with beginnings of decline or with decline well underway but still reversible in order to encourage owners to invest in their properties before abandonment advanced so far that intervention could not stop it.[29]

Arguments for social equity, neighborhood self-help, and community development countered the triage advocates' views. Abandonment is unnecessary, according to this view, a result of racism, suburbanization, federal policies, and deindustrialization. Land use policies and tax base sharing could prevent abandonment by discouraging sprawl of settlements outside the city.[30] Putting such measures in place *after* abandonment might not bring about repopulation of central cities, however. Because abandonment was unnecessary, from this perspective, the efforts of residents and community organizations with public support could bring about neighborhood revival.[31] An argument that this transformation was possible in all city neighborhoods became harder to maintain as population loss and abandonment continued into the 2000s. Even so, at a 2010 Brookings Institution meeting on the future of auto communities, the president of the Ford Foundation exhibited before and after photos of the South Bronx to demonstrate the potential transformation of neighborhoods given up for lost.[32] This view overlooked the differences in regional economic conditions between New York and regions dependent on manufacturing and the differences in the strength and diversity of the economic base of cities.

When land becomes vacant with no near-term prospects for redevelopment, planners can take new approaches to "greening the city," another perspective argued. Addressing the scale of vacant and abandoned properties in previously industrial cities requires greening strategies that convert vacant properties into environmental benefits that can enhance nearby property as well, argued Schilling and Logan.[33] Vacant areas can act as "ripening assets"[34] that may have other uses in the future. Vacant land can become an ecological asset that improves water and soil condition, neighborhood attractiveness, and quality of life and increases property values.[35]

While scholars have begun to tackle issues around planning in the context of decline, numerous lawyers, judges, policy specialists, and city and county officials have detailed ways to address the challenge and realize the opportunity of vacant property. They develop administrative approaches to managing vacant land and structures; controlling abandoned property through reformed legal systems; and using code enforcement creatively, for instance.[36] The National Vacant Properties Campaign, now subsumed under the Center for Community Progress, disseminated these ideas and produced guides for specific cities to strengthen approaches to addressing vacant property.[37] Some of these ideas have contributed to plans, rather than remaining sets of strategies and tactics; recommendations have considered strategic choices about where measures could have greatest effect, laid out priorities, and articulated goals. Usually, however, an innovative practice, such as vacant property registration or a housing court judge's strict treatment of slum landlords, remains isolated from a vision of what a place can become, although the approach may be a useful tool for achieving a vision. Perspectives from urban planning have contributed less to this work than those of policy analysts and lawyers.

Scholars elsewhere in the world have also studied population loss and the effects of efforts to address this loss where redevelopment is not possible. For American planners, the contrast in experiences offers perspective. European central governments, for instance, have more authority over land use than in the United States. Central governments devote much greater resources to decline-oriented planning than in the United States. Government efforts to address property disinvestment, nevertheless, confront complicated public-private relationships, although different from those in the United States, which mean planned changes do not necessarily occur. Governmental structures, legal frameworks, settlement patterns, racial and ethnic tensions, and other social, political, and institutional factors differ so much that solutions in other countries do not necessarily apply in the United States.[38]

Efforts to plan in ways that accept decline have not fared well politically.[39] In St. Louis in 1974, consultants advised the Planning Commission to designate "depletion areas" for a "no growth policy."[40] When a newspaper report misconstrued the recommendations, resident protests led the city administration to dismiss the consultants' suggestions. In New York City in 1976, the director of the Housing and Development Administration advocated accepting that parts of the city such as the South Bronx would lose substantial population. "If the city is to survive with a smaller population," he said, "the population must . . . concentrate itself in the sections that remain alive. . . . The remaining families can be offered relocation benefits to move."[41] His proposal met intense opposition.[42] In Cleveland, planning director Norman Krumholz called the focus on attracting population and employment back to the city "a delusion." Instead, he said, planners should manage stasis and decline.[43] His department moved in this direction, although city officials never accepted that growth would not continue.[44]

As these examples show, strong forces interfere with acceptance of population and employment loss and of planning for a smaller city. The city's function as a "growth machine"[45] means that city officials and elites have much to gain from growth and increases in land value.[46] Further, by the early 1970s, urban renewal had cleared many African American and other high-minority neighborhoods without providing better or even adequate alternative places to live.[47] Therefore, hints of clearance of minority-race areas raised the specter of more neighborhood destruction and inequitable treatment and led to strong resistance. Finally, acceptance of decline in place of growth "smacks of surrender," as a Flint mayoral candidate said in 2009,[48] or, as a columnist wrote, communicates a decision not to "rise to the great challenges before us" and to watch "greatness . . . steadily slipping away."[49]

Planning After Large-Scale Loss of Population: Lessons from Youngstown and Flint

Despite the lack of guidance in planning literature, the absence of planning perspectives in much policy work related to vacant properties, and politics that align with planning for growth, some planners are tackling planning in the context of large-scale loss of population and widespread property abandonment and disinvestment. Morrison and Kelly are inventing and adapting ways to make a better city in this context. They use numerous ideas, principles, and ways of thinking that a planner would draw on anywhere, but planning in the context of this scale of population loss differs from planning in growing places in important respects.

The following sections reflect a perspective on urban planning with several themes and underlying beliefs. First, planners have the uncomfortable, although exciting, job of figuring out a different paradigm. They need to envision what a city can become without new development. Second, the injustices residents have suffered in the past profoundly complicate the process of reaching a commitment to work together on a shared vision. Third, no one can save much of the built city. Hardly anyone wants it, except possibly historic preservationists in the case of a few architecturally significant buildings. The structures met demand for industrial, commercial, and residential space during an industrial era that no longer exists. Facilitating the transition from the old built form to a new one for which demand exists is an important part of the planners' role. Fourth, physical cues have profound influence on the everyday decisions of residents, potential residents, business owners, and others about where to locate and whether to invest in property. Planners need to manage these cues to encourage commitments to stay and decisions to locate. Ways to do this differ among types of neighborhoods and areas with different volumes of traffic.

Understand that urban planning is a profession that manages "change," not just "growth."
In cities that have experienced significant population loss, planners need to reframe their mission from managing "growth" to managing "change." This is difficult because the "planning business is almost totally focused on growth," Morrison stated. "When growth does not happen, we all too often 'blame the victim,' believing that the place alone has somehow caused the problem." Morrison elaborated:

> The planning profession needs to develop the language, data, tools, and pedagogic frameworks that deal with the reality of America's shrinking industrial cities. The smart growth movement and new urbanism have provided few tools to historically industrial cities like Detroit, Youngstown, Cleveland, and Flint as they try to transition from a past dominated by heavy industry to a sustainable future economy. Too often my colleagues from the country's growing regions dismissively describe the Great Lakes region and its industrial communities as "underperforming." They offer a description of current reality but fail to propose realistic strategies to create a more hopeful future.
>
> We have no generally accepted language in the planning profession or in any of its allied design and development professions for describing what is going on and suggesting what should happen in cities experiencing little if any growth. . . . [In most cities of the Great Lakes region,] the issue of growth management is confined to the sprawling suburbs while the core city and many of the inner ring suburbs continue to experience population loss and property abandonment.

In order to reframe the challenge facing such cities, planners need ways to think differently about what could happen in cities with substantial loss of population. "We need better words," Kelly said. "Shrinking, rightsizing, and downsizing all have pejorative meanings, and people have immediate, negative reactions."

Morrison agrees. "We need to develop a robust, honest name to describe our class of cities. 'Shrinking cities' is too pejorative for many people. 'Cities in Transition,' on the other hand, is too anodyne and general to be of much use; every city is always 'in transition.'" At an April 2011 meeting of the American Assembly on the future of cities experiencing substantial population loss, participants proposed "legacy cities."

Morrison and Kelly articulate struggles with a shift in paradigm. The most common perspective of planners—to encourage and manage growth and development projects—does not fit their situations. Rather than figuring out how to do more infill housing in disinvested areas or how to transform derelict neighborhood commercial districts with main street programs, they are making progress on developing different approaches, as Gans, Krumholz, Thompson, and others recommended in the 1970s.

Pursue a planning process that addresses the legacy of the past.
In cities that have declined, the planning process has to allow residents to address the wrongs and divisions of the past. Racism, class divisions, and the disruption of urban renewal and interstate-highway construction remain vivid memories. In the most disinvested areas, few new homeowners have arrived over the last few decades, so discussions about what such areas should become raise alarm particularly in minority-race residents and elderly homeowners who have endured the changes that destroyed their neighborhoods.

Divisions based on class, race, and ethnicity continue to inform discussions in cities such as Youngstown and Flint. As these cities developed in the late nineteenth and early twentieth centuries, the owners and managers of large manufacturing corporations used race and class divisions to slow unionization and control workers. Segregated neighborhoods reinforced the divisions that existed within the factories. During the 1960s and 1970s, urban renewal, highway construction, and white flight to suburbs disrupted these neighborhoods while reinforcing views on race and class. Plant shutdowns throughout the 1980s eliminated tens of thousands of good-paying manufacturing jobs.[50] Unemployment and tax and mortgage foreclosures increased, and the widespread abandonment of working-class neighborhoods accelerated. Long-time residents who remained have seen an increase in rental property, the arrival of slumlords, high turnover among renters, increasing disinvestment, falling property values, demolition of many structures, and the abandonment of entire neighborhoods.

To make progress toward figuring out what cities like Youngstown or Flint can become in the future, the planning process has to address the heritage of feelings of injustice, distrust, and loss. Kelly stated,

> My planning education taught me how to script meetings to present information and get feedback without acknowledging the power dynamics created by racial and class difference. This kind of engagement in Flint has proven ineffective because of the legacy of racism, top-down decision making, and white flight. Through work with community partners experienced in community engagement and social justice work, I have learned that the foundations of effective engagement are equity, respect, and honesty. As a white person working for a county authority that holds the majority of its properties in mostly black areas, I now recognize the importance of publicly acknowledging structural and historical racism and classism that helped to create today's challenges. Through my work with a team of black and white facilitators that is led by a black woman, I have learned how to create engagement processes that are structured enough to achieve specific outcomes and allow all participants to have a voice while, at the same time, they are flexible enough to be responsive to residents' feelings and concerns. I have been in meetings where the agenda and flow change on the spot to address a conflict or feelings of anger or disrespect that come up.

With others, Kelly facilitated such sessions on "Strengthening Our Community in the Face of Population Decline" in fall 2009. These encouraged discussion of Flint's challenges and of strategies to strengthen neighborhoods and make better use of abandoned land. Inez Brown, Flint's city clerk, connecting to memory, told the audience that she had experienced the "I-475 relocation" in the 1970s when her house was taken, but she called for openness to new approaches. Flint residents "must look on this as opportunity, not a negative," she said. Residents should "put aside turf wars, put aside animosities from the past, and think about our children."

In Youngstown, Jay Williams (director of the community development agency, later mayor) led "town halls" to talk about race, where he invited attendees to talk about their views on race with the aim of moving toward a better future for the city. Williams laid out ground rules and showed a video overview of the city's history of race and class conflict.[51]

"People talked for a full hour, and it was crystal clear that people had more to say," Morrison recalled. "Jay and I huddled with the producer and agreed to resume the dialogue the next week. The second show, like the first, was both hard-hitting and therapeutic. And at the end of the hour, we agreed to continue and taped a third hour segment, which aired the following week. The strategy of going live and discussing difficult and, at times, inflammatory issues in an open civic forum was risky. But it was necessary. And it cleared the air and convinced the public that Youngstown 2010 was not just another public planning process that pretended to listen to people—and then largely ignored what they said."

"These town hall meetings were critical to the success of the Youngstown 2010 process," Morrison said. "Citizens of Youngstown were on live television talking to each other—and the Northeast Ohio region—about the difficult issues of race and class. It was like a family intervention: heartfelt, honest, direct discussion about issues from people's shared past that too often held Youngstown back." He concluded:

> The lesson for me is clear. Historically industrial cities like Youngstown and Flint are, in many ways, big extended families with long memories of past slights. The past is always present in the decisions of the day. Planners, particularly those who are not "from here," have to understand that they are in the third or fourth act of a very long drama. We don't have the luxury of thinking that all things can, will—or should—be made new. Like skilled social workers or family therapists, we have to start where individuals and their communities are and work with them to move forward. And we have to listen—very intently—as people talk about their history as well as their aspirations.

Urban planning is a "white, middle-class field" and increasingly suburban, Kelly said. "There's something wrong about our deciding what to do about working-class black and ethnic neighborhoods" in central cities. Therefore, the process of addressing issues of race, poverty, and industrial dislocation is essential in order collectively to envision the future of Flint.

"A community's industrial history can be an asset as well as a liability," Morrison stated:

As my colleagues, Sherry Linkon and John Russo have noted, these are communities of "shared memory" with a strong sense of community identity that defines the collective personality of their citizens.[52] As planners, we must explore this shared memory if we are to craft physical and economic development strategies that are true to a place's unique "genetic code." We need to appreciate what makes each shrinking industrial city a distinct place and work with those assets—human, environmental, and economic—to develop place-specific strategies for moving the community forward.

Kelly, Morrison, and others have learned through reflective practice[53] what some planning scholars have derived from planning processes related to loss and in multicultural settings. As Marris wrote of planning with groups that had experienced collective loss such as slum clearance, "Every attempt to preempt conflict, argument, protest by rational planning can only be abortive: however reasonable the proposed changes, the process of implementing them must still allow the impulse of rejection to play itself out."[54] Marris recommended three principles for managing change in such circumstances: expecting and encouraging conflict, respecting the autonomy of different kinds of experience, and taking time and exercising patience in the process. Sandercock argued that some tragic "core stories" that define and reproduce a group of people with shared past and culture need to be transformed in a healing process, so that change becomes possible. A process to accomplish this involves "public telling of the story in a way that accepts its truth and acknowledges its power and pain," an exchange that settles differences, a ceremony or ritual that acknowledges a new beginning, and ongoing commitment and trust in a new approach.[55] Such efforts do not necessarily succeed; Forester points out that deliberative planning processes that acknowledge and work through collective suffering can either encourage or interfere with reaching conclusions about future direction.[56]

Pursue a planning process that enables residents to develop a shared vision for a smaller city.
The participation and involvement of residents has to extend beyond addressing the legacy of distrust and division. In Youngstown, "the vision emerged from the involvement of hundreds of people in focus groups," Morrison said:

People were ready for change. Fourteen hundred people showed up for the presentation of the Youngstown 2010 Vision. That audience was five to ten times as large as any attending a public planning meeting in Cleveland when I was that city's planning director. There was a sense of hope in the audience—mixed with deep frustration at past revitalization efforts that offered grand gestures and silver bullets but ultimately failed to deliver. People thirsted for a different, more realistic path to the future.[57]

After the initial meeting, volunteers created elements of the plan. After two years of work, 1,300 people attended a second community meeting to hear and comment on a public presentation of the finished plan.[58] At the end of the process, residents were committed to strengthening Youngstown as a smaller city.

"The Vision for Youngstown 2010 has four pillars: accepting that Youngstown is a smaller city and resolving to become a sustainable mid-sized city; adjusting to the new regional and global economies; addressing community image and quality of life; and taking action.[59] Of the four pillars, acceptance of the reality that Youngstown is a smaller place has been the most liberating and energizing," Morrison said. "The community no longer feels compelled to pursue unrealistic expectations and instead feels free to rewrite its narrative. The new narrative contemplates a Youngstown that goes from 'gray' to 'green' and becomes a model sustainable, mid-sized city rather than a gritty industrial boom town."

City residents often embrace the idea of a smaller city more quickly than their elected officials and city appointees, both Kelly and Morrison said. "Residents know that Flint is going to be smaller," Kelly said. "They see and feel the changes that are happening around them. Houses that were once occupied are now vacant or demolished. Gardens are sprouting up on lots throughout the city. . . . If Flint leaders initiate a process that involves authentic engagement to create a vision for Flint's future, I think that residents will acknowledge that Flint is becoming a smaller city. I have heard lots of ideas from residents about how they want to use the abundance of available land to create a stronger, safer, and greener city, ideas I hope would come out in a master planning process."

"Planners need to . . . give [people] the facts [about prospects for growth]," Morrison said:

When we do that, we gain credibility and can help a community envision a realistic future. The people are often far ahead of the planners and the politicians in accepting the reality of shrinkage in their community. As we have seen in several Youngstown neighborhoods, people often are comfortable with lower density provided the city removes blighted buildings, addresses crime, and maintains basic city services. Elected officials generally are another story. Mayors and councilpersons have a problem accepting the reality of sustained population loss and insist that their communities will be restored to past glory. By contrast, Youngstown's public officials embrace and promote the community's new narrative of a smaller and more sustainable city. This new political language is the direct result of the Youngstown 2010 planning process. Developing this language is, perhaps, Youngstown's most significant contribution to the emerging national debate on the future of America's historically industrial cities.

During the planning process, how can planners aid acceptance of becoming a smaller city? "Planners need to be both interpreters and visionaries," Morrison said. "Planners need to understand and communicate the changes taking place in their community and put them in larger regional, mega regional and global contexts. By taking this approach, we have seen that what has happened to Youngstown since 1978 has happened in industrial communities throughout the Great Lakes states and, in fact, throughout Europe's historic industrial regions. We are not alone. That is an empowering insight." Morrison continued:

We also have come to understand and explain Youngstown's emerging role within the megaregion stretching between Cleveland and Akron on the west to Pittsburgh on the east. Youngstown is in the middle of a region with a population in excess of seven million people and can connect to assets concentrated at both ends. That is an actionable insight. Our congressman, Tim Ryan, and his Pennsylvania colleague, Congressman Jason Altmire, have labeled this region the "Tech Belt" and have encouraged bistate collaboration on economic development and transportation initiatives. The community's development strategies now embrace that larger, regional geography.

Planners must also be visionaries. We need to help our communities think about a sustainable future without significant population growth. We can bring the most current technologies to this critical discussion. Just as fast-growing communities are using GIS [geographic information systems]-based simulation to explore alternative ways to handle anticipated population growth, we need to employ these same tools to explore alternative ways to restructure our shrinking industrial cities in the face of anticipated slow- or no-growth demographic trends.

"Data are key," Kelly said:

Using data and maps helps to show patterns and relationships in a different way. People have become accustomed to seeing vacant lots in Flint. However, showing a map of the city with more than 12,000 dots, each dot representing a vacant lot, allows people to see just how much vacant land Flint has. When you overlay the racial make-up of Flint residents on top of the map of vacant lots, it creates a powerful image of a highly segregated city with vacant land concentrated in mostly African American neighborhoods up through the core of the city along the industrial corridor. When I showed this map at a community meeting recently, a resident said, "It almost makes it look like racism is systemic." Maps and other graphics become great tools to help residents make connections and engage in difficult conversations that they might otherwise not have. Through this experience, people realize that Flint is not about growth.

We don't know the answers ourselves. This is a civic learning process, and it is not about planners deciding what to do on their own. It is about figuring out how to design a process that provides information and creates enough structure to have difficult conversations, acknowledge past mistakes, and create plans for the future.

Kelly and Morrison articulate an iterative process of achieving a vision of a smaller city. Residents, business owners, and others see the futility of an entirely growth-oriented approach before city leaders do, and planners can help citizens and decision makers see the city's prospects more clearly through maps and data. In addition to envisioning a smaller city, planners and citizens can reorient their vision for the future to encompass a region larger than the city.

Focus on community assets and magnets.

A planner should always be asking, "What are the assets?" said Kelly and Morrison.[60] One strategy for cities following decline is to identify how a city can build on "core assets" that will likely be in place for many decades where greater demand for property may exist. "What will be here in a hundred years? What is enduring?" Morrison asked. In both Flint and Youngstown, Kelly and Morrison see universities as anchors where demand for land and buildings exists and people still want to live. "Youngstown State University celebrated its hundredth anniversary several years ago," Morrison said. "We can be reasonably certain that the university will be here 100 years from now. We cannot be as certain about the future of many of our other community assets. If you want to build a sustainable future in cities like Youngstown, build off the assets you know will be there for the long haul."

This is "asset-based resizing," Morrison said. In Flint, Kelly considers the hospitals assets and anchors of activity as well. The presence of the University of Michigan-Flint just off the main downtown street has begun to support the development of new housing for students who could bring greater activity to downtown if they lived there.

"We should also be thinking about what the community's 'magnets' are," Morrison said. "These are the institutions and corporations that draw people in to work and learn. Some of the people who come to the city might choose to live there, especially in downtown or in an historic neighborhood. Cities like Youngstown can develop niche housing strategies that target their universities' students and new faculty, their hospitals' interns and residents and their downtown office workers." Kelly agreed: "Thousands of government workers, service workers connected to judicial processes, university and hospital employees come to downtown Flint every day. If even a few of these chose to live downtown, their activity could help strengthen that area of the city."

"We agree with those national advocates for stronger approaches to addressing vacant properties who recommend taking a strategic approach to assembling and developing vacant land and buildings," Kelly said:

> We partnered with Kettering University, the City of Flint, and others to create a plan for the river district, a residential and commercial

area adjacent to downtown and centered around a 140-acre concrete slab that was a former auto manufacturing plant. The area is bounded by two universities and a major medical center. Through partnerships with public and nonprofit developers, we renovated two blighted hotels and an old apartment building to create 138 affordable and market rate apartments within the district. We also purchased, remediated and sold a former auto repair shop adjacent to one of the old hotels. The building was completely renovated and converted into a deli and antique shop.

Part of the planners' job, according to Beckley, is to create "self-fulfilling prophecies" in connection with assets. Self-fulfilling ideas are strong property reuse ideas so compelling that many others build on them or continue their implementation; they create a momentum that leads to strengthening assets without planners' continuing involvement.[61]

Rediscover the urban landscape.
Many of America's previously industrial cities developed rapidly without benefit of a plan. In the rush to build workforce housing, people leveled forests, channeled streams into culverts, filled wetlands and obliterated other natural features. The abandonment of working-class neighborhoods offers these cities an opportunity to restore natural features and position them as assets for the future. "We can ask what [Frederick Law] Olmsted and his colleagues might have done if urban land now vacant and the water course no longer used industrially had been available when they did their work a century ago," Morrison said. "The loss of population, industries, and housing allows those of us in Youngstown to see the land again," he continued. "We can see more clearly the vistas and water courses that were hidden by the mills and tight working-class neighborhoods." In Youngstown, the Mahoning River, long a sewer running behind a wall of steel mills, is now a prominent downtown landscape feature.

In Flint, local organizations and institutions formed the Flint River Corridor Alliance to continue implementing the strategy and thinking about the river as an asset.[62] "Thinking about enhancing the landscape is a major way we build on assets in our planning," Kelly said.

Planners can think about how to "connect the dots" of a city's parks and open spaces and recreate natural systems. One of Youngstown's legacies is a good park system. The Youngstown plan suggests linking the city's parks and leveraging them as assets. The plan proposes using vacant land to complete parks unfinished during the industrial era and to connect parks with a network of trails and bikeways.[63]

Planners can also repurpose vacant land to restore natural systems. The Youngstown plan suggests assembling large tracts of vacant formerly residential land with hydric soils for urban wetlands and wildlife sanctuaries and proposes converting vacant riverfront industrial sites into naturalized areas for stormwater retention.

"Without the population pressure, Youngstown can consider ripping up asphalt areas and daylighting streams," Morrison said. "We can take pressure off some of our aging combined sewers by removing abandoned hardscapes and reducing the outflow."

In Flint, the Land Bank staff seeks to use vacant property for stormwater management and, in doing so, to provide ecological assets that enhance quality of life. Spring Grove was a tax-foreclosed property with a natural spring that was once a construction dumpsite. After securing a grant from the U.S. Environmental Protection Agency and a local foundation, the Land Bank worked with the neighborhood association to restore the wetland and reintroduce native plants. Students from the University of Michigan Landscape Architecture Program offered design ideas for the planning process with the neighborhood. Kelly and Morrison agree that planners working in cities such as Youngstown and Flint need to bring landscape design to the discussion, either by acquiring the skills themselves or by partnering with landscape architects.

Find ways to reuse neighborhood land without rebuilding.
As a city becomes smaller, planners need to manage planning processes for neighborhood change. Neighborhood planning and community development usually focus on redevelopment, rebuilding, and revitalization. This perspective is not sufficient for cities that have lost large shares of population but need improvement in quality of life in disinvested neighborhoods. Kelly said, in Flint, people are dealing with "emerging vacant land instead of vanishing vacant land."

Planners must recognize that some neighborhoods will not exist, or they will not exist in the way they once did, Morrison noted:

We need to look at surplus housing in our shrinking industrial cities unsentimentally. The housing in many of Youngstown's neighborhoods truly is obsolete and not worthy of renovation for today's market. This housing was built quickly 75 to 100 years ago to provide workforce housing. It has not met the test of time; like a dry snake skin, this housing has done its job and has no viable future. The same can be said of many of our older neighborhoods. They did their job housing workers for factories that no longer exist, offering a close-knit supportive community for recent immigrants, and providing the first rung on the ladder of the American Dream for many families. But their purpose is past. These neighborhoods need to be repurposed to meet current and future needs.

What does depopulation mean for Flint's neighborhoods? Kelly states that planning needs to focus on encouraging dialogue about what population loss means for land use, building coalitions around neighborhood change, tapping resources of other organizations whose work relates to land use, and building neighborhood capacity for planning and implementing change. "We are planning to *do*," she said:

> The purpose is to work with people in neighborhoods to find ways to enhance neighborhoods through the reuse of land held by the Land Bank. The Land Bank has a range of programs to accomplish the reuse of abandoned property: adopt-a-lot, side lot transfer, demolition, housing rental, garden resources, and others. These programs constitute the *doing* that could be better integrated if we had a plan for the city. In the absence of that, we work through a collaborative of groups and individuals to give residents the skills they need to work with other residents to create their own plans to guide the change they want to see in their neighborhoods. Through their own process, they learn to connect to other residents and create plans collectively. At the same time, they become better equipped to engage in other planning processes. . . . We also connect neighborhoods with planning resources wherever we can find them.

In the emptiest, most abandoned areas, the appropriate approach may be "urban land fallowing," said Morrison. Youngstown's residents backed a framework for managing depopulated neighborhoods. "The plan suggests that we should 'be generous' with our urban land and not feel compelled to put something new on every parcel. We can let our urban land lie fallow until viable new purposes emerge. The plan also recommends not scattering new development randomly. As a result, the city no longer approves the building of Low Income Housing Tax Credit housing on streets that are largely abandoned and instead focuses on streets that are still intact."

Youngstown experimented with encouraging residents in largely abandoned neighborhoods to relocate to intact streets. When residents from these neighborhoods requested repair funding, city planners offered them $50,000 to buy a new home in an intact neighborhood. As of fall 2010, no homeowner had accepted the incentive.[64]

As an alternative to engaging homeowners when they seek funds for renovation, cities like Youngstown and Flint could consider intervening when a homeowner, or his family or estate, seeks to sell the house and confronts a buyers' market limited to absentee landlords seeking cheap property. A city government or a land bank could take the position of "patient buyer," acquiring property in largely abandoned neighborhoods only when a homeowner seeks to leave or dies, if the purchasing entity has the legal standing to buy such property.[65]

The Land Bank owns many properties in largely abandoned neighborhoods where most houses show signs of advanced disinvestment. "When you have a portfolio of abandoned properties," Kelly said, "when you control land, you can encourage people to come forward to do things. It's not centralized planning as much as it is creating access to the land and facilitating engagement in planning and decision-making. . . . We look for ways to enable people to use land in new ways. We want to give people land and let them choose what to do with it," within some limits. The Land Bank seeks to support new uses that give purpose to vacant land without rebuilding—encouraging community gardens, for instance.

Kelly wants to explore uses of vacant land that can provide people with income. "Can we be a recycling center?" Kelly asked. Scrap and junkyards already operate along an old commercial corridor in Flint. "How can pieces of old houses find use elsewhere? Can we encourage deconstruction businesses? How can agriculture, community gardening, biofuel production, composting, and tree nurseries, for example, find appropriate locations and provide income and property tax revenue?"

In Flint, obsolete codes hamper land use change. "Many of the city's codes and ordinances don't make sense any longer" because they apply to a built-up city addressing new development, Kelly said. City agencies need to collaborate in new ways to enable reuse of vacant land. Flint has an array of practices that discourage gardening, for instance. The city cuts off water to lots without someone who pays the water bill. Municipal trucks do not pick up garbage when no house exists; gardeners have to haul waste to a property with a house on it. After demolishing a house, the city fills the lot with clay, so gardeners have to bring in soil. No city composting exists. A greenhouse violates the city building and zoning codes because it is an auxiliary use; a house has to exist for an auxiliary use to be permitted.

"When people are willing to do something with land," Kelly said, "we try to support them" while, at the same time, listening to neighbors' views. The Land Bank has supported gardening on Land-Bank-owned lots by advocating for changes to local ordinances and by providing resources to growers, including seeds, plants, and services in tilling, clearing, soil testing, and compost delivery. However, providing support to urban gardeners has not met with universal approval. Kelly related that, during a meeting, a resident said, "We came from sharecropping and don't want white people to turn our neighborhood into farms. That was a hard life, not a good life, and we don't want chickens in the back yard."

The Land Bank focuses on improving conditions for people in poverty, a population most vulnerable to the negative effects of neighboring abandonment. The Land Bank began a rental program when staff found former renters and homeowners living in properties the Land Bank had received through tax foreclosure.

Concern for the here-and-now often dominates the Land Bank's neighborhood meetings. "Residents talk about what they do not want," Kelly said. "It's hard to get people beyond the immediate issue—'stop the shooting!' It's hard to get people to think big about the future." Many residents say they would leave if they could.

The planner's role in cities like Youngstown and Flint is to deal with the fear and talk people through the immediate issues to get beyond these to a vision. "The key," said Kelly, "is to get people to the point where they are 'planning to stay.'"[66] If residents' perspectives change, they will invest in their homes and neighborhoods. They see positive features of their neighborhood and want to improve it.

Kelly and her colleagues look for ways to reinforce neighborhoods where people still want to live. "We move forward with our programs to encourage reuse of available land and support neighborhood-level planning even without the city endorsing the idea of making a smaller, better city," Kelly said. "So much can happen outside of city government."

The Land Bank has taken the initiative in several ways. It sells adjacent vacant lots to homeowners and makes agreements with individuals or groups to care for property. The Land Bank also enables homeowners to acquire vacant lots around their homes.

The Land Bank staff find ways to develop plans for neighborhoods that have enough assets and are sufficiently organized that residents want a plan.[67] Then the neighbors pitch the plan to others to get it implemented. For instance, in the Grand Traverse District, a few blocks west of downtown, residents got cleanup of a contaminated site and restoration of a wetland, pressed for conversion of one-way streets to two-way to slow traffic, attracted investments in a park, and built several Habitat for Humanity houses.

Act expeditiously to get rid of liabilities.
Besides building on and enhancing assets, planners need to address liabilities. With strong demand for land, a burned building or a vacated industrial site quickly gets reused, with exceptions when ownership uncertainty and environmental liabilities cause delay. In contrast, a city that has experienced large-scale population and employment loss cannot rely on demand to reuse abandoned property. City officials must act quickly to remove the surplus housing and commercial property that depresses other property values, discourages reinvestment, and often harbors criminal activities.

City officials need to get rid of derelict industrial structures, secure contaminated sites, and demolish ruined houses and abandoned commercial districts. "Addressing this large-scale, long-term structural abandonment is a problem for stressed cities such as Youngstown and Flint," Morrison said. "Federal and state housing and environmental policies have thus far failed to recognize the scale of the abandonment problem confronting these communities. The 'one size fits all' approaches we too often see coming out of Washington and Columbus need to change if we are to remove the detritus of the past and position our communities for the future."

Demolition of derelict housing needs to occur quickly to reduce harm to neighbors and encourage them to maintain their own property. Discussions of strategic demolition also need to reflect neighborhood realities, Kelly said. "How can you possibly not do demolition everywhere? You can't leave the mom with five kids to live in a house between burned out structures."

In places with development pressures, conservationists have pointed rightly to the need to adapt buildings, especially significant, old ones, to new uses rather than demolish them. This situation differs from that in cities with extensive population loss and property disinvestment where the number of buildings far exceeds that needed for residential, commercial, and industrial uses; demolition removes destroyed structures. The most extensive residential disinvestment occurs first where people do not want to live—where the housing stock is poor quality, close to highways or busy streets and to contaminated sites—so reuse is least possible there.

Focusing demolition efforts on cleaning up the entries to the city is part of Youngstown's strategy because gateways give people their first impression of the city. "Interstates and arterials need to be attractive, well lit, well signed and well maintained," Morrison said:

> Since adopting Youngstown 2010, the city has collaborated with the State of Ohio, the Youngstown State University, Lien Forward [the Mahoning County land bank] and CityScape [an urban open space advocacy group] to upgrade freeway bridges, clean up urban arterials, improve lighting, and beautify gateway focal points. We have targeted demolitions on highly visible sites along gateway arterials on the theory that these properties are "billboards of blight" that only reinforce Youngstown's popular reputation as a Rust Belt city. There has been a significant change in people's attitude toward the city as a result of taking these actions.

Conclusion

"Planners, like nature, abhor a vacuum" Morrison says. "Our impulse is to redevelop, rebuild and fill the gaps in the street and the neighborhood." However, if the thinking of planners such as Kelly and Morrison becomes more widespread, planners will look differently at cities that have lost large amounts of population and where little demand remains for housing and other kinds of property. Planners' thinking needs to shift from focusing on redeveloping and revitalizing to restructuring and reinventing.

Kelly's and Morrison's assertions about different ways of planning in cities with extensive disinvestment help to reframe how planners can approach work in such cities. Their views in this brief chapter also overlook important issues that planners in such settings need to address. First, an urban planner who sees that a city will not gain population and has few prospects for growth needs to find ways to deal with progrowth politics. Morrison arrived in Youngstown when leadership had become open to a change; Kelly had to work with thousands of abandoned properties regardless of whether the mayor wanted to acknowledge Flint's lack of prospects for growth. Planners in other cities, however, might need to find ways to work within a pro-growth context or help change it. As the efforts of Norman Krumholz and others showed in the 1970s, such work can confront considerable opposition.[68] Second, as population leaves and disinvestment proceeds, the poverty rate rises. The middle class moves away. Therefore, the work of planners in the context of decline needs to address social equity concerns quite consciously in implementing change. Planners should address social equity wherever they work, but in previously industrial cities planners face the challenge of improving conditions for people living in the worst neighborhood conditions while, for example, also building on assets and getting rid of visible liabilities. Every decision about the use of scarce resources needs to confront this issue. Third, this discussion has not addressed ways to handle derelict and obsolete commercial corridors. These corridors no longer serve dense neighborhoods and cannot accommodate the changed shopping habits and retail location patterns. They contribute to blight of nearby residential properties. Finally, such cities face many challenges beyond the built environment, and planners have much to contribute in these areas. For instance, how can city officials deal with declining revenues and rising costs in the city budget, and how could adjustments in services reduce costs? How can the use of resources such as federal Community Development Block Grants become more effective?

Training of planners needs to change, Morrison and Kelly asserted, to help them plan for smaller, better cities. "The language of smart growth and new urbanism haven't helped us much," Morrison said. Indeed, if planning education directly addresses the challenges of cities that have lost large amounts of population, where new development is rarely a choice, new planners will more easily adapt to a different paradigm in creating a better city with little new development.

NOTES

Introduction

1. In this chapter we often refer to "race," but many of the conditions apply to minority ethnicities. Like the U.S. Census Bureau, we treat Hispanic as an ethnicity, not a race.

2. Center for Urban and Regional Studies, Youngstown State University, "Population Comparisons: All Data for 1950, 1970, 2000, and the 2008 Estimate," http://cfweb.cc.ysu.edu/psi/planning.htm.

3. Tim Rieniets, "Global Shrinkage," in *Shrinking Cities*, vol. 1, ed. Philipp Oswalt (Ostfildern-Ruit, Germany: Hatje Cantz, 2005), 20–34.

4. Robert A. Beauregard, "Urban Population Loss in Historical Perspective: USA, 1820–2000," *Environment and Planning A* 41 (2009): 520.

5. For example, Ann O'M. Bowman and Michael A. Pagano, *Terra Incognita: Vacant Land and Urban Strategies* (Washington, D.C.: Georgetown University Press, 2004).

6. The term "abandonment" has varying definitions. See contrasting definitions in Alan Mallach, *Bringing Buildings Back* (Montclair, N.J.: National Housing Institute, 2006); David Wilson, Harry Margulis, and James Ketchum, "Spatial Aspects of Housing Abandonment in the 1990s," *Housing Studies* 9, 4 (1994): 493–510; Benjamin Scafidi, Michael Schill, Susan Wachter, and Dennis Culhane, "An Economic Analysis of Housing Abandonment," *Journal of Housing Economics* 7 (1998): 287–303. Mallach defines abandonment as property whose owner has stopped carrying out basic functions and which is therefore vacant or will soon become vacant. Wilson et al. count abandoned houses as those that have been withdrawn from the housing market and that the owner does not intend to return to the market for the same use. Scafidi et al. define "abandonment" in terms of building owners who have stopped paying taxes and whose property subsequently has been demolished by city government. For discussion of the term, see Amy Hillier, Dennis Culhane, Tony Smith, and C. Dana Tomlin, "Predicting Housing Abandonment with the Philadelphia Neighborhood Information System," *Journal of Urban Affairs* 25, 1 (2003): 91–105. Hillier et al. suggest that abandonment is a process or a cycle, with three possible aspects: functional,

meaning a property is no longer used as a dwelling; financial, meaning the property owner is not meeting minimal financial obligations; or physical, when owners neglect upkeep.

7. John Iceland, Daniel Weinberg, and Erika Steinmetz, *Racial and Ethnic Residential Segregation in the United States*, Census 2000 Special Reports, Washington, D.C., 2002.

8. For example, John F. Kain, "The Distribution and Movement of Jobs and Industry," in *The Metropolitan Enigma*, ed. James Q. Wilson (Cambridge, Mass.: Harvard University Press, 1968), 1–43; Reynolds Farley, Sheldon Danziger, and Harry J. Holzer, *Detroit Divided* (New York: Russell Sage, 2000); June Manning Thomas, *Redevelopment and Race* (Baltimore: Johns Hopkins University Press, 1997); Anthony Downs, "The Challenge of Our Declining Big Cities," *Housing Policy Debate* 8, 2 (1997): 359–408; Beauregard, "Urban Population Loss in Historical Perspective"; William W. Goldsmith and Edward J. Blakely, *Separate Societies* (Philadelphia: Temple University Press, 1992); Camille Zubrinsky Charles, "The Dynamics of Racial Residential Segregation," *Annual Review of Sociology* 29 (2003): 167–207.

9. For example, Barry Bluestone and Bennett Harrison, *The Deindustrialization of America* (New York: Basic Books, 1982).

10. George Sternlieb, *The Tenement Landlord* (New Brunswick, N.J.: Rutgers University Press, 1966); George Sternlieb, Robert W. Burchell, James W. Hughes, and Franklin J. James, "Housing Abandonment in the Urban Core," *Journal of the American Institute of Planners* 40, 5 (1974): 321–32; Michael A. Stegman, *Housing Investment in the Inner City* (Cambridge, Mass.: MIT Press, 1972); Anthony Downs, *Neighborhoods and Urban Development* (Washington, D.C.: Brookings Institution, 1981).

11. Alex F. Schwartz, *Housing Policy in the United States* (New York: Routledge, 2006), 238.

12. R. J. King, "MCA Exec Pleads Guilty to Fraud," *Detroit News*, August 29, 2001; Cameron McWhirter, "Homes Can't Hide Blight," *Detroit News*, September 28, 1999; Dan Immergluck, *Foreclosed* (Ithaca, N.Y.: Cornell University Press, 2009).

13. Robert Burchell, George Lowenstein, William R. Dolphin, and Catherine C. Galley, *Costs of Sprawl—2000*, Transit Cooperative Research Program Report 74 (Washington, D.C.: National Academy Press, 2002).

14. For example, Philipp Oswalt, ed., *Shrinking Cities*, vol. 2 (Ostfildern, Germany: Hatje Cantz, 2006); Philipp Oswalt, Tim Rieniets, and Henning Schirmel, eds., *Atlas of Shrinking Cities* (Ostfildern, Germany: Hatje Cantz, 2006); Karina Pallagst, "Shrinking Cities: Planning Challenges from an International Perspective," in *Cities Growing Smaller*, ed. Steve Rugare and Terry Schwarz (Cleveland: Kent State University, 2008), 6–16; Larry S. Bourne and Jim Simmons, "New Fault Lines?" *Canadian Journal of Urban Research* 12, 1 (2003): 22–47.

15. For example, Camilo Vergara, *American Ruins* (New York: Monacelli Press, 1999); Michael Chanan and George Steinmetz, *Detroit*, film released March 15, 2005,

http://www.detroitruinofacity.com/; Sean Hemmerle, "The Remains of Detroit," photo essay, *Time*, December 4, 2008; Andrew Moore and Philip Levine, *Detroit Disassembled* (Bologne: Damiani, 2010); Yves Marchand and Romain Meffre, *The Ruins of Detroit* (Göttingen: Steidl, 2010).

16. Noreen Malone, "The Case Against Economic Disaster Porn," *New Republic*, January 22, 2011.

17. Mark Bittman, "Imagining Detroit," *Opinionator* (blog), *New York Times*, May 17, 2011.

18. This area is census tract 5436 bounded by Fenkell on the north, Lamphere on the west, Lyndon on the south, and Kentfield on the east.

19. U.S. Census Bureau, "Total Population," Census 1990 Summary File 1, Table P1; Census Bureau, "Race," Census 2010 National Redistricting Data Summary File, Table P1; Census Bureau, Census 2010 TIGER/Line Files; Census Bureau, "Poverty Status in the Past 12 Months by Sex by Age," "Sex of Workers by Place of Work-Place Level," and "Sex by Age by Employment Status for the Population 16 Years and Over," American Community Survey 2005–2009 5-Year Estimates, Tables B17001, B08008, B23001.

20. U.S. Census Bureau, "Age Groups and Sex," Census 2010, Table QT-P1; U.S. Census Bureau, "Sex by Educational Attainment for the Population 25 Years and Over," American Community Survey 2005–2009 5-Year Estimates, Tables B01001, B15002; Census Bureau, "Fact Sheet for Detroit, Michigan," American Community Survey 2005–2009 5-Year Estimates.

21. U.S. Census Bureau, "Occupancy Status," Census 2010 National Redistricting Data Summary File, Table H1; U.S. Census Bureau, Census 2010 TIGER/Line Files; Data Driven Detroit, "Detroit Residential Parcel Survey," 2009, http://www.detroit parcelsurvey.org/index.php; U.S. Census Bureau, "Tenure, Household Size, and Age of Householder," Census 2010 SF 1, Tables QT-H2, H4; Census Bureau, "Tenure by Age of Householder," American Community Survey 2005–2009 5-Year Estimates, Table B25007; Census Bureau, "Fact Sheet for Detroit, Michigan," American Community Survey 2005–2009 5-Year Estimates.

22. Michigan Department of Agriculture and Rural Development, "Food Establishment Licensing Data" (Table FI-107, data file, 2011), http://www.michigan.gov /mdard/0,1607,7-125-1569_16958_16974-173898-,00.html; Data Driven Detroit, "Detroit Residential Parcel Survey"; U.S. Census Bureau, Census 2010TIGER/Line Files; U.S. Department of Agriculture, *Access to Affordable and Nutritious Food*, report to Congress, June 2009, http://www.ers.usda.gov/Publications/AP/AP036/AP036fm.pdf; Michigan Department of Energy, Labor, and Economic Growth, Statewide Search for Child Day Care Centers and Homes, 2010, http://www.dleg.state.mi.us/brs_cdc/sr_lfl .asp; Michigan Department of Energy, Labor, and Economic Growth, Barbershop and Nail Salon Licensing Data, 2010, http://www.michigan.gov/lara/0,1607,7-154-35299 _35414_35454-139498-,00.html.

23. Calculated from "Crimes for 54 Block Area, January 1, 2011–May 15, 2011," City of Detroit Police Department data on CrimeMapping.com, accessed May 24, 2011; City of Detroit Police Department, "Reported Crime Statistics for Detroit," http://www.ci.detroit.mi.us/LinkClick.aspx?fileticket=QTmqVqvC1qo%3d&tabid=1189&mid=4527.

24. Detroit Public Schools, "Performance Reports," http://detroitk12.org/schools/reports/; Detroit Public Schools, attendance areas, http://detroitk12.org/schools/docs/school_boundaries_elementary.pdf; http://detroitk12.org/schools/docs/school_boundaries_high.pdf; https://secure.detroitk12.org/schools/docs/school_boundaries_middle.pdf.

25. Margaret Dewar and Robert Linn, "Remaking Brightmoor," in *Mapping Detroit*, ed. June Manning Thomas and Henco Bekkering, draft book manuscript; Tobias Armborst, Daniel D'Oca, and Georgeen Theodore, "Improve Your Lot!" in Rugare and Schwarz, *Cities Growing Smaller*, 45–64.

26. Data based on field research, September 2010.

27. Catherine Coenen et al., "From Revenue to Reuse: Managing Tax-Reverted Properties in Detroit," Urban and Regional Planning Program, University of Michigan, Ann Arbor, 2011, http://sitemaker.umich.edu/urpoutreachreports/all_reports; Dewar and Linn, "Remaking Brightmoor."

28. Jeff Gerritt, "Bing: Let's Move Detroiters into the City's Viable Areas," *Detroit Free Press*, December 9, 2010.

29. James Holston, "Spaces of Insurgent Citizenship," in *Making the Invisible Visible: A Multicultural Planning History*, ed. Leonie Sandercock (Berkeley: University of California Press, 1998), 37–56.

30. John R. Logan and Harvey Molotch, *Urban Fortunes* (Berkeley: University of California Press, 1987); Peter Eisinger, "The Politics of Bread and Circuses," *Urban Affairs Review* 35, 3 (2000): 316–33.

31. George Galster, Peter Tatian, and John Accordino, "Targeting Investments for Neighborhood Revitalization," *Journal of the American Planning Association* 72, 4 (2006): 457–74.

32. Witold Rybczynski, "Downsizing Cities," *Atlantic Monthly*, October 1995, 36–40; Deborah E. Popper and Frank J. Popper, "Small Can Be Beautiful," *Planning* (July 2002): 20–23; Witold Rybczynski and Peter D. Linneman, "How to Save Our Shrinking Cities," *Public Interest* 135 (Spring 1999): 30–44; Justin B. Hollander, Karina M. Pallagst, Terry Schwarz, and Frank J. Popper, "Planning Shrinking Cities," in Hilda Blanco et al., eds., "Shaken, Shrinking, Hot, Impoverished and Informal: Emerging Research Agendas in Planning," special issue, *Progress in Planning* 72 (2009): 223–24.

33. Cleveland Land Lab, *Reimagining a More Sustainable Cleveland*, Cleveland Urban Design Collaborative (Cleveland: Kent State University, 2008); Cleveland Land Lab, *Reimagining Cleveland*, Cleveland Urban Design Collaborative (Cleveland: Kent State University, 2009); Cleveland Urban Design Collaborative, *Oak Hill Community Design Charrette, Youngstown, Ohio* (Cleveland: Kent State University, February 2006).

34. American Institute of Architects Sustainable Design Assessment Team, *Leaner, Greener Detroit*, report, October 30–November 1, 2008, http://www.aia.org /aiaucmp/groups/aia/documents/pdf/aiab080216.pdf, 59.

Chapter 1. Community Gardens and Urban Agriculture as Antithesis to Abandonment: Exploring a Citizenship-Land Model

1. J. Blaine Bonham, Gerri Spilka, and Darl Rastorfer, *Old Cities/Green Cities* (Chicago: American Planning Association, 2002); Jerome Kaufman and Martin Bailkey, "Farming Inside Cities Through Entrepreneurial Urban Agriculture," in *Recycling the City*, ed. R. Greenstein and Y. Sungu-Eryilmaz (Cambridge, Mass.: Lincoln Institute of Land Policy, 2004), 177–99. For designers' propositions, see Stephen Vogel, "DIY City Services" and Ingo Vetter, "Urban Agriculture," in *Shrinking Cities*, ed. Philipp Oswalt, vol. 1 (Ostfildern-Ruit, Germany: Hatje Cantz, 2005), 462–69, 484–93.

2. Vicki Been and Ioan Voicu, "The Effect of Community Gardens on Neighboring Property Rights," Law and Economics Working Paper Series, New York University, 2006; Anne Bellows, Katherine Brown, and Jac Smit, *Health Benefits of Urban Agriculture*, report for Community Food Security Coalition North American Initiative on Agriculture, 2003; Gloria Ramirez, "Social and Nutritional Benefits of Community Gardens for Hispanic Americans in New York City and Los Angeles," master's thesis, Kansas State University, 1995.

3. Duany Plater-Zyberk and Co., *Agricultural Urbanism*, draft report, March 25, 2009, http://www.lindroth.cc/pdf/QuickReadAgf.pdf. Examples of resources on planning community-based agricultural efforts include Kami Pothukuchi, "Community Food Assessment," *Journal of Planning Education and Research* 23, 4 (2004): 356–77; Megan Masson-Minock and Deirdra Stockmann, "Creating a Legal Framework for Urban Agriculture," *Journal of Agriculture, Food Systems, and Community Development* 1, 2 (2010): 91–104.

4. American Community Gardening Association, "What Is a Community Garden?" http://communitygarden.org/learn/.

5. Mark Francis, *Urban Open Space* (Covelo, Calif.: Island Press, 2003), 17.

6. Been and Voicu, "The Effect of Community Gardens on Neighboring Property Rights."

7. For examples, see the Guerrilla Gardening website, www.guerrillagardening. org; for refutations of guerrilla gardening, see Ben Helphand, "Garden Is Not Warfare," *AREA Chicago*, October 1, 2010, http://www.areachicago.org/p/issues/institutions-and -infrastructures/garden-not-warfare/. For a history of community gardening, see Thomas Bassett, "Reaping the Margins," *Landscape Journal* 25, 2 (1981): 1–8; Laura Lawson, *City Bountiful* (Berkeley: University of California Press, 2005).

8. New York Association for Improving the Conditions of the Poor, "Cultivation of Vacant City Lots by the Unemployed," *AICP Notes* 1, 1 (1895): 1–48. The Association

also extended to farmland, with hopes of permanent use of land that never material-
ized. Philadelphia Vacant Lot Cultivation Association annual reports noted the problem of losing sites when development pressure rebuilt.

9. Brian Trelstad, "Little Machines in Their Gardens," *Landscape Journal* 16, 2
(1997): 161–73.

10. Most gardens from World War II reverted to previous land uses after the war;
however, a few victory gardens persisted, such as the Fenway Community Garden in
Boston, Rainbow Victory Garden in Chicago, and several gardens on National Park
Service property in Washington.

11. Lawson, *City Bountiful*, 225–29. The USDA Urban Garden Program lasted
until 1993 when it was cut from the federal budget. The 23 cities that had the program
differed in how to address local expectations for ongoing urban gardening support.
Some dismantled their programs, while others shifted the work to nonprofits.

12. American Community Gardening Association, *National Community Gardening Survey*, Philadelphia, 1992, 1998.

13. Pamela R. Kirshbaum, "Making Policy in a Crowded World," *Community
Greening Review* 10 (2000): 2–11; Jane E. Schukoske, "Community Development
Through Gardening," *Legislation and Social Policy* 3 (2000): 351–92.

14. Lawson, *City Bountiful*, 257–63; Laura Lawson, "The South Central Farm,"
Cultural Geographies 14, 4 (2007): 611–16.

15. June Hicks, "City Farms Flourish," *Detroit News*, July 7, 1975; Betty Frankel,
"They Till the Soil of the City," *Detroit Free Press*, May 2, 1981; Sara Parker, "Conservation Comes to the City," *Missouri Conservationist* 58, 4 (1997): 22–25.

16. Janice Crossland, "The New City Common," *Environment* 17, 3 (1975): 26–28.
Jamie Jobb, *The Complete Book of Community Gardening* (New York: William Mor-
row, 1979) noted that Respond, the group Crossland mentioned, had left St. Louis and
the number of gardens had dwindled from 50 to fewer than 24. For example, see Peter
Gavrilovich, "Gardens Growing in Place of Trash," *Detroit Free Press*, June 15, 1975.

17. American Community Gardening Association, *National Community Gardening Survey*, 1992.

18. Margaret Dewar, "Selling Tax-Reverted Land," *Journal of the American Planning Association* 72, 2 (2006): 167–8.

19. David Garcia, "The Greening of Detroit," *America Magazine*, June 21–28,
2010, 11.

20. City of Detroit Planning and Development Department, *Neighborhood Stabilization Program Plan*, 2009, http://www.detroitmi.gov/Portals/0/docs/planning/pdf
/NSP_Approved/detroitNSP_R31_29_09_2.pdf.

21. Detroit Land Bank Authority website, http://www.detroitlandbank.org/.

22. U.S. Census Bureau, "Total Population," Census 2000 and 2010 Summary File
1, Table P1.

23. With each phase of garden promotion, popular articles would appear in local
papers praising Pingree Potato Patches as emblematic of Detroit self-sufficiency: "Po-

tatoe Patch 1894 Reminder," *Detroit Free Press*, February 3, 1911; "Hoeing Potatoes on Pingree Patch in 1894," *Detroit News*, February 26, 1917; Judd Arnett, "Pingree Potatoe Patches Eased Welfare Crisis," *Detroit Free Press*, January 5, 1972.

24. Michigan State University Extension Office website, http://www.msue.msu.edu /portal/. Michigan State University Extension has had a historical presence in farming efforts and more recently has offered educational resources, including youth gardening education, general horticulture classes, nutrition classes, and a Master Gardener certification program, plus extensive educational materials on its website.

25. Kami Pothukuchi, professor, SEED Wayne, Wayne State University College of Liberal Arts and Sciences, interview with authors, Detroit, June 23, 2010.

26. Grown in Detroit website, http://detroitagriculture.net/farms-and-markets /grown-in-detroit/.

27. Detroit Black Community Food Security Network website, http://detroitblack foodsecurity.org/.

28. Olga Bonfiglio, "Delicious in Detroit," *Planning* 75 (2009): 32–37; Detroit Food Policy Council, "City of Detroit Policy on Food Security," http://www.detroitfood policycouncil.net/Page_2.html.

29. Michigan Land Bank Fast Track Authority, Michigan Department of the Treasury, "Adjacent Lot Disposition Application," http://www.michigan.gov/documents /dleg/Adjacent_Lot_Disposition_Program_Application_04_01_09_273728_7.pdf.

30. Michigan Land Bank Garden for Growth Program, Michigan Department of the Treasury, http://www.michigan.gov/treasury/0,1607,7-121-34176-200357-,00.html.

31. University of Michigan School of Social Work, Good Neighborhoods Initiative, "Accessing Vacant Land Manual," 2010, http://www.ssw.umich.edu/public/cur rentProjects/goodNeighborhoods/accessing%20land%20manual_10_1[1].pdf.

32. Our assertion is based on publicly available statements by Detroit-based organizations, including websites, policy briefs and press releases.

33. Ashley Atkinson, Director of Project Development and Urban Gardening, Greening of Detroit, interview with Lawson, Detroit, April 2010.

34. Detroit Food Policy Council, "City of Detroit Policy on Food Security."

35. Ibid.

36. Hantz Farms Detroit, "World's Largest Urban Farm Planned for the City of Detroit," press release, March 23, 2009, http://www.hantzfarmsdetroit.com/press .html.

37. David Whitford, "Can Farming Save Detroit?" *Fortune* 161, 1 (2010): 78.

38. Garcia, "Greening of Detroit," 83; Whitford, "Can Farming Save Detroit," 13.

39. James A. Cloar, "Downtown St. Louis Reborn," *Economic Development Journal* (Spring 2004): 21–26.

40. Antonio D. French, "Quiet Conspiracy," *Public Defender*, October 3, 2002. The Team Four Plan was developed in the mid-1970s as an update to the city's 1947 Comprehensive Plan. Also see Eric Sandweiss, *St. Louis* (Philadelphia: Temple University Press, 2001).

41. Gwenne Hayes-Stewart, executive director, Gateway Greening, interview with authors, St. Louis, June 1, 2010.

42. Mark Tranel and Larry B. Handlin, "Metromorphosis," *Journal of Urban Affairs* 28, 2 (2006): 153.

43. Sara Parker, "Conservation Comes to the City," *Missouri Conservationist* 58, 4 (1997): 22–25.

44. Audrey Spalding and Thomas Duda, "Standstill," policy brief 27, Show-Me Institute, April 2011, http://www.showmeinstitute.org/publications/policystudy/red-tape/507-standstill.html.

45. Ibid.

46. T. Post, "Yes, There Is a Pulse," *Forbes* 164 (1999): 98–103; Linda Tucci, "In the Arch's Shadow, Signs of Revival," *New York Times*, March 30, 2005; Tranel and Handlin, "Metromorphosis."

47. Doug Moore, "Community Gardeners Fear Development in City May Take Bloom off Their Efforts," *St. Louis Post-Dispatch*, October 29, 2003.

48. Theresa Tighe, "Gardens' Success Sows Seeds of Their Demise," *St. Louis Post-Dispatch*, April 15, 2004.

49. Ibid.

50. Hayes-Stewart, interview.

51. Gateway Greening, "Whitmire Study," http://www.gatewaygreening.org/about -us/whitmire-study.html; Tranel and Handlin, "Metromorphosis."

52. Tranel and Handlin, "Metromorphosis."

53. Hayes-Stewart, interview.

54. Nicholas Blomley, *Unsettling the City* (New York: Routledge, 2008); Karl Linn, *Building Commons and Community* (Oakland, Calif.: New Village Press, 2007); Jeffrey Hou, Julie Johnson, and Laura Lawson, *Greening Cities, Growing Communities* (Seattle: University of Washington Press, 2009).

55. Donald Krueckeberg, "The Difficult Character of Property," *Journal of the American Planning Association* 61, 3 (1995): 301–9.

56. Blomley, *Unsettling the City*.

57. Nicholas Blomley, "Enclosure, Common Right and the Property of the Poor," *Social and Legal Studies* 17, 3 (2008): 316.

58. Krueckeberg, "Difficult Character of Property."

59. Lawson, "The South Central Farm."

60. Pamela Kirschbaum, "Borrowed Land, Borrowed Time," *Community Greening Review* 8 (1998): 2–11.

61. NeighborSpace, "Land Use Guidelines for Community Projects on NeighborSpace-Protected Land," www.neighbor-space.org/pdf/guidelines_site.pdf.

62. Helphand, "Garden Is Not Warfare."

63. Quoted in Marc Brelav, "Community Gardens Are Not Forever," *ACGA Community Greening Review* (1995), reprinted in *Community Greening Review* 13 (2004–5): 113. The OpenLands language is subtle but savvy; social services often rely on

moral claims—that those provided for are worthy of the services or that society has a "duty" to provide the services. See Don Mitchell, *Rights to the City* (New York: Guilford Press, 2003).

64. Lynn Staeheli, Don Mitchell, and K. Gibson, "Conflicting Rights to the City in New York's Community Gardens," *GeoJournal* 58 (2002): 197–205.

65. James Kelly, "Land Trusts that Conserve Communities," *DePaul Law Review* 59 (2009): 88.

66. Ibid.

Chapter 2. Building Affordable Housing in Cities After Abandonment: The Case of Low Income Housing Tax Credit Developments in Detroit

The author thanks Qingyun Shen, Thomas Skuzinski, and Peter Winch for their excellent research assistance. The Center for Local, State, and Urban Policy at the University of Michigan funded her work.

1. Michael H. Schill and Susan M. Wachter, "Principles to Guide Housing Policy at the Beginning of the Millennium," *Cityscape* 5, 2 (2001): 5–19.

2. Alan Mallach, *Building a Better Urban Future* (Montclair, N.J.: National Housing Institute, 2005).

3. Lan Deng, "Comparing the Effects of Housing Vouchers and Low-Income Housing Tax Credits on Neighborhood Integration and School Quality," *Journal of Planning Education and Research* 27 (2007): 20–35.

4. Jean L. Cummings and Denise DiPasquale, "The Low Income Housing Tax Credit: An Analysis of the First Ten Years," *Housing Policy Debate* 10, 2 (1999): 251–307.

5. Alex Schwartz, *Housing Policy in the United States*, 2nd ed. (New York: Routledge, 2009).

6. Ibid.

7. Michigan State Housing Development Authority, "Allocation of 2006 Low Income Housing Tax Credit," 2008, http://www.michigan.gov/documents/mshda/mshda_li_sr_2006_lihtc_allocations_185771_7.pdf.

8. Ibid.

9. Deng, "Comparing the Effects," 20–35.

10. U.S. Census Bureau, "Year Structure Built," American Community Survey 2007 1-Year Estimates, Table B25034.

11. I observe a similar pattern in Flint, Michigan, also suffering from industrial decline and abandonment. In Flint, LIHTC projects accounted for about half of new housing construction.

12. U.S. Department of Housing and Urban Development, "National Low Income Housing Tax Credit (LIHTC) Database: Projects Placed in Service Through 2007," updated Feb. 15, 2010, http://www.huduser.org/Datasets/lihtc/tables9507.pdf.

13. Ibid.

14. Neil Mayer and Kenneth Temkin, *Housing Partnerships*, final report for The Urban Institute, Washington, D.C., March 2007, http://www.urban.org/publications /411454.html; Lan Deng, "The External Neighborhood Effects of Low-Income Housing Tax Credit Projects Built by Three Sectors," *Journal of Urban Affairs* 33, 2 (2011): 143–66.

15. Community Legal Resources, "Community Development Advocates of Detroit (CDAD) Survey Summary," Detroit, 2008.

16. Nandini Bhaskara Rao and Margaret Dewar, "Streamlining Acquisition of City-Owned Land for Affordable Housing Development," working paper, Urban and Regional Research Collaborative, University of Michigan, 2004.

17. Lance Freeman, "Comment on Kirk McClure's 'The Low-Income Housing Tax Credit Program Goes Mainstream and Moves to the Suburbs'," *Housing Policy Debate* 17, 3 (2006): 447–59.

18. According to this developer, IRS requires that all LIHTC projects meet Uniform Physical Conditions Standards (UPCS) intended for multifamily projects, rather than the Housing Quality Standards (HQS) for single-family housing. HQS is also the standard used for city inspections and Section 8 inspections. Since he often used LIHTC to renovate Section 8 properties, the developer had to pay for and accommodate three inspections, which cost more than the tax credit benefits and discouraged him from continued participation in the program.

19. U.S. Census Bureau, "Median Gross Rent (Dollars)," Census 2000 Summary File 3, Table H63.

20. Dennis Quinn (senior vice president, Great Lakes Capital Fund), interview with the author, Detroit, July 2007.

21. Schill and Wachter, "Principles to Guide Housing Policy," 5–19.

22. Michael H. Schill, Ingrid Gould Ellen, Amy Ellen Schwartz, and Ioan Voicu, "Revitalizing Inner-City Neighborhoods," *Housing Policy Debate* 13, 3 (2002): 529–66; Ingrid Gould Ellen, Michael H. Schill, Scott Susin, and Amy Ellen Schwartz, "Building Homes, Reviving Neighborhoods," *Journal of Housing Research* 12, 2 (2002): 185–216; Amy Ellen Schwartz, Ingrid Gould Ellen, Michael H. Schill, and Ioan Voicu, "The External Effects of Place-Based Subsidized Housing," *Regional Science and Urban Economics* 36 (2006): 679–707.

23. Sean Zielenbach, "Assessing Economic Change in HOPE VI Neighborhoods," *Housing Policy Debate* 14, 4 (2003): 621–55; Sean Zielenbach, "Catalyzing Community Development," *Journal of Affordable Housing and Community Development Law* 13, 2 (2003): 40–80; Sean Zielenbach and Richard Voith, "HOPE VI and Neighborhood Economic Development," *Cityscape* 12, 1 (2010): 99–131.

24. Zielenbach, "Assessing Economic Change"; Zielenbach, "Catalyzing Community Development"; Zielenbach and Voith, "HOPE VI and Neighborhood Economic Development."

25. Michael H. Schill and Susan M. Wachter, "The Spatial Bias of Federal Housing Law and Policy," *University of Pennsylvania Law Review* 143 (1995): 1285–1342; George

Galster, Peter Tatian, and Robin Smith, "The Impact of Neighbors Who Use Section 8 Certificates on Property Value," *Housing Policy Debate* 10, 4 (1999): 879–917.

26. When I conducted this analysis, only 1990 and 2000 census data were available at the census tract or block group level, so I had to limit the study to LIHTC projects built by 1999. Since December 2010, the American Community Survey has released data for these small areas, which would allow me to examine all LIHTC projects in Detroit in future research.

27. The cluster analysis used 1990 census data. A comparison of 1990 and 2000 data shows that some white neighborhoods continued to lose white population and became predominantly black by the 2000 census.

28. June Manning Thomas, *Redevelopment and Race* (Baltimore: Johns Hopkins University Press, 1997), 55–80.

29. Joe T. Darden, Richard Child Hill, June Thomas, and Richard Thomas, *Detroit: Race and Uneven Development* (Philadelphia: Temple University Press, 1987), chap. 5, "City Redevelopment Policies," 151–200.

30. Ibid.

31. Thomas, *Redevelopment and Race*, 167.

32. Ibid.

33. Darden et al., "City Redevelopment Policies," 151–200.

34. In 2011, the citizens' district council in Jefferson-Chalmers continued to promote the area's redevelopment.

35. Thomas, *Redevelopment and Race*, 149–177.

36. Darden et al., "City Redevelopment Policies," 151–200.

37. Christopher Walker, "Nonprofit Housing Development," *Housing Policy Debate* 4, 3 (1993): 369–414; Rachel Bratt, "Nonprofit and For-Profit Developers of Subsidized Rental Housing," *Housing Policy Debate* 19, 2 (2008): 323–65.

38. A Z-score for indicator A is calculated as follows: (Change in indicator A experienced by the LIHTC neighborhood–mean changes in indicator A experienced by the comparison group) / (standard deviation of changes in indicator A experienced by the comparison group).

39. For poverty rate, a negative Z-score indicates positive change since it reflects a larger decline in poverty rate. For the other three indicators, a positive Z-score reflects positive change. I, thus, take the opposite sign for the Z-score for poverty rate and add it to the Z-scores for the other three indicators. Dividing the sum by 4 produces an average Z-score per indicator in each neighborhood. The higher the Z-score, the more economic improvement a neighborhood had.

40. I was unable to identify neighborhood change types for 5 of the 34 census block groups, due to lack of census data on some indicators or lack of a comparison group in the same zip code area.

41. The Rivertown area, to the south of Elmwood Park along the Detroit River, does not have as many LIHTC projects as the three areas discussed before, but it has also been at the center of the city's redevelopment efforts.

42. Maureen McDonald, "Victoria Park Sparks Growth in City's Once Blighted Areas," *Detroit News*, February 12, 2002.

43. Brent D. Ryan, "Morphological Change Through Residential Redevelopment," *Urban Morphology* 10, 1 (2006): 5–22.

44. Neighborhoods in the Jefferson-Chalmers area experienced more socioeconomic improvement than many other parts of the city, thanks to redevelopment efforts of city government and participation of local citizen groups.

45. Darden et al., "City Redevelopment Policies,"151–200.

46. More LIHTC projects have been built in some of these neighborhoods since 2000. Since the American Community Survey has released neighborhood-level data collected from 2005 to 2009, future research can examine whether the increased concentration of these projects has made a difference in these neighborhoods.

Chapter 3. Detroit Art City: Urban Decline, Aesthetic Production, Public Interest

1. According to Richard Florida, "Open culture on the macro level is a spur to societal innovation, entrepreneurship, and economic development." *Cities and the Creative Class* (New York: Routledge, 2004), 6; Florida, *The Rise of the Creative Class* (New York: Basic Books, 2002).

2. Robin Pogrebin, "New Endowment Chairman Sees Arts as Economic Engine," *New York Times*, August 7, 2009.

3. For example, Mark J. Stern and Susan C. Seifert, "Cultural Clusters," *Journal of Planning Education and Research* 29, 3 (2010): 262–79; Carl Grodach, "Art Spaces in Community and Economic Development," *Journal of Planning Education and Research* 31, 1 (2011): 74–85.

4. Neil Smith and Michele LeFaivre, "Class Analysis of Gentrification," in *Gentrification, Displacement and Neighborhood Revitalization*, ed. J. John Palen and Bruce London (Albany: State University of New York Press, 1984), 43–63.

5. Alexandra Alter, "Artists vs. Blight," *Wall Street Journal*, April 17, 2009.

6. For example, Sharon Zukin, *Loft Living* (New Brunswick, NJ: Rutgers University Press, 1989); Rosalyn Deutsche, *Evictions* (Cambridge, Mass.: MIT Press, 1996).

7. My use of "modernist" follows that of Peter Bürger, who distinguishes "modernist" and "avant-garde" art on the basis of the former's investment in art as an autonomous form-based practice. Peter Bürger, *Theory of the Avant-Garde* (Minneapolis: University of Minnesota Press, 1984).

8. Toby Barlow, "For Sale," *New York Times*, March 19, 2009.

9. For example, Miwon Kwon, *One Place After Another* (Cambridge, Mass.: MIT Press, 2002); Grant H. Kester, *Conversation Pieces* (Berkeley: University of California Press, 2004); Claire Doherty, *From Studio to Situations* (London: Black Dog, 2004); Gerald Raunig, *Art and Revolution* (New York: Semiotext(e), 2007); Blake Stimson,

ed., *Collectivism After Modernism* (Minneapolis: University of Minnesota Press, 2007); Charles Esche, ed., *Art and Social Change* (London: Tate, 2008).

10. Nicolas Bourriaud, *Relational Aesthetics*, trans. Simon Pleasance and Fronza Woods (Paris: Presses du Réel, 2002).

11. Ibid., 15.

12. Ibid., 13, 45.

13. Ibid., 15, emphasis original.

14. Grant H. Kester, "Collaboration, Art and Subcultures," *Caderno Videobrasil* 2 (2007): 20.

15. Claire Bishop, "The Social Turn," *Artforum*, February 2006, 183.

16. I follow the trajectory of Rosalyn Deutsche, who argues that one must "dislodge public art from its ghettoization within the parameters of aesthetic discourse, and resituate it, at least partially, within critical urban discourse"; see Deutsche, *Evictions*, 63.

17. Thomas Sugrue, *The Origins of the Urban Crisis*, rev. ed. (Princeton, N.J.: Princeton University Press, 2005).

18. Joe T. Darden, Richard Child Hill, June Thomas, and Richard Thomas, *Detroit: Race and Uneven Development* (Philadelphia: Temple University Press, 1987), chap. 5, "City Redevelopment Policies"; Brent Ryan, "Morphological Change Through Residential Development," *Urban Morphology* 10, 1 (2006): 5–22; Peter Eisinger, "Reimagining Detroit," *City and Community* 2, 2 (2003): 85–99. As early as the 1970s, CDBG expenditures in Detroit included funds for "clearance, demolition and rehabilitation"; see June Manning Thomas, *Redevelopment and Race* (Baltimore: Johns Hopkins University Press, 1997), 140.

19. Jennifer Dixon and Darci McConnell, "HUD Hands Detroit a $160-Million Gift Days Before Election," *Detroit Free Press*, October 29, 1997.

20. Cameron McWhirter and Brian Harmon, "Derelict Buildings Haunt School Kids," *Detroit News*, September 24, 2000; M. L. Elrick, "Demolition Slowdown," *Detroit Free Press*, June 3, 2004; David Josar, "Demolition of Detroit Homes Slows," *Detroit News*, June 27, 2006; Charlie LeDuff, "Detroit Lags on Vacant House Demolitions," *Detroit News*, November 12, 2010.

21. Data on demolitions are dispersed among several municipal offices: the departments of Buildings and Safety Engineering, Public Works, and Planning and Development. In short, the magnitude of the demolition program remains difficult to track. The databases are those of the Detroit Executive Budget, Budgets of Buildings and Safety Engineering Department and Department of Public Works, http://www .detroitmi.gov/DepartmentsandAgencies/BudgetDepartment/Archive/tabid/527/De fault.aspx (2005–present); Detroit Planning and Development Department, Building Permits, http://www.detroitmi.gov/Departments/PlanningDevelopmentDepartment /Planning/InformationServiceandMapping/CommunityInformationandMapping /AdvancedMaps/DownloadGISFiles/tabid/2105/Default.aspx.

22. "Bing's State of the City Address," *Detroit News*, March 23, 2010.

23. According to the Detroit Residential Parcel Survey, about 10,400 of the city's vacant houses were "vacant, open, and dangerous" as of fall 2009. Data Driven Detroit, "Detroit Residential Parcel Survey," February 15, 2010, http://www.detroitparcelsurvey .org/pdf/reports/DRPS_citywide_VOD_fire.pdf; Associated Press, "Downsizing Detroit," *MLive*, April 1, 2010, http://www.mlive.com/news/detroit/index.ssf/2010/04 /demolitions_to_start_on_first.htm.

24. Christine MacDonald and Darren A. Nichols, "Detroit's Desolate Middle Makes Downsizing Tough," *Detroit News*, March 9, 2010.

25. Brent D. Ryan, "The Restructuring of Detroit," *Urban Design International* (2008): 1–13.

26. Recent downtown buildings built on parcels of demolished buildings include Comerica Park, MGM Casino, and the Compuware Building. Also, Nancy Kaffer, "Detroit Authority to Pay For Demolition of Ilitch Company Buildings," *Crain's Detroit Business*, December 11, 2008, http://www.crainsdetroit.com/article/20081211/FREE /812119975#.

27. "Towers of Neglect," *Detroit Free Press,* May 2004.

28. Andrew Herscher, "Detroit Unreal Estate Agency," *Volume* 18 (2008): 94–96.

29. Dan Pitera, "FireBreak," 2001, http://dailydesignidea.wordpress.com/tag/fire break/

30. David Harvey, "The Art of Rent," chap. 18 in *Spaces of Capital* (New York: Routledge, 2002), 410.

31. The Heidelberg Project sits in a U.S. census tract where 28 percent of families were below the poverty line, with almost 50 percent of families with a child under five below this line in 1999. The tract had 771 housing units (down from around 2,500 in 1960), of which 20 percent were vacant, compared to an 11 percent housing vacancy rate in Detroit as a whole. U.S. Census, "Poverty Status in 1999 of Families by Family Type by Presence of Related Children Under 18 Years by Age of Related Children," "Housing Units," and "Occupancy Status," Census 200 Summary File 3, Tables P90, H1, and H6.

32. Michael H. Hodges, "Heidelberg and the Community," in *Connecting the Dots: Tyree Guyton's Heidelberg Project* (Detroit: Wayne State University Press, 2007), chap. 4.

33. John Beardsley, "Art or Eyesore?" in *Connecting the Dots*, chap. 3.

34. Jerry Herron, *AfterCulture* (Detroit: Wayne State University Press, 1993), 199.

35. Marion E. Jackson, "Trickster in the City," in *Connecting the Dots*, chap. 2; Grant H. Kester, *Conversation Pieces*, 62.

36. Hodges, "Heidelberg and the Community," 51.

37. DDD Project, "Detroit. Demolition. Disneyland." *Detroiter*, November 2005.

38. Ibid.

39. "Bright Orange," *Good*, November 22, 2006, http://www.good.is/post/bright -orange-2/.

40. DDD Project, "Detroit. Demolition. Disneyland."

41. Ibid.

42. From the critique of the gesture of critical exposure in Eve Kosofsky Sedgwick, *Touching Feeling: Affect, Pedagogy, Performativity* (Durham, N.C.: Duke University Press, 2003).

43. Dani Lawton, director, "Rebuilding Detroit," http://www.blightbusters.org.

44. Aaron Foley, "Motor City Blight Busters Knocking Down Detroit's Abandoned Homes One At a Time," *Mlive*, August 8, 2009, http://www.mlive.com/news/detroit/index.ssf/2009/08/motor_city_blight_busters_knoc.html.

45. Chrissa Swanson, "Blight Busters Beautifies City," *Hush Your Mouth!*, Fall 2002, http://www.hushyourmouth.com/motor_city_blight_busters.htm.

46. Motor City Blight Busters, "The Motor City Blight Buster Volunteer Network Gets the Job Done," http://www.blightbusters.org/detroit-charity.

47. This neighborhood is in a census tract where 27 percent of households were below the poverty line in 1999, around the average for Detroit as a whole, and around 13 percent of homes were vacant, compared to 11 percent for Detroit as a whole. U.S. Census Bureau, "Poverty Status in 1999 of Households by Household Type by Age of Householder" and "Occupancy Status," Census 2000 Summary File 3, Tables P92, H6.

48. Mamey Rich Keenan, "Blight Busters Celebrates Revitalized Block in Old Redford," *Detroit News*, November 4, 2009.

49. Motor City Blight Busters, "Artist Village," http://www.blightbusters.org/artistvillage.html.

50. Jeff Gerritt, "Artistic Stroke Fights City's Blight," *Detroit Free Press*, September 29, 2008.

51. The Power House is in a census block group that differs from neighborhoods in Detroit as a whole. For example, in 2000, 72 percent of households in this block group were families and 51 percent were married couples. In Detroit as a whole, 65 percent of households were families but only 28 percent were married couples. In the Power House block group, 100 percent of vacant housing units were rented or sold (44 of 44 units), compared to 15 percent overall. Designation of the neighborhood as "challenging" is only true relative to urban conditions outside Detroit. U.S. Census Bureau, "Household Size by Household Type by Presence of Own Children Under 18 Years" and "Vacancy Status," Census 2000 Summary File 3, Tables P10,d H8.

52. As of mid-2011, Design 99 owned four properties in north Hamtramck: the Power House, a nearby building that serves as home and studio, a nearby house altered by five architects from the University of Michigan, and another nearby house being converted into artist residences.

53. Design 99, "The Project," http://www.powerhouseproject.com/index.php?/updates/info-statements/.

54. Ibid.

55. Ibid.

56. The Power House may be the most cited contemporary work of community-based art in Detroit; for some of these citations, see Power House Productions press page, http://www.powerhouseproject.com/index.php?/updates/press/.

57. Kester, *Conversation Pieces*, 8.

58. Charles Esche, "Detroit and Support," *VAM Kitchen* (blog), January 21, 2009, http://thekitchen.vanabbe.nl/2009/01/25/detroit-and-support/#more-173.

59. "Guided by Another Hope: An Interview with Charles Esche," by Christian Ernsten, *Volume* 22 (2009): 62–64.

60. Kester, *Conversation Pieces*, 8.

Chapter 4. Decline-Oriented Urban Governance in Youngstown, Ohio

1. Angela Barbanente and Valeria Monno, "Changing Images and Practices in a Declining 'Growth Pole' in Southern Italy," *Magazin Städte im Umbruch Ausgabe* 2 (2004): 36–44; Mario Polèse and Richard Shearmur, "Why Some Regions Will Decline," *Papers in Regional Science* 85, 1 (2006): 23–46; Michael Punch, "Global Economic Restructuring, Urban Social Change and the State," *Magazin Städte im Umbruch Ausgabe* 2 (2004): 10–17; John Lovering, "The Relationship Between Urban Regeneration and Neoliberalism," *International Planning Studies* 12, 4 (2007): 343–66; Gordon Dabinett, "Uneven Spatial Development Regeneration Outcomes in the UK," *Magazin Städte im Umbruch Ausgabe* 2 (2004): 18–22; Richard Shearmur, "The New Knowledge Aristocracy," *Work Organisation, Labour and Globalisation* 1, 1 (2006): 31–47.

2. Deborah E. Popper and Frank J. Popper, "Small Can Be Beautiful?" *Planning* 68, 7 (2002): 20–23; Polèse and Shearmur, "Why Some Regions Will Decline"; Joseph Schilling and Jonathan Logan, "Greening the Rust Belt," *Journal of the American Planning Association* 74, 4 (2008): 451–66.

3. Christopher Leo and Kathryn Anderson, "Being Realistic About Urban Growth," *Journal of Urban Affairs* 28, 2 (2006): 169; Alan DiGaetano and Paul Lawless, "Urban Governance and Industrial Decline," *Urban Affairs Review* 34, 4 (1999): 546–77.

4. Leo and Anderson, "Being Realistic," 169.

5. Liz Boardman, "As Residents Leave, Locals Shrink Smartly," *American City and County*, July 1, 2008; Gordon Russell, "Faded Midwestern Cities Offer Ways New Orleans Could Slim Down to Match Its Smaller Population," *Times Picayune*, November 24, 2008. Other cities such as Pittsburgh, Detroit, Cleveland, and Flint have not been as willing as Youngstown to accept contraction publicly but have addressed the by-products of shrinking, such as deteriorating infrastructure and budget shortages. Russell calls these strategies "less daring" than Youngstown's but asserts they still bear watching.

6. John Minnery, "Stars and Their Supporting Cast," *Urban Policy and Research* 25, 3 (2007): 333.

7. Jon Pierre, "Comparative Urban Governance," *Urban Affairs Review* 40, 4 (2005): 446–62; Gerry Stoker, *Governance as Theory* (Oxford: Blackwell 1998); Harvey L. Molotch, "The City as Growth Machine," *American Journal of Sociology* 82, 2

(1976): 309–30; John R. Logan and Harvey L. Molotch, *Urban Fortunes* (Berkeley: University of California Press, 1987); Clarence Stone, *Regime Politics* (Lawrence: University Press of Kansas, 1989). Under the "urban governance" umbrella, several analytic frameworks help explain the role of entities beyond formal government in urban policy. The best-known concepts are urban growth coalitions (Molotch; Logan and Molotch) and urban regimes (Stone). The concept of growth coalitions argues that local economic and political elites work together to accomplish the mutually beneficial aim of more land intensive development. Urban regime theory explains cooperation between state and market in local policy making and implementation. Both are subsets of the urban governance perspective. Because the urban governance perspective is better able than urban regime theory to "conceptualize the heterogeneity of actors on the urban political scene" (Pierre, "Comparative Urban Governance," 450), I use the broader "urban governance" perspective in this chapter.

8. Minnery, "Stars," 330.

9. Alan DiGaetano, "Urban Governing Realignments in Comparative Perspective," *Urban Affairs Review* 32, 6 (1997): 844–70; Jonathan S. Davies, "The Governance of Urban Regeneration," *Public Administration* 80, 2 (2002): 301–22; Pierre, "Comparative Urban Governance"; Stoker, *Governance as Theory*; Jon Coaffee and Patsy Healey, "'My Voice: My Place',", *Urban Studies* 40, 10 (2003): 1979–99.

10. Jon Pierre, "Models of Urban Governance," *Urban Affairs Review* 34, 3 (1999): 372–96; DiGaetano, "Urban Governing Realignments"; Matthias Bernt, "Partnerships for Demolition," *International Journal of Urban and Regional Research* 33, 3 (2009): 754–69.

11. Minnery, "Stars"; DiGaetano, "Urban Governing Realignments"; DiGaetano and Lawless, "Urban Governance and Industrial Decline."

12. Stoker, *Governance as Theory*, 22.

13. Gerry Stoker, "New Localism, Participation and Networked Community Governance," University of Manchester Institute for Political and Economic Governance, 2004, http://www.ipeg.org.uk.

14. Anne Mette Kjaer, "Governance and the Urban Bureaucracy," in *Theories of Urban Politics*, ed. Jonathan S. Davies and David L. Imbroscio (Los Angeles: Sage, 2009), 142.

15. Stoker, "New Localism."

16. Kjaer, "Governance," 141.

17. Stoker, *Governance as Theory*, 23.

18. Jörg Röber, "Governance in Urban Development Crisis Situations," *Annals of the Croatian Political Science Association* 5 (2008): 323–46; Bernt, "Partnerships for Demolition"; Martin Franz, Orhan Güles, and Gisela Prey, "Place-Making and 'Green' Reuses of Brownfields in the Ruhr," *Tijdschrift voor Economische en Sociale Geografie* 99 (2008): 316–28.

19. Ulf Matthiesen, "Governance Milieus in Shrinking Post-Socialist City Regions—and Their Respective Forms of Creativity," *DisP* 163, 3 (2005): 53–61; Henry J. Mayer

and Michael R. Greenberg, "Coming Back from Economic Despair," *Economic Development Quarterly* 20, 3 (2001): 232–58.

20. Matthiesen, "Governance Milieus."

21. Minnery, "Stars"; Pierre, "Models of Urban Governance"; Kjaer, "Governance"; DiGaetano, "Urban Governing Realignments"; Stoker, *Governance as Theory*; Stephen Greasley and Gerry Stoker, "Mayors and Urban Governance," *Public Administration Review* (July/August 2008): 722–30.

22. Minnery, "Stars," 222.

23. Ibid.; Pierre, "Models of Urban Governance"; Pierre, "Comparative Urban Governance."

24. Pierre, "Models of Urban Governance;" Minnery, "Stars."

25. Minnery, "Stars."

26. Pierre, "Models of Urban Governance"; "Minnery, "Stars"; Kjaer, "Governance."

27. This discussion is based on document review (the *Youngstown 2010 Plan*, media reports, and Internet sources) and interviews with sixteen key informants (including planners, academics, politicians, members of local social organizations, and planning consultants) conducted between 2007 and 2008 in Youngstown and Toronto. Key informants were identified through document review and the "snowball" technique of asking interviewees to suggest other interview subjects. Interviews were open ended and focused on what the *Youngstown 2010 Plan* was trying to achieve, how the process was undertaken, and why the decline-oriented approach was adopted. All interviews were conducted with the understanding that the interviewees' names would be withheld. Laura Schatz, "What Helps or Hinders the Adoption of 'Good Planning' Principles in Shrinking Cities?" Ph.D. dissertation, University of Waterloo, 2010.

28. Sean Safford, *Why the Garden Club Couldn't Save Youngstown* (Cambridge, Mass.: Harvard University Press, 2009); Terry F. Buss and F. Stevens Redburn, *Shutdown at Youngstown* (Albany: State University of New York Press, 1983).

29. Sherry Lee Linkon and John Russo, *Steeltown U.S.A.* (Lawrence: University Press of Kansas, 2002).

30. Ibid.; Buss and Redburn, *Shutdown at Youngstown*.

31. U.S. Census Bureau, "Total Population," Census 2010 Summary File 1, Table P1.

32. Personal interview with Youngstown official, December 5, 2007.

33. City of Youngstown, *Youngstown 2010 Citywide Plan*, Youngstown, Ohio, 2005.

34. Ibid., 17.

35. Ibid.; Belinda Lanks, "The Incredible Shrinking City," *Metropolis Magazine*, April 17, 2006; Christopher Swope, "Smart Decline," *Governing*, November 2006, http://www.governing.com/topics/economic-dev/Smart-Decline.html.

36. City of Youngstown, *Youngstown 2010*, 135, emphasis original.

37. Timothy Aeppel, "Shrink to Fit," *Wall Street Journal*, May 3, 2007; Haya El Nassar, "As Older Cities Shrink, Some Reinvent Themselves," *USA Today*, December 27, 2006; Jonathan Logan, "NVPC Participates in Shrinking Cities Symposium," National Vacant Properties Campaign, http://www.vacantproperties.org/resources /ShrinkingCities.pdf (site discontinued), accessed June 6, 2007; Swope, "Smart Decline"; Associated Press, "Youngstown Planners Turn Shrinking Population into Positive," June 19, 2007; Russell, "Faded Midwestern Cities."

38. City of Youngstown, *Youngstown 2010*, 137.

39. Lanks, "Incredible Shrinking City"; Boardman, "Locals Shrink Smartly."

40. Joe P. Tone, "Dream Small," *Cleveland Scene Magazine*, April 18, 2007, http://www.clevescene.com/gyrobase/dream-small/Content?oid=1498290, emphasis original.

41. Harwood Group, *Waiting for the Future*, report prepared for the Charles Stewart Mott Foundation, 1999; Thomas A. Finnerty, "Youngstown Embraces Its Future," *Planning* 69, 8 (2003): 14–19; Boardman, "Locals Shrink Smartly."

42. Personal interview with YSU administrator, July 30, 2007.

43. Finnerty, "Youngstown Embraces," 1.

44. Personal interview with YSU administrator, December 5, 2007.

45. Tone, "Dream Small."

46. Personal interview with Youngstown official, July 30, 2007.

47. Personal interview with YSU administrator, July 30, 2007.

48. Personal interview with YSU administrator, July 30, 2007.

49. Barbara Faga, *Designing Public Consensus: The Civic Theater of Community Participation for Architects, Landscape Architects, Planners, and Urban Designers* (Hoboken, N.J.: Wiley, 2006).

50. Finnerty, "Youngstown Embraces," 1.

51. Ibid., 2.

52. Faga, *Designing Public Consensus*, 55.

53. Roger G. Smith, "Last, Best Chance," *Planning*, 2007, http://www.cityofy oungstownoh.com/about_youngstown/youngstown_2010/news_information/na tional/PlanningApril2007.pdf.

54. Swope, "Smart Decline."

55. Finnerty, "Youngstown Embraces," 4.

56. Smith, "Last, Best Chance."

57. American Planning Association, "'Youngstown 2010' Honored with Award for Public Outreach," December 19, 2006, http://www.planning.org/newsreleases/2006 /dec19-8.htm.

58. Telephone interview with urban designer/shrinking cities researcher, March 26, 2008.

59. Personal interview with Youngstown official, July 30, 2007.

60. Personal interview with YSU administrator, July 30, 2007.

61. Finnerty, "Youngstown Embraces," 2.

62. Personal interview with YSU administrator, July 30, 2007.

63. Faga, *Designing Public Consensus*, 58.

64. Personal interview with planning consultant, July 20, 2007.

65. Faga, *Designing Public Consensus*, 59.

66. Ibid.

67. Finnerty, "Youngstown Embraces," 3.

68. Ibid.; Faga, *Designing Public Consensus*, 61–62.

69. Personal interview with planning consultant, July 20, 2007.

70. Personal interview with Youngstown official, July 30, 2007.

71. Faga, *Designing Public Consensus*, 61, emphasis original.

72. Ibid., 61.

73. Personal interview with Youngstown official, July 30, 2007.

74. Personal interview with Youngstown official, July 30, 2007.

75. Ibid.; City of Youngstown, *Youngstown 2010.*

76. Personal interview with Youngstown official, July 30, 2007.

77. Telephone interview with urban designer/shrinking cities researcher, March 26, 2008.

78. City of Youngstown Planning Department and Ohio State University, *Idora Neighborhood Comprehensive Neighborhood Plan*, Youngstown, 2008, 3.

79. Personal interview with Youngstown official, December 5, 2007.

80. Youngstown Cityscape website, http://www.youngstowncityscape.com/wick -park-history.

81. Personal interview with Youngstown official, November 24, 2008.

82. Personal interview with Youngstown official, December 5, 2007.

83. Personal interview with Youngstown official, July 30, 2007.

84. DiGaetano, "Urban Governing Realignments"; Pierre, "Models of Urban Governance"; Kjaer, "Governance."

85. Bernt, "Partnerships for Demolition."

86. Matthiesen, "Governance Milieus," 59.

87. Telephone interview with urban designer/shrinking cities researcher, March 26, 2008.

88. Minnery, "Stars," 328.

89. Ibid., 336.

Chapter 5. Targeting Neighborhoods, Stimulating Markets: The Role of Political, Institutional, and Technical Factors in Three Cities

1. For the variations of and rationale for strategic geographic targeting, see Dale E. Thomson, "Strategic, Geographic Targeting of Housing and Community Development Resources," *Urban Affairs Review* 43, 5 (2008): 629–62.

2. Ibid.

3. Paul C. Brophy and Kim Burnett, "Building a New Framework for Community Development in Weak Market Cities," paper prepared for Community Development Partnership Network, 2003, http://www.community-wealth.org/_pdfs/articles-publications/cdcs/paper-brophy-burnett.pdf.

4. Ingrid Gould Ellen, Michael H. Schill, Scott Susin, and Amy Ellen Schwartz, "Building Homes, Reviving Neighborhoods," *Journal of Housing Research* 12, 2 (2002): 185–216; Ingrid G. Ellen and Ioan Voicu, "Nonprofit Housing and Neighborhood Spillovers," *Journal of Policy Analysis and Management* 25, 1 (2006): 31–52; George Galster, Peter Tatian, and John Accordino, "Targeting Investments in Neighborhood Revitalization," *Journal of the American Planning Association* 72, 4 (2006): 457–74; George Galster et al., "Measuring the Impact of Community Development Block Grant Spending on Urban Neighborhoods," *Housing Policy Debate* 15, 4 (2004): 903–34.

5. See William C. Baer, "On the Death of Cities," *Public Interest* 45 (Fall 1976): 3–19; Anthony Downs, "Using the Lessons of Experience to Allocate Resources in the Community Development Program," in *Recommendations for Community Development Planning* (Chicago: Real Estate Research Corporation, 1976), 1–28; Nancy Kleniewski, "Triage and Urban Planning," *International Journal of Urban and Regional Research* 10, 4 (1986): 563–79.

6. Robert K. Yin, *Case Study Research* (Thousand Oaks, Calif.: Sage, 1994), 13.

7. Ibid.

8. The targeting initiatives serve as embedded cases within the broader city cases.

9. David Boehlke, "Great Neighborhoods, Great City," paper prepared for Goldseker Foundation, Baltimore, 2004, http://www.goldsekerfoundation.org/GNGC.pdf.

10. Ibid.

11. Ibid.

12. Ibid.

13. Maryland senator Barbara Mikulski secured the earmark to address consequences of property flipping but ensured that the funds went to neighborhoods that became part of the HNI pilot.

14. Brophy and Burnett, "Building a New Framework," 15.

15. The city government officially recognizes 238 neighborhoods. The original 6 pilot organizations served 11 neighborhoods. For Baltimore, I classify middle neighborhoods as those with lower stable or transitional housing markets based on the 2008 neighborhood market typology developed by Baltimore Housing and described later in the chapter. These categories reflect the middle range of markets in the typology.

16. Calculated from IRS 990 forms for each foundation.

17. Healthy Neighborhoods, Inc., "Healthy Neighborhoods NSP2 Application (Application Identification: 308558434)," Baltimore, 2009, http://www.healthyneighborhoods.org/buyandrenovate/NSP2_Application_Final.pdf.

18. Based on data from the city's Ordinance of Estimates, Budget Summaries, and Capital Plan.

19. The $5.8 million include $4.1 million from NSP provided directly to the city of Baltimore and $1.7 million provided to Baltimore through the State of Maryland. About 57 percent of this funding was targeted to HNI areas in the original plan. Quarterly Performance Reports show that the share decreased to about 44 percent by June 2010.

20. Statistics from NPI FY 1999–2009 IRS 990 forms.

21. For example, see Tony Proscio, *From Improvement to Recovery*, report for Cleveland and George Gund Foundations, Cleveland, 2003.

22. Some CDCs excluded from SII received operating funding from NPI in sub-stantially smaller amounts than those provided to SII CDCs.

23. Village Capital Corporation, *Investing in City Life* (Cleveland: Village Capital, 2007).

24. For Cleveland, I define middle neighborhoods as those where a significant portion falls in the "transitional" market classification in Cleveland's Neighborhood Market Typology. Transitional markets lie in the mid-range of markets in Cleveland based on nine indicators. They are historically stable neighborhoods where the hous-ing market is viable but showing signs of deterioration.

25. City of Cleveland Department of Community Development, "Year 36 Com-munity Development Block Grant CDC Competitive Grant Program Application," 2010, http://www.city.cleveland.oh.us/clnd_images/PDF/CD/BlockGrantApp.pdf.

26. This estimate assumes $120,000 for each of 20 Housing Trust Fund Model Blocks; $1,600,000 annual, three-year commitment to Opportunity Homes; and $1,400,000 to the CDC Competitive Grant for FY11. Some funding came from NSP, but most commitments preceded NSP.

27. The $8.6 million came from a variety of sources, including CDBG, HOME, general obligation bonds, and NSP. Targeted funds as a percent of total funding from all these programs would be lower than reported here. I used CDBG and HOME dol-lars as the denominator because these totals are a more accurate though not exhaus-tive indicator of city funding for community development.

28. This figure includes Opportunity Homes and six Model Blocks funded through the city's Housing Trust Fund.

29. Cuyahoga County Land Reutilization Corporation, *Neighborhood Stabiliza-tion Program Action Plan*, report for the U.S. Department of Housing and Urban Development, 2010, http://hudnsphelp.info/media/GAReports/A_B-09-CN-OH-0032 .pdf.

30. Local Initiatives Support Corporation, "Detroit LISC Announces Plans for Its Largest Effort in Detroit—The $40M 'Neighborhoods Now' Campaign," news release, February 15, 2005, http://www.prnewswire.com/news-releases/detroit-lisc-announces -plans-for-its-largest-effort-in-detroit—the-40m-neighborhoods-now-campaign -54072292.html.

31. Local Initiatives Support Corporation, *2008 Annual Report to the Community*, Detroit, 2009.

32. For an account of NDNI's experience, see Dale E. Thomson, "Strategic Geographic Targeting in Community Development," *Urban Affairs Review* 47, 4 (2011): 564–94.

33. Ibid.

34. NSP regulations required cities to target areas with greatest need; however, almost all block groups in Detroit, including many in middle neighborhoods, met HUD's definition of greatest need, which emphasized number of foreclosures and risk of future foreclosures. A similar situation was evident in Baltimore and Cleveland, though less so than in Detroit.

35. NDNI targeted three tiers of neighborhoods, but the political selection process resulted in target areas that were either overwhelmingly low-income with distressed markets or with significantly higher income levels than those associated with middle neighborhoods.

36. John R. P. French and Bertram Raven, "The Bases of Social Power," in *Studies in Social Power*, ed. Dorwin Cartwright (Ann Arbor, Mich.: Institute for Social Research, 1959), 150–67.

37. Ibid.; Paul Hersey, Kenneth H. Blanchard, and Walter E. Natemeyer, "Situational Leadership, Perception, and the Impact of Power," *Group and Organizational Studies* 4, 4 (1979): 418–28.

38. Thomson, "Strategic Geographic Targeting in Community Development."

39. Thirty-four percent of CDBG and HOME dollars, less allocations for administration, nonprofit homeless services, and AIDS prevention services. City of Cleveland Department of Community Development, *Community Planning and Development Programs Proposed 2010–2011 Action Plan for Public Review and Comment*, report for U.S. Department of Housing and Urban Development, March 11, 2010.

40. Mayor's Council on City Living, *The Mayor's Council on City Living Report*, Baltimore, 2003, http://fallcreekconsultants.com/documents/Baltimore%20Mayors%20Council%20on%20City%20Living.pdf.

41. Thomson, "Strategic Geographic Targeting in Community Development."

42. Ibid.

43. HUD calculates AMI using census estimates of median income for each metropolitan area adjusted for varying family sizes.

44. Percentages reflect total targeted funding reported earlier in the chapter divided by total annual HUD CDBG and HOME appropriations. http://www.hud.gov/offices/cpd/communitydevelopment/budget/. Targeted funds also came from other sources, including general obligation bonds, used for activities other than community development. Targeted funds as a share of total funding from all these programs would be a much lower percentage. However, CDBG and HOME funds provide a more reasonable approximation of community development expenditures in a given year.

45. I derived these percentages from the foundations' IRS 990 reports, cross-checked against grant awards listed on each foundation's website, where available.

46. Two HNI target areas reflected the HNI criteria less obviously than the others. Southern Mondawmin was poorer than most HNI neighborhoods, but community organizations and institutions in the area were building good partnerships. Mt. Vernon was wealthier than most, but its CDC was assisting preservation of many historic properties. Selection team members felt these neighborhoods warranted inclusion as a means of testing the Healthy Neighborhoods model in different contexts. No evidence of influence of external parties on inclusion of these areas was found. Other neighborhoods team members had hoped to include were excluded because of inadequate proposals.

Chapter 6. Recovery in a Shrinking City: Challenges to Rightsizing Post-Katrina New Orleans

1. U.S. Census, Profile of General Population and Housing Characteristics: 2010, City of New Orleans; Allison Plyer and Elaine Ortiz, "Benchmarks for Blight," *Greater New Orleans Community Data Center*, October 27, 2010, http://www.gnocdc.org /BenchmarksForBlight/index.html.

2. David Brooks, "Katrina's Silver Lining," *New York Times*, September 8, 2005; Brookings Institution Metropolitan Policy Program, "New Orleans After the Storm," http://www.brookings.edu/reports/2005/10metropolitanpolicy.aspx; Urban Land Institute, *A Strategy for Rebuilding New Orleans, Louisiana*, report, Washington, D.C., 2005.

3. Melissa Schigoda, "Hurricane Katrina Impact," *Greater New Orleans Community Data Center*, August 19, 2011, http://www.gnocdc.org/Factsforfeatures/Hurri caneKatrinaImpact/index.html.

4. John R. Logan, "The Impact of Katrina," report for American Communities Project, Brown University, 2006, http://www.s4.brown.edu/katrina/report.pdf.

5. Chester W. Hartman and Gregory D. Squires, *There Is No Such Thing as a Natural Disaster* (New York: Routledge, 2006); Logan, "The Impact of Katrina"; Christina Finch, Christopher T. Emrich, and Susan L. Cutter, "Disaster Disparities and Differential Recovery in New Orleans," *Population and Environment* 31, 4 (2010): 179–202.

6. U.S. Census Bureau, "2007 Hurricane Season Begins," http://www.census.gov /newsroom/releases/archives/facts_for_features_special_editions/cb07-ffse03.html; Greater New Orleans Community Data Center, "Population Loss and Vacant Housing in New Orleans Neighborhoods," April 15, 2010, http://www.gnocdc.org/Population LossAndVacantHousing/index.html.

7. U.S. Census Bureau, "New Orleans Was Nation's Fastest-Growing City in 2008," July 1, 2009, http://www.census.gov/newsroom/releases/archives/population/cb09-99 .html.

8. U.S. Census Bureau, "Annual Estimates of the Resident Population for Counties of Louisiana," April 1, 2000, to July 1, 2009, Table 1; Census Bureau, New Orleans city, 2010 Demographic Profile Table.

9. Plyer and Ortiz, "Benchmarks for Blight."

10. Finch, Emrich, and Cutter, "Disaster Disparities"; Lisa Bates and Rebekah Green, "Housing Recovery in the Ninth Ward," in *Race, Place and Environmental Justice After Hurricane Katrina*, ed. Robert D. Bullard and Beverly Wright (Boulder, Colo.: Westview Press, 2009), 229–45. How quickly neighborhoods recovered was determined by depth of flooding, amount of physical damage, preexisting social vulnerabilities of the population, and the availability and accessibility of recovery resources. In the heavily flooded Lower Ninth Ward neighborhood where recovery was particularly slow, for instance, low- and moderate-income African American homeowners faced greater obstacles and received fewer rebuilding resources than their counterparts in predominately white areas of the city with similar levels of damage.

11. In the absence of overall population growth, households will likely relocate into these neighborhoods as these developments are completed, increasing vacancies in sending neighborhoods.

12. Allison Plyer, "Neighborhood Recovery Rates," *Greater New Orleans Community Data Center*, July 1, 2010, http://www.hurstvillesecurity.com/images/page _uploads/Recovery%20-%20Neighborhood%20Recovery%20(GNOCDC)%20(June %202010).pdf.

13. Gordon Russell, "It's Time for New Orleans to Admit It's a Shrinking City, Some Say," *Times-Picayune*, November 22, 2008.

14. Richard Campanella, "New Orleans Population Density over the Years," *Times-Picayune*, November 22, 2008.

15. Russell, "It's Time for New Orleans"; Richard Campanella, *Above-Sea-Level New Orleans* (New Orleans: Center for Bioenvironmental Research at Tulane and Xavier Universities, 2007); Campanella, "New Orleans Population Density." From 1960 to 2000, population density decreased from 17,053 to 7,266 people per square mile.

16. Coleman Warner, "A Blight on the City," *Times-Picayune*, May 9, 1999.

17. Greg Thomas, "Home Ownership Climbs Block by Block in N.O.; But Renters Still Are Bulk of City," *Times-Picayune*, May 22, 2001.

18. Martha Carr, "City Takes on Blight in Sweeping Program," *Times-Picayune*, January 7, 2005.

19. Plyer and Ortiz, "Benchmarks for Blight." Total unoccupied residential addresses include blighted and vacant but habitable residences, and empty residential lots.

20. Census vacancy rates underestimate the extent of unused property in distressed neighborhoods because vacant lots and vacant units exposed to the elements, condemned, or slated for demolition are not included in the housing inventory. Census vacancy rates likely overestimate the vacant properties in areas, like the French Quarter, with a large share of units for occasional or seasonal recreational use.

21. Greater New Orleans Community Data Center, "Population Loss and Vacant Housing in New Orleans Neighborhoods."

22. Transition New Orleans Blight Task Force, *Task Force Report*, April 2010, http://www.transitionneworleans.com/SiteContent/Static/Documents/Blight.pdf.

23. Greater New Orleans Community Data Center, "Population Loss and Vacant Housing in New Orleans Neighborhoods."

24. Yael Allweil, "Shrinking Cities," *Places* 19, 1 (2006): 92.

25. James Heilbrun, "On the Theory and Policy of Neighborhood Consolidation," *Journal of the American Planning Association* 45, 4 (1979): 417–27; Michael Pagano and Ann Bowman, *Terra Incognita* (Washington, D.C.: Georgetown University Press, 2004).

26. Roger Starr, "Making New York Smaller," *New York Times Magazine*, November 14, 1976; Roger Starr, "The Changing Life of Cities," in *How Cities Can Grow Old Gracefully*, prepared for Committee on Banking, Finance, and Urban Affairs, Subcommittee on the City, 95th Cong., 1st sess. (Washington, D.C., 1977); Wilbur Thompson, "Land Management Strategies for Central City Depopulation" and S. Jerome Pratter, "Strategies for City Investment," in *How Cities Can Grow Old Gracefully*; Heilbrun, "Neighborhood Consolidation."

27. Karina Pallagst, "The End of the Growth Machine," paper presented at Association of Collegiate Schools of Planning Conference, Kansas City, 2005; Philipp Oswalt, ed., *Shrinking Cities*, vol. 2 (Ostfildern-Ruit, Germany: Hatje Crantz, 2006); Justin Hollander et al., "Planning Shrinking Cities," *Progress in Planning* 72, 1 (2009): 223–32.

28. Starr, "Making New York Smaller," "Changing Life of Cities"; Thompson, "Land Management Strategies"; Heilbrun, "Neighborhood Consolidation."

29. Frank Popper and Deborah Popper, "Small Can Be Beautiful," *Planning*, July 2002, 20–23; Witold Rybczynski, "Downsizing Cities," *Atlantic Monthly*, October 1995, 36–47.

30. Laura Reese, "Economic Versus Natural Disasters," *Economic Development Quarterly* 20, 3 (2006): 219–31.

31. Bring New Orleans Back Commission website, http://www.bringneworleans back.org.

32. Bureau of Governmental Research, "Wanted: a Realistic Development Strategy," 2005, http://www.bgr.org/files/news/BGR_Reports_Realistic_Development _Strategy_12_22_05.pdf.

33. Marla Nelson, Renia Ehrenfeucht, and Shirley Laska, "Planning, Plans and People," *Cityscape* 9, 3 (2007): 23–52.

34. Ibid.; Mtangulizi Sanyika, "Katrina and the Condition of Black New Orleans," in Bullard and Wright, eds., *Race, Place and Environmental Justice After Hurricane Katrina*, 87–111.

35. Website of the New Orleans Neighborhood Rebuilding Plan, http://www.no lanrp.com.

36. Renia Ehrenfeucht and Marla Nelson, "Planning, Population Loss and Equity in New Orleans after Hurricane Katrina," *Planning Practice and Research* 26, 2 (2011): 129–46.

37. Nelson, Ehrenfeucht and Laska, "Planning, Plans, and People."

38. Website of the Unified New Orleans Plan, http://www.unifiedneworleansplan.com/home3/.

39. Starr, "Making New York Smaller"; Starr, "Changing Life of Cities"; Thompson, "Land Management Strategies"; Pratter, "Strategies for City Investment"; Heilbrun, "Neighborhood Consolidation."

40. Robert A. Beauregard, "Strategic Thinking for Distressed Neighborhoods," this volume.

41. Hollander et al, "Planning Shrinking Cities"; Pratter, "Strategies for City Investment."

42. Thompson, "Land Management Strategies," 73.

43. Ibid.; Heilbrun, "Neighborhood Consolidation."

44. Peter Marris, *Loss and Change* (New York: Pantheon, 1974), 124.

45. City of New Orleans City Planning Commission, *New Century New Orleans Land Use Plan*, 1999, 201. In its 1999 *New Century New Orleans Land Use Plan*, for instance, the City Planning Commission promoted undeveloped, flood-prone portions of New Orleans East as urban growth areas, stating that "long term, these development opportunities represent not only population increases but also significant potential employment for the city."

46. Christine Hauser, "Mayor Announces Layoffs of City Workers," *New York Times*, October 5, 2005.

47. New Orleans Redevelopment Authority, *New Orleans Redevelopment Authority Transition Report*, prepared for Mayor Landrieu's Transition Team on the State of NORA, 2010, http://www.noraworks.org/index.php/resources/studies-and-analytics/.

48. Ehrenfeucht and Nelson, "Planning, Population Loss, and Equity."

49. Heilbrun, "Neighborhood Consolidation"; Joseph Schilling and Jonathan Logan, "Greening the Rust Belt," *Journal of the American Planning Association* 74, 4 (2008): 451–66.

50. The Road Home program also included a small rental program that offered competitive grants to owners of rental properties with one to four units. Rental property owners did not have the option of conveying properties to the state.

51. In 2010, NORA had implemented Phase II of the program in only two areas, both with relatively strong market demand: Lakeview and the Oak Park subdivision of the Filmore neighborhood.

52. Although abutting property owners could have a house on the property, in practice existing structures were demolished before neighboring property owners took possession, and in the short term Lot Next Door conveyed vacant lots and became a de facto program to reduce housing density.

53. Margaret Dewar, "Remaking Cities Through Property Tax Foreclosure and Sale of Tax-Reverted Property," paper presented at the Association of Collegiate Schools of Planning Conference, Milwaukee, 2007.

54. Justin Hollander, "Moving Toward a Shrinking Cities Metric," *Cityscape* 12, 1 (2010): 133–51.

55. Allison Plyer et al., *Housing Production Needs: Three Scenarios for New Orleans*, Greater New Orleans Community Data Center Annual Report, November 2009, http://www.gnocdc.org.

56. Email correspondence with NORA staff member, September 2010.

57. Michelle Krupa, "A N.O. Program Has Given New Life to 1,000 Blighted Properties," *Times-Picayune*, June 13, 2011.

58. Margaret Dewar, "Selling Tax-Reverted Land," *Journal of the American Planning Association* 72, 2 (2006): 167–80.

59. Pre-Katrina Neighborhood Data, Greater New Orleans Community Data Center.

60. New Orleans Redevelopment Authority, *Transition Report*.

61. George Galster, Peter Tatian, and John Accordino, "Targeting Investments for Neighborhood Revitalization," *Journal of the American Planning Association* 72, 4 (2006): 457–74.

62. New Orleans Redevelopment Authority, *Transition Report*.

63. Ibid.

64. Ibid.

65. Lolis Elie, "Oretha Castle Haley Boulevard Gets Help from the City as It Tries to Turn a Corner," *Times-Picayune*, August 2, 2009.

66. Alan Mallach, *Mayors' Resource Guide on Vacant and Abandoned Properties* (Washington, D.C.: U.S. Conference of Mayors Housing Task Force, National Vacant Properties Campaign, Fannie Mae Foundation, 2006).

67. Jeffrey S. Lowe and Lisa K. Bates, "Missing New Orleans," this volume.

68. Alan Altshuler and David Luberoff, *Mega-Projects* (Washington, D.C.: Brookings Institution Press, 2003).

Chapter 7. Missing New Orleans: Lessons from the CDC Sector on Vacancy, Abandonment, and Reconstructing the Crescent City

1. U.S. Census, "Occupancy Status," Census 2000 Summary File 3, Table H6.

2. Senate Ad Hoc Subcommittee on Disaster Recovery of the United States Senate Committee on Homeland Security and Governmental Affairs, "Testimony of Mayor C. Ray Nagin Regarding 'FEMA's Project Worksheets,'" July 7, 2007, http://www.hsgac.senate.gov/download/71007-testimony-c-ray-nagin, accessed November 29, 2009.

3. Heather Burke, "New Orleans, 80% Flooded After Katrina, Plans Evacuation," *Bloomberg*, August 31, 2005, http://www.bloomberg.com/apps/news?pid=newsarchive &sid=aIJBD0M13h8M&refer=canada; *Field Hearings on Solving the Affordable Housing Crisis in the Gulf Coast Region Post-Katrina, Part I, Before the Subcommittee on Housing and Community Opportunity of the Committee on Financial Services, House of Representatives*, 110th Cong. (2007) (statement of Dr. Sherece Y. West, CEO, Louisiana Disaster Recovery Foundation).

4. Statement of Sherece West; U.S. Census Bureau, "Occupancy Status" and "Vacancy Status," American Community Survey 2008 1-Year Estimates, Tables B25002, B25004.

5. Gordon Russell, "Vacant, Ruined Properties Put N.O. at Top of Heap," *Times-Picayune*, August 21, 2008; Allison Plyer and Elaine Ortiz, "Benchmarks for Blight," *Greater New Orleans Community Data Center*, October 27, 2010, http://www.gnocdc.org/BenchmarksForBlight/index.html.

6. Rachel G. Bratt, *Rebuilding a Low-Income Housing Policy* (Philadelphia: Temple University Press, 1989); Avis Vidal, *Rebuilding Communities* (New York: New School for Social Research, Community Development Research Center, 1992); Edward Goetz, *Shelter Burden* (Philadelphia: Temple University Press, 1993); Keith P. Rasey, "The Role of the Neighborhood-Based Housing Nonprofits in the Ownership and Control of Housing in U.S. Cities," in *Ownership, Control, and the Future of Housing Policy*, ed. R. Allen Hayes (Westport, Conn.: Greenwood, 1993), 195–224; Sara E. Stoutland, "Community Development Corporations," in *Urban Problems and Community Development*, ed. Ronald F. Ferguson and William T. Dickens (Washington, D.C.: Brookings Institution Press, 1999), 193–240; Herbert J. Rubin, *Renewing Hope Within Neighborhoods of Despair* (Albany: State University of New York Press, 2000).

7. Harry Berndt, *New Rulers in the Ghetto* (Westport, Conn.: Greenwood, 1977); Robert Halpern, *Rebuilding the Inner City* (New York: Columbia University Press, 1995); W. Dennis Keating, Keith P. Rasey, and Norman Krumholz, "Community Development Corporations," in *Government and Housing*, ed. Willem van Vliet and Jan Van Weesep (Newbury Park, Calif.: Sage, 1990), 206–18; Nicholas Lemann, "Rebuilding the Ghetto Doesn't Work," *New York Times*, January 9, 1994; Randy Stoecker, "The CDC Model of Urban Redevelopment," *Journal of Urban Affairs* 19, 1 (1997): 1–22.

8. Ronald F. Ferguson and Sara E. Stoutland, "Reconceiving the Community Development Field," in Ferguson and Dickens, eds., *Urban Problems and Community Development*, 33–75.

9. June Manning Thomas, "Redevelopment and Redistribution," in *Rebuilding America's Cities*, ed. Paul R. Porter and David C. Sweet (New Brunswick, N.J.: Center for Urban Policy Research, 1986), 143–59; Herbert J. Rubin, "There Aren't Going to Be Any Bakeries Here If There Is No Money to Afford Jellyrolls," *Social Forces* 41, 3 (1994): 401–24.

10. Christopher Walker, "Nonprofit Housing Development," *Housing Policy Debate* 4, 3 (1993): 369–414; Jordan S. Yin, "The Community Development Industry System," *Journal of Urban Affairs* 20, 2 (1998): 137–57; Norman J. Glickman and Lisa J. Servon, "More Than Bricks and Sticks," *Housing Policy Debate* 9, 3 (1998): 497–539; Christopher Walker and Mark Weinheimer, *Community Development in the 1990s*, report for Urban Institute, Washington, D.C., 1998; Nancy Nye and Norman J. Glickman, "Working Together," *Housing Policy Debate* 11, 1 (2000): 163–98; Margaret Dewar, "What Helps or Hinders Nonprofit Developers in Reusing Vacant, Abandoned, and Contaminated Property?" this volume.

11. Ferguson and Stoutland, "Reconceiving the Community Development Field."

12. Peirce F. Lewis, *New Orleans: The Making of an Urban Landscape* (Cambridge, Mass.: Ballinger, 1976).

13. Richard Campanella, *Geographies of New Orleans* (Lafayette: Center for Louisiana Studies, University of Louisiana at Lafayette, 2006).

14. Elizabeth Mullener and Christopher Cooper, "City Offers Few Solutions," *Times-Picayune*, January 22, 1992.

15. U.S. Census Bureau, "Occupancy Status," Census 1990 Summary File 3, Table H004; Coleman Warner, "Morial Asks Community to Play Role," *Times-Picayune*, August 25, 1994.

16. Ross Gittell and Avis Vidal, *Community Organizing* (Thousand Oaks, Calif.: Sage, 1998).

17. Mullener and Cooper, "City Offers Few Solutions."

18. Coleman Warner, "Candidates Vow to Help Turn Abandoned Houses into Homes," *Times-Picayune*, November 7, 1993.

19. Coleman Warner and Leslie Williams, "Tonight, City to Get Blueprint for Saving Abandoned Homes," *Times-Picayune*, August 24, 1994; Warner, "Morial Asks Community"; Coleman Warner, "Bankers Leery, but Like N.O. Housing Plan," *Times-Picayune*, August 26, 1994.

20. Aquati Gibson, executive director, New Orleans Neighborhood Development Collaborative, in interview with Lowe, New Orleans, February 18, 2000.

21. Coleman Warner, "ACTs of Faith," *Times-Picayune*, October 23, 1994; Bruce Nolan, "Second Church-Based Group Ready to Help Change City," *Times-Picayune*, October 24, 1994.

22. Warner, "ACTs of Faith."

23. Warner and Williams, "Tonight, City to Get Blueprint."

24. Gibson, interview.

25. Warner, "Bankers Leery."

26. Kristen Delguzzi and Coleman Warner, "Morial Intrigued by Program's Ability to Finance Housing," *Times-Picayune*, February 13, 1999.

27. Gibson, interview.

28. Ibid.

29. Jeffery S. Lowe, *Rebuilding Communities the Public Trust Way* (Lanham, Md.: Lexington, 2006).

30. Ibid.

31. Larry Schmidt, executive director, Community Resource Partnership, and Jane Apffel, assistant director, Community Resource Partnership, in interview with Lowe, New Orleans, February 22, 2000.

32. NORA, "Sustainable Stabilization," application for Neighborhood Stabilization Program funding, 2009, http://www.noraworks.org.

33. U.S. Census Bureau, "Occupancy Status" and "Vacancy Status," Census 2000 Summary File 1, Tables H3, H5.

34. U.S. Census Bureau, "Occupancy Status" and "Vacancy Status," American Community Survey 2008 1-Year Estimates, Tables B25002, B25004.

35. NORA, "Parish Redevelopment and Disposition Plan for Louisiana Land Trust Properties, Orleans Parish," http://thinknola.com/files/chat/revisedLRA_NORA_sub _12_7_07.pdf; Ommeed Sathe, NORA strategic policy director, in interview with author, New Orleans, August 14, 2007.

36. Marla Nelson, Renia Ehrenfeucht, and Shirley Laska, "Planning, Plans and People," *Cityscape* 9, 3 (2007): 23–52; Robert B. Olshansky, "Planning After Hurricane Katrina," *Journal of the American Planning Association* 72, 2 (2006): 147–53.

37. Renia Ehrenfeucht and Marla Nelson, "Recovery in a Shrinking City," this volume.

38. Under Louisiana law, "expropriation" refers to eminent domain where a government takes property for specified purposes. Properties that fail to sell at tax auctions following tax foreclosure become property of the local government as a "tax-adjudicated" property. Frank S. Alexander, "Louisiana Land Reform in the Storms' Aftermath," *Loyola Law Review* 53, 4 (2007): 727–61. Titles to adjudicated properties are clouded due to inadequate notice to persons with an interest in the property, previous owners' rights to redemption of their property, and other issues. David A. Marcello, "Housing Redevelopment Strategies in the Wake of Katrina and Anti-Kelo Constitutional Amendments," *Loyola Law Review* 53, 4 (2007), 766–838. The lengthy notice and redemption periods further prevent transfer of property.

39. Under the Road Home grant program, homeowners could either receive funds to rebuild/repair their properties or sell them to the state's land trust and relocate. The Louisiana Land Trust (LLT) was established in 2007 to hold these properties and distribute them to designated parish agencies according to their state-approved redevelopment plans.

40. Alexander, "Louisiana Land Reform."

41. Frank Donze, "Seized N.O. Houses May Alleviate Shortage," *Times-Picayune*, August 2, 2006.

42. Tax-adjudicated properties have been transferred to the city following non-payment of taxes and failure to sell at tax auctions; blighted properties are those

designated based on their physical condition. The owners of these properties can redeem them by paying past-due property taxes or making needed repairs. Before the properties can be transferred, the city must place advertisements and attempt to contact the owner for the opportunity to redeem the title.

43. Greg Thomas, "Developers Bidding for Blighted Properties in N.O.," *Times-Picayune*, June 24, 2006.

44. Donze, "Seized N.O. Houses."

45. Christopher Walker, *Community Development Corporations and their Changing Support Systems*, report for Urban Institute, 2002, http://www.urban.org/url.cfm?ID=410638.

46. NORA, *Orleans Parish Redevelopment and Disposition Plan*.

47. The Road Home pipeline report for New Orleans for May 2010 showed 5,514 properties would transfer from LLT to NORA when NORA was ready for disposition to new owners.

48. Thomas, "Developers Bidding for Blighted Properties."

49. NORA, "Sustainable Stabilization," application for Neighborhood Stabilization Program funding, 2008, http://www.noraworks.org.

50. Lisa K. Bates and Rebekah Green, "Housing Recovery in the Ninth Ward," in *Race, Place, and Environmental Justice After Hurricane Katrina*, ed. Robert D. Bullard and Beverly Wright (Boulder, Colo.: Westview, 2009), 229–45; Kenneth A. Weiss, "Clearing Title in Katrina's Wake," *Probate and Property* 20, 5 (2006): 42–44.

51. Bruce Eggler, "$2.4 Million in Grants Awarded for N.O. Housing," *Times-Picayune*, February 14, 2008.

52. NORA, *Orleans Parish Redevelopment and Disposition Plan*.

53. Louisiana Loan Fund, "Louisiana Loan Fund Description," http://www.louisianaloanfund.org/description.asp.

54. Ibid.

55. Molly Reid, "Communities Find New Tool for Rebuilding," *Times-Picayune*, December 30, 2006.

56. Jainey Bavishi and Rachel Wilch, *New Orleans' Post-Katrina Community Organizing Landscape: Current Efforts, Unmet Needs*, report for the Unitarian Universalist Service Committee, March 2006, 7–8. The UUA-UUSC ultimately funded staff positions at six organizations, including Neighborhood Housing Services, a CDC.

57. Jainey Bavishi and Rachel Wilch, *New Orleans' Post-Katrina Community Organizing Landscape: From Action to Policy*, report for Unitarian Universalist Service Committee, April 2006, 10.

58. Jainey Bavishi and Rachel Wilch, *New Orleans' Post-Katrina Community Organizing Landscape: Building Relationships to Rebuild New Orleans*, report for UUSC, June 2006, 6–7.

59. Pablo Eisenberg, "After Katrina," *Chronicle of Philanthropy*, January 26, 2006, http://philanthropy.com/article/After-Katrina-What/57869/.

60. Jordan Flaherty, "Catastrophic Failure," *Left Turn*, December 16, 2006, http://www.leftturn.org/catastrophic-failure-foundations-nonprofits-and-continuing-crisis-new-orleans.

61. Eisenberg, "After Katrina."

62. Bavishi and Wilch, *Building Relationships*.

63. Ibid.

64. City of New Orleans, "Mayor Unveils Comprehensive Blight Eradication Strategy," news release, September 30, 2010, http://www.nola.gov/PRESS/City Of New Orleans/All Articles/.

65. Greater New Orleans Foundation, *Learning in Two Directions*, organizational report, August, 2009, http://www.gnof.org/wp-content/uploads/2009/09/crf-state-of-the-fund-2009_public.pdf.

66. Timothy F. Green and Robert B. Olshansky, "Homeowner Decisions, Land Banking, and Land Use Change in New Orleans after Hurricane Katrina," working paper, Lincoln Institute of Land Policy, Cambridge, Mass., 2009, https://www.lincolninst.edu/pubs/dl/1728_948_Olshansky%20Final.pdf.

67. Nicole Wallace, "Fight for Survival Revives New Orleans Neighborhood," *Chronicle of Philanthropy* 20, 14 (2008): 17.

68. NORA staff, in interview with Bates, New Orleans, May 9, 2010.

69. John Marshall, NORA counsel, in interview with Bates, New Orleans, May 13, 2010.

70. NORA, Application for NSP funding, 2009.

71. Ommeed Sathe, NORA strategic policy director, in interview with Bates, New Orleans, May 8, 2010.

72. NORA, *Orleans Parish Redevelopment and Disposition Plan*.

73. U.S. Census Bureau, "Total Population," Census 2000 and 2010 Summary File 1, Table P1; U.S. Census Bureau, "Poverty Status in the Past 12 Months by Sex by Age," American Community Survey 2009 1-Year Estimates, Table B17001.

74. Campanella, "Geographies of New Orleans."

75. Louis Armstrong (a New Orleans native) and Billie Holiday performed "Do You Know What It Means to Miss New Orleans?" in the 1947 movie *New Orleans*. Eddie DeLange and Louis Alter wrote the song.

Chapter 8. What Helps or Hinders Nonprofit Developers in Reusing Vacant, Abandoned, and Contaminated Property?

1. In many cities, for-profit developers partnered with nonprofit developers to build Low Income Housing Tax Credit housing where they could earn the developer fee but avoid property management responsibility, according to interviews in Cleveland and Detroit. Also, Lan Deng, "Building Affordable Housing in Cities After Abandonment," this volume.

2. Margaret Dewar and Sabina Deitrick, "The Role of Community Development Corporations in Brownfield Redevelopment," in *Recycling the City: The Use and Reuse of Urban Land*, ed. Rosalind Greenstein and Yesim Sungu-Eryilmaz (Cambridge, Mass.: Lincoln Institute of Land Policy, 2004), 159–74; George Galster, Peter Tatian, and John Accordino, "Targeting Investments for Neighborhood Revitalization," *Journal of the American Planning Association* 72, 4 (Autumn 2006): 457–74; Ingrid Gould Ellen and Ioan Voicu, "Nonprofit Housing and Neighborhood Spillovers," *Journal of Policy Analysis and Management* 25, 1 (2006): 31–52.

3. Nancy Green Leigh, "Survey of State-Level Policies to Address Urban Vacant Land and Property Reuse," in Greenstein and Sungu-Eryilmaz, eds., *Recycling the City*, 111–34; Ann O. Bowman and Michael A. Pagano, "The Different Contexts of Vacant Urban Land," in *Terra Incognita: Vacant Land and Urban Strategies* (Washington, D.C.: Georgetown University Press, 2004), chap. 1.

4. James R. Cohen, "Abandoned Housing," *Housing Policy Debate* 12, 3 (2001): 415–16; John Kromer, "Vacant-Property Policy and Practice," discussion paper, Brookings Institution, Washington, D.C., 2002, http://www.brookings.edu/es/urban/publications /kromervacant.pdf: 6; Mark Alan Hughes, "Dirt into Dollars," Brookings Institution, 2000, http://www.brookings.edu/articles/2000/summer_metropolitanpolicy_hughes .aspx; Margaret Dewar, "Selling Tax-Reverted Land," *Journal of the American Planning Association* 72, 1 (2006): 167–80.

5. GAO, "Superfund," GAO/RCED-96-125, Washington, D.C., June 1996; U.S. Census Bureau, "Total Population," Census 2010 Summary File 1, Table P1; Nora J. Beck et al., "New Directions for Vehicle City," Urban and Regional Planning Program, University of Michigan, Ann Arbor, April 2005, http://sitemaker.umich.edu/urpout reachreports/economic_development__c_/da.data/504802/ReportFile/new_direc tions_for_vehicle_city.pdf. This number for Flint does not include properties that Michigan law classifies as brownfields because a land bank owned them.

6. City of Cleveland, *City Record* 75, 3865 (January 6, 1988)–92, 4770 (May 11, 2005); City of Detroit Planning and Development Department, "Detroit City Property Inventory" (data file, 2006); Revitalife, "Records of Sale of State-Owned Tax-Reverted Property in Detroit" (data file, 2007). Under Michigan property tax foreclosure procedures prior to 1999, the state foreclosed on tax-delinquent property and eventually transferred the property to the city of Detroit. In the mid- to late 1990s state officials stopped transferring the property to the city and therefore accumulated a substantial stock of tax-reverted Detroit property. J. Taylor Teasdale, "Land Acquisition Procedures Manual," Legal Assistance for Urban Communities Clinic, University of Michigan Law School, Ann Arbor, 2000; Jennifer Dixon, "Tax-Seized Detroit Properties Given to Nonprofits," *Detroit Free Press*, July 27, 2001.

7. Aerial photos of Detroit and Cleveland, 2005, accessed May–August 2007, maps.google.com and maps.live.com (site discontinued); Aerial photos of Detroit, 2005, Southeast Michigan Council of Governments (SEMCOG).

8. Michigan Department of Labor and Economic Growth (MI-DLEG), Business Entity Database, http://www.dleg.state.mi.us/bcs_corp/sr_corp.asp; Ohio Secretary of State, Business Filings, http://www2.sos.state.oh.us/pls/bsqry/f?p=100:1 :3307527243366664, both accessed May–August 2007.

9. Aerial photos of Detroit, maps.live.com, and SEMCOG.

10. Northeast Ohio Community and Neighborhood Data for Organizing (NEO CANDO), "Properties of Community Development Corporations Through 2003" (data file, May 2007), http://neocando.case.edu/cando/index.jsp.

11. Aerial photos of Wayne County, 1998 Michigan State Center for Geographic Information, http://www.mcgi.state.mi.us/mgdl/doqs_zip/1998_Series_htm/wayne /index.html, accessed May–August 2007; Aerial photos of Cleveland, 1991, USGS, Cleveland Public Library; Digital orthophoto quadrangle for Cleveland, 1994 and 2000, USGS, Center for Earth Resources Observation and Science; Aerial photos of Detroit, SEMCOG.

12. City of Detroit Planning and Development Department, "Detroit City Property Inventory"; City of Cleveland, *City Record*; Revitalife, "Records of Sale of State-Owned Tax-Reverted Property in Detroit."

13. Sanborn, Cleveland maps, 1968–72, Cleveland Public Library; Sanborn, Detroit maps, 1977–78, Detroit Public Library; Michigan Department of Environmental Quality, "Properties with a Baseline Environmental Assessment" (data file received by e-mail, October 2007); Ohio Environmental Protection Agency, "Properties in the Voluntary Action Program" (data file received by e-mail, October 17, 2007).

14. Dewar, "Selling Tax-Reverted Land"; Nandini B. Rao and Margaret Dewar, "Streamlining Acquisition of City-Owned Land for Affordable Housing Development," working paper, Urban and Regional Planning Program, University of Michigan, Ann Arbor, 2004, http://sitemaker.umich.edu/urrcworkingpapers/all_urrc_working_papers &mode=single&recordID=539848&nextMode=list; Christopher Ash et al., "Growing Stronger," Urban and Regional Planning Program, University of Michigan, Ann Arbor, 2009, http://sitemaker.umich.edu/urpoutreachreports/all_reports/da.data/2946211/Re portFile/growingstrongerred.pdf.

15. In both cities, the nonprofit developers submitted applications explaining their planned development in order to purchase land. City of Cleveland Department of Community Development, sample letter sent to applicant for purchase of land for development, Cleveland, OH, 2004; Cleveland Land Reutilization Program, "Disposition Policy of the City of Cleveland Land Reutilization Program" (handout available from City of Cleveland Community Development Department, 2003). In Detroit, policies and implementation shifted over the years, but in general, nonprofit developers submitted a concept plan and perhaps a site plan. City of Detroit Planning and Development Department, *Development Review Process Manual: Concept Plan Review*, 2001, http://www.ci.detroit.mi.us/plandevl/CPR_Manual_ALLPAGES.pdf (site discontinued), accessed August 29, 2001.

16. Norman J. Glickman and Lisa J. Servon, "More Than Bricks and Sticks," *Housing Policy Debate* 9, 3 (1998): 497–539.

17. Avis C. Vidal, *Rebuilding Communities* (New York: Community Development Research Center, 1992).

18. Ross Gittell and Margaret Wilder, "Community Development Corporations," *Journal of Urban Affairs* 21, 3 (1999): 341–62.

19. William M. Rohe and Rachel G. Bratt, "Failures, Downsizings, and Mergers Among Community Development Corporations," *Housing Policy Debate* 14 (2003): 1–46; Spencer M. Cowan, William Rohe, and Esmail Baku, "Factors Influencing the Performance of Community Development Corporations," *Journal of Urban Affairs* 21, 3 (1999): 325–40.

20. Sara E. Stoutland, "Community Development Corporations," in *Urban Problems and Community Development*, ed. Ronald F. Ferguson and William T. Dickens (Washington, D.C.: Brookings Institution, 1999), 193–240.

21. Langley C. Keyes et al., "Networks and Nonprofits," *Housing Policy Debate* 7, 2 (1996): 201–29.

22. Christopher Walker and Mark Weinheimer, *Community Development in the 1990s*, report for Urban Institute, Washington, D.C., 1998, 7.

23. Christopher Walker, *Community Development Corporations and Their Changing Support Systems*, report for the Urban Institute, Washington, D.C., 2002.

24. Norman J. Glickman and Lisa J. Servon, "By the Numbers," *Journal of Planning Education and Research* 22 (2003): 240–56; Nancy Nye and Norman J. Glickman, "Working Together," *Housing Policy Debate* 11, 1 (2000): 163–98.

25. Neil Mayer and Langley Keyes, *City Government's Role in the Community Development System*, report for Urban Institute, Washington, D.C., June 2005, http://www.urban.org/uploadedPDF/311218_city_government.pdf.

26. Jordan Yin, "The Community Development Industry System," *Journal of Urban Affairs* 20, 2 (1998): 137–57.

27. City of Cleveland Department of Community Development, "Tables of Community Development Block Grant Allocations to Community Development Agencies by Program Area and Program Year, 2002–06" (data file, 2007); Ash et al., "Growing Stronger," 42.

28. City of Detroit City Planning Commission, "2010–11 CDBG Category Funding Amounts," 2010, http://www.detroitmi.gov/Portals/0/docs/legislative/cpc/pdf/City%20Council%202010-11%20FINAL%20allocations.pdf.

29. Community Legal Resources, "CDAD Community Development Block Grant (CDBG) Briefing Paper," Detroit, 2006.

30. City of Detroit, "Who Got Funded Last Year: 2008–09 Community Development Block Grant," handout at CDBG proposal session, March 3, 2009; Ash et al., "Growing Stronger," 20.

31. Dale Thomson, assistant professor, University of Michigan-Dearborn, "The Detroit CDBG System," presentation, University of Michigan, September 28, 2010.

32. Edward C. Banfield and James Q. Wilson, "Electoral Systems," in *City Politics* (New York: Vintage, 1963), chap. 7.

33. Elise M. Bright, *Reviving America's Forgotten Neighborhoods* (New York: Garland 2000); Background materials, Government Action on Urban Land, 2002, Cuyahoga County Treasurer.

34. Joe T. Darden, Richard Child Hill, June Thomas, and Richard Thomas, "City Redevelopment Policies," in *Detroit* (Philadelphia: Temple University Press, 1987), chap. 5; Marion Orr and Gerry Stoker, "Urban Regimes and Leadership in Detroit," *Urban Affairs Quarterly* 30, 1 (1994): 48–73; Alan DiGaetano, "Urban Political Regime Formation," *Journal of Urban Affairs* 11, 3 (1989): 261–81.

35. Peter Eisinger, "Reimagining Detroit," *City and Community* 2, 2 (2003): 85–99.

36. Brent Ryan, "Morphological Change Through Residential Redevelopment," *Urban Morphology* 10, 1 (2006) 5–22.

37. Dale E. Thomson, "Strategic Geographic Targeting in Community Development," *Urban Affairs Review* 47 (2011): 564–94.

38. Dewar, "Selling Tax-Reverted Land."

39. Ibid.; Rao and Dewar, "Streamlining Acquisition of City-Owned Land."

40. Walker, *Community Development Corporations*, 48.

41. Mark McDermott, "National Intermediaries and Local Community Development Corporation Networks," *Journal of Urban Affairs* 26, 2 (2004): 171–76; Y. Thomas Liou and Robert C. Stroh, "Community Development Intermediary Systems in the United States," *Housing Policy Debate* 9, 3 (1998): 575–94; Nye and Glickman, "Working Together." LISC left Cleveland in 2007.

42. Diana Tittle, *Rebuilding Cleveland* (Columbus: Ohio University Press, 1992), 88–93.

43. Neighborhood Progress, Inc., website, http://www.neighborhoodprogress.org/ (site under construction), accessed May 15, 2011.

44. Jeffrey S. Lowe, *Building Community Development Capacity in Cleveland*, report for the Ford Foundation, Center for Urban Policy Research, Rutgers, N.J., December 1998, http://policy.rutgers.edu/cupr/ford/cleve.pdf; OMG Center for Collaborative Learning, *A Decade of Development*, January 2001; Neighborhood Progress, Inc., website; Nye and Glickman, "Working Together"; Yin, "The Community Development Industry System"; Ash et al., "Growing Stronger," 39.

45. Michael McQuarrie, "Unified Means and Divergent Goals," paper presented at the annual meeting of the American Sociological Association, New York, August 2007, http://citation.allacademic.com/meta/p_mla_apa_research_citation/1/8/3/3/9/pages183395/p183395-1.php.

46. Nye and Glickman, "Working Together."

47. Ash et al., "Growing Stronger," 9, 14–18; Thomson, "Targeting Neighborhoods, Stimulating Markets," this volume.

48. Rao and Dewar, "Streamlining Acquisition of City-Owned Land."

49. Christopher Warren, "Housing," in *Cleveland: A Metropolitan Reader*, ed. W. Dennis Keating, Norman Krumholz, and David C. Perry (Kent, Oh.: Kent State University Press, 1995), 355; Yin, "The Community Development Industry System."

50. Cleveland Housing Network, website, http://www.chnnet.com/.

51. Ibid.

52. Yin, "The Community Development Industry System"; Norman Krumholz, "The Provision of Affordable Housing in Cleveland," in *Affordable Housing and Urban Redevelopment in the United States*, ed. Willem VanVliet (Thousand Oaks, Calif.: Sage, 1997), 52–72; Warren, "Housing."

53. Warren, "Housing," 361.

54. Neil Mayer and Kenneth Temkin, *Housing Partnerships*, final report for Urban Institute, Washington, D.C., March 2007, http://www.urban.org/publications/411454.html.

55. Cleveland Neighborhood Development Coalition website, http://www.cndc2.org/.

56. NEO CANDO website, http://neocando.case.edu/cando/index.jsp.

57. Janice L. Bockmeyer, "A Culture of Distrust," *Urban Studies* 37, 13 (2000): 2417–40.

58. Southwest Detroit Development Collaborative, "Governance Structure and Membership Information," http://www.richardcannnon.com/Governance%20Membership%20Info%20-%20Board%20Approved.doc (site discontinued), accessed November 28, 2007.

59. Community Development Advocates of Detroit website, http://www.cdad.org.

60. Based on annual reports of the Cleveland, George Gund and St. Luke's Foundations; Ash et al., "Growing Stronger," 38–39.

61. Gund Foundation, "Economic Development and Community Revitalization," http://www.gundfdn.org/what-we-fund/economic-development/economic-development; Tittle, *Rebuilding Cleveland*.

62. Based on annual reports of Hudson-Webber, Kresge, Skillman, and McGregor Foundations and Community Foundation for Southeast Michigan. Ash et al., "Growing Stronger," 27.

63. Langley C. Keyes, "Housing, Social Capital, and Poor Communities," in *Social Capital and Poor Communities*, ed. Susan Saegert, J. Phillip Thompson, and Mark R. Warren (New York: Russell Sage, 2001), 136–64.

64. Bockmeyer, "A Culture of Distrust."

65. Ibid.

66. Todd C. Shaw, "Holding Them Responsible," in Shaw, *Now Is the Time! Detroit Black Activists and Grassroots Activism* (Durham, N.C.: Duke University Press, 2009), chap. 5.

67. *Jumpstarting the Motor City*, quoted in Bockmeyer, "A Culture of Distrust," 2433.

68. Todd C. Shaw and Lester K. Spence, "Race and Representation in Detroit's Community Development Coalitions," *Annals of the American Academy of Political and Social Science* 594 (2004): 125–42.

69. Dewar, "Selling Tax-Reverted Land," 172; Data Driven Detroit, Detroit Residential Parcel Survey, *Citywide Report for Vacant and Non-Vacant Housing*, February 16, 2010, http://www.detroitparcelsurvey.org/pdf/reports/DRPS_citywide_vacancy _housing.pdf.

70. Lavea Brachman, "Greater Southwest Development Corporation, 'The Silver Shovel' Case," case study prepared for symposium "Reuse of Brownfields and Other Underutilized Land," Lincoln Institute of Land Policy, Cambridge, Mass., January 26–28, 2003; Dewar and Deitrick, "The Role of Community Development Corporations in Brownfield Redevelopment."

71. Kevin Bush et al., "Building Better Blocks: Transforming Detroit's CDBG Sub-recipient System," Urban and Regional Planning Program, University of Michigan, Ann Arbor, January 2011, http://www.tcaup.umich.edu/planning/pdfs/buildingbet terblocks.pdf.

72. U.S. Census Bureau, "Total Population," Census 2010 Summary File 1, Table P1; U.S. Census Bureau, "Poverty Status in the Past 12 Months by Sex by Age," American Community Survey 2009 1-Year Estimates, Table B17001; Initiative for a Competitive Inner City, "Foreclosures and the Inner City," briefing paper, Boston, 2008, http://www.icic.org/ee_uploads/publications/ICICReport-Foreclosures-InnerCity -080421.pdf; U.S. Census Bureau, "Occupancy Status," Census 2000 and 2010 Summary File 1, Table H1.

Chapter 9. Targeting Strategies of Three Detroit CDCs

1. Dale E. Thomson, "Strategic, Geographic Targeting of Housing and Community Development Resources," *Urban Affairs Review* 43, 5 (2008): 629–62; George Galster, Peter Tatian, and John Accordino, "Targeting Investments for Neighborhood Revitalization," *Journal of the American Planning Association* 72, 4 (2006): 457–74.

2. Ingrid Ellen and Ioan Voicu, "Nonprofit Housing and Neighborhoods Spillovers," *Journal of Policy Analysis and Management* 25, 1 (2006): 31–52.

3. Michael Schill et al., "Revitalizing Inner-City Neighborhoods," *Housing Policy Debate* 13, 3 (2002): 529–66.

4. Galster et al., "Targeting Investments."

5. John Accordino, George Galster, and Peter Tatian, "The Impact of Targeted Public and Nonprofit Investment on Neighborhood Development" (Richmond, Va.: Federal Reserve Bank, July 2005), 8, 57–63.

6. See description of the "HOME Investment Partnerships Program" as cited in HUD's "Overview of the HOME Program," chap. 1 in *Building HOME*, 2010, http:// www.hud.gov/offices/cpd/affordablehousing/training/materials/building/ch01.pdf, 1.

7. Schill et al., "Revitalizing Inner-City Neighborhoods"; Brent Smith, "Neighborhood Housing Markets," *Urban Affairs Review* 39, 2 (2003): 181–204; Ellen and Voicu, "Nonprofit Housing."

8. George Galster, "On the Nature of Neighbourhood," *Urban Studies* 38, 12 (2001): 2111–24.

9. Roberto Quercia and George Galster, "Threshold Effects and Neighborhood Change," *Journal of Planning Education and Research* 20, 2 (2000): 146–62; Camille Z. Charles, "Can We Live Together?" in *The Geography of Opportunity*, ed. Xavier de Souza Briggs (Washington, D.C.: Brookings Institution Press, 2005), 45–80.

10. The term "legacy city" stems from the 110th American Assembly, an assemblage of diverse participants that met in Detroit April 14–17, 2011. See "Reinventing America's Cities," http://www.cumc.columbia.edu/americanassembly/.

11. The need for planners to target their housing rehabilitation and construction activities may only be implied in materials offering guidance on neighborhood planning; see Bernie Jones, *Neighborhood Planning* (Chicago: Planners Press, American Planning Association, 1990). Illustrations for this book offer sketches of needed improvements for neighborhoods but in sketches (e.g., 92–93) related to housing construction or rehabilitation focus on much smaller areas.

12. June Thomas, *Redevelopment and Race* (Baltimore: Johns Hopkins University Press, 1997).

13. Margaret Dewar, "What Helps or Hinders Nonprofit Developers in Reusing Vacant, Abandoned, and Contaminated Property?" this volume.

14. Robert Yin, *Case Study Research*, 4th ed. (Thousand Oaks, Calif.: Sage, 2009); Robert Stake, *The Art of Case Study Research* (Thousand Oaks, Calif.: Sage, 1995).

15. Nandini Rao and Margaret Dewar, "Streamlining Acquisition of City-Owned Land for Affordable Housing Development," working paper, Urban and Regional Research Collaborative, URRC 04-07, Urban and Regional Planning Program, University of Michigan, Ann Arbor, 2004.

16. Stake, *The Art of Case Study Research*.

17. Rao and Dewar, "Streamlining Acquisition."

18. Ibid.

19. Rodd Monts, "Snapping Back," *Model D*, January 9, 2007, http://www.modeld media.com/features/usnap76.aspx.

20. Katherine Beebe and Associates, *Brightmoor Alliance Revitalization Strategy Overview*, Detroit, February 2001, http://www.aabds.com/Dreamweaver%20-%20 Brightmoor%20Stuff/Brightmoor%20Alliance%20Revit%20Strategy%20Overview .pdf.

21. City of Detroit, *Modified Development Plan for Jefferson-Chalmers Neighborhood Development Project Michigan A-4-1*, February 2001.

22. Nancy Moss et al., "The Mack Alter Redevelopment Project," cosponsored by Detroit Eastside Community Collaborative, Urban and Regional Planning Program, University of Michigan Community Outreach Partnership Center, Ann Arbor, 1996,

http://sitemaker.umich.edu/urpoutreachreports/all_reports/da.data/55279/Report File/mack_alter_redevelopment_project.pdf; Smith Group Urban Solutions, *MorningSide Commons II,* Detroit, 1998.

23. Reynolds Farley, "Detroit: The History and Future of the Motor City," 2010, http://detroit1701.org/.

24. Kimiko Doherty et al., "A Land Use Plan for Brightmoor," Urban and Regional Planning Program, University of Michigan, Ann Arbor, April 2008, http://sitemaker.umich.edu/urpoutreachreports/all_reports/da.data/2408151/ReportFile/final_bookopt.pdf.

25. Beebe and Associates, *Brightmoor Alliance Revitalization,* 16–17, for ACORN Market Segments analysis; see p. 21 and following pages for city-owned percentage for various sectors.

26. Detroit is overwhelmingly African American, so whites who are "white only" are the anomaly. The U.S. Census for 2000 used "two or more races" to identify mixed race and "black or African American only" to identify blacks, but these categories could overlap. In 2000, the percentage of blacks or African Americans was 81.6, with 12.3 percent white and 2.3 percent of two races. By 2008, the white proportion had declined to 11.1 percent. Hispanics of any race were 5.0 percent in 2000 and increased to 6.9 percent in 2008. U.S. Census Bureau, "Race" and "Hispanic or Latino, or not Hispanic or Latino By Race," Census 2000 Summary File 1, Tables P3 and P4; U.S. Census Bureau, "Race" and "Hispanic or Latino Origin by Race," American Community Survey 2008 1–Year Estimates, Tables B02001, B03002.

27. McKenna Associates and AAB Development Strategies, LLC, *Brightmoor Neighborhood Plan,* July, 2009, http://www.mcka.com/work/neighborhood-brightmoor.html, 2–12.

28. Margaret Dewar and Robert Linn, "Remaking Brightmoor," in *Mapping Detroit,* ed. June Thomas and Henco Bekkering, draft book manuscript.

29. U.S. Census Bureau, "Poverty Status in 1999 by Age," Census 2000 Summary File 3, Table P87.

30. Sunny Cooper et al., "Creekside Revitalization Plan," Urban and Regional Planning Program, University of Michigan, Ann Arbor, December 1998, http://sitemaker.umich.edu/urpoutreachreports/all_reports/da.data/55293/ReportFile/creekside_revitalization_plan.pdf, 6–7.

31. Rao and Dewar, "Streamlining Acquisition," 24–25.

32. All target areas were in QCTs, according to U.S. Department of Housing and Urban Development, 2010, Qualified Census Tracts and Difficult Development Areas, http://www.huduser.org/portal/datasets/qct.html/.

33. Jones, *Neighborhood Planning.*

34. Kimberly Johnson, "Community Development Corporations, Participation, and Accountability," *Annals of the American Academy of Political and Social Science* 594 (July 2004): 109–24.

35. Norman Glickman and Lisa Servon, "More Than Bricks and Sticks," *Housing Policy Debate* 9, 3 (1998): 497–539.

36. Ibid.; Norman Glickman and Lisa Servon, "By the Numbers," *Journal of Planning Education and Research* 22, 3 (2003): 240.

37. Rachel Bratt and William Rohe, "Organizational Changes Among CDCs," *Journal of Urban Affairs* 26, 2 (2004): 197–220.

38. Lance Freeman, "Comment on Kirk McClure's 'The Low-Income Housing Tax Credit Program Goes Mainstream and Moves to the Suburbs,'" *Housing Policy Debate* 17, 3 (2006): 447–59.

39. Rao and Dewar, "Streamlining Acquisition."

40. Margaret Dewar and Kris Wernstedt, "Challenges in Reusing Vacant, Abandoned, and Contaminated Urban Properties," *Land Lines*, Lincoln Institute of Land Policy, April 2009, 2–7.

41. Thomas, *Redevelopment and Race.*

42. City of Detroit, *Community Reinvestment Strategy*, 1997, http://www.detroitmi.gov/DepartmentsandAgencies/PlanningDevelopmentDepartment/Planning/LongRangeandCommunityPlanning/1997CommunityReinvestmentStrategy.aspx.

43. City of Detroit, *Master Plan*, 1992, http://www.detroitmi.gov/DepartmentsandAgencies/PlanningDevelopmentDepartment/Planning/LongRangeandCommunityPlanning/1992MasterPlan.aspx; City of Detroit, *Community Reinvestment Strategy*, 1997; City of Detroit, *Draft Master Plan*, 2004; City of Detroit, *Master Plan*, 2009, http://www.detroitmi.gov/DepartmentsandAgencies/PlanningDevelopmentDepartment/Planning/LongRangeandCommunityPlanning/CurrentMasterPlan.aspx.

44. Freeman, "Comment."

45. Kristopher Rengert, "Comment on Kirk McClure's 'The Low-Income Housing Tax Credit Program Goes Mainstream and Moves to the Suburbs,'" *Housing Policy Debate* 17, 3 (2006): 473–90.

46. Michael Hollar and Kurt Usowski, "Low-Income Housing Tax Credit Qualified Census Tracts," *Cityscape* 9, 3 (2007): 153–59; U.S. GAO, *Tax Credits: Characteristics of Tax Credit Properties and Their Residents*, Resources, Community, and Economic Development Division, Washington, D.C., 2000; U.S. GAO, *Tax Credits: Opportunities to Improve Oversight of the Low Income Housing Program*, Washington, D.C., 2000.

47. Nathaniel Baum-Snow and Justin Marion, "The Effects of Low-Income Housing Tax Credit Developments on Neighborhoods," *Journal of Public Economics* 93, 5 (2009): 654–66.

48. Deirdre Oakley, "Locational Patterns of Low-Income Housing Tax Credit Developments," *Urban Affairs Review* 43, 5 (2008): 599–628.

49. William Rohe and Lance Freeman, "Assisted Housing and the Role of Residential Segregation," *Journal of the American Planning Association* 67, 3 (2001): 279–92.

50. David Varady, "Comment on Kirk McClure's 'The Low-Income Housing Tax Credit Program Goes Mainstream and Moves to the Suburbs,'" *Housing Policy Debate* 17, 3 (2006): 461–72.

51. Kirk McClure, "The Low-Income Housing Tax Credit Program Goes Mainstream and Moves to the Suburbs," *Housing Policy Debate* 17, 3 (2006): 419–46; Michigan State Housing Development Authority, "Prior Year LIHTC Allocations," 2010, http://www.michigan.gov/mshda/0,1607,7-141-5587_5601-37847-,00.html.

52. Christopher Ash et al., "Growing Stronger," Urban and Regional Planning Program, University of Michigan, Ann Arbor, 2009, http://sitemaker.umich.edu/urpoutreachreports/all_reports/da.data/2946211/ReportFile/growingstrongerred.pdf, 25; Lan Deng, "Building Affordable Housing in Cities After Abandonment," this volume.

53. Rengert, "Comment."

Chapter 10. Strategic Thinking for Distressed Neighborhoods

The author thanks Robert Beckley, James Defilippis, Margaret Dewar, Marla Nelson, Susan Saegert, June Manning Thomas, Avis Vidal, and Matthew Weber for their helpful comments.

1. Phil Fairbanks, "Albany and Washington Shine Light on Buffalo Housing Blight," *Buffalo News*, November 2, 2009; Brian Meyer, "Housing Activists Hail Paterson Strategy," *Buffalo News*, January 8, 2010; Governor's Office of the State of New York, "Time to Rebuild New York," news release, January 6, 2010.

2. U.S. Census Bureau, "Housing Occupancy," American Community Survey 2006–2008 3-Year Estimates, Table B25002. In July 2010, the Governor's Office announced Buffalo would receive $500,000 to revitalize a 20-block area containing a high proportion of vacant structures.

3. Phil Fairbanks, "Shrinking of Cities Catches Traction," *Buffalo News*, June 14, 2010; Steve Rugare and Terry Schwarz, eds., *Cities Growing Smaller* (Cleveland: Cleveland Urban Design Collaborative, Kent State University, 2008); Susan Saulny, "Razing the City to Save the City," *New York Times*, June 21, 2010; Meghan Stromberg, "Tough Love in Buffalo," *Planning*, October 2005, 6–11; Christopher Swope, "Smart Decline," *Governing*, November 2006, 46–52.

4. My examples come from material on the nine large central cities of the United States that lost population every decade between 1950 and 2000, plus Flint, Michigan, and Youngstown, Ohio, the two cities most often mentioned in the discussion of shrinking cities. For each city, I searched newspaper articles, academic writings, and city government websites. The nine are Baltimore, Buffalo, Cincinnati, Cleveland, Detroit, Philadelphia, Pittsburgh, St. Louis, and Washington.

5. Website of National Vacant Properties Campaign, www.vacantproperties.com, accessed March 23, 2010 (site discontinued). After its formation in 2004, the NVPC provided technical assistance to over 30 cities including Youngstown, Buffalo, Philadelphia, Indianapolis, and St. Louis.

6. Jennifer R. Leonard and Joseph M. Schilling, "Lessons from the Field," *Real Estate Review* 36, 3 (2007): 33.

7. David L. Birch, "Toward a Stage Theory of Urban Growth," *Journal of the American Institute of Planners* 37, 2 (1971): 78–87; Anthony Downs, *Neighborhoods and Urban Development* (Washington, D.C.: Brookings Institution Press, 1981), 153–71; William A. Schwab, "The Predictive Value of Three Ecological Models," *Urban Affairs Quarterly* 23, 2 (1987): 295–308; Kent P. Schwirian, "Models of Neighborhood Change," *Annual Review of Sociology* 9 (1983): 83–102.

8. Rob Gurwitt, "Betting on the Bulldozer," *Governing*, July 2002, 28–34; Gregory Heller, "We Want a Victory for Philadelphia!" *Next American City*, July 2004; John Kromer, *Fixing Broken Cities* (New York: Routledge, 2010); Stephen J. McGovern, "Philadelphia's Neighborhood Transformation Initiative," *Housing Policy Debate* 17, 3 (2006): 529–70.

9. Happy Fernandez, "Community Effort Turns Blight to Beauty," *Philadelphia Tribune*, June 30, 1998.

10. McGovern, "Philadelphia's Neighborhood Transformation Initiative," 536.

11. Gurwitt, "Betting on the Bulldozer," 29.

12. Kromer, *Fixing Broken Cities*, 116–21. Regional Choice markets had older housing in good condition whose residents had high credit scores and were financially well off, while High Value/Appreciating markets resembled Regional Choice markets except that their housing values were not the city's highest. Stressed markets had older, deteriorated housing, low housing values, and a high concentration of vacant buildings; Reclamation markets had the oldest, lowest value housing and highest levels of vacancy and deterioration.

13. Dan Barry, "Amid Ruin of Flint, Seeing Hope in a Garden," *New York Times*, October 19, 2009; Kathleen Gray, "Land Banks Gain Popularity as a Way to Fight Urban Blight," *USA Today*, July 9, 2009; Dan T. Kildee, "Reusing Forgotten Urban Land," *Housing Facts & Findings* 6, 2 (2004): 3–5; David Streitfeld, "In Flint, Mich., Fighting to Save a Failing Town by Shrinking It," *New York Times*, April 22, 2009.

14. Gray, "Land Banks."

15. Joseph Schilling and Jonathan Logan, "Greening the Rust Belt," *Journal of the American Planning Association* 74, 4 (2008): 458.

16. Swope, "Smart Decline."

17. Timothy Aeppel, "Shrink to Fit: As Its Population Declines, Youngstown Thinks Small," *Wall Street Journal*, May 3, 2007.

18. Katie Seminara, "Vacant Property Surveys Aim to Revive Neighborhoods in Youngstown, Ohio," *McClatchy-Tribune Business News*, January 23, 2009.

19. Title III of the Housing and Economic Recovery Act of 2008 authorized the NSP, which was originally designed to enable borrowers in danger of losing their homes to refinance. Municipal governments could also use the funds to buy and rehabilitate foreclosed properties.

20. Other programs relevant to downsizing and the demolition of abandoned housing are Richmond, Virginia's Neighborhoods in Bloom created in 1998, Cleveland's Neighborhood Stabilization Strategy, and Detroit's Next Detroit Neighborhood Initia-

tive. In 2007, Buffalo launched its "5 in 5" plan, similar to that in Baltimore, to demolish 5,000 properties in five years. Joseph Schilling, "Buffalo as a Living Laboratory for Reclaiming Vacant Properties," in Rugare and Schwarz, *Cities Growing Smaller*, 43.

21. John Kromer, "Vacant-Property Policy and Practice," discussion paper for Brookings Institution Center for Urban and Metropolitan Policy and CEOs for Cities, Washington, D.C., 2002.

22. John Fritze, "Land Bank Against Blight," *Baltimore Sun*, October 10, 2007.

23. This emphasis on abandonment and infrastructure downsizing has roots in the much-maligned "planned shrinkage" proposal of the late 1970s. Roger Starr, "Making New York Smaller," *New York Times Magazine*, November 14, 1976.

24. McGovern, "Philadelphia's Neighborhood Transformation Initiative."

25. In contrast, Washington's Vacant and Abandoned Property Action Plan has the singular goal to acquire and then sell abandoned properties to developers with little coordination with other neighborhood interventions (Debbi Wilgoren, "District Has Big Plans for Vacant Homes," *Washington Post*, January 16, 2002). The Genesee County Land Bank is a county-based entity, and coordination with city agencies is not automatic.

26. Dale E. Thomson, "Strategic, Geographic Targeting of Housing and Community Development Resources," *Urban Affairs Review* 43, 5 (2008): 629–62.

27. Colin Gordon, *Mapping Decline: St. Louis and the Fate of the American City* (Philadelphia: University of Pennsylvania Press, 2008); Arnold R. Hirsch, *Making the Second Ghetto* (Cambridge: Cambridge University Press, 1983), 1–39.

28. Gordon, *Mapping Decline*.

29. Ira S. Lowry, "Filtering and Housing Standards," *Land Economics* 36, 4 (1960): 362–70.

30. Thad Williamson, David Imbroscio, and Gar Alperovitz, *Making a Place for Community* (New York: Routledge, 2002).

31. Leonard and Schilling, "Lessons from the Field," 33. The NSP was modified in 2009 by the American Recovery and Reinvestment Act to allow grants to be used for "whole neighborhoods," with 25 percent of the funds mandated for the preservation and rehabilitation of foreclosed and abandoned homes. A city can also use the funds to establish a land bank. Going even farther toward a "holistic regeneration model" is the 2009 federal Community Regeneration, Sustainability, and Innovation Act, which focuses on areas of large-scale housing vacancy and abandonment caused by long-term employment and population loss.

32. Jennifer Steinhauer, "A Cul-de-Sac of Lost Dreams, and New Ones," *New York Times*, August 23, 2009.

33. James DeFilippis, *Unmaking Goliath* (New York: Routledge, 2004); David Imbroscio, *Urban America Reconsidered* (Ithaca, N.Y.: Cornell University Press, 2010).

34. Alan Mallach, "Abandoned Property," *Housing Facts & Findings* 6, 2 (2004): 5–7; Schwab, "Predictive Value," 296.

35. I have considered intergovernmental relations only tangentially. On this issue, in 2009 Senator Charles E. Schumer (D., N.Y.) introduced in the U.S. Senate the Com-

munity Regeneration, Sustainability, and Innovation Act to address widespread property abandonment in a fashion similar to that proposed by the NVPC. NSP funds and New York State's Sustainable Neighborhood Project are intergovernmental, and land banks require state enabling legislation.

36. Mark A. Hughes, "Dirt into Dollars," *Brookings Institution*, Summer 2000, http://www.brookings.edu/articles/2000/summer_metropolitanpolicy_hughes.aspx.

37. Schilling and Logan, "Greening the Rust Belt," 460–61.

38. Judith Innes and David Booher, "Reframing Public Participation," *Planning Theory & Practice* 5, 4 (2004): 419–36.

39. Margaret Dewar, "Selling Tax-Reverted Land," *Journal of the American Planning Association* 72, 2 (2006): 167–80.

40. Declining cities are also prone to political corruption. I know of no research on this, but anecdotal evidence from New Orleans; Detroit; Camden, New Jersey; Bridgeport, Connecticut; and Toledo, Ohio, suggests such a hypothesis.

41. Norman J. Glickman and Lisa J. Servon, "By the Numbers: Measuring Community Development Corporations' Capacity," *Journal of Planning Education and Research* 22, 3 (2003): 240–56.

42. DeFilippis, *Unmaking Goliath*.

Chapter 11. The Promise of Sustainability Planning for Regenerating Older Industrial Cities

1. Devashree Saha and Robert G. Paterson, "Local Government Efforts to Promote the 'Three Es' of Sustainable Development," *Journal of Planning Education and Research* 28, 1 (2008): 21–37; Edward J. Jepson, "The Adoption of Sustainable Development Policies and Techniques in U.S. Cities," *Journal of Planning Education and Research* 23, 3 (2004): 229–41.

2. Philip R. Berke, "Does Sustainable Development Offer a New Direction for Planning?" *Journal of Planning Literature* 17, 1 (2002): 21–36.

3. Catherine Tumber, "Small, Green, and Good," *Boston Review*, March 2009, 2.

4. Joseph Schilling and Jonathan Logan, "Greening the Rust Belt," *Journal of the American Planning Association* 74, 4 (2008): 451–66.

5. Jennifer Vey, John C. Austin, and Jennifer Bradley, "The Next Economy," *Brookings Institution*, 2010, http://www.brookings.edu/papers/2010/0927_great_lakes.aspx.

6. Maria M. Conroy and Timothy Beatley, "Getting It Done," *Planning, Practice, & Research* 22, 1 (2007): 25–40.

7. United Nations GAOR, 42nd Sess., Supp. 25, UN Doc. A/42/427, *Report of the World Commission on Environment and Development*, August 4, 1987, http://worldinbalance.net/pdf/1987-brundtland.pdf.

8. Kent E. Portney, *Taking Sustainable Cities Seriously* (Cambridge, Mass.: MIT Press, 2003).

9. Mark Roseland, *Toward Sustainable Communities* (Gabriola Island, BC: New Society, 2005).

10. Scott Campbell, "Green Cities, Growing Cities, Just Cities?" *Journal of the American Planning Association* 62, 3 (1996): 296–312.

11. David R. Godschalk, "Land Use Planning Challenges," *Journal of the American Planning Association* 70, 1 (2004): 5–13.

12. Portney, *Taking Sustainable Cities Seriously*.

13. Peter Newman and Isabella Jennings, *Cities as Sustainable Ecosystems* (Washington, D.C.: Island Press, 2008).

14. Tumber, "Small, Green, and Good."

15. Robert Pollin et al., *Green Recovery*, report prepared for the Center for American Progress, 2008, http://www.peri.umass.edu/fileadmin/pdf/other_publication_types /peri_report.pdf.

16. Pollin et al., *Green Recovery*; Joan Fitzgerald, *Emerald Cities* (New York: Oxford University Press, 2010).

17. Judy Keen, "Toledo Reinvents Itself as a Solar-Power Innovator," *USA Today*, June 15, 2010, http://www.usatoday.com/money/industries/energy/2010-06-15-toledo15 _CV_N.htm.

18. Vicki Been et al., *Building Environmentally Sustainable Communities*, report prepared for the Urban Institute, Washington, D.C., 2010, http://www.urban.org/url .cfm?ID=412088.

19. Alan Mallach, "Facing the Urban Challenge," Metropolitan Policy Program Brookings Institution, 2010, http://www.brookings.edu/~/media/Files/rc/papers/2010 /0518_shrinking_cities_mallach/0518_shrinking_cities_mallach.pdf.

20. Been et al., "Building Environmentally Sustainable Communities."

21. Fitzgerald, *Emerald Cities*.

22. Federal and state brownfields redevelopment policies introduced in the 1990s encourage the redevelopment of contaminated properties. Brownfields programs also seek to redress past environmental injustices by building the capacity of community-based organizations to participate in local development decision making and in brownfields policy making. Robert Hersh et al., *REUSE—Creating Community-Based Brownfields Redevelopment Strategies*, report for the American Planning Association, 2010, http://www.planning.org/research/brownfields/pdf/brownfieldsguide.pdf.

23. Portney, *Taking Sustainable Cities Seriously*, 36.

24. International Council of Local Environmental Initiatives (ICLEI), "Sustainability Planning Toolkit," 2010, http://www.icleiusa.org/action-center/planning/sus tainability-planning-toolkit.

25. U.S. Conference of Mayors website, http://www.usmayors.org/.

26. No widely accepted index of population loss and property abandonment exists—two critical indicators in identifying the older industrial shrinking city. However, the cities that have substantial percentages of "other" vacant housing units, according to the U.S. Census, corresponds to the older industrial cities with losses in

population of 20 percent or more since 1970. U.S. Census Bureau, "Vacancy Status," American Community Survey 2010 1–Year Estimates, Table B25004; U.S. Census Bureau, "Total Population," Census 1970–2010 Summary File 1, Table P1.

27. ICLEI website, http://www.icleiusa.org/.

28. Conroy, "Getting It Done."

29. Maria Conroy, "Moving the Middle Ahead," *Journal of Planning Education and Research* 26, 1 (2006): 18–27.

30. Philip Berke and Maria Conroy, "Are We Planning for Sustainable Development?" *Journal of the American Planning Association* 66, 1 (2000): 21–33.

31. Mallach, "Facing the Urban Challenge."

32. Everett M. Rogers, *Diffusion of Innovations* (New York: Free Press, 2003).

33. Since climate action plans focus almost exclusively on reducing greenhouse gas emissions and do not cover the range of sustainability policies, we chose not to include them in this analysis.

34. Buffalo was a member of ICLEI from 2006–2008; see archived ICLEI roster at http://ci.golden.co.us/Files/ICLEI_USA_Members-9064.pdf.

35. City of Baltimore Office of Sustainability, *The Baltimore Sustainability Plan*, 2009, http://www.baltimorecity.gov/LinkClick.aspx?fileticket=DtRcjL%2fIBcE%3d&tabid=128; City of Philadelphia Mayor's Office of Sustainability, *Greenworks Philadelphia*, 2010, http://www.phila.gov/green/greenworks/pdf/Greenworks_OnlinePDF_FINAL.pdf.

36. Baltimore Office of Sustainability website, http://www.baltimoresustainability.org/contact/index.aspx.

37. City of Philadelphia Mayor's Office of Sustainability website, http://www.phila.gov/green/.

38. American Planning Association, *Sustaining Places: The Role of the Comprehensive Plan*, revised task force report, September 6, 2011.

39. Cleveland City Planning Commission, *Connecting Cleveland*, http://planning.city.cleveland.oh.us/cwp/contents.html; City of Buffalo, *The Queen City in the 21st Century*, 2003, http://www.ci.buffalo.ny.us/files/1_2_1/Mayor/COB_Comprehensive_Plan/index.html.

40. Congress of New Urbanism, "CNU Announces 2009 Charter Award Recipients," March 25, 2009, http://www.cnu.org/node/2750.

41. Buffalo, *The Queen City*.

42. Philip Berke and David Godschalk, "Searching for the Good Plan," *Journal of Planning Literature* 23, 3 (2009): 227–40.

43. Ibid., 229.

44. Buffalo, *The Queen City*, 67.

45. Philadelphia Mayor's Office of Sustainability, *Greenworks Philadelphia*, 94.

46. Baltimore Office of Sustainability, *The Baltimore Sustainability Plan*, 13.

47. Richard K. Norton, "Using Content Analysis to Evaluate Local Master Plans and Zoning Codes," *Land Use Policy* 25, 3 (2008): 432–54.

48. In *Taking Sustainability Seriously*, Portney built an index of thirty-four sustainability policies from his examination of twenty-four city sustainability initiatives underway as of 2000.

49. Cleveland City Planning Commission, *Connecting Cleveland*, 14.

50. Baltimore Office of Sustainability, *The Baltimore Sustainability Plan*, 30–37.

51. Philadelphia Mayor's Office of Sustainability, *Greenworks Philadelphia*, 7.

52. Baltimore Office of Sustainability, *The Baltimore Sustainability Plan*, 110.

53. Living Cities, "Green Cities," May 2009, http://www.livingcities.org/knowledge/media/?action=download&id=6.

54. Vancouver, *Policy Report, Social Development*, report to Vancouver City Council, May 10, 2005, http://vancouver.ca/ctyclerk/cclerk/20050524/documents/p1.pdf, 3.

55. Portney, *Taking Sustainable Cities Seriously*.

56. States (except New York) with large numbers of older industrial cities with substantial population loss generally do not have strong planning frameworks that give the comprehensive plan enforceability and weight.

57. Patricia E. Salkin, "Sustainability and Land Use Planning," *William & Mary Environmental Law & Policy Review* 34, 1 (2009): 121–70.

58. Carol-Ann Beswick and Sasha Tsenkova, "Overview of Urban Regeneration Policies," in *Urban Regeneration*, ed. Sasha Tsenkova (Calgary: University of Calgary, Faculty of Environmental Design, 2002), 9–17.

59. Urban regeneration, like sustainability, can suffer from too broad a definition that includes virtually all facets of urban policy that involve the redevelopment or revitalization of places.

60. Translating planning models and terms across countries is challenging given different legal, policy, and political dimensions. David Dolowitz and Dale Medearis, "Considerations of the Obstacles and Opportunities to Formalizing Cross-National Policy Transfer to the United States," *Environment and Planning C* 27, 4 (2009): 684–97. Despite these barriers, the UK urban regeneration model offers lessons for the revitalization of older industrial cities in the U.S.

61. Beswick and Tsenkova, "Overview of Urban Regeneration Policies."

62. Sasha Tsenkova, "Partnerships in Urban Regeneration," in Tsenkova, ed., *Urban Regeneration*, 73–92.

63. Alan Mallach, *Bringing Buildings Back*, 2nd ed. (Montclair, NJ: National Housing Institute, 2010); Jennifer Leonard and Alan Mallach, *Restoring Properties, Rebuilding Communities*, report by Center for Community Progress, 2010, http://www.communityprogress.net/filebin/pdf/RestoringProperties_Final.pdf.

64. As part of the AIA Sustainable Development Assessment Team (S-DAT) process, six planners and designers in the fall 2008 created a policy and planning framework to reconfigure Detroit as a more sustainable city. The report suggests that Detroit repurpose the city's surplus land to create a greener, more sustainable city. Alan Mallach et al., *Leaner, Greener Detroit*, report by the AIA, 2008, http://www.aia.org/aiaucmp/groups/aia/documents/pdf/aiab080216.pdf.

65. New East Manchester, Ltd., *East Manchester Strategic Regeneration Framework 2008–2018*, http://www.east-manchester.com/downloads/1/strategic-regeneration-framework-2008-2018/index.htm.

Chapter 12. Rightsizing Shrinking Cities: The Urban Design Dimension

1. Richard Campanella, *Bienville's Dilemma* (Lafayette: Center for Louisiana Studies, 2008), 344–50; Renia Ehrenfeucht and Marla Nelson, "Recovery in a Shrinking City," this volume.

2. John Reps, *The Making of Urban America* (Princeton, N.J.: Princeton University Press, 1965).

3. Camilo Vergara, *American Ruins* (New York: Monacelli Press, 2003); Andrew Moore and Philip Levine, *Detroit Disassembled* (Akron, Ohio: Akron Art Museum, 2010); Yves Marchand and Roland Meffre, *The Ruins of Detroit* (London: Steidl, 2010).

4. For the purposes of this chapter, "abandonment" means permanently vacant buildings as well as the vacant land that results from the demolition of such structures.

5. In this chapter, diagrams of a hypothetical city illustrate problems and solutions at both the city scale (Figures 12.1–12.4) and neighborhood scale (Figures 12.5–12.7). This hypothetical city contains elements of several shrinking cities in the American Rust Belt but does not represent real conditions in any one.

6. John Kromer, *Fixing Broken Cities* (New York: Routledge, 2010), 107–28; City of Buffalo Department of Administration, Finance, Policy and Urban Affairs, "Mayor Brown's '5 in 5' Demolition Plan," *Moving Buffalo Forward: Policy Briefs from the Brown Administration*, August 2007, http://www.ci.buffalo.ny.us/files/1_2_1/Mayor/PublicPolicyPublication/5in5_DemoPlan.pdf.

7. Jane Jacobs, *The Death and Life of Great American Cities* (New York: Vintage, 1961).

8. Brent Ryan et al., "Project 1," *Shrinking City Buffalo Urban Design Studio*, MIT School of Architecture and Planning, Cambridge, MA, 2010, http://shrinkingcitystudio.wordpress.com/final-proposals-for-buffalo/final-project-1/.

9. Christine MacDonald and Darren A. Nichols, "Bing Moves to Jump-Start Plans to Reshape Detroit," *Detroit News*, August 18, 2010.

10. Ryan et al., "Project 1."

11. Ibid.

12. Charles Waldheim, ed., *The Landscape Urbanism Reader* (Princeton, N.J.: Princeton Architectural Press, 2006).

13. Kevin Lynch, *Good City Form* (Cambridge, Mass.: MIT Press, 1981); Alexander Cuthbert, *The Form of Cities* (London: Wiley-Blackwell, 2006).

14. Paul Davidoff, "Advocacy and Pluralism in Planning," *Journal of the American Institute of Planners* 31, 4 (1965): 544–55.

15. Richard Dagenhart and David Sawicki, "Architecture and Planning," *Journal of Planning Education and Research* 12, 1 (1992): 1–16.

16. Bernard Tschumi, "The Environmental Trigger," in *A Continuing Experiment*, ed. James Gowan (London: Architectural Association, 1975), 89–99.

17. Brent Ryan, *Design After Decline* (Philadelphia: University of Pennsylvania Press, 2012).

18. Peter G. Rowe, *Modernity and Housing* (Cambridge, Mass.: MIT Press, 1993).

19. John Kromer, *Neighborhood Recovery* (New Brunswick, NJ: Rutgers University Press, 2001); Kromer, *Fixing Broken Cities*; Ryan, *Design After Decline*.

20. City of Philadelphia Office of Housing and Community Development, *Learning from Yorktown*, report, Philadelphia, 1996.

21. David L. A. Gordon, ed., *Directions for New Urban Neighborhoods*, conference proceedings, Ryerson Polytechnic Institute, Toronto, November 17–18, 1989.

22. Shrinking City Buffalo Urban Design Studio, MIT School of Architecture and Planning, Cambridge, Mass., 2010, http://shrinkingcitystudio.wordpress.com/; Aftercity: Baltimore Urban Design Studio, Massachusetts Institute of Technology School of Architecture and Planning, Cambridge, Mass., 2011, http://aftercity.mit.edu/.

23. Philadelphia Office of Housing and Community Development, *Home in North Philadelphia*, report, 1993; Kromer, *Neighborhood Recovery*; Ryan, *Design After Decline*.

24. Rowe, *Modernity and Housing*.

25. Jonathan Barnett, *Urban Design as Public Policy* (New York: McGraw-Hill, 1974).

26. Richard Plunz, *A History of Housing in New York City* (New York: Columbia University Press, 1990).

27. Susan Fainstein, "New Directions in Planning Theory," *Urban Affairs Review* 35, 4 (2000): 451–78.

28. Henry Cisneros and Lora Engdahl, eds., *From Despair to Hope* (Washington, D.C.: Brookings Institution, 2009).

29. Philadelphia Office of Housing and Community Development, *Home in North Philadelphia*.

30. Justin Hollander, *Sunburnt Cities* (New York: Routledge, 2011), 42–45.

31. Waldheim, *The Landscape Urbanism Reader*.

32. Ryan et al., "Project 1."

33. Edmund N. Bacon, *Design of Cities*, rev. ed. (London: Penguin, 1974).

34. Norma Evenson, *Two Brazilian Capitals* (New Haven, Conn.: Yale University Press, 1973).

35. Andres Duany and Elizabeth Plater-Zyberk, *Towns and Town-Making Principles* (New York: Rizzoli, 1991).

36. Kevin Lynch, "The Pattern of the Metropolis," *Daedalus* 90, 1 (1960): 79–98.

37. Andres Duany and Emily Talen, "Making the Good Easy," *Fordham Urban Law Journal* 29, 4 (2002): 1445–68.

38. Interboro Partners, "Improve Your Lot!" in *Verb Crisis*, ed. Mario Ballesteros (Barcelona: Actar, 2008), 240–69.

39. John Chase, John Kaliski, and Margaret Crawford, *Everyday Urbanism*, 2nd ed. (New York: Monacelli Press, 2008).

40. Ryan et al., "Project 1."

41. William Julius Wilson, *The Truly Disadvantaged* (Chicago: University of Chicago Press, 1987), 57.

42. Vergara, *American Ruins.*

43. Ryan et al., "Project 1."

44. Ryan, *Design After Decline.*

45. Ibid.

46. Kromer, *Neighborhood Recovery,* 22.

47. Ryan, *Design After Decline.*

48. Brent Ryan et al., "Project 2," *Shrinking City Buffalo*, Urban Design Studio, MIT School of Architecture and Planning, Cambridge, Mass., 2010, http://shrinkingcitystudio.wordpress.com/final-proposals-for-buffalo/final-project-2/.

49. Ryan et al., "Project 4," *Shrinking City Buffalo.*

50. Ibid.

51. Norman Fainstein and Susan Fainstein, *Restructuring the City* (New York: Longman, 1986), 18–20.

52. Alexander Garvin, *The American City* (New York: McGraw Hill, 1996).

53. Ryan, *Design After Decline.*

Chapter 13. Planning for Better, Smaller Places After Population Loss: Lessons from Youngstown and Flint

The authors thank Robert Beauregard, June Thomas, and Alan Mallach for helpful comments on an earlier draft.

1. For a review, Margaret Dewar and Matthew Weber, "City Abandonment," in *Oxford Handbook of Urban Planning*, ed. Rachel Weber and Randall Crane (New York: Oxford University Press, 2012).

2. Gary Hack et al., *Local Planning* (Washington, D.C.: ICMA Press, 2009).

3. Ibid., 71–72, 88, 146.

4. Alan Mallach, *Bringing Buildings Back* (Montclair, N.J: National Housing Institute, 2006); J. Blaine Bonham, Jr., Gerri Spilka, and Darl Rastorfer, *Old Cities/Green Cities*, Planning Advisory Service Report 506/507 (Chicago: American Planning Association, 2002).

5. City of Youngstown, *Youngstown 2010 Citywide Plan*, 2005.

6. Harwood Group, *Waiting for the Future*, prepared for Charles Stewart Mott Foundation, Bethesda, Md., 1999.

7. City of Youngstown, *Youngstown 2010*, 18.

8. Belinda Lanks, "Creative Shrinkage," *New York Times Magazine*, December 10, 2006; American Planning Association, "National Planning Awards 2007," 2007, http://www.planning.org/awards/2007/index.htm.

9. City of Youngstown, *Youngstown 2010*, 7.

10. Ibid., 18.

11. Daniel T. Kildee, "Reusing Forgotten Urban Land," *Housing Facts and Findings* 6, 2 (2004): 3–5; Frank Alexander, *Land Bank Authorities* (New York: Local Initiatives Support Corporation, 2005); Mike Brown et al., "White Paper on Flint Strategy," paper prepared for Auto Communities Roundtable on Repositioning Land and Infrastructure for Economic and Environmental Opportunities, March 11, 2010, http://www.metro-community.org/index.php?option=com_content&view=article&id=277:whitepaper-on-flint-strategy&catid=70:features&Itemid=226 ; Genesee County Land Bank, "About Us," 2009, http://thelandbank.org/aboutus.asp; Daniel Kildee, "Genesee County Land Bank," lecture, Wayne State University, Detroit, April 2009; Ash Center, "Urban Land Reform Initiative" (Harvard University, Cambridge, Mass., 2007), http://www.innovations.harvard.edu/awards.html?id=52621.

12. Christina Kelly, draft letter to Ruth Mott Foundation, 2010.

13. Robert Beckley, "Managing Change," paper for Symposium on the City After Abandonment, University of Michigan, Ann Arbor, June 24–25, 2010.

14. Andrew R. Highsmith, "Demolition Means Progress," *Journal of Urban History* 35, 3 (2009): 348–68.

15. Kristin Longley, "Off-the-Cuff Suggestion Prompts Discussion on What to Do with Abandoned Neighborhoods in Flint," *Flint Journal*, March 17, 2009; Ron Fonger, "Land Bank Chairman Dan Kildee Wants More Discussion About Shrinking Flint," *Flint Journal*, March 20, 2009.

16. Dave Weiland, "Abandoned Property in Flint," unpublished data sheet, Genesee County Land Bank, Flint, Mich., April 2009.

17. City of Youngstown, *Youngstown 2010*.

18. *How Cities Can Grow Old Gracefully*, prepared for Committee on Banking, Finance, and Urban Affairs, Subcommittee on the City, 95th Cong., 1st sess. (Washington, D.C., 1977), viii.

19. Herbert J. Gans, "Planning for Declining and Poor Cities," *Journal of the American Institute of Planners* 41, 5 (1975): 306–7.

20. Philipp Oswalt, ed., *Shrinking Cities*, vol. 1 (Ostfildern-Ruit, Germany: Hatje Cantz, 2005), 16.

21. Justin B. Hollander et al., " Planning Shrinking Cities," in Hilda Blanco et al., "Shaken, Shrinking, Hot, Impoverished and Informal," *Progress in Planning* 72 (2009): 223.

22. Witold Rybczynski, "Downsizing Cities," *Atlantic Monthly*, October 1995, 36–38 .46–47.

23. Wilbur R. Thompson, "Land Management Strategies for Central City Depopulation," in *How Cities Can Grow Old Gracefully*, 67–78.

24. James Heilbrun, "On the Theory and Policy of Neighborhood Consolidation," *Journal of the American Planning Association* 45, 4 (1979): 417–27.

25. Ibid.; Thompson, "Land Management Strategies."

26. Witold Rybczynski and Peter D. Linneman, "How to Save Our Shrinking Cities," *Public Interest* 135 (Spring 1999): 30–44.

27. Dale E. Thomson, "Strategic, Geographic Targeting of Housing and Community Development Resources," *Urban Affairs Review* 43, 5 (2008): 629–62.

28. George Galster, Peter Tatian, and John Accordino, "Targeting Investments for Neighborhood Revitalization," *Journal of the American Planning Association* 72, 4 (2006): 467.

29. Anthony Downs, "Using the Lessons of Experience to Allocate Resources in the Community Development Program," in *Recommendations for Community Development Planning* (Chicago: Real Estate Research Corporation, 1976), 1–28.

30. Casey J. Dawkins and Arthur C. Nelson, "State Growth Management Programs and Central-City Revitalization," *Journal of the American Planning Association* 69, 4 (2003): 381–96.

31. Peter Marcuse, Peter Medoff, and Andrea Pereira, "Triage as Urban Policy," *Social Policy* 12, 3 (1982): 33–37; Peter Medoff and Holly Sklar, *Streets of Hope* (Boston: South End Press, 1994); Evelyn Gonzalez, *The Bronx* (New York: Columbia University Press, 2004).

32. Luis Ubiñas, "Opening Remarks," Brookings Summit on Auto Communities and the Next Economy, Washington, D.C., May 18, 2010, http://www.fordfoundation.org/newsroom/speeches/376.

33. Joseph Schilling and Jonathan Logan, "Greening the Rust Belt," *Journal of the American Planning Association* 74, 4 (2008): 451–66.

34. Joan I. Nassauer et al., *Vacant Land as a Natural Asset*, research report for the Genesee Institute, University of Michigan, Ann Arbor, April 2008, http://www-personal.umich.edu/~nassauer/UrbanDesign/Links/FlintReport_FINAL.pdf.

35. Joan I. Nassauer, Brady Halverson, and Steve Roos, "Bringing Garden Amenities into Your Neighborhood," Department of Landscape Architecture, University of Minnesota, Minneapolis, June 1997, http://www-personal.umich.edu/~nassauer/MetropolitanWatersheds/Maplewood/Maplewood.html; Cleveland Urban Design Collaborative, *Reimagining a More Sustainable Cleveland* (Cleveland, Oh.: Kent State University, 2008); Cleveland Urban Design Collaborative, *Reimagining Cleveland* (Cleveland, Oh.: Kent State University, 2009).

36. Mallach, *Bringing Buildings Back*; Alan Mallach, Lisa M. Levy, and Joseph Schilling, *Cleveland at the Crossroads*, report for National Vacant Properties Campaign, Washington, D.C., 2005, http://www.usmayors.org/brownfields/library/cleveland0605.pdf; Joseph Schilling, Lisa Schamess, and Jonathan Logan, *Blueprint Buffalo*, report for National Vacant Properties Campaign, Washington, D.C., 2006, http://buffalolisc.org/documents/BlueprintBuffalo_Action_Plan%20FINAL.pdf.

37. Website of the National Vacant Properties Campaign, http://www.vacantprop erties.org/ (site discontinued), accessed January 31, 2010,

38. For example, Bernhard Müller and Stefan Siedentop, "Growth and Shrinkage in Germany," *German Journal of Urban Research* 43, 1 (2004), http://www.difu.de/node /6053; Matthias Bernt, "Partnerships for Demolition," *International Journal of Urban and Regional Research* 33, 3 (September 2009): 754–69; Matthias Koziol, "The Consequences of Demographic Change for Municipal Infrastructure," *German Journal of Urban Studies* 43, 1 (2004), http://www.difu.de/publikationen/german-journal-of-urban -studies-vol-44-2004-no-1/the-consequences-of-demographic-change-for-municipal .html; Discussions among Italians and Germans at a conference, "Shrinking Cities, Smaller Cities," Lehman Center, Columbia University, New York, September 30– October 1, 2010. Because Detroit, Youngstown, and Flint have become destinations for international visitors interested in cities that have experienced considerable population loss and property abandonment, these statements also reflect the authors' discussions with planners and scholars from the Netherlands, Germany, Japan, Italy, and China.

39. Patrick Cooper-McCann, "Rightsizing Detroit," senior honor's thesis, College of Literature, Science, and the Arts, University of Michigan, Ann Arbor, 2010.

40. S. Jerome Pratter, "Strategies for City Investment," in *How Cities Can Grow Old Gracefully*.

41. Roger Starr, "Making New York Smaller," *New York Times*, November 14, 1976.

42. Cooper-McCann, "Rightsizing Detroit."

43. Norman Krumholz, "The Aging Central City," in *How Cities Can Grow Old Gracefully*.

44. Todd Swanstrom, *The Crisis of Growth Politics* (Philadelphia: Temple University Press, 1985).

45. Harvey Molotch, "The City as a Growth Machine," *American Journal of Sociology* 82, 2 (1976): 309–32; John R. Logan and Harvey L. Molotch, *Urban Fortunes* (Berkeley: University of California Press, 1987).

46. Stephen L. Elkin, *City and Regime in the American Republic* (Chicago: University of Chicago Press, 1987).

47. June Manning Thomas, *Redevelopment and Race* (Baltimore: Johns Hopkins University Press, 1997); Highsmith, "Demolition Means Progress."

48. Anthony Brooks, "Flint, Mich.: Growing Stronger by Growing Smaller?" National Public Radio, July 13, 2009, http://www.npr.org/templates/story/story.php?sto ryId=106492824.

49. Bob Herbert, "When Greatness Slips Away," *New York Times*, June 22, 2010.

50. Stephen P. Dandaneau, *A Town Abandoned* (Albany: State University of New York, 1996); Sherry Lee Linkon and John Russo, *Steeltown U.S.A.* (Lawrence: University Press of Kansas, 2002); Highsmith, "Demolition Means Progress"; Sean Safford, *Why the Garden Club Couldn't Save Youngstown* (Cambridge, Mass.: Harvard University Press, 2009).

51. Western Reserve Public Media, "Race and Youngstown 2010," parts 1 and 2, Northeastern Public Educational Television of Ohio, September 25, November 30, 2004, http://westernreservepublicmedia.org/ytow2010.htm.

52. Linkon and Russo, *Steeltown U.S.A.*

53. Donald A. Schön, *The Reflective Practitioner* (New York: Basic Books, 1983).

54. Peter Marris, *Loss and Change* (London: Routledge and Kegan Paul, 1974), 155.

55. Leonie Sandercock, "Out of the Closet," *Planning Theory and Practice* 4, 1 (2003): 11–28; Graeme Dunstan and Wendy Sarkissian, "Goonawarra," in *Community Participation in Practice, Casebook*, ed. Wendy Sarkissian and Kevin Walsh (Perth, Australia: Institute of Sustainability Policy, 1994), 75–91, quoted in Sandercock.

56. John Forester, "On Not Leaving Your Pain at the Door," chap. 7 in *The Deliberative Practitioner* (Cambridge, Mass.: MIT Press, 1999).

57. See also Laura Schatz, "Decline-Oriented Urban Governance in Youngstown, Ohio," this volume.

58. American Planning Association, "National Planning Awards 2007."

59. City of Youngstown, *Youngstown 2010*, 135.

60. See Beckley, "Managing Change," 14–19.

61. Ibid.

62. Sasaki Associates, Inc., *Flint River District Strategy*, July 2005, http://www.frcalliance.org/documents/Flint%20River%20District%20Strategy.pdf.

63. City of Youngstown, *Youngstown 2010*, 47.

64. Les Christie, "You Can't Pay Them Enough to Leave," *CNNMoney*, April 24, 2008, http://money.cnn.com/2008/04/15/real_estate/Youngstown_plan_roadblock/index.htm; William D'Avignon, Community Development Agency director, Youngstown, Ohio, in discussion with University of Michigan students, Youngstown, October 2009.

65. Daniel Kildee et al., *Regenerating Youngstown and Mahoning County Through Vacant Property Reclamation*, report for National Vacant Properties Campaign, Washington, D.C., 2009, http://www.smartgrowthamerica.org/documents/youngstown-assessment.pdf.

66. William R. Morrish and Catherine R. Brown, *Planning to Stay* (Minneapolis: Milkweed Editions, 2000).

67. Christopher Bryant et al., "Creating a Neighborhood of Choice," Urban and Regional Planning Program, University of Michigan, Ann Arbor, 2005, http://sitemaker.umich.edu/urpoutreachreports/housing_community_development_h_/da.data/1199583/ReportFile/grand_traverse_district_neighborhood_plan_2006.pdf; Tara AuBuchon and Krista Trout-Edwards, "Reclaiming the Neighborhood," Urban and Regional Planning Program, University of Michigan, Ann Arbor, 2009, http://www.tcaup.umich.edu/planning/pdfs/reclaiming_the_neighborhood.pdf.

68. Krumholz, "The Aging Central City"; Gans "Planning for Declining and Poor Cities."

Lisa K. Bates teaches urban studies and planning at Portland State University She has written numerous pieces that critically evaluate the challenges and opportunities of post-Katrina redevelopment in New Orleans. These include "Overcoming the Challenges of Post-Disaster Planning in the Ninth Ward of New Orleans: Lessons from the ACORN Housing University Collaborative," *Journal of Planning Education and Research*, and "Impediments to Recovery in New Orleans' Upper and Lower Ninth Ward One Year After Hurricane Katrina," *Disasters.*

Robert A. Beauregard is Professor of Urban Planning in the Graduate School of Architecture, Planning and Preservation at Columbia University. His research focuses on urbanization in the United States with particular emphasis on declining (shrinking) cities. He is the author of *Voices of Decline: The Postwar Fate of U.S. Cities* and *When America Became Suburban.*

Lan Deng is Associate Professor of Urban and Regional Planning at the University of Michigan. Her research lies at the intersection of housing policy and economics, real estate development and finance, and local public finance. She is the author of "Comparing the Effects of Housing Vouchers and Low Income Housing Tax Credits on Neighborhood Integration and School Quality," *Journal of Planning Education and Research*, and "The External Neighborhood Effects of Low-income Housing Tax Credit Projects Built by Three Sectors," *Journal of Urban Affairs.*

Margaret Dewar is Professor of Urban and Regional Planning at the University of Michigan. Her research addresses urban economic development, environmental planning, and land use, particularly in cities facing disinvestment and property abandonment. Her publications related to vacant and abandoned property include "Selling Tax-Reverted Land," *Journal of* *the American Planning Association*, and "The Role of Community Development Corporations in Brownfield Redevelopment" in *Recycling the City*, ed. Rosalind Greenstein and Yesim Sungu-Eryilmaz.

Renia Ehrenfeucht is Associate Professor in the Planning and Urban Studies Department at University of New Orleans, where she coordinates the MS and PhD in Urban Studies programs. Among her publications, she has co-authored two papers with Marla Nelson about planning efforts in post-Katrina New Orleans: "Planning, Population Loss and Equity in New Orleans after Hurricane Katrina," *Planning Practice and Research* and "Planning, Plans and People: Professional Expertise, Local Knowledge and Governmental Action in Post-Katrina New Orleans," *Cityscape*.

Andrew Herscher is Associate Professor at the University of Michigan with appointments in the Taubman College of Architecture and Urban Planning, Department of Slavic Languages and Literatures, and Department of the History of Art. His work focuses on the architectural and urban media of political violence, cultural memory, collective identity, and human rights. He is author of *Violence Taking Place: The Architecture of the Kosovo Conflict*.

Christina Kelly is lead planner at the Genesee County Land Bank, Flint, Michigan, where she has worked since 2003. She directs research and planning activities to bring abandoned, Land Bank-owned properties in Flint back to life and works with community partners, consultants, and universities in the region to develop plans, site designs and strategies to position abandoned properties in the city for greening and re-use. She has master's degrees in urban planning and in natural resources from the University of Michigan.

Laura Lawson is Professor and Chair of the Department of Landscape Architecture at Rutgers, The State University of New Jersey. She has published numerous works on the significance of urban gardens in community development, most notably as co-author of *Greening Cities/Growing Communities: Urban Community Gardens in Seattle*, and as author of *City Bountiful: A History of Urban-Garden Programs in America, 1890s to Present*.

Jeffrey S. Lowe is Visiting Associate Professor of Urban Planning in the Graduate School of Architecture, Planning and Preservation at Columbia

University. His research addresses racial equity, urban sustainability and community development; the role of philanthropy, universities, and faith-based partnerships in community transformation; and the politics of post-disaster planning. He is author of *Rebuilding Communities the Public Trust Way* and "Policy Versus Politics: Post-Katrina Lower Income Housing Restoration in Mississippi," *Housing Policy Debate.*

Abbilyn Miller is a PhD candidate in the Department of Landscape Architecture at the University of Illinois Urbana Champaign. She has worked for the East St. Louis Action Research Project, an interdisciplinary service learning and community engagement program, where she developed a seminar on improving conditions of homelessness and organized with a local tent community. Her research investigates the social accessibility of community landscapes and has received funding from the U.S. Department of Housing and Urban Development Doctoral Dissertation Research Grant.

Hunter Morrison is Executive Director of the Northeast Ohio Sustainable Communities Consortium. He served as Director of the Cleveland City Planning Commission from 1980 through 2001 and most recently as Director of Campus Planning and Community Partnerships at Youngstown State University. Plans he has developed have twice won national awards from the American Planning Association—*Cleveland's Civic Vision 2000* and *Youngstown 2010.*

Marla Nelson is Associate Professor in the Department of Planning and Urban Studies at the University of New Orleans where she coordinates the Master of Urban and Regional Planning program and teaches and conducts research in local economic development. Her current research focuses on how cities cope with population decline, whether sudden or prolonged, sustained or temporary. Her work on New Orleans, co-authored with Renia Ehrenfeucht, addresses planning and policy interventions to deal with vacant and abandoned property and the difficulties city officials face in translating the desire for a safer, better city into policies that could direct a just redevelopment.

Brent D. Ryan teaches urban design and public policy in the School of Architecture and Planning at the Massachusetts Institute of Technology. His teaching and research interests focus on the physical dimensions of urban revitalization, particularly in older cities suffering from disinvestment and deindustrialization. He authored *Design After Decline: How America Rebuilds Shrinking Cities.*

Laura Schatz is a lecturer in the Geography and Urban Studies Program at the University of Western Sydney, Australia, and a member of the Shrinking Cities International Research Network. She wrote (with Dr. Laura Johnson) "Smart City North: Economic and Labour Force Impacts of Call Centres in Sudbury, Ontario" in *Defragmenting: Towards a Critical Understanding of the New Global Division of Labor,* ed. Ursula Huws.

Joseph Schilling is Research Assistant Professor in the School of Public and International Affairs and Associate Director of the Metropolitan Institute at Virginia Tech in Alexandria, where he also leads the Sustainable Communities Initiative. As a co-founder of the National Vacant Properties Campaign (now part of the Center for Community Progress), he championed the continued study of vacant properties and has authored and co-authored numerous studies, including "Greening the Rust Belt: A Green Infrastructure Model for Right Sizing America's Shrinking Cities," *Journal of the American Planning Association.*

June Manning Thomas is Centennial Professor of Urban and Regional Planning at the University of Michigan. In 2003 she was inducted as a Fellow in the American Institute of Certified Planners. She writes about diversity in the planning profession, planning history, and social equity in neighborhoods and urban revitalization. Her books related to cities and abandonment include *Redevelopment and Race: Planning a Finer City in Postwar Detroit,* the co-edited *Urban Planning and the African American Community: In the Shadows,* the co-authored *Detroit: Race and Uneven Development,* and the forthcoming, co-edited *Mapping Detroit.*

Dale E. Thomson, Associate Professor of Political Science at the University of Michigan-Dearborn, where he teaches courses including public administration, political science, and public policy. He also directs the Institute for Local Government, which provides training and technical assistance to local governments. His current research foci include community development policy, the role of foundations and community development organizations in city policy making, and performance measurement in nonprofit organizations.

Raksha Vasudevan graduated from the Urban Affairs and Planning program at Virginia Tech in Alexandria, with a concentration in sustainable community development. As a research assistant for the Metropolitan Institute, she worked on papers and policy briefs that evaluated more than 25 sustainability plans. She is Sustainability Associate at the National League of Cities and 2011–2012 Groundwork USA Fellow at the Center for Community Progress.

INDEX

ACKNOWLEDGMENTS

Creating a cohesive book that addresses an issue that literature covers well—the distress of U.S. central cities, particularly where manufacturing has declined—and yet focuses with depth on a topic that is not addressed well at all—how to understand and what to do about cities that have experienced high levels of abandonment, as a whole and in their neighborhoods—proved a difficult task. We tackled this challenge with our authors with a great deal of research, revision, and rounds of dialogue and feedback.

We thank the Center for Local, State, and Urban Policy at the University of Michigan for funding for research assistance and for a symposium, held in summer 2010, which brought this volume's authors together to critique each other's drafts. Our ability to bring together most of the authors and several other commentators helped us develop coherence of vision and refine our purpose. Research assistants Catherine Coenen, Erin Evenhouse, Diana Flora, Angela Fortino, Kate Humphrey, Sophonie Joseph, Robert Linn, Daniel Stern, and Erin Thoresen contributed enormously. Robert Linn also provided cartography for individual chapters and brought consistency to the book's maps. Debbie Becher, Robert Beckley, Robin Boyle, Daniel D'Oca, Dennis Keating, Brian Larkin, Avis Vidal, and Matthew Weber provided helpful feedback on many chapters and on the book as a whole, and many chapter authors offered comments, either in the symposium or in memos, on others' work. In subsequent months authors obligingly revised their chapters several times, strengthening the quality of the whole. All this helped make this truly a collaborative project.

We thank as well the editors of Penn Press and of the City in the Twenty-First Century Series for their support throughout the process of publishing this book—Peter Agree, Eugenie Birch, and Susan Wachter. They encouraged our proposed manuscript; they immediately believed in the project and its merit and offered helpful advice along the way to final product.

The co-editors were also chapter authors. Margaret Dewar thanks the Lincoln Institute of Land Policy and the faculty director fund from the Ginsberg Center, University of Michigan, for funding the research for Chapter 8. Melon Wedick, Erin Thoresen, Emily Schemper, Claire Vlach, Lisa Morris, Mark Hansford, Ashley Fuller, Janet Nelson, and Kelly Koss contributed research assistance. Roz Greenstein, Dan Immergluck, Dennis Keating, Alan Mallach, Avis Vidal, Christopher Walker, and participants in several symposia provided very helpful comments. June Thomas thanks the Office of the Vice President for Research and the Taubman College of Architecture and Urban Planning, University of Michigan, for funding the research for Chapter 9. She thanks as well the graduate students who supported this project, Angela Fortino, Brian Larkin, Scott Pitera, and Robert Linn. Other helpful reviewers included Eric Dueweke, Robert Beauregard, Margaret Dewar, and one anonymous scholar.